From Instruction to Delight

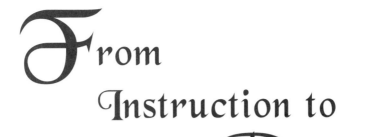

From Instruction to Delight

An Anthology of Children's
Literature to 1850

Second Edition

Edited by Patricia Demers

OXFORD
UNIVERSITY PRESS

1904 ❦ 2004

100 YEARS OF
CANADIAN PUBLISHING

OXFORD
UNIVERSITY PRESS

70 Wynford Drive, Don Mills, Ontario M3C 1J9
www.oup.com/ca

Oxford University Press is a department of the University of Oxford.
It furthers the University's objective of excellence in research, scholarship,
and education by publishing worldwide in

Oxford New York

Auckland Bangkok Buenos Aires Cape Town Chennai
Dar es Salaam Delhi Hong Kong Istanbul Karachi Kolkata
Kuala Lumpur Madrid Melbourne Mexico City Mumbai Nairobi
São Paulo Shanghai Taipei Tokyo Toronto

Oxford is a trade mark of Oxford University Press
in the UK and in certain other countries

Published in Canada
by Oxford University Press

Copyright © Oxford University Press Canada 2004

The moral rights of the authors have been asserted

Database right Oxford University Press (maker)

First published 2004

National Library of Canada Cataloguing in Publication

From instruction to delight; an anthology of children's literature to 1850 /
edited by Patricia Demers. – 2nd ed.

ISBN 0–19–541889–1

1. Children's literature, English. I. Demers, Patricia

PN1109.F76 2003   820.8'09282   C2003–904603–6

2 3 4 – 05 04

This book is printed on permanent (acid-free) paper ∞.

Printed in Canada

CONTENTS

ILLUSTRATIONS

For Gordon and in memory of Alison

—colleagues, mentors, friends

PREFACE

He who combines the useful and the pleasing wins out by both instructing and delighting the reader.

—Horace

In his critical treatise, *The Art of Poetry*, Horace proposed a formula for literary success that has been the hallmark of the best children's books for over two centuries. Historians of children's literature have used his dictum to chart the progress of that literature from its rude beginnings to its Golden Age. Prior to the middle of the eighteenth century, they maintain, the emphasis fell heavily and deliberately on instruction—so much so that before 1744 there were, properly speaking, no children's books. In that year John Newbery produced *A Little Pretty Pocket-Book*, which heralded the beginning of *delight* and, along with the ubiquitous chapbooks, ushered in a new era in children's reading. In the century that followed, the quality of works written for children varied according to the degree of their authors' acceptance or rejection of Horace's advice. But by 1850 there had emerged a body of literature whose unashamed *raison d'être* was to give pleasure to children. This anthology illustrates that development.

In the two decades since the appearance of the first edition of *From Instruction to Delight*, the field of children's literature itself has grown and diversified. Studies of its underpinning bourgeois ideology, of the influential gestalt of business and market realities, and deconstructions of the discourse aimed at disciplining subordinate populations have enriched and complicated views of its history and traditions, its innovations and repressions. One constant, however, is the need for access to primary materials. Even in the age of cyberculture, the search for examples to support the complex development of writing for children is still a daunting task. Histories of children's books and reading practices usually give brief quotations from early key works, which themselves can often be seen only in a few rare-book collections or with their covers displayed on websites. It is the intention of this anthology to include—and discuss in new, enlarged introductions—enough important examples to clarify the different approaches to writing for children that provide the basis for an historical tradition, one that is linked to the emergence of the child as an individual. The updated bibliography contains suggestions for further reading and identifies a companion website with a selected number of well maintained weblinks. <www.oup.com/ca/he/companion/demers>

From Aelfric's Colloquy (*c*. 1000) to the English version of Heinrich Hoffmann's *Struwwelpeter* (1848) and Jane Cotton's illustrated manuscript poem for her young daughter, *The Sad Tale of Mrs Mole and Mrs Mouse* (*c*. 1849), this edition presents over 100 literary 'gems', arranged in historical groupings, that reveal the long, slow transition from instruction in various forms and voices to the equally diverse pleasures of amusement. Glimmerings of creative genius anticipate some of the riches to come after 1850. While a few of the later selections are well known, most are drawn from works that are known by name or reputation only; a few have been rescued from obscurity. Collectively they represent an amazing variety of literary forms, including a charming Latin dialogue in a monastic school, Puritan exhortations, gentle Christian lyrics, psychologically intense narratives, and nonsense ditties. The second edition adds more texts and more literary forms that make the divide between writing for adults and for children very permeable. Opening and closing chapters feature juvenilia, where youngsters themselves display the effects of their learning. Mothers' poignant advice books and the witty sophistication of their illustrated manuscript verse convey the cultural value of the child. Female poets whose work about their own children—alive or dead—straddles the line between adult and child fare are rarely included in a narrow definition of children's literature; this edition seeks to loosen or dissolve those boundaries by sampling the work of Katherine Philips, Lady Mary Chudleigh, Anne Bradstreet, Mary Barber, and Jane Cave. This wonderfully diverse literature not only reveals a steady increase in playful and entertaining devices, which enliven both the content and format of the tales and poems, but also illuminates attitudes toward children and writing that shape our own understanding of contemporary children's literature. Such an historical perspective helps to unsettle stereotypes about parents from earlier centuries, with the realization that fondness and sternness could—and often did—coexist. Moreover, the borrowings and adaptations that advance the tradition of writing for children show what a creative matrix it was.

The year 1850 is not merely an arbitrary frontier date: it marks the beginning of a period of remarkable artistic productivity. Although most works for children at this time were still under the influence of Dr Watts and wagged a disapproving finger 'against idleness and mischief'—which reach heights of joyous misrule in the cover subject, 'The Village School in an Uproar' (*c.* 1820)—by the mid-nineteenth century their tone was less uniformly repressive and more sympathetically expressive than that of previous children's books. As the balance began to tip in favour of delight, striking changes occurred in the content. The tales of Perrault had been translated as early as 1729, but by the nineteenth century the compiling and composing of folk and fairy stories were vigorous activities. The Grimms' *Kinder-und Hausmarchen* was translated into English in 1823, and by 1846 Andersen's volume of fairy tales, *Eventyr*, was also available in English. After the publication of the books discussed in the last chapter of this book, the curtain was ready to rise on the fairy tales of Ruskin and Thackeray, the fantasies of Carroll and MacDonald, and the stylized art of Caldecott, Crane, and Greenaway.

Happily, however, this anthology contains more than preparatory and formative material: much is still delightful and humorous—whether intentionally so or not. The early years of children's literature provide many surprises that do not deserve to languish on library shelves.

Over two decades ago, when my senior colleague, Gordon Moyles, graciously invited me to join him in co-editing the first edition of *From Instruction to Delight*, he started a process of discovery that continues to sustain me and to offer neglected yet invigorating routes through which to orient myself in the space of cultural studies. Working with Gordon and with our now deceased colleague, Alison White, who were always so encouraging and generous with access to their libraries, was a good part of the delight for me of that first edition: the dedication only hints at my indebtedness. Memories of sessions with our first editor, William Toye, flooded back as I worked on this project; I remain deeply grateful to 'Bill' for his exacting care. In the extended interval I have learned much more about the field from hundreds of undergraduate students, and especially from graduate students—Lynn Gergens, Bonnie Herron, Barbara Miron, John Murray, Andrew O'Malley, Erika Rothwell, Jean Stringam, and Elizabeth Walker-Green, among them—all of whom are championing the cause of children's literature in the academy. At the Osborne and Lillian H. Smith Collections of the Toronto Public Library, the director, Leslie McGrath, and her knowledgeable staff have been exceptionally helpful; thanks to Leslie's assistance I am able to introduce the splendid *Mrs Mole and Mrs Mouse* for the first time in published form. The librarians at the Bruce Peel Special Collections Library of the University of Alberta, John Charles, Jeannine Green, Carol Irwin, and Jeff Papineau, have unlocked doors and cracked mysteries for me. Sara Cooke has been a keen, invaluable research assistant. For extraordinary technological assistance—and often at extraordinary hours—I thank Kris Calhoun, Leona Erl, Kevin Moffitt, and Mina Patel for their patience and expertise.

ACKNOWLEDGEMENTS

In addition to the generous and sustained support of colleagues in the Bruce Peel Special Collections Library and the Children's Historical Collection of the University Alberta and The Osborne Collection of Early Children's Books, Toronto Public Library, I wish to acknowledge specific permissions to include material. The manuscript poems of William Paget and George Berkeley (Chapter One) are included by permission of the syndics of Cambridge University Library. Mary Downing's letter (Chapter One) from *Winthrop Papers* 3: 214–215 is included courtesy of the Massachusetts Historical Society. The first publication of Jane Cotton's illustrated manuscript poem is permitted courtesy of The Osborne Collection, Toronto Public Library.

1. EARLY LESSONS AT HOME AND SCHOOL

The child that nature has given you is nothing but a shapeless lump, but the material is still pliable, capable of assuming any form, and you must so mould it that it takes on the best possible character. . . . If you apply yourself, you will fashion, if I may use such a bold term, a godlike creature.

—*Erasmus*, On Liberal Education for Children (De Pueris Instituendis) [1529]

We have all been children. But our experience of childhood is vastly different from that of youngsters in Anglo-Saxon, medieval, and early modern England. The cultural ideologies that shaped our twentieth-century upbringing, including an abundance of child-centred books, theatre and films, the outlawing of corporal punishment, and the view of public, national education as a prime means of scaling the social ladder, were foreign notions centuries ago. Yet parental expectations from the ninth to the seventeenth centuries, however antique and remote their expression might seem, were equally moulded by cultural ideologies and as shaped by concepts of class, gender, and nation as prevailing notions today. Though children were instructed and admonished in sermons, school exercises, courtesy manuals, and religious primers, books especially designed to entertain them were unheard of. Though fond clerics, from the Church Father John Chrysostom to the scholastic theologian, Anselm, Archbishop of Canterbury, and the eloquent humanist Erasmus, enveighed against rough punishment, the rod—in accord with biblical directive (Proverbs 13. 24)—

was not spared in many homes and schools. Though literature written specifically for children developed in response to the needs of an educational system, the purpose of hearing instruction (Proverbs 8. 33) and, in some cases, reading and writing it, was to instill the fundamentals of faith; knowledge of prayers and the alphabet promoted the cultural design of the obedient, pious, dependent child.

Historians of childhood have debated whether a concept of the child, as an individual with unique needs as opposed to a miniature adult, actually existed. The speculations of Norbert Elias, Philippe Ariès, and Lloyd de Mause, about the slight distance between adult and child, have been contextualized by the more archivally precise investigations of Keith Wrightson, Linda Pollock, Shulamith Shahar, and Hugh Cunningham, among others, establishing that a concept of childhood as a distinct phase did in fact exist—although as Zohar Shavit notes, it left little room for the 'extravagance of childhood'. One way of pinning down the elusive sense of childhood in the early centuries of English civilization is to consider developments in cognate notions of education and literacy, as they absorbed the influence of such historical transformations as the Norman Conquest, the invention of printing, and the settlement of the New World.

Erasmus observed that we cannot eat, walk, or speak without instruction. The kinds of instruction provided for children reflected cultural expectations about the aims and extent of education. Before the eleventh century there were two types of educational establishments, both of which relied on Roman and, to a lesser extent, Alexandrian, models of instruction. Song and Grammar schools, or public clerical schools, were connected with the cathedrals and run by parish priests or deacons. Their pupils were sons of the nobility or of yeomen (freeholders of small, landed

estates); lessons included Latin grammar, rhetoric, logic, geometry, and music, and were aimed at creating an educated laity along with candidates for the priesthood. Private monastic schools affiliated with specific orders were a second centre of education. Stressing an equally strong grounding in Latin, they usually prepared their pupils for membership in a religious community. These were institutions for boys only; girls' education, if it existed beyond the precincts of convents, was strictly domestic.

With the Norman Conquest and the new emphasis on chivalric manners and etiquette, a third kind of seminary achieved prominence: the aristocratic home. Here nobly born boys and girls who might one day enter the service of the monarch boarded as pages, squires, and maids of honour while they learned the rudiments of subjects normally taught in the Grammar school. Unlike the preparation of a social elite, a lowlier form of instruction relying on vernacular primers, upper- and lower-case alphabets, and syllabicated nouns occurred in village, dame, petty, and ABC schools, humble institutions whose numbers tripled in the fifteenth century.

In all these early schools instruction was primarily oral—the rote-learned lessons were based on a manuscript manual usually possessed only by the master. With the establishment of William Caxton's printing press in the 1480s, however, the education of children could be textual as well as oral. From the fourth century, the compact, portable codex (manuscript volume) had replaced the single-sided scroll as the predominant book form, a development closely linked with the expansion of Christianity. (This dating is actually conservative, for a codex fragment of the Gospel of John has been reliably dated at 125 CE [Gr. Pap. 457, John Rylands University Library, Manchester].) Late in the fifteenth century, the circulation of printed information, in contrast to the limited availability of manuscripts, made learning accessible to other than privileged children and contributed forcibly to the spread of literacy.

If by literacy we understand the capacity of being Latinate, as *litteratus* would imply, the numbers who would qualify would be limited to clergy who read and directed Latin liturgies and professionals who copied documents and witnessed wills. But, if by literacy we understand the ability to read and write in English, for the purposes of devotion, information, and pleasure, then the percentages are larger, though the process is still economically determined. The ability to read and write distinguished pupils who stayed in school until at least the age of eight from those who had to leave to contribute to the family's welfare after learning to read. Gender and locale provide further distinctions, for the actual geographical spread of literacy was patchy and numbers involving children are ferociously difficult to ascertain. While in seventeenth-century London 78 per cent of the population was literate, including a high proportion of merchants' and guild members' wives, national literacy outside the metropolis hovered at around 30 per cent; throughout the early modern period, when more than half the population was under the age of twenty-five, only 11 per cent of English women were literate.

Although the advent of printing from movable type expanded the network of textual circulation, in both manuscript and print cultures elements of individual personalities and a hunger for entertainment influenced reading practices and flavoured a largely theological diet. Ninth-century Carolingian manuscripts, comprising the writings of Insular polymaths Bede and Alcuin, introduced diagrams as ways of visualizing and interpreting ideas, an innovation soon followed by such crucial developments in book decoration as illuminated

letters and capitals, and pictures. The *mise-en-page* of the text in early medieval manuscripts was part of a process of persuasion and literacy. Fifteenth-century manuscript quires (MS. Advocates 19. 3. 1, National Library of Scotland) which sandwiched blood and thunder romances between courtesy and prayer books show one scribe's editorial principles aimed both at instructing and delighting readers. Within print culture similar blends appeared. Among Caxton's first publications were three books of moral instruction—*A Book of Curteyse* (1477), *The History of Reynard the Fox* (1481), and *Aesop's Fables* (1484)— that were designed for popular consumption. The concise text, pithy morals, and crude woodcuts (borrowed from a German edition) of the Aesop were enjoyed by old and young alike.

Like the range of reading material, the full scope of adult attitudes toward children dislodges the single stereotype of the grim, foreboding parent or master. Sternness and fondness coexisted, as sermons, educational manuals, and recorded experience testify. The preaching about children, collected in the Communiloquium (1268–70) of the Franciscan scholar John of Wales, charges both parents with the responsibility of fitting their male and female children to lead a useful life, which embraces a knowledge of the Psalter and other prayers along with basic medicine and correct grammar. Parental expectations combined views of the vulnerability and potentiality of childhood. Martin Luther's profound grief over the deaths of his eight-month-old and thirteen-year-old daughters was matched by Thomas More's concern for the household education of his three daughters and one son. In a letter to their tutor William Gonell in 1518, More described this activity as a germinating crop since 'the seeds of good precepts have been sown'. The archery and alphabet games More created to make learning enjoyable for his own household school were examples of 'cups aflow with sweet milk', which he advised in the Latin epigrams he had supplied to *Anglice Mylke for Chyldren* (1499) at the request of the author, John Holt, a teacher at More's alma mater, Cardinal Morton's School at Lambeth Palace. As More quipped in one epigram,

What good is a strong larder if a door which you cannot open keeps you from sumptuous food?

Early writing on education is studded with metaphors of promised development: the planted garden, the temple under construction, the slate being written on, and soft wax being shaped. At Archbishop Thomas Cranmer's urging, Grammar schools admitted both gentlemen's sons and poor men's children who showed aptitude. Richard Mulcaster, headmaster of the second largest endowed Grammar school in England, the Merchant Taylors' School in London, for its first twenty-five years until 1586, clarified the social utility and national importance of this undertaking in his *Positions Concerning the Training Up of Children* (1581). Dedicating his pedagogical principles for 'one good and profitable uniformitie' of instruction in English to Queen Elizabeth, Mulcaster, whose pupils included Edmund Spenser, Thomas Kyd, and Lancelot Andrewes, defined the aim of education as 'the bringing up of one, not to live alone, but amongst others'.

Parents from every station echoed this purpose, for a remarkable feature of early publishing activity was the amount of educational material equipping young learners to gain both worldly preferment and, more important, a heavenly reward. Between 1549 and 1646 over 280 different catechetical forms were published; designed for domestic, parish, and school use and often incorporating scriptural texts, the catechism was a question-and-answer

exchange between a teacher and a learner about religious doctrine. The production and sale of hornbooks, single-sheet lessons containing the alphabet and the Lord's Prayer pasted to a wooden board and covered by a sheet of transparent horn, spread throughout the sixteenth and seventeenth centuries. Mothers' advice books and rare examples of early modern juvenilia confirm the co-existence of a serious godly outlook and warm family ties.

The Puritan settlers in New England transplanted the notion of special publications for children to America. Hurt under Jacobean disfavour and persecuted after the close of the Interregnum (1649–60), Puritans of both Congregational and Independent views emigrated in increasing numbers to a new and promisingly tolerant land. Among these early emigrants were university-educated preachers, who saw the formation of the young as an awesome responsibility, and London-trained printers who had suffered for their religious views. Together they not only brought current English primers and catechisms to the colonies but also encouraged the adaptation of these texts to suit the religious and philosophical climate of New England. The first text produced in America, *The Whole Booke of Psalmes Faithfully Translated into English Metre*, which became known as *The Bay Psalm Book*, was printed at Harvard College in 1640; reprinted for over a century, this new translation, altering the sturdy rhymes of Sternhold and Hopkins, claimed to preserve the scriptural text's 'native purity'. Since the colonies were originally experimental religious communities, it is not surprising that the literature they offered the young was intensely doctrinal. Presses and printing shops were among the first buildings erected, and Boston quickly became a focus of publishing activity.

The extracts that follow illustrate the distinctions between Latin and vernacular, elite and plebeian, manuscript and print, prepared and received education. Collectively they provide their own evidence of the expansion of children's literature.

Monks and friars knew a good deal about children's needs and capacities. Aelfric's Colloquy, by a tenth-century Benedictine homilist, hagiographer, and teacher, communicates directly with children rather than adults. It was probably composed as a manual for his pupils while Aelfric was teaching at Cerne Abbas (987–1002). A revealing portrait of monastic instruction, in which Master and pupils talk about various occupations, the Colloquy calls upon the respondents to answer, always in correct Latin, as a monk or a ploughman, an oxherd, a huntsman, a fowler, a merchant, a cook, or a blacksmith. The exercise was meant to model a conversational ease in the generally stern business of learning Latin. The popular and widely translated encyclopedia of medieval lore compiled in the mid-thirteenth century by the English Franciscan, Bartholomew, *De Proprietatibus Rerum, On the Properties of Things*, borrows from Greek and Arabic sources. Although Bartholomew endorses the ancient practice of swaddling, apparently to prevent deformities, his comments on boys and girls—influenced by the gender essentialism of the age—also show a knowledge of real children.

The represented century and a half of courtesy books, from *The ABC of Aristotle* to Francis Seager's *The Schoole of Vertue*, illustrate the pithy power of verse to warn against social *faux pas*. Gentlemanly attendants or henchmen are advised not to belch, scratch their head or face, pare their nails at table, or pick their teeth with knives. Without the concessions which four centuries later Robert Louis Stevenson would allow in his poem 'Whole Duty of Children', mannerly pages were never gluttonous, presumptuous, or interrupting. They served their lord in secular society

much as acolytes would assist the priest at the liturgy of the Mass. After this preliminary training in courtesy, they could look forward to becoming esquires. Some notable henchmen acquired further distinctions: Thomas Howard became Duke of Norfolk; Thomas More rose to be Chancellor of England; Roger Ascham served in turn both Princess Elizabeth as tutor and her Catholic half-sister Queen Mary as Latin secretary. Sometimes these young gentlemen continued their studies at Oxford or Cambridge, or travelled on the Continent, taking lessons in Paris or Padua or Montpellier.

More universal, democratic, and numerous than the courtesy books were primers and hornbooks. Chaucer's Prioress gives us a glimpse of a young student, the widow's son who is murdered, unfortunate 'litel clergeon, seven yeer of age', who in studying to be a cleric learns his alphabet and prayers 'as he sat in the scole at his prymer' (*Canterbury Tales*, l. 1707). Although the child did not yet know his Latin, 'for he was yong and tendre was of age', he learned hymns by rote and strove above all to praise Mary. Pre-Reformation primers usually contained the Little Office of the Blessed Virgin, the beginnings of the four Gospels, the Athanasian and other creeds, and prayers for confession and communion; post-Reformation primers deleted much of the Marian and sacramental content. Offering preliminary religious instruction for every child attending a church school, the primer appeared in more than 180 editions between 1525 and 1560.

The hornbook, a smaller and less sectarian tool, had an even wider distribution. It consisted of a single sheet, printed in either black letter (Gothic) or Roman type, pasted to a thin piece of wood in the shape of a paddle or batlet, and covered with a sheet of transparent horn fixed by a narrow band of brass. Thus the content of the page was protected from little soiled fingers. In *A Jewell House of Art and Nature,* Sir Hugh Plat's suggestion of letter-engraved dice to make a game of learning the alphabet shows an enlightened understanding of the link between fun and instruction. Nearly a century after the hornbook came into use another popular educational device was created: the battledore. It was a three-leaf cardboard lesson-book that contained a surprising variety of printed matter, including prayers, verses, and lists of vowels and consonants, often with some appealing wood-engravings. Its format was borrowed by monarchs in the Royal Primers they commissioned to promote literacy in the nation.

Rare examples of early modern children's own writing, juvenilia, display their personalities along with the results of their learning. While Henry Stanford was employed as tutor in the Paget, and subsequently the Berkeley, households, his young charges, boys between the ages of nine and thirteen, composed occasional poetry in English and Latin. Both aristocrats later studied at Christ Church, Oxford. Addressing relatives and friends, the boys' verse exhibits their erudition and reflects many of the views of the privileged class in early modern England. Mary Downing, a Puritan youngster who was separated from her father and stepmother for five years before they joined her in Massachusetts, writes a lively letter defending her request for money for clothes by showing what a dutiful child she is.

The earliest stage of children's literature is a hybrid of at least three types of writing. Through it all the boundaries between writing for and about children are very permeable. By far the largest component, the work of anxious adults, is lessons to instruct children. Within this group, the genre of mothers' manuals, combining proverbial advice and moral guidance, highlights a particular form of expressly female communication. The advice books of Elizabeth Grymeston, Dorothy Leigh, Elizabeth Joscelin, and Elizabeth Richardson illustrate a diverse register of personally inflected, at times confessional, voices. Conveying much more than the role of the mother as a godly mentor, they reveal insights into fears about safe deliveries, family dynamics, and aspirations for living or unborn children. The mother's grief of Katherine Philips and Lady Mary Chudleigh, expressed in their elegies for dead children, discloses the ways these early modern women reconciled themselves to loss and sheds light on the immense cultural value of the child. Parents and schoolmasters also wrote about children to assist or enlarge the understanding of youngsters' aptitudes and needs. Johan Amos Comenius, Bishop of the Unity of Czech Brethren, was a remarkable innovator who used parallel columns of Latin and vernacular texts describing the enumerated detail of a woodcut to encourage the learning of Latin. In addition to the encyclopedic sweep of its lessons, his *Orbis Sensualium Pictus* shows the intelligence of a true pedagogue at work. Just as Aelfric realized that conversational exchanges helped in learning vocabulary, so Comenius affirms the value of the picture—already acknowledged in medieval manuscripts—as an aid to understanding, when he leads his readers into a *Visible World,* the 1659 English title of the *Pictus.*

The second and third types of writing that comprised early children's literature are smaller and more difficult to chart. The rare, extant reactions to educational practice and parental expectations of children themselves are a second element in this mix. The third is the borrowed and sometimes imperfectly understood work possessed by parents and schoolmasters, such as Topsell's bizarre, exotic, and potentially terrifying *Histories* of beasts and serpents. Then as now, children appropriated books that were not meant for them; they listened and learned, but they also fed their curiosity with glances at higher shelves.

As this brief sketch of books written for children until the end of the seventeenth century shows, the predominant impulse was didactic. It was literature of improvement, aimed at explaining doctrine, laying down rules for behaviour, and dispensing information. However, as the example of juvenile writers and grieving mothers attests, this formative literature also allowed for and anticipated the expression of strong feelings. The open appeal to children's emotions would be the product of developments in the offing: the commercial success and expansion of the embryonic field of literature for children.

AELFRIC (*c.* 955–1020)
From the *Colloquy* (*c.* 1000)

The prominence given to the ploughman because he provides food underlines the solid common sense of the tenth-century monk who composed this Latin dialogue. The teacher is stern, but kind; hence, while upholding his position of authority, he accedes to the boys' requests that he use a vocabulary they can understand. The lesson of contributing at one's station and according to expectations is reinforced throughout. Although a less scholarly contemporary of Aelfric wrote an interlinear gloss in Anglo-Saxon, the editor has provided a translation in modern English.

Aelfric's Colloquy

PUPILS *Nos pueri rogamus te, magister, ut doceas nos loqui latialiter recte, quia idiote sumus et corrupte loquimur.*
We children ask you, oh master, that you will teach us to speak Latin correctly, because we are ignorant and speak brokenly.

MASTER *Quid vultis loqui?*
What do you want to speak about?

PUPILS *Quid curamus quid loquamur, nisi recta locutio sit et utilis, non anilis aut turpis.*
We are not concerned with what we talk about, except that it be correct and useful conversation, and not superstitious or foul.

MASTER *Vultis flagellari in discendo?*
Are you willing to be flogged while learning?

PUPIL *Carius est nobis flagellari pro doctrina quam nescire. Sed scimus te mansuetum esse et nolle inferre plagas nobis, nisi cogaris a nobis.*
It is dearer to us to be beaten for the sake of learning than not to know. But we know that you are gentle and unwilling to inflict blows on us unless we force you to.

MASTER *Interrogo te, quid mihi loqueris? Quid habes operis?*
I ask you, what do you say to me? What sort of work do you do?

PUPIL 'MONK' *Professus sum monachus, et psallam omni die septem sinaxes cum fratribus, et occupatus sum lectionibus et cantu, sed tamen vellem interim discere sermocinari latina langua.*
I am a professed monk, and I sing every day seven times with the brothers, and I am busy with reading and singing, but for all that I want in the meantime to learn to converse in the Latin language.

MASTER *Quid sciunt isti tui socii?*
What do your comrades do?

PUPIL 'MONK' *Alii sunt aratores, alii opiliones, quidam bubulci, quidam etiam venatores, alli piscatores, alli aucupes, quidam mercatores, quidam sutores, quidam salinatores, quidam pistores, coci.*
Some are ploughmen, others are shepherds, some oxherds, some again huntsmen, some fishermen, others fowlers, some merchants, some cobblers, some salters, some bakers.

MASTER *Quid dicis tu, arator? Quomodo exerces opus tuum?*
What do you say, ploughman? How do you perform your work?

PUPIL 'PLOUGHMAN' *O, mi domine, nimium laboro. Exeo diluculo minando boves ad campum, et iungo los ad aratrum; non est tam aspera hiems ut audeam latere domi pro timore domini mei, sed iunctis bobus, et confirmato vomere et cultro aratro, omni die debeo arare integrum agrum aut plus.*
Oh, my Lord, I work a great deal. I go out at dawn driving the oxen to the plain, and yoke them to the plough; there is not so severe a winter that I would dare conceal myself at home for fear of my master, but having yoked the oxen and fastened the share and coulter to the plough, every day I must plough a whole acre or more.

[The Pupils describe the occupations of the Shepherd, Oxherd, Huntsman, Fowler, Merchant, Shoemaker, Salter, Baker, and Cook.]

MASTER *Quid dicis tu, sapiens? Que ars tibi videtur inter istas prior esse?*
What do you say, wise one? Which skill seems to you among all these to be of first importance?

PUPIL 'COUNSELLOR' *Dico tibi, mihi videtur servitium Dei inter istas artes primatum tenere, sicut legitur in evangelio: 'Primum querite regnum Dei et iustitiam eius, et haec omnia adicientur vobis.'*
I tell you, it seems to me that the service of God among these skills holds the first place, just as it reads in the gospel: 'Seek first the kingdom of God and his justice and all things will be added to you.'

MASTER *Et qualis tibi videtur inter artes seculares retinere primatum?*
And which among the secular crafts seems to you to hold the first place?

PUPIL 'COUNSELLOR' *Agricultura, quia arator omnes pascit.*
Agriculture, because the ploughman feeds everybody.

PUPIL 'SMITH' *Ferrarius dicit: unde aratori vomer aut culter, qui nec stimulum habet nisi ex arte mea? Unde piscatori hamus, aut sutori subula sive sartori acus? Nonne ex meo opere?*
The blacksmith says: where does the ploughman get the ploughshare or coulter or even goad except through my skill? Where does the fisherman get his hook, or the cobbler his awl or the tailor his needle? Is it not from my work?

PUPIL 'COUNSELLOR' *Consilarius respondit: Verum quidem dicis, sed omnibus nobis carius est hospitari apud te aratorem quam apud te, quia arator dat nobis panem et potum; tu, quid das nobis in officina tua nisi ferreas scintillas et sonitus tundentium malleorum et flantium follium?*
The Counsellor says: What you say is true, but it would be more esteemed by all of us to live near you, ploughman, than to live near to you, because the ploughman gives us bread and drink; you, what do you give us in your workshop except iron sparks and the noise of hammers beating and bellows blowing?

PUPIL 'CARPENTER' *Lignarius dicit; quis vestrum non utitur arte mea, cum domos et diversa vasa et naves omnibus fabrico?*
The carpenter says: Which of you does not use my skill, when I make houses and different utensils and boats for everyone?

PUPIL 'SMITH' *Ferrarius respondit; O, lignare, cur sic loqueris, cum nec saltem unum foramen sine arte mea vales facere?*
The blacksmith says: Oh, carpenter, why do you speak thus, when without my skill you could not pierce even one hole?

PUPIL 'COUNSELLOR' *Consilarius dicit: O, socii et boni operarii, dissolvamus citius has contentiones, et sit pax et concordia inter vos, et prosit unusquisque alteri arte sua, et conveniamus semper apud aratorem, ubi victum nobis et pabula equis nostris habemus. Et hoc consilium do omnibus operariis, ut unusquisque artem suam diligenter exerceat, quia qui artem suam dimiserit, ipse dimittatur ab arte. Sive sis sacerdos, sive monachus, seu laicus, seu miles, exerce temet ipsum in hoc, et esto quod es; quia magnum dampnum et verecundia est homini nolle esse quod est et quod esse debet.*

The counsellor says: Oh, comrades and good workmen, let us break up these arguments quickly, let peace and concord be between us, and let each one help the others by his skill, and let us always be in harmony with the ploughman from whom we have food for ourselves and fodder for our horses. And I give this counsel to all workmen, that each one perform his craft diligently, since the man who abandons his craft will be abandoned by his craft. Whoever you be, whether priest or monk, whether laymen or soldier, exercise yourself in this and be what you are; because it is a great injury and shame for a man not to want to be what he is and what he ought to be.

MASTER *O, pueri, quomodo vobis placet ista locutio?*
Oh, boys, how does this speech please you?

PUPIL *Bene quidem placet nobis, sed valde profunde loqueris et ultra etatem nostram protrahis sermonem: sed loquere nobis uixta nostrum intellectum, ut possimus intelligere que loqueris.*
It pleases us well, but you certainly talk profoundly and use discourse beyond our ability; but talk to us according to our perception, so that we can understand what you say.

MASTER *Interrogo vos cur tam diligenter discitis?*
I ask you, why are you learning so diligently?

PUPIL *Quia nolumus esse sicut bruta animalia, que nihil sciunt, nisi herbam et aquam.*
Because we do not wish to be as stupid animals, who know nothing except grass and water.

MASTER *Et quid vultis vos?*
And what do you want?

PUPIL *Volumus esse sapientes.*
We wish to be prudent.

MASTER *Qua sapientia? Vultis esse versipelles aut milleformes in mendaciis, astuti in loquelis, astuti, versuti, bene loquentes et male cogitantes, dulcibus verbis dediti, dolum intus alentes, sicut sepulchrum depicto mausoleo, intus plenum fetore?*
What sort of prudence? Do you want to be sly or cunning in lies, adroit in speech, clever, wily, speaking well and thinking

evil, given to agreeable words, feeding anguish within, just like a sepulchre, painted like a splendid monument, and full of a stink inside?

PUPIL *Nolumus sic esse sapientes, quia non est sapiens, qui simulatione semet ipsum decipit.*
We do not want to be clever in that way, because he is not clever who deceives himself with false show.

MASTER *Sed quomodo vultis?*
But how do you want to be?

PUPIL *Volumus esse simplices sine hipochrisi, et sapientes ut declinemus a malo et faciamus bona. Adhunc tamen profundius nobiscum disputas, quam etas nostra capere possit; sed loquere nobis nostro more, non tam profunde.*
We want to be upright without hypocrisy, and wise so that we avoid evil and do good. However, you are still debating with us more deeply than our years can take; therefore, speak to us in our own way, not so deeply.

MASTER *Et ego faciam sicut rogatis. Tu, puer, quid fecisti hodie?*
And I will do as you ask. You, boy, what did you do today?

PUPIL *Multas res feci. Hac nocte, quando signum audivi, surrexi de lectulo et exiui ad ecclesiam, et cantavi nocturnam cum fratribus; deinde cantavimus de omnibus sanctis et matutinales laudes; post haec primam et VII psalmos cum letaniis et primam missam ; deinde tertiam, et fecimus missam de die: post haec cantavimus sextam, et manducavimus et bibimus et dormivimus, et iterum surreximus et cantavimus nonam; et modo sumus hic coram te, parati audire quid nobis dixeris.*
I did many things. Last night, when I heard the bell, I got up from bed and went to church, and sang matins with the brothers; then we sang of all the holy ones and the morning praises; after this the six o'clock service and the seven psalms with the litanies and the first mass; then the nine o'clock service, and we celebrated the mass of the day; after this we sang the noon service, and ate and drank and slept and we got up a second time and sang the three o'clock service; and now we are here in your presence, ready to hear what you will say to us.

* * *

MASTER *O, probi pueri et venusti mathites, vos hortatur vester eruditor ut pareatis divinis disciplinis et observetis vosmet eleganter ubique locorum. Inceditis morigerate cum auscultaveritis ecclesie campanas, et ingredimini in orationem, et inclinate suppliciter ad almas aras, et state disciplinabiliter, et concinite unanimiter, et intervenite pro vestris erratibus, et egredimini sine scurrilitate in claustrum vel in gimnasium.*

O, good boys and charming students, your teacher encourages you to obey the divine commandments and to conduct yourselves with taste in every situation. Proceed in a reverent fashion when you hear the church bells, and enter in prayer, and bow humbly towards the dear altars, and stand as you have been instructed, and sing all together, and pray for your wrongdoings and go out either into the cloister or school without any buffoonery.

BARTHOLOMEW THE ENGLISHMAN (*fl.* 1240–1250)
From *De Proprietatibus Rerum* (*c.* 1250), translated by John of Trevisa as *On the Properties of Things* (1398)

The encyclopedia, a digest of widely held views and superstitious lore, was a popular medieval form. Translated into French, Dutch, Spanish, and English, Bartholomew's nineteen-book *De Proprietatibus Rerum* was known to Chaucer and Shakespeare. Enlivened by real-life observation, not without a dose of clerical sexism, its commentaries on the elements of the created universe blend borrowings from Aristotle (384–322 BCE) and Pliny (d. 79) with etymologies from Isidore, Bishop of Seville (d. 636), and natural history from the Arab physician Avicenna (980–1036). The following excerpts from the Sixth Book, devoted to the ages of mankind, show an awareness of fidgety, perpetually hungry boys and a celibate's suspicion about delicate looking but potentially malicious girls. Bartholomew's first English translator, John de Trevisa (1326–1412), served as the chaplain of Thomas, fourth baron Berkeley; a revised version of this translation, with additions by Stephen Batman (known as *Batman on Bartolome*), was printed as late as 1582.

De Puero

A childe that is bitwene seven yere and fourtene hatte [is called] *puer* in latyn, and hath that name of *puritas* 'clennes and purenes.' So seith Isidre [Isidore]. For the childe is propirliche clepid *puer* when he is iwanied [weaned] from melk and departid from the brest and the tete, and knoweth good and evel. . . . Than soche children be neisch [soft] of fleisch, lethy [lithe] and pliant of body, abel and light to mevynge, witty to lerne caroles, and withoute busines, and they lede here lif withoute care and busines and tellen pris onliche [set their courages only] of merthe and likynge, and dreden no perile more than betinge with a gerde [rod]. . . . They desiren and coveiten all thinges that they see, and prayeth and asketh hem with voys and with honde. They love talkynges and counsailes of suche children as they bene and forsaken and voyden companye of olde men. They holde no counsaile but they tellen out alle that they see and here. Sodeynly they laughe and sodeynly they wepe. Alwey they crie and jangle and jape and make mowes; unneth [hardly] they ben stille while they slepe. Whanne they bene iwassche of filthe anon they defoulen [dirty] hemself eft [again]. Whanne the modir [mother] wasschith and kempith hem they kyken [kick] and praunsen and putte with feet and hondis, and withstonde with al here myght and strength. Thei coveiten and desiren to ete and drinke alwey. Unnethe they risen out of bed and axen [ask for] mete anon.

De puella

A maiden childe and a wenche hatte [called] *puella*, as it were clene and pure as the blake of the eye, as seith Isidre. For among alle that is iloved in a wenche chastite and clennes is iloved most. Men scahl take hede of wenches for they bene hote and moist of complexioun; and tendre, smal, pliaunt, and faire of disposicioun of body; schamefast, fereful, and mury [merry], touchinge the affeccioun; delicat in clothinge. . . . *Puella* is a name of soundenes withoute wem [fault], and also of honeste. So seith Isidre. . . . Aristotles seith that everiche womman generalich hath more neische [wavier] and softe here [hair] and more pliant than a man, and lengere necke. And the colour of wommen is more white thanne of men, and here face and semblant [appearance] is glad, softe, bright and plesinge. . . . And for a womman is more mylde than a man (sche wepith sonner than a man), and is more envyous and more lovynge. And malice of soule is more in a womman than in a man, and sche is of feble kynde, and sche maketh mo lesinges [more lies], and is more schamefast and more slow in worchinge and in mevynge thanne is a man. So seith Aristotle.

ANONYMOUS
The ABC of Aristotle (*c.* 1430)

In some manuscripts this alliterative alphabet of courtesy bears the alternate title 'Lerne or be Lewde (i.e. ignorant)'. Despite the claim that it is the work of a child, this punctilious catalogue of traits to avoid was obviously penned by a demanding though practical adult. The abecedary is secular, yet its injunctions promoting conservative social conduct definitely comply with Christian teaching. Although emphasis on the ascetic life of the spirit is understandably absent, this lesson does uphold the Aristotelian mean of good sense and temperance.

The ABC of Aristotle

Who-so wilneth to be wijs*, & worship desirith,	wise
Lerne he oo* lettir, & looke on anothir	one
Of the .a. b. c. of aristotil: argue not agen that:	
It is councel for right manye clerkis & knyghtis	
5 a thousand,	

And eek it myghte ameende* a man ful oft   *amend*
For to leerne lore of oo lettir, & his lijf save;
For to myche of ony thing was nevere holsum.
Reede ofte on this rolle, & rewle* thou ther aftir;   *rule*
10 Who-so be greved* in his goost*, governe him bettir;   *grieved; ghost*
Blame he not the barn* that this .a. b. c. made,   *bairn, child*
But wite* he his wickid will & his werk aftir;   *blame*
It schal nevere greve a good man though the gilti
    be meendid*.   *mended*
15 Now herkeneth & heerith how y bigynne.

A to amerose*, to avnterose*, ne argue not to myche.   *amorous; adventurous*
B to bolde, ne to bisi, ne boorde* not to large.   *babble*
C to curteis, to cruel, ne care not to sore*.   *sorely*
D to dul, ne to dreedful, ne drinke not to ofte.
E to elenge*, ne to excellent*, ne to eernesful* neither.   *melancholy; haughty; earnest.*
F to fers*, ne to famuler, but freendli of cheer.   *fierce*
G to glad, ne to gloriose, & gelosie thou hate.
H to hasti, ne to hardi, ne to hevy in thine herte.
I to iettynge*, ne to iangeline*, ne iape* not to ofte.   *ostentatious; chattering; joke*
K to kinde, ne to kepynge, & be waar* of
    knave tacchis*.   *wary; tricks*
L to looth for to leene, ne to liberal of goodis.
M to medelus*, ne to myrie, but as mesure wole
    it meeve   *meddling*
N to noiose*, ne to nyce, ne use to new iettis*.   *annoyed; devices*
O to orped*, ne to overthwart*, & ooth* thou hate.   *overbold; obstinate; oaths*
P to presing*, ne to prevy with princis ne with dukis;   *praising*
Q to queynte, ne to quarelose, but queeme* well   *please*
    youre sovereyns.
R to riotus, to reveling, ne rage not to rudeli.
S to straunge, ne to stirynge, ne straungeli to stare.
T to toilose*, ne to talewijs*, for temperaunce is beest.   *toiling; tale-bearing*
V to venemose, ne to veniable*, & voide al vilonye.   *envious*
W to wielde*, ne to wrathful, neither waaste, ne waade   *wild*
    not to depe
For a mesurable meene* is evere the beste of alle.   *mean*

FRANCIS SEAGER (*fl.* 1549–1563)
From *The Schoole of Vertue and Booke of Good Nurture* (1557)

Poet and translator, from a Devonshire yeoman family, Seager (sometimes spelled Segar) published a setting of nineteen Psalms before *The Schoole of Vertue*, whose twelve chapters of doggerel celebrate a trig, prepared, earnest schoolboy.

From *The Schoole of Vertue*

Downe from thy chamber when thou shalte go,
Thy parentes salute thou, and the famely also;
Thy handes se thou washe, and thy head keame,
And of thy rayment se torne be no seame;
5 Thy cappe fayre brusht, thy hed cover than,
Takynge it of In speakynge to any man.
Cato doth councel thee thyne elders to reverence
Declarynge therby thy dutye and obedience.
Thy shyrte coler fast to thy necke knyt;
10 Comely thy rayment loke on thy body syt.
Thy gyrdell about thy wast then fasten,
Thy hose fayre rubd thy showes se be cleane.
A napkyn se that thou have in redines
Thy nose to clense from all fylthynes.
15 Thy nayles, yf nede be, se that thou payre;
Thyne eares kepe cleane, thy teath washe thou fayre.
If ought about thee chaunce to be torne,
Thy frendes therof shewe howe it is worne,
And they wyll newe for thee provyde,
20 Or the olde mende, In tyme beinge spyde,
This done, thy setchell and thy bokes take,
And to the scole haste see thou make.
But ere thou go, with thy selfe forthynke.
That thou take with thee pen, paper, and ynke;
25 For these are thynges for thy study necessary,
Forget not then with thee them to cary.
The souldiar preparynge hym selfe to the fielde
Leaves not at home his sworde and his shielde,
No more shulde a scoler forget then truly
30 what he at scole shulde nede to occupy.
These thynges thus had, Take strayght thy way
Unto the schole without any stay.

HUGH RHODES (*fl.* 1550)
From *The Boke of Nurture, or Schoole of Good Manners* (1577)

This Devonshire-born gentleman of the King's Chapel was not only an acute observer of gross table manners but an adroit strategist in his own right. He maintained his position, much like that of a master, in the chapels of Henry VIII, and his Protestant son, King Edward VI, and Catholic daughter, Queen Mary. Rhodes composed *The Song of the Chyld-byshop* (1555) in Mary's praise. *The Boke of Nurture* was first printed in 1550, with a new edition, from which this excerpt is taken, appearing in 1577.

From *The Boke of Nurture*

Looke that your knyfe be sharp & kene to cut your meate withall;
So the more cleanlyer, be sure, cut your meate you shall.
Or thou put much bread in thy pottage, looke thou doe it assay:
Fill not thy spoone to full, least thou loose somewhat by the way.

. . .

And sup not lowde of thy Pottage, no tyme in all thy lyfe:
Dip not thy meate in the Saltseller, but take it with thy knyfe.
When thou haste eaten thy Pottage, doe as I shall thee wish:
Wype clean thy spone, I do thee read, leave it not in the dish;
Lay it downe before thy trenchoure, thereof be not afrayde;
And take heede who takes it up, for feare it be convayde.
Cut not the best peece for thy selfe, leave thou some parte behynde:
Bee not greedye of meate and drinke; be liberall and kynde.
Burnish no bones with thy teeth, for that is unseemly;
Rend not thy meate asunder, for that swarves from curtesy;
And if a straunger syt neare thee, ever among now and than
Reward thou him with some daynties: shew thyselfe a Gentleman.
If your fellow sit from his meate and cannot come thereto,
Then cutte for him such as thou haste; he may lyke for thee doe.

. . .

Scratche not thy head with thy fyngers when thou arte at thy meate;
Nor spytte you over the table boorde; see thou doest not this forget.
Pick not thy teeth with thy knyfe nor with thy fyngers ende,
But take a stick, or some cleane thyng, then doe you not offende.

. . .

Fyll not thy mouth to full, leaste thou perhaps of force must speake;
Nor blow not out thy crums when thou doest eate.
Fowle not the place with spitting whereas thou doest syt,
Least it abhore some that syt by: let reason rule thy wyt.
If thou must spit, or blow thy nose, keepe thou it out of sight,
Let it not lye upon the ground, but tread thou it out right.

SIR HUGH PLAT (1552–1608)
From *A Jewell House of Art and Nature* (1594)

Educated as a fellow-commoner at Cambridge, Hugh Plat (or Platt), the son of a wealthy brewer, devoted his relatively privileged life to literary studies, natural science, mechanical inventions, and agricultural experiments. His first publication, *Floures of Philosophie* (1572), consisting of over eight hundred terse statements from Seneca, was adapted by the contemporary poet Isabella Whitney for her *Sweet Nosegay* (1573). Plat's last publications were collections of recipes for preserving fruit, making cosmetics, and dyeing hair, *Delights for Ladies* (1602), and advice on gardening, *Floraes Paradise* (1608). *A Jewell House*, which he dedicated to the Earl of Essex, conveys Plat's interests in experiments in such diverse fields as horticulture, distillation, metal casting and, as the excerpt makes clear, progressive ideas about learning to read.

A ready way for children to learn their A.B.C.

CAufe 4 large dice of bone or wood to be made, and upon every fquare, one of the fmal letters of the crofs row to be graven, but in fome bigger fhape, and the child ufing to play much with them,

 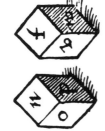 and being alwayes told what letter chanceth, will foon gain his Alphabet, as it were by the way of fport or paftime. I have heard of a pair of cards, whereon moft of the principall

Grammer rules have beenprinted, and the School-Mafter hath found good fport thereat with his fchollers.

Uncovered oaken hornbrook
of the later period

THE HORNBOOK

Whether handwritten or printed from type, this little lesson book is known from manuscript evidence to have existed from the fourteenth century. The parchment or paper lesson-sheet pasted onto the board was protected by a leaf of horn. (This material was made from the horns of sheep and goats; after having been softened and then boiled in water, they yielded the true horn that could be pressed and cut into sheets.) The covering was fixed to the small board by means of a brass or latten border held by minute tacks with raised heads; these slightly raised tacks protected the horn itself from scratches when the 'book' was laid face down. In the earliest examples the alphabet was preceded by the Cross; hence, the format was called the Criss-Cross row. In later Puritan examples the Cross was omitted.

Early uncovered hornbrook
in black letter

THE BATTLEDORE

The racquet in the game of battledore and shuttlecock, a forerunner of badminton, was modelled on the washerwoman's board or paddle ('batyldoure'). Just as the shuttlecock evolved into a very light object, usually a cork stuck with feathers, so the battledore also became lighter; early ones consisted of parchment, inscribed with lessons, stretched over a wooden frame.

A still lighter battledore, made of stiff paper, displayed a pictorial alphabet and prayers on both sides. Since it was folded, this battledore held more information than the hornbook sheet. The battledore was popular well into the nineteenth century, and developed an increasingly sophisticated format.

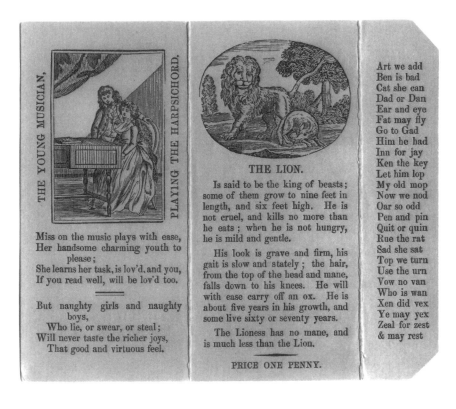

THE YOUNG MUSICIAN,

PLAYING THE HARPSICHORD.

Miss on the music plays with ease,
Her handsome charming youth to please;
She learns her task, is lov'd, and you,
If you read well, will be lov'd too.

But naughty girls and naughty boys,
Who lie, or swear, or steal;
Will never taste the richer joys,
That good and virtuous feel.

THE LION.

Is said to be the king of beasts; some of them grow to nine feet in length, and six feet high. He is not cruel, and kills no more than he eats; when he is not hungry, he is mild and gentle.

His look is grave and firm, his gait is slow and stately; the hair, from the top of the head and mane, falls down to his knees. He will with ease carry off an ox. He is about five years in his growth, and some live sixty or seventy years.

The Lioness has no mane, and is much less than the Lion.

PRICE ONE PENNY.

Art we add
Ben is bad
Cat she can
Dad or Dan
Ear and eye
Fat may fly
Go to Gad
Him he had
Inn for jay
Ken the key
Let him lop
My old mop
Now we nod
Oar so odd
Pen and pin
Quit or quin
Rue the rat
Sad she sat
Top we turn
Use the urn
Vow no van
Who is wan
Xen did vex
Ye may yex
Zeal for zest
& may rest

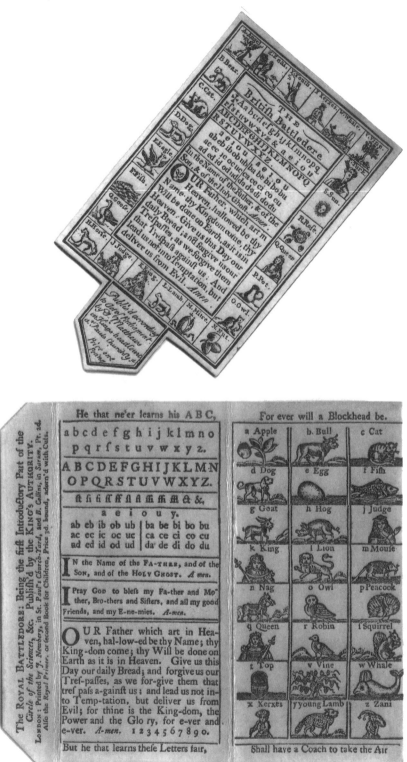

WILLIAM PAGET (1572–1629), later Fourth Lord Paget
From Manuscript Juvenilia preserved in Henry Stanford's *Miscellany*
(MS Dd 5.75 [F], University Library, Cambridge)

William Paget was an only child. At the time of his New Year's poem to his grandmother, with whom he was living at West Drayton, Middlesex, his parents were separating. This nine-year-old shows an awareness of what we would call the consumerism of the gift-giving season. His picture of Christmastide festivities has a broad social sweep—from the swish of silks at court during the visit of the Queen's suitor to the bids of farmers and citizens for favour. Paget's understanding of the pervasiveness of flattery, though conventional, is quite remarkable for a child. With allusions to Homer and Cicero ('Tullie') and the concluding pun on his name, he wears his learning openly, but he also makes an affecting display of his 'loving mynd'.

A new yeres gift (1581)

The tyme is ronne about & Phebus golden sphere
by revolution just beginneth I hope a happie year
And Janus doble faced doth now put us in mynd
of tyme that is past & for to wishe good successe to
5   our frend
And all both riche & poore prepare giftes to present
to thos to whom in hart they ar & goodwill frendly bent
The countrie farme he his hennes & capons sendes
And maides & wyves such giftes provides as fortune to
10   them lendes
The citisens wch have of worldly welthe no lacke
provyde for to present ther frendes wth wares of
    pedlars packe
The little wanton boy & pretie Mopsie mayd
15 present som comfites or som toye to make ther
    parentes glad
The coart now swymes in sylke, & Monsieur* playes
    his part
And lordes of fraunce & English dames do stryve to
20   shew yr art
Who shall to frend present the thing of greatest price
or may by gallant gift advance, himself in bravest wise
Ther brodered purses flie, wth store of pelf well fraught
& plate of silver & of gold, & velvete derely bought
25 The Indian precious pearl & Jewels passing brave
are ther presented for to shew, what mynd the givers have

Duc D'Alençon, one
of Queen Elizabeth's
suitors, was in
England from Oct.
1581 to Feb. 1582.

wch thing when I do thinke, yt makes my hart full sad

that I for you my Grandam dear, no gift can get (though bad)

for thoughe I be a boy, in yeres & wit a child

30 yet none in dutie doth me passe, yf I be not beguiled

The countrie farmers giftes, are sent for privy gayne

that they therbie ther landlordes grace, & favour may retayn

The wafers wch are sent, of wyves & maydes to frendes

are rather thinges of course & use, then signes of loving myndes

35 The Citisen hath lerned, to flatter & speake fair

his newyeres giftes are but a bait, to utter well his ware

Althoughe the little child, wth no dissembling is clad

yet for to bear a great good will, his yong wittes are to bad

The court the place is thought, where flatterie cheif doth raign

40 I dare say som would wish ther giftes, might brede to frendes yr bane

But I my ladie dear, & Grandham most beloved

do bear to you suche great good, will as seldom hath byn proved

I thinke yf Homer lyved, wth streames of golden speache

he could not to my loving mynd, wth all his witt now reache

                 skill

45 nor Tullie wth his ~~witt~~ & lerned sugred worke

could halfe expresse the dutie w^ch, w^thin my mynd doth lurke

[f. I] My love is pure & true, I never lerned to flatter

nor never tyme or thing shall cause, yt for to move or totter

Since then the case thus standes, & that no store I have

50 of pedlars ware or parfumed gloves, wch me from shame

    might save

lest that I might now seme, more rude then clounishe swayn

yf that I nothing should present, wch so much bound remayn.

In verses thes I gyve, my hart & willing mynd

55 wch for to dwell alwayes wth you yt fullie now I bynd

before that I do shrinke or from this promise swarve

the rockes shall swyme in toppes of seas, & meat shall make

    men starve

Trent* shall I say before, run over scowfill hill*

60 & mountes shall move out of ther place, & run the seas untill

And monsters uncouthe strange, shall yoyn in league of love

before that any worldly thing do cause my mynd to move

for tripping stag shall chuse, the tigre for his make

And dove the Eagle for his fear, as then shall not forsake

65 nor seelie shepe the paw, of lion feirce shall fear

And clyming goat in salt seas foames, to swym then we

    shall hear

before that I forget, what dutie that I owe

or cease wth wordes or thoughtes or deedes, yt alwayes

70   forth to shooe

Receave for new yeres gift, this shew of loving mynd

& in all dutie & good will, me slacke you shall not fynd

I pray almightie god, wch rules the golden sphear

The river Trent ran past the Paget estates at Beaudesert, Staffordshire; Scawfell or Scafell, Cumbria, is the second highest peak in England

to graunt to you all happines, & many a merye year
75 And that when you shall passe, out of this vaile of payn
you may wth him in cristall skyes, always in pleasure raigne.

> Your little sonne Will Paget dothe
> thes verses to you send
> W^ch in good will gives place to none
80 & thus he makes an end.

GEORGE BERKELEY (1601–1658), later eighth Lord Berkeley
From Manuscript Juvenilia preserved in Henry Stanford's *Miscellany*
(MS Dd 5.75 [F], University Library, Cambridge)

Ten-year-old George Berkeley wrote to a wider circle of subjects—his grandparents, family friends, and a servant—than William Paget. Both boys may have benefited from a rhetorical handbook of allusions and images which their tutor likely possessed. Berkeley's poems are shorter and keener to display his learning and sense of duty than Paget's. Playing on the Latin meaning of the name of his mother's servant (*cave*: beware), this junior patriarch tries to balance the urge to lecture and the desire for friendship.

George Bercklay to his Grandfather (1610)

Trice honourd lord the prop & cheifest stay
of my poore state & of my tender yeares
my duty biddes me this same new yeares day
to shew my mynd & to congratulate
5 An asse did speake as scripture dothe us show*   Numbers 22. 28
king Cræsus son born dumb being movd did speake*   Herodotus, Book 1, chap. 85
Augustus was saluted by a crow*   Pliny, Book 10, §121
No mervail then yf that I silence breake
All hail deere Grandsire & long live in joy
10 Yf I deserve then count me still your boy.

George to Mrs Cave his mothers wayting woman

My Cave I wishe the this new yeare suche fortune & suche hap
As they do use to prove wch sit in lady fortunes lap
long life & store of worldly wealth, & husband the to love
of whom thou maist have store of brattes & joyes of
5   wedlocke prove
Thie name I trow a sentence is, & willes the to take hede
Ile deskant of yt by thy leave, for yt may profite brede

Take [hede] you be not made I say wth flattring speaches drunke
For fawning smiling speache hath made, an honest wenche
10   a punke*   *prostitute*
Take hede thou be not led wth gaine for Covetise is a vice
and gold of honest wenche hath made full oft a Cockatrice*   *serpent hatched*
Take hede thou be not arrogant, for that will the disgrace   *from a cock's egg*
A prowd & haughty cariage marrs full oft a pleasing face
15   Take hede of Anger it becomes, feirce beastes & ugly creatures
more than thy milde & gentle sex, wch hath so goodly features
But I surcease for see thy name, doth yeald to large a theame
my only purpose was to tell how much I the esteme
live happie I will the regard & wishe the as my freinde
20   Doe thou the like yf so thou please, & thus I make an ende.

MARY DOWNING (*fl.* 1630s)
A Letter to Her Father: Mary Downing to Emmanuel Downing (1635)

Following her mother's death and father's remarriage to Lucy Winthrop, Mary Downing, along with a brother and sister, was sent to Boston to board with an aunt and uncle. The children's uncle, John Winthrop, was Governor of the Bay Colony. Mary Downing's Puritan pedigree is impeccable. The following letter reveals the anxieties of a youngster living at a great distance from her parents, pleading for money for new clothes, and attempting respectfully to answer her stepmother's complaints about prodigality. The Downings did not emigrate to join the children until 1638, following the birth of Lucy Winthrop Downing's sixth child. Although the strained relationship with her stepmother is evident, so too is the young Puritan's ability to cite scripture to prove her acceptance, to appeal to a sense of family shame that her clothes offend elders, and to sidestep the issue of conversion until the time is right.

Mary Downing to Emmanuel Downing

Worthy Sir, Deare Father,

The continuall experience that I enjoy of your tender love and care to a child, though I confesse an undeservinge one [yet] your love emboldens mee to present my humble duty and respect I owe and shall render with my might and power to your selfe soe longe as it pleaseth the Lord to continue my life. I have found soe much your love and see that neither time nor distance of place doth diminish or blast the same. . . . Father I trust in him who hath the harts and the disposinge of them in his hand, that I have not provoked you to harbor soe ill an opinion of mee as my mothers letters do signifie and give me to understand, the ill opinion and hard perswasion which shee beares of mee, that is to say, that I should abuse your goodnes, and bee prodigall of your purse neglectfull of my brothers bands and of my slatterishnes and lasines. for my brothers bands I will not excuse my selfe, but I thinke not worthy soe sharpe a reproofe, for the rest I must needs excuse, and cleare my selfe If I may be beleived. I doe not know my selfe guilty of any of them. for myne owne part I doe not desire to bee myne owne judge, but am willinge to be judged by them, with whom I live and sees my course, whether I bee addicted to such thinges or noe. for my habitt, it is meane, for the most as many servants, and if I had not had money which I had for some thinges here I might have wanted many necessaries which I could not have bin without, except I should have made you a scoare [debt] here, which I was not willing to doe: I writt to my mother for lace not out of any prodigall or proud mind but onely for some crosscloathes [linen worn across the forehead], which is the most allowable and commendable dressinge here. Shee would have me weare dressings which I did soe longe as they would suffer mee, whilest the elders with others intreated mee to leave them of; for they gave great offence and seeinge it hath pleased the Lord to bringe mee hither amongst his people, I would not willingly doe any thinge amongst them that should be displeasing unto them, but for myne owne part since my sendinge for things gives such offence I will be more sparinge in that kind hereafter but leave it to the Lord to deale with mee according to his mercy earnestly desireinge him to give mee an hart to bee content with my porcion, knowinge that nothinge can beefall mee but that, that hee hath appointed. I may take that verse in the 106th Psalme 17th verse, fooles because of their transgressions and their iniquities are afflicted soe I thinke that just it is, whatsoever affliction shall come unto mee. Deare Father I am farr distant from you, and knowe not how longe it will please the Lord to continue it soe, but howsoever I desire to rest satisfied with his will and doe earnestly desire to submitt my selfe in all duty and obedience as belongeth unto a child to your selfe and my mother, as if I were with you. Father I perceive by your lettres that you would very willingly to have mee change my condition [to convert to being a 'Saint'] which I must confesse I might soe may with divers if the Lord pleased to move my hart to accept any of them, but I desire to wayte upon him that can change my hart at his will. thus with my humble duty to your selfe and my mother craving pardon of you both and of her If I have given her any offence, and soe desiringe your prayers to him, who is able to give wisedome and direccion to me in all thinges I rest: Your obedient Daughter till death

Mary Downinge
Boston, 27th of Novemb 1635

LADY ELIZABETH GRYMESTON (1563–1602/3)
From *Miscelanea. Meditations. Memoratives* (1604)

Lady Grymeston addressed her *Miscelanea. Meditations. Memoratives* to her son Bernye, the only surviving child of her nine children. Knowing herself to be 'a dead woman among the living', she presents him with 'this portable *veni mecum* [as] Counseller, in which to see the true portrature of [his] mothers minde.' The picture that emerges is of a learned woman who delights in quoting Latin and Greek, borrows a verse paraphrase of psalms (Chapter XIII), and, as this excerpt illustrates, distills proverbial wisdom into pithy directives.

Memoratives

In all temptations it is safer to flie, than to fight with Satan.

Shun occasion of doing evill, and thou hast halfe overcome him.

Examine thy thoughts. If thou findest them to be good; there is the Spirit: Quench not the Spirit. If bad; forbid them entrance: for once admitted, they straightwayes fortifie, and are expelled with more difficultie, than not admitted. Think from whence thou camest, and blush; where thou art, and sigh; and tremble to remember whither thou shalt goe.

Where proportion keeps not the doore, there confusion will quickly enter.

Labour in youth gives strong hope of rest in olde age.

Let wit be thy friend, thy minde thy companion, thy tongue thy servant.

Let vertue be thy life, valour thy love, honour thy fame and heaven thy felicity.

On the anvill of upbraiding is forged the office of unthankfulnesse.

Let thy speeche be the shadow of thy deed.

Innocencie groweth in despight of oppression.

Dominion is always attended by envy.

Fortune is always a friend to a froward minde.

He never gives in vaine that gives in zeale.

Courtesie is the true character of a good minde.

Trueth is the centre of religion.

Dominion is safest, where obedience is best nourished.

DOROTHY LEIGH
From *The Mothers Blessing* (1616)

A widow who saw herself 'going out of the world,' Dorothy Leigh addressed her posthumously published advice book to her three sons, George, John, and William, probably grammar school pupils at the time. Designed to be 'profitable for all Parents to leave as a Legacy to their Children', *The Mothers Blessing* clearly met a demand: the text had twenty-three editions in less than sixty years. Hoping to see her sons 'grow in godlinesse', this 'fearefull, faithfull and carefull Mother' combines purposiveness and humility. As the following chapter of this forty-four-chapter text illustrates, Leigh mortifies the self while she provides a continuous string of scriptural allusions to map a path for her sons. Concerned that her exhortation not mould unused, she relies on practical examples with no sugarcoating.

Chapter 2

The first cause of writing, is a Motherly affection.

But lest you should marvaile, my children, why I doe not, according to the usuall custome of women, exhort you by word and admonitions, rather then by writing, a thing so unusuall among us, and especially in such a time, when there bee so manie godly bookes in the world, that they mould in some mens studies, while their Masters are mard, because they will not meditate upon them; as many mens garments motheate in their chests, while their Christian bretheren quake with cold in the street for want of covering; know therfore, that it was the motherly affection that I bare unto you all, which made me now (as it often hath done heretofore) forget my selfe in regard of you: neither care I what you or any shall thinke of mee, if among many words I may write but one sentence, which may make you labour for the spirituall food of the soule, wch must be gathered every day out of the word, as the children of Israel gathered Manna in the wildernesse. By the which you may see it is a labour: but what labour? a pleasant labour, a profitable labour: a labour without the which the soule cannot live. For as the children of Israel must needs starve, except they gath'red every day in the wildernesse and fed of it, so must your soules, except you gather the spiritual Manna out of the word every day, and feed of it continually: for as they by this Manna cóforted their harts, strengthened their bodies, and preserved their lives; so by this heavenly Word of God, you shall comfort your soules, make them strong in Faith, and grow in true godlinesse, and finally preserve them with great joy, to everlasting life, through Faith in Christ; whereas if you desire any food for your soules, that is not in the written Word of God, your soules die with it even in your harts and mouthes; even as they that desired other food (Numbers 11. 3) dyed with it in their mouthes, were it never so dainty: so shall you, and there is no recovery for you.

ELIZABETH JOSCELIN (1595–1622)
From *The Mothers Legacie to her unborne Childe* (1624)

Elizabeth Joscelin began the incomplete *Mothers Legacie*, discovered posthumously in a writing desk, during her first pregnancy. She died of puerperal fever nine days after the birth of her daughter (Theodora) on 12 October 1622. The text enjoyed considerable popularity, with seven editions within eleven years; there were five nineteenth-century editions. The posthumous publication, the ardour of the prefatory letter to her husband, and the poignant blend of fear of death and spirited mentoring are some of the reasons for this enduring appeal. *The Mothers Legacie* introduces thirteen directions with the following preliminary notice.

From *The Mothers Legacie to her unborne Childe*

Having long, often and earnestly desired of God, that I might be a mother to one of his children, and the time now drawing on, which I hope hee hath appointed to give thee unto mee: It drew me into a consideration both wherefore I so earnestly desired thee, and (having found that the true cause was to make thee happy) how I might compasse this happinesse for thee.

I knew it consisted not in honour, wealth, strength of body or friends (though all these are great blessings) therefore it had beene a weake request to desire thee onely for an heire to my fortune. No, I never aimed at so poore an inheritance for thee, as the whole world: Neither would I have begged of God so much paine, as I know I must endure, to have only possest thee with earthly riches, of which to day thou maist bee a great man, tomorrow a poore begger. Nor did an hope to dandle thy infancy move mee to desire thee. For I know all the delight a Parent can take in a childe is hony mingled with gall.

But the true reason that I have so often kneeled to God for thee, is, that thou mightest bee an inheritour of the Kingdome of Heaven. To which end I humbly beseech Almightie God thou maist bend all thy actions and (if it bee his blessed will) give thee so plentifull a measure of his grace, that thou maist serve him as his Minister, if he make thee a man.

It is true that this age holds it a most contemptible office, fit only for poore mens children, younger brothers, and such as have no other means to live. But for Gods sake bee not discouraged with these vaine speeches; but fortifie your selfe with remembring of how great worth the winning of one soule is in Gods sight, and you shal quickly finde how great a place it is to be a Priest unto the living of God. If it will please him to move your heart with his holy Spirit, it will glow and burne with zeale to doe him service. The Lord open thy lips, that thy mouth may shew forth his praise. . . .

And if thou beest a daughter, thou maist perhaps thinke I have lost my labour; but reade on, and thou shalt see my love and care of thee and thy salvation is as great, as if thou wert a sonne, and my feare greater.

It may peradventure when thou comest to some discretion, appeare strange to thee to receive these lines from a Mother that died when thou wert borne; but when thou seest men purchase land, and store up treasure for their unborne babes, wonder not at mee that I am carefull for thy salvation, being such an eternall portion: and not knowing whether I shall live to instruct thee when thou art borne, let mee not bee blamed though I write to thee before. Who would not condemne mee if I should bee carelesse of thy body while it is within me? Sure a farre greater care belongs to thy soule; to both these cares I will endeavour my selfe so longe as I live.

Againe, I may perhaps bee wondred at for writing in this kinde, considering there are so many excellent bookes, whose least note is worth all my meditations. I confesse it, and thus excuse my selfe. I write not to the world, but to mine own childe, who it may be, will more profit by a few weake instructions comming from a dead mother (who cannot every day praise or reprove it as it deserves) than by farre better from much more learned. These things considered, neither the true knowledge of mine owne weaknesse, nor the feare this may come to the worlds eie, and bring scorne upon my grave, can stay my hand from expressing how much I covet thy salvation.

Therefore deare childe, reade here my love, and if God take mee from thee, be obedient to these instructions, as thou oughtest to bee unto mee, I have learnt them out of Gods Word, I beseech him that they may be profitable to thee.

ELIZABETH RICHARDSON (1576–1651)
From *A Ladies Legacie to her Daughters* (1645)

Written over a span of approximately forty years from 1606 to 1645, *A Ladies Legacie* charts Richardson's progress through two marriages and final widowhood. Book One, a calendar of prayers associated with specific liturgies and composed between 1606 and 1625, is addressed to her four daughters (three unmarried at the time). Significantly she excludes her sons who, 'being men', will misconstrue her intention. In 1620 with the death of John Ashburnham, her first husband who had been imprisoned for debt, she was a widow with six children and a precarious future. Yet her letter reproduced here, though noting her daughters' 'want of preferments', rehearses the sense of assurance in providential guidance. Book Two, composed after the death in 1634 of her second husband, Sir Thomas Richardson, Lord Chief Justice of the King's Bench, is a weekly exercise of prayer. Book Three contains prayers on the topics of widowhood, affliction, sickness, and death.

A Letter to my foure Daughters

My deare Children:

I have long and much grieved for your misfortunes, and want of preferments in the world: but now I have learned in what estate soever I am, therewith to be content, and to account these vile and transitorie things to be but vaine and losse, so

I may win Christ the fountaine of all blisse, wishing you with me, to condemne that which neglecteth you, and set your hearts and affections on better subjects, such as are above, more certaine and permanent: and feare not but what is needfull for this present life shall be supplyed by him who best knows our wants: and had it not been for your sakes (whose advancements love and nature bindeth me to seeke) I had prevented the spite of my enemies, and forsaken the World before it despised me: But though I am so unhappy as to be left destitute, not able to raise you portions of wealth, yet shall I joy as much to adde unto the portion of Grace, which I trust, and pray, that God will give to each of you, to whose mercy I daily commit you, nothing doubting but that he will receive you into the number of those fatherlesse he graciously taketh care of, if you omit not to serve and depend on him faithfully, for he never faileth them that trust in him. God is as free and ready to give us as we to aske, and contrary to the World, he grows not weary of importunate suters, but often deferreth his blessings to make us the more earnest for them. Neither hath the Lord withdrawn his favour so from us as to leave us utterly desolate to despair, but hath graciously raised us comfort by honourable friends to be carefull and deare parents unto us, whom God preserve and shew mercy to them and theirs, as they have done to us. And here I send you a motherly remembrance, and commend this my labour unto your loving acceptance, that in remembring your poor mother, you may be also put in minde to performe your humble duty and service to our heavenly Father, who hath created us to his own glory and service; and all we can performe, comes far short of what we owe unto him; yet is he well pleased if we returne (for all his mercies) but obedience, and the sacrifice of praise and calling upon his holy Name. Now prayer being the winged messenger to carry our requests and wants into the ears of the Lord (as David saith) he will praise the Lord seven times a day, and prevent the light to give thanks unto God; and indeed, who can awake to enjoy the light and pleasure of the day, and not begin the same with an intreaty of the Lords gracious direction in all things, and desire of his blessing upon us, and all that we have or doe? Or how can we possesse or hourely receive so many favours and benefits from God, and not offer unto him an evening sacrifice of thanksgiving? Or who dares adventure to passe the dreadfull night, the time of terror, and yeeld themselves to sleep, the image of death, before they are at peace with God, by begging pardon for their sins, and craving his protection and care over them in the night?

I know you may have many better instructers then my self, yet can you have no true mother but me, who not only with great paine brought you into the world, but do now still travell in care for the new birthe of your soules; to bring you to eternall life, which is my chiefest desire, and the height of my hopes: And howsoever this my endeavour may be contemptible to many, (because a womans) which makes me not to joyne my sons with you, lest being men, they misconstrue my well-meaning; yet I presume that you my daughters will not refuse your Mothers teaching (which I wish may be your ornament, and a crown of glory to you) who I hope will take in the best part my carefull industrie, for your present and future happinesse, towards which I have not failed to give you the best breeding in my power, to bring you to vertue and piety, which I esteem the greatest treasure; and sure I am, it leads you to him that is the giver of all good things, both spirituall and temporall; to whose infinite mercy I most humbly commend you, who I trust will fulfill all your necessities, through the riches of his grace, and make you perfect in all good workes to doe his will. And the God of peace sanctifie you throughout, that your whole spirits, soules and bodies, may bee kept blamelesse unto the comming of our Lord Jesus Christ, which shall be the endlesse joy of your most loving Mother,

Eliz. Ashbournham

KATHERINE PHILIPS (1632–1664)
From *Poems* (1664)

Philips's early death at age thirty-two contributed to the legend of her precocity, which was amplified by a well-received production of her translation of Corneille and several editions of her collection of letters and poems on friendship sent by 'Orinda', the pseudonym she adopted, to a coterie of select, primarily female, friends. Her marriage to James Philips, MP for Cardiganshire in Wales and a widower three decades her senior, was childless for seven years. The focus of her mature poetry, circulated in manuscript in the 1650s, was both public and private,

national and local. It ranges over topics from the regicide, which she denounced, to the country life, disputes in religion, the marriages of friends, the absences of her husband, and the death of children, particularly her only son, for whom she wrote an epitaph and this elegy in quatrains. According to the 'Epitaph', Hector Philips lived 'less then six weeks'. Therefore, the date in the title of the elegy, which conveys with poignant feeling the fragility of life, may be a misprint for June 2. The setting by Philips's friend, the musician Henry Lawes, has not survived.

**On the death of my first and dearest childe, Hector Philipps,
borne the 23^d of Aprill, and dy'd the 2^d of May 1655. set by Mr Lawes**

> Twice Forty moneths in wedlock I did stay,
>   Then had my vows crown'd with a lovely boy.
> And yet in forty days he dropt away;
>   O! swift vicissitude of humane Joy!
>
> 5 I did but see him, and he disappear'd,
>   I did but touch the Rose-bud, and it fell;
> A sorrow unfore-seen and scarcely fear'd,
>   Soe ill can mortalls their afflictions spell.
>
> And now (sweet Babe) what can my trembling heart
> 10   Suggest to right my doleful fate or thee?
> Tears are my Muse, and sorrow all my Art,
>   So piercing groans must be thy Elogy.

Thus whilst no eye is witness of my mone,
 I grieve thy loss (Ah, boy too dear to live!)
15 And let the unconcerned World alone,
 Who neither will, nor can refreshment give.

An Off'ring too for thy sad Tomb I have,
 Too just a tribute to thy early Herse;
Receive these gasping numbers to thy grave,
20 The last of thy unhappy Mother's Verse.

LADY MARY CHUDLEIGH (1656–1710)
From *Poems on Several Occasions* (1703)

Restoration feminist, Mary, Lady Chudleigh, wrote essays and poems experimenting with satire and biblical paraphrases, which went through four editions. Her marriage to Sir George Chudleigh, the third baronet of Ashton, Devon, was apparently unhappy, but productive. Four of her six children, including both daughters, died, and she herself suffered from debilitating rheumatism, which caused her death. She took great delight in reading, especially English verse translations of the classics, and in corresponding through assumed pastoral names with a female literary circle, for whom Chudleigh became 'Marissa' and her correspondents, 'Clorissa', 'Eugenia', 'Cleanthe', or 'Lucinda'. The death of her beloved mother, Mary (Sydenham) Lee, immortalized as 'Philinda', was followed closely by the death of her youngest child, the eight-year-old Eliza Maria. The dialogue reproduced here discloses the vulnerability of the grieving, exhausted mother and the instruction between women about the role of reason in ruling the passions of a generous mind.

On the Death of my dear Daughter *Eliza Maria Chudleigh*: A Dialogue between *Lucinda* and *Marissa*

Marissa. O my *Lucinda!* O my dearest Friend!
Must my Afflictions never, never End!
Has Heav'n for me no Pity left in Store,
Must I! O must I ne'er be happy more,
5 *Philinda's* Loss had almost broke my Heart,
From her, Alas! I did but lately part:
And must there still be new Occasions found
To try my Patience, and my Soul to wound?
Must my lov'd Daughter too be snatch'd away,
10 Must she so soon the Call of Fate obey?
In her first Dawn, replete with youthful Charms,
She's fled, she's fled from my deserted Arms.

Long did she struggle, long the War maintain,
But all th'Efforts of Life, alas! were vain.
15 Could Art have sav'd her she had still been mine,
Both Art and Care together did combine,
But what is Proof against the Will Divine!
    Methinks I still her dying Conflict view
And the sad Sight does all my Grief renew;
20 Rack'd by Convulsive Pains she meekly lies,
And gazes on me with imploring Eyes,
With Eyes which beg Relief, but all in vain,
I see, but cannot, cannot ease her Pain:
She must the Burthen unassisted bear,
25 I cannot with her in her Tortures share:
Wou'd they were mine, and she stood easie by;
For what one loves, sure 'twere not hard to die.
    See, how she labours, how she pants for Breath,
She's lovely still, she's sweet, she's sweet in Death!
30 Pale as she is, she beauteous does remain,
Her closing Eyes their Lustre still retain:
Like setting Suns, with undiminish'd Light,
They hide themselves within the Verge of Night.
    She's gone! she's gone! she sigh'd her Soul away!
35 And can I! can I any longer stay!
My Life, alas! has ever tiresome been,
And I few happy, easie Days have seen;
But now it does a greater Burthen grow,
I'll throw it off and no more Sorrow know,
40 But with her to calm peaceful Regions go.
    Stay thou, dear Innocence, retard thy Flight,
O stop thy Journey to the Realms of Light,
Stay till I come: To thee I'll swiftly move,
Attracted by the strongest Passion, Love.

45 *Lucinda.* No more, no more let me such Language hear,
I can't, I can't the piercing Accents bear:
Each Word you utter stabs me to the Heart:
I cou'd from Life, not from *Marissa* part:
And were your Tenderness as great as mine,
50 While I were left, you would not thus repine.
My Friends are Riches, Health, and all to me,
And while they're mine, I cannot wretched be.

Marissa. If I on you cou'd Happiness bestow,
I still the Toils of Life wou'd undergo,
55 Wou'd still contentedly my Lot sustain,
And never more of my hard Fate complain:
But since my Life to you will useless prove,

O let me hasten to the Joys above:
Farewel, farewel, take, take my last adieu,
60 May Heav'n be more propitious still to you
May you live happy when I'm in my Grave,
And no Misfortunes, no Afflictions have:
If to sad Objects you'll some Pity lend,
And give a Sigh to an unhappy Friend,
65 Think of *Marissa*, and her wretched State,
How she's been us'd by her malicious Fate,
Recount those Storms which she has long sustain'd
And then rejoice that she the Port has gain'd,
The welcome Haven of eternal Rest,
70 Where she shall be fore ever, ever blest;
And in her Mother's, and her Daughter's Arms,
Shall meet with new, with unexperienc'd Charms.
O how I long those dear Delights to taste;
Farewel, farewel; my Soul is much in haste.
75 Come Death and give the kind releasing Blow;
I'm tir'd with Life, and over-charg'd with Woe:
In thy cool, silent, unmolested Shade,
O let me be by their dear Relicks laid;
And there with them from all my Troubles free,
80 Enjoy the Blessings of a long Tranquillity.

Lucinda. O thou dear Suff'rer, on my Breast recline
Thy drooping Head, and mix thy Tears with mine:
Here rest a while, and make a Truce with Grief,
Consider; Sorrow brings you no Relief,
85 In the great Play of Life we must not chuse,
Nor yet the meanest Character refuse
Like Soldiers we our Gen'ral must obey,
Must stand our Ground, and not to Fear give way,
But go undaunted on till we have won the Day.
90 Honour is ever the Reward of Pain,
A lazy Virtue no Applause will gain,
All such as to uncommon Heights would rise,
And on the Wings of Fame ascend the Skies,
Must learn the Gifts of Fortune to despise.
95 They to themselves their Bliss must still confine,
Must be unmov'd, and never once repine:
But few to this Perfection can attain,
Our Passions often will th'Ascendant gain,
And Reason but alternately does reign;
100 Disguis'd by Pride, we sometimes seem to bear
A haughty Port, and scorn to shed a Tear;
While Grief within still acts a tragick Part,
And plays the Tyrant in the bleeding Heart.

Your Sorrow is of the severest kind,
105 And can't be wholly to your Soul confin'd:
Losses like yours, may be allow'd to move
A gen'rous Mind, that knows what 'tis to love.
Who that her innate Worth had understood,
Wou'd not lament a Mother so divinely good?
110 And who, alas! without a Flood of Tears,
Cou'd lose a Daughter in her blooming Years:
An only Daughter, such a Daughter too,
As did deserve to be belov'd by you;
Who'd all that cou'd her to the World commend,
115 A Wit that did her tender Age transcend,
Inviting Sweetness, and a sprightly Air,
Looks that had something pleasingly severe,
The Serious and the Gay were mingl'd there:
These merit all the Tears that you have shed,
120 And could Complaints recall them from the Dead,
Could Sorrow their dear Lives again restore,
I here with you for ever would deplore:
But since th'intensest Grief will prove in vain,
And these lost Blessings can't be yours again,
125 Recal your wand'ring Reason to your Aid,
And hear it calmly when it does persuade;
'Twill teach you Patience, and the useful Skill
To rule your Passions, and command your Will;
To bear Afflictions with a steady Mind,
130 Still to be easie, pleas'd, and still resign'd,
And look as if you did no inward Trouble find.

Marissa. I know, *Lucinda,* this I ought to do,
But oh! 'tis hard my Frailties to subdue:
My Head-strong Passions will Resistance make,
135 And all my firmest Resolutions shake:
I for my Daughter's Death did long prepare,
And hop'd I shou'd the Stroke with Temper bear,
But when it came, Grief quickly did prevail,
And I soon found my boasted Courage fail:
140 Yet still I strove, but 'twas, alas! in vain,
My Sorrow did at length th'Ascendant gain:
But I'm resolv'd I will no longer yield;
By Reason led, I'll once more take the Field,
And there from my insulting Passions try
145 To gain a full, a glorious Victory:
Which till I've done, I never will give o'er,
But still fight on, and think of Peace no more;
With an unwaery'd Courage still contend,
Till Death, or Conquest, does my Labour end.

EDWARD TOPSELL (1572–1625)
From *The Historie of Four-footed Beastes* (1607)

Born in Kent and educated at Cambridge (BA 1591; MA 1595), Topsell was an ordained minister of the Church of England, holding a succession of livings in Sussex, Lincolnshire, Northamptonshire and, finally, Aldersgate. This clergyman and naturalist wrote a series of religious tracts and scriptural commentaries. But by far his most famous works are the illustrated folios, *The Historie of Four-footed Beastes* (1607) and *The Historie of Serpents* (1608), which were combined with Thomas Moffet's *Theatre of Insects* in *The History of Four-footed Beasts and Serpents and Insects* in 1658. Topsell's study of birds, *The Fowles of Heaven*, derived from the fourteen-volume Latin work of the Italian ornithologist Ulisse Aldrovani (1522–1605), is an incomplete illustrated manuscript. Topsell's source for the first two books was the Swiss zoologist Conrad Gesner (1516–65). His dedication supplies a theological justification for the study of natural history, which 'might profit and delight the Reader' by allowing him or her to 'passe away the Sabbaths in heavenly meditations upon earthly creatures'. Like Gesner, from whose work he borrowed the often fantastic illustrations, Topsell made no distinction between real and fabulous beasts. Expanding the popular medieval tradition of the bestiaries (allegorical poems or stories on legendary animals with Christian morals appended), Topsell's *Histories*, the only major study of animals in English before the dawn of the new science, combine philology, mythology, and anecdote.

Of the Lamia

This word *Lamia* hath many significations, being taken sometimes for a beast of *Lybia*, sometimes for a fish, and sometimes for a Spectre or apparition of women called Phairies. And from hence some have ignorantly affirmed, that either there were no such beastes at all, or else that it was a compounded monster of a beast and a fish, whose opinions I will briefly set downe. *Aristophanes* affirmeth, that he heard one say, that he saw a great wilde Beast having severall parts resembling outwardly an Oxe, and inwardly a Mule, and a beautifull woman, which he called afterwards *Empusa*.

When *Appollonius* and his companions travailed in a bright Moone shine night, they saw a certaine apparition of Phairies, in *Latine* called *Lamiae*, and in Greeke, *Empusae*, changing themselves from one shape into another, being also sometimes visible, and presently vanishing out of sight againe: as soone as he perceaved it, he knew what it was and did rate it with very contumelious and despightfull words, exhorting his fellowes to do the like, for that is the best remedie against the invasion of Phairies. And when his companions did likewise raile at them, presently the vision departed away.

The Poets say, that *Lamia* was a beautifull woman, the daughter of *Bellus* and *Lybia*, which *Jupiter* loved, bringing her out of *Lybia* into *Italie*, where he begot upon hir many sonnes, but Juno jealous of her husband, destroied them as soone as they were borne, punishing *Lamia* also with a restlesse estate, that she could never be able to sleepe, but live night and day in continuall mourning, for which occasion she also stealeth away and killeth the children of others, whereupon came the fable of changing of children: Jupiter having pitty upon her, gave exemptile eyes that might be taken in and out at hir own pleasure, & likewise power to be transformed into what shape she would. . . .

Plutarch also affirmeth, that they have exemptile eies as aforesaid, and that as often as they go from home, they put in their eies, wandring abroad by habitations, streetes, and cross waies, entring into the assemblies of men, and prying so perfectly into every thing, that nothing can escape them, be it never so well covered: you wil thinke (saith hee) that they have the eies of Kites, for there is no small mote but they espie it, nor any hole so secret but they finde it out, and when they come home againe, at the very entrance of their howse they pul out their eies, and cast them aside, so being blinde at home, but seeing abroad. If you ask me (saith he) what they do at home, they sit singing and making of wool, and then turning his speech to the *Florentines* speaketh in this manner: O ye Florentines, did you ever see such Phairies, which were busie in prying into the affairs of other men, but yet ignorant of their own? Do you denie it? yet do there commonly walke uppe and downe the Cittie, phairies in the shapes of men.

There were two women called *Macho*, and *Lamo*, which were both foolish and madde, and from the strange behaviours of them, came the first opinion of the Pharies: there was also an auncient *Lybian* woman called *Lamia*, and the opinion was, that if these Pharies had not whatsoever they demaunded, presently they would take away live children, according to these verses of Horace.

> *Nec quodcunque volet, poscat sibi fabula credi*
> *Neu pransæ Lamiæ vivum puerum extrahat alvo*

> [Let not your play demand belief for whatever absurdities it exhibits, nor take out of a witch's belly a living child whom she has eaten.]

It is reported of *Menippus* the Lycian, that he fell in love with a strange woman, who at that time seemed both beautifull, tender, and rich, but in truth there was no such thing, and all was but fantasticall ostentation; she was said to insinuate her selfe into his familiaritie, after this manner: as he went upon a day alone from *Corinth* to *Senchrea* hee met with a certaine phantasme or spectre like a beautifull woman, who tooke him by the hand, and told him that she was a *Phoenician* woman, and of long time had loved him dearely, having sought many occasions to manifest the same, but could never find opportunitie untill that day, wherefore she entreated him to take knowledge of her house which was in the Suburbes of *Corinth*, therewithall pointing unto it with her finger, and so desired his presence: The young man seeing himselfe thus wooed by a beautifull woman was easily overcome by her allurements, and did oftentimes frequent her company.

Ther was a certaine wise man and a Philosopher which espied the same, and spake unto *Menippus* in this manner. O faire *Menippus* beloved of beautifull women, art thou a serpent and dost nourish a serpent? by which words he gave him his first admonition, or inclining of a mischiefe; but not prevayling, *Menippus* purposed to marry with this spectre, her house to outward shew being richly furnished with all manner of houshold goods, then said the wise man againe unto *Menippus*, this gold, silver, and ornaments of house, are like to *Tantalus* Apples, who are said by *Homer* to make a faire shew, but to containe in them no substance at all: even so whatsoever you conceave of this riches, there is no matter or substance in the things which you see, for they are onely inchaunted images and shadowes, which that you may beleeve, this your neate bride is one of the *Empusae*, called *Lamiae* or *Mormoliciae* wonderfull desirous of copulation with men, and loving their flesh above measure, but those whom they doe entice, with their veneriall marts, afterwards they devoure without love or pittie, feeding upon their flesh: at which words the wise man caused gold and silver plate and houshold stuffe, Cookes and servants, to vanish all away; Then did the spectre like unto one that wept, entreate the wise man that he would not torment her, nor yet cause her to confesse what manner of person she was, but he on the other side being inexorable, compelled her to declare the whole truth, which was, that she was a Phairy, and that she purposed to use the companie of *Menippus*, and feede him fat with all manner of pleasures, to the entent that afterward she might eate up and devour his body, for all their kinde love was but onely to feede upon beautifull yong men. . . .

Of the Mantichora

The beast or rather Monster is bred among the Indians, having a treble row of teeth beneath and above, whose greatnesse, roughnesse, and feete are like a Lyons, his face and ears like unto a mans, his eies gray, and collour red, his taile like the taile of a Scorpion of the earth, armed with a sting, casting forth sharp pointed quils, his voice like the voice of a small trumpet or pipe, being in course as swift as a Hart; His wildnes such as can never be tamed, and his appetite is especially to the flesh of man. His body like the body of a Lyon, being very apt both to leape and to run, so as no distance or space doth hinder him, and I take it to bee the same Beast which *Avicen* [Avicenna] calleth *Marion*, and *Maricomorion*, with her taile she woundeth her Hunters whether they come before her or behind her, and presently when the quils are cast forth, new ones grow up in their roome, wherewithal she overcommeth all the hunters: and although India be full of divers ravening beastes, yet none of them are stiled with a title of *Andropophagi*, that is to say, Men-eaters; except onely this *Mantichora*. When the Indians take a Whelp of this beast, they all to bruise the buttockes and taile thereof, that so it may never be fit to bring sharp quils, afterwards it is tamed without peril. This also is the same beast which is called *Leucrocuta* about the bignesse of a wilde Asse, being in legs and hoofes like a Hart, having his mouth reaching on both sides to his eares, and the head & face of a female like unto a Badgers, It is called also *Martiora*, which in the Persian tongue signifieth a devourer of men.

JOHAN AMOS COMENIUS (1592–1670)
From *Orbis Sensualium Pictus* (1659)

Comenius strove throughout his life to prove the might of the pen and the mind. As rector of the German school at Fulnek, he conducted botany classes outdoors and added honey to the local diet by introducing beehives to the town. Eventually forced out of his homeland by the constant Hapsburg plundering of Bohemia, and finding temporary homes in England, Sweden, Poland, and the Netherlands, this advocate of Pansophism—the harmonious system uniting all knowledge through education—still clung tenaciously to his motto: *omnia sponte fluant absit violentia rebus* (all things should develop of their own free will with complete absence of violence). Known to the royalty and literati of Europe for such works as *The Labyrinth of the World, Janua Linguarum Reserata / The Door to Languages Opened,* and *Via Lucis / The Way of Light,* Comenius enlivened and revolutionized the teaching of Latin with the *Pictus*. First published in a German-Latin version in Nuremburg in 1658, it was translated by the London schoolmaster Charles Hoole and made available in an English-Latin version by the next year.

XXXVII.

Septem Ætates Hominis.

The Seven Ages of Man.

A Man is first an *Infant*, 1.
then a *Boy*, 2.
then a *Youth*, 3.
then a *Young-man*, 4.
then a *Man*, 5.
after that, an *Elderly Man*, 6
and at last a *decrepid old man*, 7.

    So also in the other *Sex*, there are,
a *Girl*, 8. a *Damosel*, 9. a *Maid*, 10.
a *Woman*, 11. an *elderly Woman*, 12.
and a *decrepid old Woman*, 13.

Homo est primum *Infans*, 1.
deinde *Puer*, 2.
tum *Adolescens*, 3.
inde *uvenis*, 4.
postea *Vir*, 5.
dehinc *Senex*, 6.
tandem *Silicernium*, 7.

    Sic etiam in altero *Sexu*, sunt
Pupa, 8. *Puella*, 9. *Virgo*, 10.
Mulier, 11. *Vetula*, 12.
Anus decrepita, 13.

XXVIII.

Jumenta.

Labouring Beaſts.

The *Ass*, 1. and the *Mule*, 2. carry burthens.

The *Horse*, 3. (which a *Mane*, 4. graceth) carryeth us.

The *Camel*, 5. carryeth the Merchant with his ware.

The *Elephant*, 6. draweth his meat with his *Trunk*, 7.

He hath two *Teeth*, 8. standing out And is able to carry full thirty men.

[Note that 4. and 5. are inverted]

Asinus, 1. & *Mulus*, 2. gestant Onera.

Equus, 3. (quam *Juba*, 4. ornat) gestat nos ipsos.

Camelus, 5. gestat Mercatorem cum mercibus suis.

Elephas, (Barrus) 6. attrahit pabulum *Proboscide*, 7.

Habet duos *dentes*, 8. prominentes, & potest portare etiam triginta viros.

XLIV.

Deformes & Monſtroſi.

Deformed and Monſtrous People.

Monstrous and *deformed* People are those which differ in the Body from the ordinary Shape, as the huge *Gyant*, 1. the little *Dwarf*, 2. One with *two bodies*, 3. One With *two Heads*, 4. and such like Monsters.

Amonst these are reckoned, The *Jolt-headed*, 5. The great nosed, 6. The *blubber-lipped*, 7. The *blub-cheeked*, 8. The *goggle-eyed*, 9. The *wry-necked*, 10. *great-throated*, 11. The *crump-backed*, 12. The *crump-footed*, 13. The *steeple-crowned*, 15. add to these The *Bald-pated*, 14.

Monstrosi, & deformes sunt abeuntes corpore à communi formâ, ut sunt, immanis *Gigas*, nanus (*Pumilio*), 2. *Bicorpor*, 3. *Biceps*, 4. & id genus monstrosa

His accesentur, *Capito*, 5. *Naso*, 6. *Labeo*, 7. *Bucco*, 8. *Strabo*, 9. *Obstipus*, 10. *Strumosus*, 11. *Gibbosus*, 12. *Lorpies*, 13. *Cilo*, 15. adde *Calvastrum*, 14.

XCVII.

Schola.

A School.

A *School*, 1. is a Shop in which *Young Wits* are fashion'd to vertue, and it is distinguish'd into *Forms*.

The *Master*, 2. sitteth in a *Chair*, 3. the *Scholars*, 4. in *Forms*, 5. he teacheth, they learn.

Some things are writ down before them with *Chalk* on a *Table*, 6.

Some sit at a Table and *write*, 7. he *mendeth* their *Faults*, 8.

Some stand and rehearse things committed to *memory*, 9.

Some talk together, 10. and behave themselves wantonly and carelessly;these are chastised with a *Ferula*, 11. and a *Rod*, 12.

Schola, 1. est Officina, in quâ *Novelli Animi* formantur ad virtutem, & distinguitur in *Classes.*

Praeceptor, 2. sedet in *Cathedra*, 3. *Discipuli*, 4. in *Subselliis*, 5. ille docet, hi discunt.

Quaedam praescribuntur illis *Cretâ* in *Tabella*, 6.

Quidam sedent ad Mensam, & *scribunt*, 7. ipse corrigit *Mendas*, 8.

Quidam stant & recitant mandata memoriae, 9.

Quidam confabulantur, 10. ac gernunt se petulantes, & negligentes; hi castigantur *Ferulâ* (baculo), 11. & *Virgâ*, 12.

CXXX.

Ludus Scenicus.

A Stage-Play.

In a *Play-house*, 1, which is trimmed with *Hangings*, 2. and covered with *Curtains*, 3. Comedies and Tragedies are acted, wherein memorable things are represented, as here, the History of the *Prodigal Son*, 4. and his *Father*, 5. by whom he is entertained, being returned home. The players act being in disguise. The *Fool*, 6. maketh Jests. The chief of the Spectators sit in the *gallery*, 7. the common sort stand on the *ground*, 8. and clap the hands if anything please them.

In *Theatro*, 1. quod vestitur *Tapetibus*, 2. & *Sipariis*, 3. tegitur aguntur Commoedia vel Tragoedia, quibus representantur res memorabiles; ut hic Historia de *Filio prodigo*, 4. & *Patre*, 5. ipsius à quo recipitur, domum redux.

Actores (*Histriones*) agunt personati. *Morio*, 6. date Jocos. Spectatorum primarii, sedent in *Orchestrâ*, 7. plebs stat in *Caveâ*, 8. & plaudit si quid arridet.

2. PURITAN 'HELL-FIRE': WARNINGS AND WARMTH

Diverse children have their different natures: some are like flesh which nothing but salt will keep from putrefaction, some again like tender fruits that are best preserved with sugar. Those parents are wise that can fit their nurture according to their nature.

—*Anne Bradstreet*, Meditations Divine and Moral (1664)

The designation 'Puritan' is broad and multi-purpose. From its first usage in the late sixteenth century until the present day, it can serve as a form of religious identification or a sneer at precise moral behaviour. Yet despite the limited usefulness of the term for conveying differences of theological temperature between Anglicans and nonconformists, the stringent—often ridiculed—beliefs of Puritanism have shaped English and American culture, including views of children and judgements about the literature deemed appropriate for their ethical and social formation.

A complex range of attitudes, enlivened by contradictions, seventeenth-century Puritanism embraced a 'sincere multitude of true professors', to borrow the term of the martyrologist John Foxe. Presbyterians, Calvinists, and Congregationalists considered themselves Puritans. The Baptist faith, a late offshoot of English Congregationalism that reconstituted the church on the basis of the believer's baptism, also represented a variety of Puritanism. Although it was anything but monolithic, a knowledge of some of Puritanism's widely held tenets should help us to understand the dourness of their writing aimed specifically at children. Prizing the Bible more than the Mass-book, Puritans sought to cleanse the church of non-essentials, which could involve the abolition of vestments, 'popish' ceremonies, and the offices of archbishop, bishop, and deacon. Puritans who emigrated to the wilderness of the New World insisted that they had left behind the true wilderness of the Established Church's pomp and glitter, often referred to as Babylon. As printing presses were dispersing new English versions of the scriptures—Tyndale, Coverdale, and Geneva

Bibles—Puritans looked to the Bible as the only acknowledged authority and blueprint for salvation. Although they fashioned themselves as attentive listeners to the expositions of scripture in sermons, which were the high point of their worship, Puritans also valued scholarship in the Calvinist humanist tradition of the study of ancient languages and biblical exegesis. The experience of being chastised by their dark and glowering God was itself an opportunity for contemplation. The Puritan, who could do nothing without God, had to accept responsibility for himself or herself. What may appear to us to be an obsessive chronicling of doubts and a paranoid concern with doom was, for the Puritan, a necessary element of the religious regimen, in which nothing was random and everything was charged with spiritual meaning.

Puritans found abiding strength in the divine gift of sanctifying grace, which, through a rigorous and proscriptive code of behaviour, promised salvation to believers. This was the rock upon which their zeal was founded. Frivolity and what we might call high spirits were in short supply. Puritans banned sabbath games and forbade instrumental music, and, in some cases, singing, in their churches. New England Puritans outlawed the observance of Christmas, with its accompanying 'profane' merriment, and replaced it with a celebration of Thanksgiving Day. Despite the severity of their beliefs, Puritans were very much people of this world: they permitted themselves to strive for both salvation and material success.

Although confident in their possession of grace, Puritans could never be smug. As the finest poetic, homiletic, and allegorical writing from within the tradition testifies, life for the Puritan was a continuing spiritual contest between conversion and backsliding. The various assaults on the town of Mansoul in Bunyan's *The Holy War*, the sloughs and mountains over which Christian must journey in *The Pilgrim's Progress*, and the observations of Mr Wiseman about the sinful end of the central character in *The Life and Death of Mr Badman* had equivalents in the daily lives of Puritans. They were constantly doubting, then restoring, their confidence in salvation.

For all the solemn finger-wagging of the Puritans, they were among the first to write specifically for children. Since many of the emigrant preachers to the Bay Colony were university-educated, they injected considerable severity and erudition into the lessons designed for the young. John Cotton's *Milk for Babes* (1646) offered spiritual nourishment in the form of a stern, though brief, catechism. In contrast to the royal primers commissioned by Tudor and Stuart monarchs to promote literacy, the Dissenters eagerly seized on the primer as a forceful means of teaching doctrine. In its many variants and over a long span of popularity, *The New England Primer* consisted of a catechism usually supplemented by pictorial alphabets and such imperative verses as:

> *Have communion with few*
> *Be intimate with one*
> *Deal justly with all*
> *Speak evil of none.*

In addition to the lessons of hornbooks, primers, and catechisms, Puritan children in the late seventeenth and early eighteenth centuries were familiar with little books of religious instruction in prose and verse designed specially for their benefit. Three well-circulated examples were James Janeway's *A Token for Children* (1672), Benjamin Keach's *War With the Devil* (1673), and John Bunyan's *A Book for Boys and Girls* (1686). These pastors wrote to awaken and sustain children's penitence. As Bunyan observed in his address 'To the Reader':

> To shoot too high doth but make
> Children gaze
> 'Tis that which hits the man, doth
> him amaze.

Janeway, an Oxford graduate, and Keach and Bunyan, self-taught preachers, hit home their lessons in different ways. These pastors suffered for their beliefs: Janeway lost his indulgence to preach; Keach was imprisoned and witnessed the public burning of his catechism; Bunyan spent long periods in Bedford jail. Yet all wrote for children because they saw them as diminutive sinners who stood in urgent need of their soul-saving admonitions.

A nonconformist preacher who died before reaching the age of forty, Janeway composed his *Token for Children* as a martyrology, consisting of thirteen examples of the holy lives and joyful deaths of young Puritans. Believing that children were 'not too little to go to hell', he catechizes the reader with eleven soul-battering questions before closing his Preface with this adjuration:

> Children, if you love me, if you love
> your Parents, if you love your Souls,
> if you would scape Hell fire, and if you
> would live in Heaven when you dye,
> do you go and do as these good children.

His virtuous exemplars are obsessed by their faith. Their chilling life stories, which conclude with sometimes powerful sermons, were meant to frighten readers into submission: a breathless, excited urgency pervades little Sarah Howley's admonitions, not only because she is aware of her approaching death but also because she is hemorrhaging. Janeway based his accounts, as he frequently affirms, on the testimony of real children. The epigraph to the last six states their purpose: 'Out of the mouths of babes and sucklings thou hast ordained strength' (Psalms 8. 2).

While Janeway's children are spiritually strong and physically weak, Keach's and Bunyan's are often healthy reprobates. The versified dialogue of Keach's *War With the Devil* concentrates on Youth in his 'natural' state: cheeky, self-absorbed, and materialistic. Because Youth's turn to conversion is delayed until the eleventh hour, Keach is able to expose—with at times unwitting entertainment—the impertinence of this almost incorrigible backslider.

In *A Book for Boys and Girls*; or, *Country Rhimes for Children*, Bunyan determines to use the medium of verse to meet his readers on their own ground:

> . . . by their Play-thinges, I would
> them entice
> To mount their thoughts from what are
> childish Toys,
> To Heav'n, for that's prepar'd for
> Girls and Boys.

He also assures them that he knows the difference between 'Boys' and 'Men', and will temper his matter accordingly:

> Our Ministers, long time by Word
> and Pen,
> Dealt with them, counting them,
> not Boys, but Men:
> Thunder-bolts they shot at them,
> and their Toys:
> But hit them not, 'cause they were
> Girls and Boys.

With the preacher's consciousness of analogies, Bunyan strives to hit the mark by extracting lessons from animal exempla, everyday occurrences, and childish pursuits. Domestic life, animals, and insects supply material for several rhymes, whether developed through prolonged metaphors, apt comparisons, or pointed one-for-one correspondences. When describing the life cycle of the fertilized egg, for instance, he furnishes an extended gloss on man's spiritual condition; with contrasting brevity, he makes the bee an emblem of sweet yet mortal sin. Diligent and steadfast, like the reliable postboy, or reckless and conceited, like the hobbyhorse rider, the children Bunyan portrays offer an assortment of behaviour models.

Dour pedagogy and the threat of imminent doom were ingredients in Puritan writing that were not reserved for adults. While children were reminded constantly of the fearful chasm separating the City of Destruction from the heavenly Sion, they were also treated to singularly fond parental vigilance. Because Puritan mothers and fathers were such solicitous guides, they knew their children's strengths and weaknesses well. The posthumously published domestic poetry of Anne Bradstreet is a revealing window into an actual Puritan home. Her prose *Meditations Divine and Moral* does not mince words about the human propensity to sin. But the undisguised affection of her maternal care for the 'eight birds hatched in one nest' and her acknowledgement of the child as a borrowed gift may help to temper our judgements about the unrelieved gloom of Puritan writing for children. Severe, earnest, and anything but saccharine, this writing grew out of an informed recognition of youngsters' willingness, openness, and suggestibility.

JOHN COTTON (1584–1652)
Milk for Babes, Drawn Out of the Breasts of Both Testaments. Chiefly for the spiritual nourishment of Boston babes in either England: but may be of like use for any children (1646)

Influential clergyman and scholar, Cotton had been lecturer, dean, and tutor at Emmanuel College, Cambridge, before he was appointed vicar in Boston, Lincolnshire, where he served for two decades until emigrating to the new Boston. At Southampton, in 1630, Cotton delivered the farewell sermon to the passengers of the Arbella, bound for Salem, co-religionists whom he joined in three years. In the Bay Colony his writing and preaching careers flourished: he was a contributing translator to *The Bay Psalm Book*; his *Way of the Churches of Christ in New England* (1645) summarized New England practice; and his sermons on Canticles, Ecclesiastes, and

Revelation, among other biblical texts, were published. He was the father of six children; his daughter, who married Increase Mather, was the mother of Cotton Mather. His catechism, taking its title from a widely used biblical metaphor (I Corinthians 3. 2; Hebrews 5. 12; I Peter 2. 2), sees humankind as sinners whose only hope of salvation lies in obeying the Commandments and the Gospel and in receiving the two sacraments. However, in contrast to Hugh Peter's *Milk for Babes and Meat for Men* (1630), the more intense catechism of another reformer who was in exile in the Netherlands at the time of its publication, Cotton's work is remarkable for the pithiness and brevity of its questions and answers.

Milk for Babes

Q. *What hath God done for you?*
A. God hath made me, He keepeth me, and He can save me.
Q. *Who is God?*
A. God is a Spirit of himself and for himself.
Q. *How many Gods be there?*
A. There is but one God in three Persons, the Father, the Sonne, and the Holy Ghost.
Q. *How did God make you?*
A. In my first Parents, holy and righteous.
Q. *Are you then born holy and righteous?*
A. No, my first father sinned and I in him.
Q. *Are you then born a sinner?*
A. I was conceived in sinne, and born in iniquity.
Q. *What is your birth-sinne?*
A. Adams sinne imputed to me, and a corrupt Nature dwelling in me.
Q. *What is your corrupt Nature?*
A. My corrupt nature is empty of Grace, bent unto sinne, and only unto sinne, and that continually.
Q. *What is sinne?*
A. Sinne is the transgression of the Law.
Q. *How many commandments of the Law be there?*
A. Ten.
Q. *What is the first Commandement?*
A. Thou shalt have no other Gods but me.
Q. *What is the meaning of the commandement?*
A. That we should worship the only true God, and no other beside him.
Q. *What is the 2d. Commandement?*
A. Thou shalt not make to thy self any graven image, etc.
Q. *What is the meaning of the Commandement?*
A. That we should worship the true God with true worship: such as God hath ordained, not such as man hath invented.
Q. *What is the third commandement?*
A. Thou shalt not take the Name of the Lord thy God in vain, etc.

Q. *What is here meant by the Name of God?*

A. God himself and the good things of God, whereby he is known, as a man by his name; as his Attributes, worship, words and works.

Q. *What is it not to take his Name in vain?*

A. To make use of God, and the good things of God, to his glory, and our good; not vainly, not unreverently, not unprofitably.

Q. *What is the fourth Commandement?*

A. Remember that thou keep holy the Sabbath day, etc.

Q. *What is the meaning of the Commandement?*

A. That we should rest from labor and much more from play on the Lords day, that we may draw nigh to God in holy duties.

Q. *What is the fifth Commandement?*

A. Honour thy Father, and thy mother, that thy dayes may be long in the land, which the Lord thy God giveth thee.

Q. *Who are here meant by Father and Mother?*

A. All our superiours, whether in Family, School, Church, and Commonwealth.

Q. *What is the honour due to them?*

A. Reverence, obedience, and (when I am able) Recompence.

Q. *What is the Sixth Commandement?*

A. Thou shalt do no murder.

Q. *What is the meaning of this Commandement?*

A. That we should not shorten the life, or health of our selves or others, but preserve both.

Q. *What is the seventh Commandement?*

A. Thou shalt not commit Adultery.

Q. *What is the sinne here forbidden?*

A. To defile ourselves or others with unclean lusts.

Q. *What is the duty here commanded?*

A. Chastity, to possesse ourselves in holinesse and honour.

Q. *What is the eighth commandement?*

A. Thou shalt not steal.

Q. *What is the stealth here forbidden?*

A. To take away another mans goods, without his leave: or to spend our own without benefit to ourselves or others.

Q. *What is the duty here commanded?*

A. To get our goods honestly, to keep them safely, and to spend them thriftily.

Q. *What is the ninth Commandement?*

A. Thou shalt not bear false witnesse against thy Neighbour.

Q. *What is the sinne here forbidden?*

A. To lye falsly, to think or speak untruly of our selves, or others.

Q. *What is the duty here required?*

A. Truth and faithfulnesse.

Q. *What is the tenth Commandement?*

A. Thou shalt not covet, etc.

Q. *What is the coveting here forbidden?*

A. Lust after the things of other men: and want of contentment with our own.

Q. *Whether have you kept all these Commandements?*

A. No, I and all men are sinners.

Q. *What is the wages of sin?*

A. Death and damnation.

Q. *How look you then to be saved?*

A. Onely by Jesus Christ.

Q. *Who is Jesus Christ?*

A. The eternall Son of God, who for our sakes became man, that he might redeem and save us.

Q. *How doth Christ redeem and save us?*

A. By his righteous life, and bitter death, and glorious resurrection, to life again.

Q. *How do we come to have part and fellowship with Christ, in his Death and Resurrection?*

A. By the power of his Word and Spirit, which bring us to Christ, and keep us in him.

Q. *What is his Word?*

A. The Holy Scriptures of the Prophets and Apostles, the Old and New Testament, Law and Gospell.

Q. *How doth the Ministery of the Law bring you towards Christ?*

A. By bringing me to know my sinne, and the wrath of God against me for it.

Q. *What are you thereby the nearer to Christ?*

A. So I come to feel my cursed estate, and need of a Saviour.

Q. *How doth the Ministery of the Gospell help you in this cursed Estate?*

A. By humbling me yet more, and then raising me up out of the Estate.

Q. *How doth the ministery of the Gospell humble you more?*

A. By revealing the grace of the Lord Jesus, in dying to save sinners: and yet convincing me of my sinne, in not believing on him, and of mine insufficiency to come to him; and so I feele my selfe utterly lost.

Q. *How then doth the Ministery of the Gospell raise you up out of this lost estate to come unto Christ?*

A. By teaching me the value and the vertue of the death of Christ, and the riches of his grace to lost sinners: By revealing the promise of grace to such, and by ministring the Spirit of grace, to apply Christ, and his promise of grace unto my selfe, and to keepe me in him.

Q. *How doth the spirit of Christ apply Christ, and his promise of grace unto you, and keepe you in him?*

A. By begetting in me faith to receive him: Prayer to call upon him: Repentance to mourne after him: and new obedience to serve him.

Q. *What is Faith?*

A. Faith is a grace of the spirit; whereby I deny my selfe: and believe on Christ for righteousnesse and salvation.

Q. *What is Prayer?*

A. It is calling upon God, in the Name of Christ, by the helpe of the Holy Ghost, according to the will of God.

Q. *What is Repentance?*

A. Repentance is a grace of the spirit, whereby I loath my sinnes, and my selfe for them, and confesse them before the Lord, and mourne after Christ for the pardon of them, and for grace to serve him in newnesse of life.

Q. *What is newnesse of life or new obedience?*

A. Newnesse of life is a grace of the spirit, whereby I forsake my former lusts, and vaine company, and walk before the Lord in the light of his word, and in the Communion of his Saints.

Q. *What is the communion of Saints?*

A. It is the fellowship of the Church in the blessings of the Covenant of grace, and seales thereof.

Q. *What is the Church?*

A. It is a Congregation of Saints joyned together in the bond of the Covenant, to worship the Lord, and to edify one another, in all his Holy Ordinances.

Q. *What is the bond of the Covenant, in which the Church is joyned together?*

A. It is the profession of that Covenant, which God hath made with his faith-full people, to be a God unto them and to their seede.

Q. *What doth the Lord binde his people to in this Covenant?*

A. To give up themselves and their seede first to the Lord to be his people, and then to the Elders and Brethren of the Church, to set forward the worship of God and their mutuall edifycation.

Q. *How do they give up themselves and their seed to the Lord?*

A. By receiving through faith, the Lord, & his Covenant, to themselves, and to their seed. And accordingly walking themselves, and trayning up their Children in the wayes of his Covenant.

Q. *How do they give up themselves and their seed to the Elders and Brethren of the Church?*

A. By confession of their sinnes and profession of their faith, and of their subjection to the Gospell of Christ. And so they and their seede are received into fellowship of the Church, and seales thereof.

Q. *What are the seales of the Covenant now in the dayes of the Gospel?*

A. Baptisme and the Lords Supper.

Q. *What is done for you in Baptism?*

A. In baptisme, the washing with water is a signe and seale of my washing with the blood and spirit of Christ, and thereby of my ingrafting into Christ: of the pardon and clensing of my Sinnes into Christ: of the pardon and cleansing of my sinnes: of my rising up out of Affliction: and also of my resurrection from the dead at the last day.

Q. *What is done for you in the Lords Supper?*

A. In the Lords Supper the receiving of the bread broken and the wine powred out, is a signe and a seal of my receiving the Communion of the body of Christ broken for me, and of his bloud shed for me. And thereby of my growth in Christ, of the pardon and healing of my sinnes: of the fellowship of his spirit: of my strengthening and quickning in Grace: and of my sitting together with Christ on his throne of glory at the last judgement.

Q. *What is the resurrection from the dead, which was sealed up to you in Baptisme?*

A. When Christ shall come to his last judgement, all that are in the graves shall arise again, both the just and the unjust.

Q. *What is the last judgement, which is sealed up to you in the Lords Supper?*

A. At the last day we shall all appear before the judgement seat of Christ, to give an accompt of our works, and to receive our reward according to them.

Q. *What is the reward that shall then be given?*
A. The righteous shall go into life eternal, and the wicked shall be cast into everlasting fire with the Devill and his angels.

ANNE BRADSTREET (1612–1672)
From *The Works of Anne Bradstreet* (1867)

Hailed as the first female poet of the New World, English-born Anne Bradstreet spent her adult life, from young bride to mother of eight children, in Massachusetts: in Newtowne (later Cambridge), Ipswich, and, from 1645, North Andover. She and her husband listened to John Cotton's sermon before they embarked on the Arbella for Salem. Her father, Thomas Dudley, and, following her death, her husband, Simon Bradstreet, were the second and third governors of the Bay Colony. Her earliest work, *The Tenth Muse* (1650), probably written between 1630 and 1642 and published without her knowledge by her brother-in-law in England, was well received. Designed as a quaternion (four poems of four books), the collection displayed her learning and her religious convictions, especially in the 'Dialogue between Old England and New', in which New England counsels her dear mother Old England at the outbreak of the Civil Wars. Bradstreet's posthumously published poetry, inserted in the 1678 edition and discovered in the Andover manuscripts printed in 1867, illuminates domestic, emotional interiors. With maternal vigilance and Christian acceptance she adapts and condenses the genre of mothers' advice books, recording sicknesses and deaths, journeys and homecomings in the prayer-like rhythms of her ballad stanzas and couplets. As crystallized in her verse 'Upon the burning of our House July 10th, 1666', Bradstreet's outlook is benedictional: 'I blest his name that gave and took'.

Upon my Son Samuel His Going for England, Nov. 6, 1657

Thou mighty God of sea and land,
I here resign into Thy hand
The son of prayers, of vows, of tears,
The child I stayed for many years.
5 Thou heard'st me then and gav'st him me;
Hear me again, I give him Thee.
He's mine, but more, O Lord, Thine own,
For sure Thy grace on him is shown.
No friend I have like Thee to trust,
10 For mortal helps are brittle dust.
Preserve, O Lord, from storms and wrack,
Protect him there, and bring him back,
And if Thou shalt spare me a space
That I again may see his face,

15 Then shall I celebrate Thy praise
And bless Thee for't even all my days.
If otherwise I go to rest,
Thy will be done, for that is best.
Persuade my heart I shall him see
20 Forever happified with Thee.

In Reference to Her Children,
23 June, 1659

I had eight birds hatched in one nest,
Four cocks there were, and hens the rest.
I nursed them up with pain and care,
Nor cost, nor labour did I spare,
5 Till at last they felt their wing,
Mounted the trees, and learned to sing;
Chief of the brood then took his flight
To regions far and left me quite.
My mournful chirps I after send,
10 Till he return, or I do end:
Leave not thy nest, thy dam and sire,
Fly back and sing amidst this choir.
My second bird did take her flight,
And with her mate flew out of sight;
15 Southward they both their course did bend,
And seasons twain they there did spend,
Till after blown by southern gales,
They norward steered with filled sails.
A prettier bird was no where seen,
20 Along the beach among the treen.
I have a third of colour white,
On whome I placed no small delight;
Coupled with mate loving and true,
Hath also bid her dam adieu;
25 And where Aurora first appears,
She now hath perched to spend her years.
One to the academy flew
To chat among that learned crew;
Ambition moves still in his breast
30 That he might chant above the rest,
Striving for more than to do well,
That nightingales he might excel.
My fifth, whose down is yet scarce gone,
Is 'mongst the shrubs and bushes flown,
35 And as his wings increase in strength,
On higher boughs he'll perch at length.
My other three still with me nest,

Until they're grown, then as the rest,
Or here or there they'll take their flight,
40 As is ordained, so shall they light.
If birds could weep, then would my tears
Let others know what are my fears
Lest this my brood some harm should catch,
And be surprised for want of watch,
45 Whilst pecking corn and void of care,
They fall un'wares in fowler's snare,
Or whilst on trees they sit and sing,
Some untoward boy at them do fling,
Or whilst allured with bell and glass,
50 The net be spread, and caught, alas.
Or lest by lime-twigs they be foiled,
Or by some greedy hawks be spoiled.
O would my young, ye saw my breast,
And knew what thoughts there sadly rest,
55 Great was my pain when I you bred,
Great was my care when I you fed,
Long did I keep you soft and warm,
And with my wings kept off all harm,
My cares are more and fears than ever,
60 My throbs such now as 'fore were never.
Alas, my birds, you wisdom want,
Of perils you are ignorant;
Oft times in grass, on trees, in flight,
Sore accidents on you may light.
65 O to your safety have an eye,
So happy may you live and die.
Meanwhile my days in tunes I'll spend,
Till my weak lays with me shall end.
In shady woods I'll sit and sing,
70 And things that past to mind I'll bring.
Once young and pleasant, as are you,
But former toys (no joys) adieu.
My age I will not once lament,
But sing, my time so near is spent.
75 And from the top bough take my flight
Into a country beyond sight,
Where old ones instantly grow young,
And there with seraphims set song;
No seasons cold, nor storms they see;
80 But spring lasts to eternity.
When each of you shall in your nest
Among your young ones take your rest,
In chirping language, oft them tell,
You had a dam that loved you well,

85 That did what could be done for young,
And nursed you up till you were strong,
And 'fore she once would let you fly,
She showed you joy and misery;
Taught what was good, and what was ill,
90 What would save life, and what would kill.
Thus gone, amongst you I may live,
And dead, yet speak, and counsel give:
Farewell, my birds, farewell adieu,
I happy am, if well with you.

A.B.

JAMES JANEWAY (1636–1674)
From *A Token for Children: Being An Exact Account of the Conversion, Holy and Exemplary Lives, and Joyful Deaths of Several young Children* (1672)

Because of his noncompliance with the Uniformity Act (1662) of the Anglican Establishment, Janeway suffered the loss of his teaching indulgence and the wreck of the meeting-house where he preached in Jamaica Row, Rotherhithe, in London. He was, however, a popular and an indefatigable preacher, who survived the plague of February 1665 and the fire of September 1666. His lengthy sermon *Heaven Upon Earth; or, the Best Friend in the Worst Times* (1669), a favourite of his first obituary subject, Sarah Howley, is a grim introduction to the idea of heaven that is embedded in the realities of disease, fire, and ruin. Janeway's *Token*, reprinted several times in the eighteenth century, began with the sobering admission that 'children are not too little to go to either heaven or hell.' It was imitated by Cotton Mather with a Massachusetts Bay setting in his equally terrifying *A Token for the Children of New England* (1700). Janeway died of consumption.

Example I

Of one eminently converted between Eight and Nine years old, with an account of her Life and Death

Mrs Sarah Howley, when she was between eight and nine years old, was carried by her Friends to hear a Sermon, where the Minister Preached upon Matthew 11.30. *My yoak is easie and my burden is light*. In the applying of which Scripture, this Child was mightily awakened, and made deeply sensible of the condition of her Soul, and her need of a Christ; she wept bitterly to think what a case she was in; and went home and got by her self into a Chamber, and upon her knees she wept and cryed to the Lord, as well as she could, which might easily be perceived by her eyes and countenance.

2. She was not contented at this, but she got her little Brother and Sister into a Chamber with her, and told them of their condition by nature, and wept over them, and prayed with them and for them.

3. After this she heard another Sermon upon *Prov.* 29. 1, *He that being often reproved, hardeneth his heart, shall suddenly be destroyed, and that without remedy*: At which she was more affected than before, and was so exceedingly solicitous about her Soul, that she spent a great part of the night in weeping and praying, and could scarce take any rest day or night for some time together; desiring with all her Soul to escape from everlasting flames, and to get an interest in the Lord Jesus; O what should she do for a Christ! what should she do to be saved!

4. She gave her self much to attending upon the Word Preached, and still continued very tender under it, greatly favouring what she heard.

5. She was very much in secret prayer, as might easily be perceived by those who listened at the Chamber Door, and was usually very importunate, and full of tears.

6. She could scarce speak of sin, or be spoke to, but her heart was ready to melt.

7. She spent much time in reading the Scripture, and a Book called *The best Friend in the worst times*; by which the work of God was much promoted upon her Soul, and was much directed by it how to get acquaintance with God, especially toward the end of that Book. Another Book that she was much delighted with, was Mr. Swinnocks *Christian Mans Calling*, and by this she was taught in some measure to make Religion her business. The *Spiritual Bee* was a great companion of hers.

8. She was exceeding dutiful to her Parents, very loath to grieve them in the least; and if she had at any time (which was very rare) offended them, she would weep bitterly.

9. She abhorred lying, and allowed her self in no known sin.

10. She was very Conscientious in spending of time, and hated idleness, and spent her whole time either in praying, reading, instructing her little Brothers, and working at her Needle, at which she was very ingenious.

11. When she was at School, she was eminent for her diligence, teachableness, meekness and modesty, speaking very little; but when she did, it was usually very spiritual.

12. She continued in this course of Religious Duties for some years together.

13. When she was about fourteen years old, she brake a Vein in her Lungs (as is supposed), and oft did spit blood, yet did a little recover again, but had several dangerous relapses.

14. At the beginning of January last she was taken very bad again, in which sickness She was in great distress of Soul. When she was first taken, she said, O Mother, pray, pray, pray, for me, for Satan is so busie that I cannot pray for my self, I see I am undone without a Christ, and a pardon! O I am undone! undone to all Eternity!

15. Her Mother knowing how serious she had been formerly, did a little wonder that she should be in such agonies; upon which her Mother asked her what sin it was that was so burdensome to her spirit: O Mother, said she, it is not any particular Sin of Omission or Commission, that sticks so close to my Conscience, as the Sin of my nature; without the blood of Christ, that will damn me.

16. Her Mother asked her what she should pray for, for her? she answered, that I may have a saving knowledge of Sin and Christ; and that I may have an assurance of Gods love to my Soul. Her Mother asked her, why she did speak so little to the Minister that came to her? She answered, that it was her duty with patience and silence to learn of them: and it was exceeding painful to her to speak to any.

17. One time when she fell into a fit, she cried out, O I am going, I am going: But what shall I do to be saved? Sweet Lord Jesus, I will lye at thy feet, and if I perish, it shall be at the Fountain of thy mercy.

18. She was much afraid of presumption, and dreaded a mistake in the matters of her Soul, and would be often putting up ejaculations to God, to deliver her from deceiving her self. To instance in one: Great and mighty God, give me faith, and true faith, Lord, that I may not be a foolish Virgin, having a Lamp and no Oyl.

19. She would many times be laying hold upon the Promises, and plead them in prayer. That in Mat. 11. 28, 29. was much in her Tongue, and no small relief to her spirit. How many times would she cry out, Lord, hast thou not said, *Come unto me all ye that are weary and heavy laden, and I will give you rest.*

20. Another time her Father bid her be of good cheer, because she was going to a better Father; at which she fell into a great passion, and said, but how do I know that? I am a poor sinner that wants assurance: O, for assurance! It was still her Note, O, for assurance! This was her great, earnest, and constant request to all that came to her, to beg assurance for her; and, poor heart, she would look with so much eagerness upon them as if she desired nothing in the world so much, as that they would pity her, and help her with their prayers; never was poor creature more earnest for any thing, than she was for an assurance, and the Light of Gods Countenance; O the piteous moan that she would make! O the agonies that her Soul was in!

21. Her Mother askt her, if God should spare her life, how she would live; truly Mother, said she, we have such base hearts that I can't tell; we are apt to promise great things; when we are sick, but when we are recovered, we are as ready to forget our selves, and to turn again unto folly; but I hope I should be more careful of my time and my soul, than I have been.

22. She was full of natural affection to her Parents, and very careful least her Mother should be tired out with much watching. Her Mother said, how shall I bear parting with thee, when I have scarce dryed my eyes for thy Brother? She answered. The God of love support and comfort you; it is but a little while, and we shall meet in Glory, I hope. She being very weak, could speak but little; therefore her Mother said, Child, if thou hast any comfort, lift up thy hand, which she did.

23. The Lords day before that in which she died, a Kinsman of hers came to see her, and asking of her, whether she knew him, she answered; yes, I know you, and I desire you would learn to know Christ: you are young, but you know not how soon you may die; and O to die without a Christ, it is a fearful thing; O redeem Time, O Time, Time, Time, precious Time! Being requested by him not to spend herself: she said, she would fain do all the good she could while she lived, and when she was dead too, if possible; upon which account, she desired

that a Sermon might be Preached at the Funeral concerning the preciousness of Time. O that young ones would now remember their Creator!

24. Some Ministers that came to her, did with earnestness, beg that the Lord would please to give her some token for good, that she might go off triumphing; and Bills of the same Nature were sent to several Churches.

25. After she had long waited for an answer of their prayers, she said, *Well, I will venture my soul upon Christ.*

26. She carried it with wonderful patience, and yet would often pray that the Lord would give her more patience, which the Lord answered to astonishment; for considering the pains and agonies that she was in, her patience was next to a wonder; Lord, Lord give me patience, said she, that I may not dishonour thee.

27. Upon Thursday, after long waiting, great fears, and many Prayers, when all her Friends thought she had been past speaking, to the astonishment of her Friends she broke forth thus with a very audible voice, and chearful Countenance: Lord, thou hast promised that whosoever comes unto thee, thou wilt in no wise cast out; Lord, I come unto thee, and surely thou wilt in no wise cast me out. O so sweet! O so glorious is Jesus! I have the sweet and glorious Jesus; he is sweet, he is sweet, he is sweet! O the admirable love of God in sending Christ! O free grace to a poor lost Creature! And thus she ran on repeating many of these things a hundred times over; but her Friends were so astonished to see her in this Divine Rapture, and to hear such gracious words, and her prayers and desires satisfied, that they could not write a quarter of what she spoke.

28. When her soul was thus ravished with the love of Christ, and her tongue so highly engaged in the magnifying of God; her Father, Brethren, and Sisters, with other of the Family were called, to whom she spake particularly, as her strength would give leave. She gave her Bible as a Legacy to one of her Brothers, and desired him to use that well for her sake, and added to him and the rest, O make use of time to get a Christ for your Souls; spend no time in running up and down in playing; O get a Christ for your Souls while you are young, remember now your Creator before you come to a sick-bed; put not off this great work till then, for then you will find it a hard work indeed. I know by experience, the Devil will tell you it is time enough; and ye are young, what need you to be in such haste? You will have time enough when you are old. But there stands one (meaning her Grand-mother) that stayes behind, and I that am but young, am going before her. O therefore make your Calling and Election sure, while you are in health. But I am afraid this will be but one nights trouble to your thoughts; but remember, these are the words of a dying Sister. O if you knew how good Christ were! O if you had but one taste of his sweetness, you would rather go to him a thousand times, than stay in this wicked world. *I would not for ten thousand, and ten thousand worlds part with my interest in Christ.* O how happy am I that am going to everlasting Joyes! I would not go back again for twenty thousand worlds; And will not you strive to get an interest in Christ?

29. After this, looking upon one of her Fathers Servants, she said, What shall I do? What shall I do at that great day, when Christ shall say to me, *Come thou Blessed of my Father inherit the Kingdom prepared for thee?* and shall say to the wicked, *Go thou cursed into the Lake that burns for ever*: What a grief is it to me to think that I shall see any of my friends that I knew upon Earth turned into

that Lake that burns for ever! O that word for ever! Remember that for ever; I speak these words to you, but they are nothing, except God speak to you too. O pray, pray, pray, that God would give you grace! and then she prayed, O Lord finish thy work upon their Souls. It will be my comfort to see you in glory; but it will be your everlasting happiness.

30. Her Grandmother told her she spent her self too much; she said, I care not for that, if I could do any Soul good. O with what vehemency did she speak, as if her heart were in every word she spoke.

31. She was full of Divine Sentences, and almost all her discourse from the first to the last in the time of her sickness, was about her Soul, Christs sweetness, and the Souls of others, in a word, like a continued Sermon.

32. Upon Friday, after she had had such lively discoveries of Gods love, she was exceeding desirous to die, and cryed out, Come Lord Jesus, come quickly, conduct me to thy Tabernacle; I am a poor creature without thee: but Lord Jesus, my soul longs to be with thee: O when shall it be? Why not now, dear Jesus? Come Lord Jesus, come quickly; but why do I speak thus? Thy time dear Lord is the best; O give me patience.

33. Upon Saturday she spoke very little (being very drowsie) yet now and then she dropt these words, How long sweet Jesus, finish thy work sweet Jesus, come away sweet dear Lord Jesus, come quickly; sweet Lord help, come away, now, now dear Jesus, come quickly; Good Lord give patience to me to wait thy appointed time; Lord Jesus help me, help me, help me. Thus at several times (when out of her sleep) for she was asleep the greatest part of the day.

34. Upon the Lords Day she scarce spoke any thing, but much desired that Bills of Thanksgiving might be sent to those who had formerly been praying for her, that they might help her to praise God for that full assurance that he had given her of his love; and seemed to be much swallowed up with the thoughts of Gods free love to her Soul. She oft commended her spirit into the Lords hands, and the last words which she was heard to speak, were these, Lord Help, Lord Jesus help, Dear Jesus, Blessed Jesus—And thus upon the Lords Day, between Nine and Ten of the Clock in the Forenoon, she slept sweetly in Jesus, and began an everlasting Sabbath, *February 19, 1670.*

BENJAMIN KEACH (1640–1704)
From *War With the Devil: or, the Young Man's Conflict with the Powers of Darkness* (1673)

Calvinistic Baptist pastor Benjamin Keach was a self-taught preacher of strong, unflinching convictions. In 1664, in his native Buckinghamshire, he was imprisoned, fined, and pilloried for his preaching, and his catechism, *A Child's Instructor*, was burned. From the late 1660s he was a controversial London preacher, attracting audiences of almost one thousand but running foul of the Baptish Church by advocating congregational singing. Father of ten children and author of over fifty publications, Keach conveyed a zealot's fervour. *War With the Devil*, a versified dialogue that went through twenty-two editions over a century, shows a rhymester's ease with iambic couplets as well as an awareness of the language of ridicule. Youth, who, in his reluctant progress from 'natural' to 'converted' states, talks with the Devil, Conscience, Truth, Companions, a Neighbour, and Jesus, finally repents. But, as in the early exchange extracted here, Keach is very successful in scripting the self-gratification and venality that muffle conscience.

YOUTH.
    Was ever Young Man thus perplex'd as I,
Who flourished in sweet Prosperity?
Where'er I go *Conscience* dogs me about,
No Quiet can I have in doors or out.
5 *Conscience*, what is the Cause you make such Strife,
I can't enjoy the Comforts of my Life?
I am so grip'd and pinched in my Breast,
I know not where to go, nor where to rest.

CONSCIENCE.

    'Cause you have wronged and offended me,
10 Loving vain Pleasures and Iniquity.
The Light you have you walk not up unto,
You know, 'tis Evil which you daily do.
My Witness I must bear continually,
For the Great GOD, whose Glorious Majesty
15 Did in thy Soul give me so large a Place,
As for to stop you in your sinful Race;
I must reprove, accuse, and you condemn,
Whilst you by Sin his Sov'reignty contemn;
I can't betray my Trust, nor hold my Peace,
20 Till I am stabbed, fear'd, or Light doth cease:
Till you your Life amend, and Sins forsake,
I shall pursue you, though your Heart doth ach.

YOUTH.

    How bold and malapert* is *Conscience* grown?   impudent
Tho' I upon this Fellow daily frown,
25 And his Advice reject, yet still doth he
Knock at my Door, as if he'd weary me.
Conscience, I'd have you know, in Truth, that I
A Person am of some Authority;
Are you so saucy as to curb and chide
30 Such a brave Spark, who can't your Ways abide?
'Tis much below my Birth and Parentage,
And it agrees not with my present Age
For to give place to you, or to regard
Those Things from you I have so often heard.

CONSCIENCE.

35   Alas! proud Flesh, dost think thyself too high
To be subject to such a one as I?
Thy Betters I continually gainsay,
If they my Motions don't with Care obey;
My Power's great, and my Commission's large,
40 There's scarce a Man but I with Folly charge;
The King and Peasant are alike to me,
I favour non of high or low Degree;
If they offend, I in their Faces fly,
Without Regard, or Fear of Standers by.

YOUTH.

45   Speak not another Word: Don't you perceive
There's scarce a Man or Woman will believe
What you do say, you're grown so out of Date?
Be silent then, and do no longer prate.

In the Country your Credit is but small,
50 There's few care for your Company at all,
The *Husbandman* the *Land-mark** can't remove   boundary
But you straitway him bitterly reprove;
Nor plough a little of his Neighbour's Land,
But you command him presently to stand.
55 There's not a man can go in the least awry,
But out against him you do fiercely fly.
The People therefore now so weary are,
They've thrust you almost out of ev'ry Shire:
And in the City you so hated be,
60 There's very few that care a Rush for thee;
For if they should believe what you do say,
Their Pride and Bravery will soon decay;
Their *Swearing, Cursing,* and their *Drunkenness,*
Would vanish quite away, or grow much less.
65 Our *Craft* of *Profit,* and our *Pleasure* too,
Would soon go down and ruin'd be by you.
The *Whore* and *Bawd,* with the *Play-houses* then
Would be contemned by all Sorts of Men.
You strive to spoil us of our sweet Delight,
70 Our Pleasures you oppose with all your Might;
The Fabrick of our Joy you would pull down,
And make our Youth like to a Country Clown;
We half *Fanaticks* should be made ('tis clear)
If unto thee we once inclined were.
75 But this among the rest doth chear my Heart,
There's very few in *London* take thy Part;
Here and there one which we do *Nick-names* give,
Who hated are, and judg'd not fit to live.
'Tis out of Fashion grown, we daily see,
80 *Conscience* for to regard i'th' least Degree:
He that can't Whore and Swear without Controul,
We do accout to be a timorous Fool.
Therefore, though you so desperately do fall
Upon poor Me, yet I do hope I shall
85 Get loose from you, and then I'll tear the Ground,
And in all Joy and Pleasure will abound.

From *The New England Primer* (*fl.* 1683–1830)

The *Primer* appeared in hundreds of editions, with many variants and additions, over its long span of popularity. Encased in a cover of thin sheets of oak spread with coloured paper, this book was literally read to pieces by its young owners. The earliest extant copy is dated 1727, but records indicate that it was printed from the 1680s. One of the first compilers of *The New England Primer* was the Boston book merchant Benjamin Harris. Formerly an enterprising London publisher (who printed the works of Benjamin Keach, among others), Harris had already printed *The Protestant Tutor* in England and had been pilloried in 1681 for issuing *The Protestant Petition*. *The New England Primer* was the staple lesson book for most young colonists. It usually contained the alphabet and a syllabarium; prayers and promises to be memorized by all dutiful children; the anti-papist testament of John Rogers, who was the first Smithfield martyr; a rhymed pictorial alphabet, which often summarized Bible history; and a Puritan catechism.

A — In *Adam's* Fall
We Sinned all.

B — Thy Life to Mend
This *Book* Attend.

C — The *Cat* doth play
And after flay.

D — A *Dog* will bite
A Thief at night.

E — An *Eagles* flight
Is out of fight.

F — The Idle *Fool*
Is whipt at School.

G — As runs the *Glaſs*
Mans life doth paſs.

H — My *Book* and *Heart*
Shall never part.

J — *Job* feels the Rod
Yet bleſſes GOD.

K — Our *K I N G* the
good
No man of blood.

L — The *Lion* bold
The *Lamb* doth hold.

M — The *Moon* gives light
In time of night.

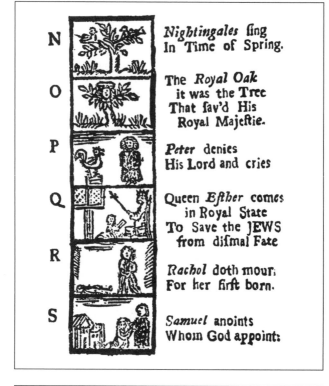

N Nightingales sing
In Time of Spring.

O The *Royal Oak*
it was the Tree
That sav'd His
Royal Majestie.

P *Peter* denies
His Lord and cries

Q Queen *Esther* comes
in Royal State
To Save the JEWS
from dismal Fate

R *Rachol* doth mour,
For her first born.

S *Samuel* anoints
Whom God appoints

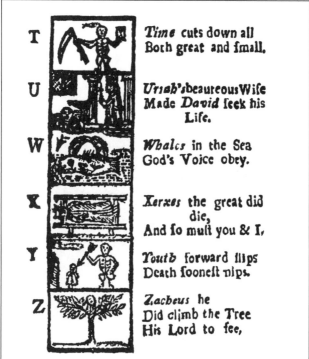

T *Time* cuts down all
Both great and small.

U *Uriah's* beauteous Wife
Made *David* seek his
Life.

W *Whales* in the Sea
God's Voice obey.

X *Xerxes* the great did
die,
And so must you & I,

Y *Youth* forward slips
Death soonest nips.

Z *Zacheus* he
Did climb the Tree
His Lord to see,

The Dutiful Child's Promises

I will fear God and honour the King.
I will honour my Father and Mother.
I will obey my Superiors.
I will submit to my Elders.
I will love my Friends.
I will hate no Man.
I will forgive my Enemies, and pray to God for them.
I will as much as in me lies, keep all God's holy Commandments.
I will learn my Catechism.
I will keep the Lord's Day holy.
I will Reverence God's Sanctuary.

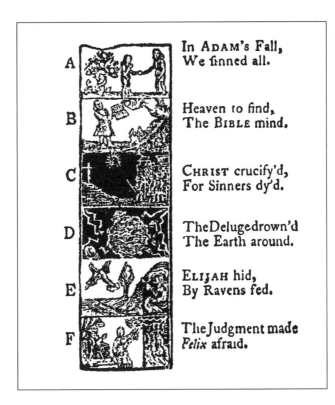

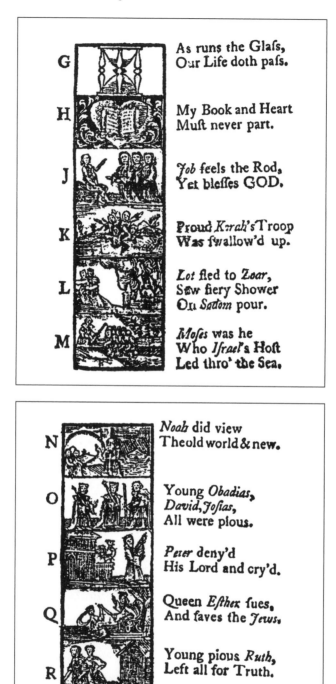

G As runs the Glaſs,
Our Life doth paſs.

H My Book and Heart
Muſt never part.

J *Job* feels the Rod,
Yet bleſſes GOD.

K Proud *Korah's* Troop
Was ſwallow'd up.

L *Lot* fled to *Zoar*,
Saw fiery Shower
On *Sodom* pour.

M *Moſes* was he
Who *Iſrael's* Hoſt
Led thro' the Sea.

N *Noah* did view
The old world & new.

O Young *Obadias*,
David, *Joſias*,
All were pious.

P *Peter* deny'd
His Lord and cry'd.

Q Queen *Eſther* ſues,
And ſaves the *Jews*.

R Young pious *Ruth*,
Left all for Truth.

S Young *Samuel* dear,
The Lord did fear.

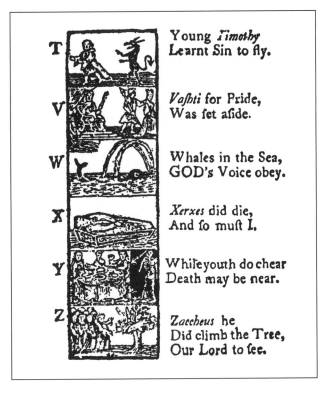

Young *Timothy*
Learnt Sin to fly.

Vashti for Pride,
Was set aside.

Whales in the Sea,
GOD's Voice obey.

Xerxes did die,
And so must I.

While youth do chear
Death may be near.

Zaccheus he
Did climb the Tree,
Our Lord to see.

JOHN BUNYAN (1628–1688)
From *A Book for Boys and Girls; or, Country Rhimes for Children* (1686)

Father of six children, itinerant mender, and 'mechanic preacher', John Bunyan gained a considerable reputation as pastor of the Baptist congregation at Bedford and author of sixty printed works. His best-known writings are the spiritual autobiography *Grace Abounding to the Chief of Sinners* (1660), recounting his conversion; the dialogue *The Life and Death of Mr Badman* (1680), exposing the hypocrisies of small-town society; the allegory *The Holy War* (1682), relating Emmanuel's recapture of the town of Mansoul from Diabolus; and the two-part dream allegory *The Pilgrim's Progress* (1677, 1684), the first part written in prison and narrating Christian's journey from the wilderness of this world to Sion. His originally unillustrated *Book for Boys and Girls* went through several editions in the eighteenth century. In an abridged form, which reduced its rhymes from seventy-four to forty-nine, *Divine Emblems; or, Temporal Things Spiritualized* often appeared adorned with woodcuts.

III
Meditations Upon an Egg

The Egg's no Chick by falling from the Hen;
 Nor man a Christian, till he's born agen.
The Egg's at first contained in the Shell;
Men afore Grace, in sins, and darkness dwell.
5 The Egg when laid, by Warmth is made a Chicken;
And Christ, by Grace, those dead in sin doth quicken.
 The Egg, when first a Chick, the shell's its Prison;
So's flesh to th'Soul, who yet with Christ is risen.
 The Shell doth crack, the Chick doth chirp and peep;
10 The flesh decays, as men do pray and weep.
 The Shell doth break, the Chick's at liberty;
The flesh falls off, the Soul mounts up on high.
 But both do not enjoy the self-same plight;
The Soul is safe, the Chick now fears the Kite.

2

15 But Chick's from rotten Eggs do not proceed;
Nor is an Hypocrite a Saint indeed.
 The rotten Egg, though underneath the Hen,
If crack'd, stinks, and is loathsome unto men.
 Nor doth her Warmth make what is rotten sound,
20 What's rotten, rotten will at last be found.
 The Hyppocrite, sin has him in Possession,
He is a rotten Egg under Profession.

3

 Some Eggs bring Cockatrices; and some men
Seem hatcht and brooded in the Vipers Den.
25 Some Eggs bring wild-Fowls; and some men there be
As wild as are the wildest Fowls that flee.
 Some Eggs bring Spiders; and some men appear
More venom than the worst of Spiders are.
 Some Eggs bring Piss ants; and some seem to me
30 As much for trifles as the Piss-ants be.
 Thus divers Eggs do produce divers shapes,
As like some Men as Monkeys are like Apes.
But this is but an Egg, were it a Chick,
Here had been Legs, and Wings, and Bones to pick.

VIII
Upon the Swallow

This pretty Bird, oh! how she flies and sings!
But could she do so had she not Wings?
Her Wings, bespeak my Faith, her Songs my Peace;
When I believe and sing, my Doubtings cease.

IX
Upon the Bee

The Bee goes out and Honey home doth bring;
And some who seek that Honey find a sting.
Now wouldst thou have the Honey and be free
From stinging; in the first place kill the Bee.

Comparison

5 This Bee an Emblem truly is of sin
Whose sweet unto a many death hath been.
Now wouldst have Sweet from sin, and yet not dye,
Do thou it in the first place mortifie.

XXI
Of the Boy and Butter Fly

Behold how eager this our little Boy,
Is of this Butter Fly, as if all Joy,
All Profits, Honours, yea and lasting Pleasures,
Were wrapt up in her, or the richest Treasures,
5 Found in her would be bundled up together,
When all her all is lighter than a feather.
He hollo's, runs, and cries out here Boys, here,
Nor doth he Brambles or the Nettles fear:
He stumbles at the Mole-Hills, up he gets,
10 And runs again, as one bereft of wits;
And all this labour and this large Out-cry,
Is only for a silly Butter-fly.

Comparison

This little Boy an Emblem is of those,
Whose hearts are wholly at the World's dispose.
15 The Butter-fly doth represent to me,
The World's best things at best but fading be.
All are but painted Nothings and false Joys,
Like this poor Butter-fly to these our Boys.
His running through Nettles, Thorns and Bryers,
20 To gratifie his boyish fond desires,

His tumbling over Mole-hills to attain
His end, namely, his Butter-fly to gain;
Doth plainly shew, what hazards some men run,
To get what will he lost as soon as won.
25 Men seem in Choice, then children far more wise,
Because they run not after Butter flies:
When yet alas! for what are empty Toys
They follow Children, like to beardless Boys.

XXIX
Upon a Ring of Bells

Bells have wide mouths and tongues, but are too weak,
   Have they not help, to sing, or talk, or speak.
But if you move them they will mak't appear,
By speaking they'l make all the Town to hear.
5   When Ringers handle them with Art and Skill,
They then the ears of their Observers fill,
With such brave Notes, they ting and tang so well
As to out strip all with their ding, dong, Bell.

Comparison

   These Bells are like the Powers of my Soul;
10 Their Clappers to the Passions of my mind:
The Ropes by which my Bells are made to tole,
Are Promises (I by experience find.)
   My body is the Steeple, where they hang,
My Graces they which do ring ev'ry Bell:
15 Nor is there any thing gives such a tang,
When by these Ropes these Ringers ring them well.
   Let not my Bells these Ringers want, nor Ropes;
Yea let them have room for to swing and sway:
To toss themselves deny them not their Scopes.
20 Lord! in my Steeple give them room to play.
If they do tole, ring out, or chime all in,
They drown the tempting tinckling Voice of Vice:
Lord! when my Bells have gone, my Soul has bin
As 'twere a tumbling in this Paradice!
25   Or if these Ringers do the Changes ring,
Upon my Bells, they do such Musick make,
My Soul then (Lord) cannot but bounce and sing,
So greatly her they with their Musick take.
But Boys (my Lusts) into my Belfry go,
30 And pull these Ropes, but do no Musick make
They rather turn my Bells by what they do,
Or by disorder make my Steeple shake.
   Then, Lord! I pray thee keep my Belfry Key,

Let none but Graces meddle with these Ropes:
35 And when these naughty Boys come, say them Nay,
From such Ringers of Musick there's no hopes.
    O Lord! If thy poor Child might have his will,
And might his meaning freely to thee tell;
He never of this Musick has his fill,
40 There's nothing to him like thy ding, dong, Bell.

XXXVII
Upon the Whipping of a Top

Tis with the Whip the Boy sets up the Top,
    The Whip makes it run round about it's Toe;
The Whip makes it hither and thither hop:
Tis with the Whip, the Top is made to go.

Comparison
5   Our Legalist is like unto this Top,
Without a Whip, he doth not Duty do.
Let *Moses* whip him, he will skip and hop;
Forbear to whip, he'l neither stand nor go.

XLVI
The Boy and Watch-Maker

This Watch my Father did on me bestow,
    A Golden one it is, but 'twill not go,
Unless it be at an Uncertainty;
But as good none, as one to tell a Lye.
5   When 'tis high Day, my Hand will stand at nine;
I think there's no man's Watch so bad as mine.
Sometimes 'tis sullen, 'twill not go at all,
And yet 'twas never broke, nor had a Fall.

Watch-maker
    Your Watch, tho it be good, through want of skill,
10 May fail to do according to your will.
Suppose the Ballance, Wheels, and Spring be good,
And all things else, unless you understood
To manage it, as Watches ought to be,
Your Watch will still be at Uncertainty
15 Come, tell me, do you keep it from the Dust?
Yea wind it also duly up you must.
Take heed (too) that you do not strain the String;
You must be circumspect in ev'ry thing.
Or else your Watch, were it as good again,
20 Would not with Time, and Tide you entertain.

Comparison

This Boy an Emblem is of a Convert;
His Watch of th'work of Grace within his heart.
The Watch-maker is Jesus Christ our Lord,
His Counsel, the Directions of his Word.
Then Convert, if thy heart be out of frame,
25 Of this Watch-maker learn to mend the same.
    Do not lay ope'thy heart to Worldly Dust,
Nor let thy Graces over grow with Rust.
Be oft renew'd in th' Spirit of thy mind,
Or else uncertain thou thy Watch wilt find.

XLIX
Upon a Lanthorn

The Lanthorn is to keep the Candle Light,
    When it is windy, and a darksome Night.
Ordain'd it also was, that men might see
By Night their way, and so in safety be.

Comparison

5   Compare we now our Lanthorn to the man,
That has within his heart a Work of Grace.
As for another let him, if he can,
Do as this Lanthorn, in its time and place:
    Profess the Faith, and thou a Lanthorn art:
10 But yet if Grace has not possessed thee:
Thou want'st this Candle Light within thy heart
And art none other, than dark Lanthorns be.

LIV
Upon the Chalk-Stone

This Stone is white, yea, warm, and also soft,
    Easie to work upon, unless 'tis naught.
It leaves a white Impression upon those,
Whom it doth touch, be they its Friends or Foes.

5   The Child of God, is like to this Chalk-Stone,
White in his Life, easily wrought upon:
Warm in Affections, apt to leave impress,
On whom he deals with, of true Godliness.

He is no sulling Coal, nor daubing Pitch,
10 Nor one of whom men catch the Scab, or Itch;
But such who in the Law of God doth walk,
Tender of heart, in Life whiter than Chalk.

LXXII
Upon Time and Eternity

Eternity is like unto a Ring.
Time, like to Measure, doth it self extend;
Measure commences, is a finite thing.
The Ring has no beginning, middle, end.

3. LYRICAL INSTRUCTION: ISAAC WATTS AND HIS CONTEMPORARIES

The Sorrows of the Mind
Be banish'd from the Place!
Religion never was design'd
To make our Pleasures less.

—*Watts*, 'Heavenly Joy on Earth',
Hymns and Spiritual Songs (1709)

Poetry can have amazing grace. The hymns, fables, and verse monologues sampled in this chapter soften the message of Christian repentance and attenuate the stress on fire and brimstone. They also highlight an increasing awareness of the behaviour of real children—not sermonizing paragons—and their quickness to borrow from adult entertainments.

The idea of tempering religious instruction to enthrall, not terrorize, the young was gaining popularity. Thomas Willis (d. 1692), an Oxford-educated, temporizing, and finally conforming minister, who served during both the Commonwealth and the Restoration, added a final section to his *The Key of Knowledg* (1682), entitled

'Apples of Gold in Pictures of Silver, For the Use and Delight of Children and Servants'. It consisted of well-known seventeenth-century religious poetry—Anglican and Catholic—abbreviated and edited to appeal to children.

Isaac Watts's Dissenting beliefs caused him to forgo Oxford and Cambridge, but his fame was neither confined nor narrow. Having studied Latin, Greek, French, and Hebrew at King Edward VI School in Southampton, he spent four years at London's Newington Green Academy under the principalship of the Reverend Thomas Rowe, a Calvinist. Even though Watts was brought up strictly within the Puritan tradition, and though he moved with ease among the learned Puritan elite, he remained free of sectarian bias. What is remarkable about his poetry, much of which is still enshrined in hymnals of different denominations, is its universal appeal born of a conscious desire to praise. In the preface to his *Divine Songs* Watts made it very clear that 'you will find here nothing that savours of a Party: the children of high and low degree, of the Church of England and Dissenters, baptized in infancy or not, may all join together in these songs'. After ministering in the Stoke Newington section of London's rich Dissenting population, Watts was appointed, in 1712, tutor and private chaplain in the home of Sir Thomas Abney, in Hertfordshire, a position he held for thirty-six years. Likely the *Divine Songs* was composed, in the first instance, for the Abney children.

Watts's preface explained his practical, spiritual intentions. Describing the easily memorized songs as 'a constant furniture for the minds of children', he concentrated on delight. 'There is something so amusing and entertaining in rhymes and metre', he observed, 'that will incline children to make this part of their business a diversion.' In the preface to the two 'Moral Songs' that were included in the 1715 edition of *Divine Songs*, he hoped that 'children might find Delight and Profit together'.

A clear indication that Watts had no desire to follow the example of the unremittingly admonitory Janeway can be seen by comparing their choice of biblical epigraphs. Watts chose 'Out of the Mouths of Babes and Sucklings Thou has perfected Praise' (Matt. 21. 16), which certainly echoes Janeway's use of Psalms 8. 2: 'Out of the mouths of Babes and Sucklings Thou has ordained Strength'. But the difference between *ordaining strength* and *perfecting praise* is significant, and it accounts for the palpable contrasts between the lyrics of Watts and the reproofs of Janeway, Bunyan,

and the Puritan primers. Though the children in his hymns are God-fearing, Watts's comparisons are invariably more positive than those of his predecessors. While Bunyan made the bee an emblem of sin, Watts makes it a symbol of spiritual industry.

In *Divine Songs* Watts demonstrates his ability to employ simple diction, rhymes, and rhythms to fashion Christian lyrics for children that artfully combine instruction, admonition, and praise. Often announcing the lessons in his titles—'Against Quarrelling and Fighting', 'Against Idleness and Mischief'—he claims the young reader's attention with homely, familiar subjects before introducing depictions of the wages of sin. Yet Watts's severity is tempered by his graceful prosody and sweetness of tone. His inimitable gentleness is most evident in 'A Cradle Hymn'. Only a poet of great compassion and delicacy would have attempted to relate the major events of Christian salvation in the form of a lullaby. While the infant is rocked and soothed to sleep, the mother or nurse sings of the Christ Child whose 'softest bed was hay', and who came to earth 'to save thee, child, from dying / Save my dear from burning flame.' Hell-fire, a plain fact in Watts's creed, has been woven naturally and unobtrusively into this lilting cradle-song.

Prominent motifs in the 'Moral Songs' are animals and plants, employed to provide ideal moral comparisons. 'The Rose' extends the lilies-of-the-field theme of the Divine Song 'Against Pride in Clothes', laying its stress on the enduring 'scent' of dutiful goodness. Watts's Moral Songs show his closest affinity to Bunyan's *Country Rhimes*; however, the differences are marked. While Bunyan's sinner was catechized by the articulate spider, Watts's 'The Ant' inculcates its lesson simply by describing that insect's activities.

Although, in his *Hymns for Children* (1763), John Wesley criticized Watts for communicating with children on their level, rather than lifting them up, Watts's lyrics continue to contribute to children's and modern hymnody. Charles Wesley wrote over 7000 hymns, and Watts fewer than seven hundred; yet two-fifths of the hymns in current hymnals are those of Isaac Watts. In Victorian times the freshness and power of his imagery made Watts's children's poems not only effective inducements to piety but sources of brilliant parody, as in Lewis Carroll's transformation of 'Against Idleness and Mischief' into 'How doth the little crocodile'. Many of Watts's poetic maxims about the Christian's responsibility to be always busy, obedient, and clean—often accepted as direct biblical injunction—have exerted an influence on Sunday School parlance to this day.

While Watts's songs are tailored for Christian instruction, the genres of fable and monologue may appear at first less suited to this end. In fact, the vigour and terseness of the fable, with punchlines delivered by articulate animals brought to life by John Gay, and the school child's monologue, as ventriloquized by an observant parent, Mary Barber, instruct the Christian in the ways—and detours—of the world. Gay makes a flea the teacher of a vain, but deflated, human being. Barber scripts her son's consternation with the tyranny of custom in the mandated change to short pants, and voices perennial parental anxieties about the career preparation—what we would call job prospects—of his expensive education. No piety drapes this secular, though lyrical, instruction. Instead, irony and humour enliven the exercise.

ISAAC WATTS (1674–1748)
From *Divine Songs Attempted in Easy Language for the Use of Children* (1715)

Dissenting poet, hymnodist, and intellectual, Watts, the son of an Independent deacon, was born in the year of Milton's death and probably came under the spell of the great Puritan poet's writings at an early age. Prior to his publications for children Watts had written *Horae Lyricae* (1706), early experiments with psalms and hymns, and

Hymns and Spiritual Songs (1707, 1709). His concern was always to clarify the text of psalmody and energize church singing. Historians of church music readily acknowledge a general indebtedness to Watts, and some pay specific tribute to his works for the young. Louis Benson in *The English Hymn* (1915; rpt. 1962) regards these poems as 'the Fountainhead of Children's Hymnody in the English Language'. Among Watts's most important prose works are *The Art of Reading and Writing English* (1734), *Logick, or the Right Use of Reason in the Enquiry after Truth* (1734), and *The Improvements of the Mind* (1741), texts which, as Selma Bishop notes, were used in academies and Oxford and Cambridge for over a century.

The Excellency of The Bible

Great God, with wonder and with praise
    On all thy works I look;
But still thy wisdom, power, and grace,
    Shine brighter in thy book.

The stars, that in their courses roll,
5   Have much instruction given;
But thy good Word informs my soul
    How I may climb to heaven.

The fields provide me food, and show
10   The goodness of the Lord;
But fruits of life and glory grow
    In thy most holy Word.

Here are my choicest treasures hid,
    Here my best comfort lies;
15 Here my desires are satisfied,
    And hence my hopes arise.

Lord, make me understand thy law;
    Show what my faults have been;
And from thy gospel let me draw
20   Pardon for all my sin.

Here would I learn how Christ has died
    To save my soul from hell:
Not all the books on earth beside
    Such heavenly wonders tell.

25 Then let me love my Bible more,
    And take a fresh delight
By day to read these wonders o'er,
    And meditate by night.

Praise to God for Learning to Read

The praises of my tongue
   I offer to the Lord,
That I was taught and learnt so young
   To read his holy Word.

5 That I am brought to know
   The danger I was in,
By nature and by practice too
   A wretched slave to sin.

That I am led to see
10   I can do nothing well;
And whither shall a sinner flee
   To save himself from hell?

Dear Lord, this book of thine
   Informs me where to go,
15 For grace to pardon all my sin,
   And make me holy too.

Here I can read, and learn
   How Christ, the Son of God,
Has undertook our great concern;
20   Our ransom cost his blood.

And now he reigns above,
    He sends his Spirit down
To show the wonders of his love,
    And make his gospel known.

25 O may that Spirit teach,
    And make my heart receive,
Those truths which all thy servants preach,
    And all thy saints believe.

Then shall I praise the Lord
30   In a more cheerful strain,
That I was taught to read his Word,
    And have not learnt in vain

Heaven and Hell

There is beyond the sky
    A heaven of joy and love;
And holy children, when they die,
    Go to that world above.

5 There is a dreadful hell,
    And everlasting pains;
There sinners must with devils dwell,
    In darkness, fire, and chains.

Can such a wretch as I
10   Escape this cursed end?
And may I hope, whene'er I die,
    I shall to heaven ascend?

Then will I read and pray,
    While I have life and breath:
15 Lest I should be cut off to-day,
    And sent to eternal death.

Against Quarrelling and Fighting

Let dogs delight to bark and bite,
    For God hath made them so;
Let bears and lions growl and fight,
    For 'tis their nature too.

5 But, children, you should never let
    Such angry passions rise;
Your little hands were never made
    To tear each other's eyes.

Let love through all your actions run,
10   And all your words be mild;
Live like the blessed Virgin's Son,
    That sweet and lovely child.

His soul was gentle as a lamb;
    And as his stature grew,
15 He grew in favour both with man,
    And God his Father too.

Now Lord of all he reigns above,
    And from his heavenly throne
He sees what children dwell in love,
20   And marks them for his own.

Against Idleness and Mischief

How doth the little busy bee
    Improve each shining hour,
And gather honey all the day
    From every opening flower!

5 How skilfully she builds her cell!
    How neat she spreads the wax!
And labors hard to store it well
    With the sweet food she makes.

In works of labour or of skill,
10   I would be busy too;
For Satan finds some mischief still
    For idle hands to do.

In books, or work, or healthful play,
    Let my first years be past,
15 That I may give for every day
    Some good account at last.

Against Pride in Clothes

Why should our garments, made to hide
Our parents' shame, provoke our pride?
The art of dress did ne'er begin,
Till Eve, our mother, learn'd to sin.

5 When first she put the covering on,
Her robe of innocence was gone;
And yet her children vainly boast
In the sad marks of glory lost.

How proud we are! how fond to shew
10 Our clothes, and call them rich and new!
When the poor sheep and silkworm wore
That very clothing long before.

The tulip and the butterfly
Appear in gayer coats than I;
15 Let me be drest fine as I will,
Flies, worms, and flowers, exceed me still.

Then will I set my heart to find
Inward adornings of the mind;
Knowledge and virtue, truth and grace,
20 These are the robes of richest dress.

No more shall worms with me compare;
This is the raiment angels wear;
The Son of God, when here below,
Put on this blest apparel too.

25 It never fades, it ne'er grows old,
Nor fears the rain, nor moth, nor mould;
It takes no spot, but still refines;
The more 'tis worn, the more it shines.

In this on earth would I appear,
30 Then go to heaven and wear it there;
God will approve it in his sight,
'Tis his own work, and his delight.

From *The Moral Songs*

By 1740 Watts's edition of *Divine Songs* included seven 'Moral Songs' as well.

The Sluggard

'Tis the voice of the sluggard; I heard him complain,
'You have waked me too soon, I must slumber again.'
As the door on its hinges, so he on his bed,
Turns his sides, and his shoulders, and his heavy head.

5 'A little more sleep, and a little more slumber;'
Thus he wastes half his days and his hours without number;
And when he gets up, he sits folding his hands,
Or walks about sauntering, or trifling he stands.

I pass'd by his garden, and saw the wild brier,
10 The thorn and the thistle, grow broader and higher;
The clothes that hang on him are turning to rags;
And his money still wastes, till he starves, or he begs.

I made him a visit, still hoping to find
He had took better care for improving his mind:
15 He told me his dreams, talk'd of eating and drinking,
But he scarce reads his Bible, and never loves thinking.

Said I then to my heart, 'Here's a lesson for me;
That man's but a picture of what I might be;
But thanks to my friends for their care in my breeding,
20 Who taught me betimes to love working and reading.'

The Ant, or Emmet

These emmets, how little they are in our eyes!
We tread them to dust and a troop of them dies,
    Without our regard or concern;
Yet as wise as we are, if we went to their school,
5 There's many a sluggard and many a fool
    Some lessons of wisdom might learn.

They don't wear their time out in sleeping or play
But gather up corn in a sunshiny day,
    And for winter they lay up their stores:
10 They manage their work in such regular forms,
One would think they foresaw all the frost and the storms,
    And so brought their food within doors.

But I have less sense than a poor creeping ant,
If I take no due care for the things I shall want,
15   Nor provide against dangers in time:
When death or old age shall stare in my face,
What a wretch shall I be in the end of my days,
    If I trifle away all their prime!

Now, now, while my strength and my youth are in bloom,
20 Let me think what will serve me when sickness shall come,
    And pray that my sins be forgiven:
Let me read in good books, and believe, and obey,
That when death turns me out of this cottage of clay,
    I may dwell in a palace in heaven.

The Rose

How fair is the Rose! what a beautiful flower.
    The glory of April and May!
But the leaves are beginning to fade in an hour,
    And they wither and die in a day.

5 Yet the Rose has one powerful virtue to boast,
    Above all the flowers of the field;
When its leaves are all dead, and fine colours are lost,
    Still how sweet a perfume it will yield!

So frail is the youth and the beauty of man,
10   Though they bloom and look gay like the Rose;
But all our fond care to preserve them is vain;
    Time kills them as fast as he goes.

Then I'll not be proud of my youth or my beauty,
  Since both of them wither and fade;
15 But gain a good name by well-doing my duty;
  This will scent, like a Rose, when I'm dead.

In the 1727 edition of *Divine Songs* 'A Cradle Hymn' appeared after two 'Moral Songs'.

A Cradle Hymn

Hush, my dear, lie still and slumber!
  Holy angels guard thy bed!
Heavenly blessings without number
  Gently falling on thy head.

5 Sleep, my babe; thy food and raiment,
  House and home, thy friends provide
All without thy care or payment,
  All thy wants are well supplied.

How much better thou'rt attended
10 Than the Son of God could be,
When from heaven he descended,
  And became a child like thee!

Soft and easy is thy cradle;
  Coarse and hard thy Saviour lay,
15 When his birthplace was a stable,
  And his softest bed was hay.

Blessed babe! what glorious features,
  Spotless fair, divinely bright!
Must he dwell with brutal creatures?
20 How could angels bear the sight!

Was there nothing but a manger
    Cursed sinners could afford,
To receive the heavenly Stranger?
    Did they thus affront their Lord?

25 Soft, my child; I did not chide thee,
    Though my song might sound too hard;
'Tis thy ⎰ mother* ⎱ that sits beside thee,
    ⎱ nurse ⎰
    And her arms shall be thy guard.

Yet to read the shameful story,
30   How the Jews abus'd their King,
How they serv'd the Lord of Glory,
    Makes me angry while I sing.

See the kinder shepherds round him,
    Telling wonders from the sky;
35 There they sought him, there they found him,
    With his virgin mother by.

See the lovely babe a-dressing;
    Lovely infant, how he smil'd!
When he wept, the mother's blessing
40   Sooth'd and hush'd the holy child.

Lo, he slumbers in his manger,
    Where the horned oxen feed;
Peace, my darling, here's no danger,
    Here's no ox a-near thy bed.

45 'Twas to save thee, child, from dying,
    Save my dear from burning flame,
Bitter groans, and endless crying,
    That thy blest Redeemer came.

Mayst thou live to know and fear him,
50   Trust and love him all thy days;
Then go dwell for ever near him,
    See his face, and sing his praise!

I could give thee thousand kisses,
    Hoping what I most desire;
55 Not a mother's fondest wishes
    Can to greater joys aspire.

* Here you may use the words, brother, sister, friend, &c. [Author's note.]

JOHN GAY (1685–1732)
From *Fables* (1727)

Poet and playwright, Gay gained and lost friends due to his satirical, tart wit. His best-known works are *Trivia, or the Art of Walking the Streets of London* (1716), a long humorous poem about the often grotesque realities of eighteenth-century life; *The Beggar's Opera* (1728), a hugely successful musical comedy, full of travesties of operatic arias—with barbs aimed at the corruption of politics and the law—delivered mainly by the highwayman-hero Macheath; and *Fables* (1727–38), a collection of sixty-six tales (with the last sixteen published posthumously). Appearing in over 350 editions, Fables attracted such illustrators as Thomas Bewick and William Blake. Mary Barber's 'A Tale', first published as an addition to Gay's Fables in 1728, relates the true story of her son's response to Gay's work: he seized the volume, was 'highly pleas'd' and 'delighted', and made observations on every page that 'the Mother thought above his Age'. In fact, Fables quickly became a staple text in school libraries. With smoothly polished couplets and contrastive exchanges, as in the following conversation between the all-important man and the seemingly insignificant insect, Gay's pithy tales use wry humour to puncture pretenses. Instead of lecturing his readers, Gay begins with an epigrammatic moral and proceeds to illustrate it with witty élan.

The Man and the Flea

Whether on earth, in air, or main,*   sea
Sure every thing alive is vain!
 Does not the hawk all fowls survey,
As destined only for his prey?
5 And do not tyrants, prouder things,
Think men were born for slaves to kings?
 When the crab views the pearly strands,
Or *Tagus*,* bright with golden sands,   Spanish-Portuguese river
Or crawls beside the coral grove,   noted for deposits of gold
10 And hears the ocean roll above;
Nature is too profuse, says he,
Who gave all these to pleasure me!
 When bord'ring pinks and roses bloom,
And every garden breaths perfume,
15 When peaches glow with sunny dyes,
Like *Laura's** cheek, when blushes rise;   Petrarch's beloved
When with huge figs the branches bend;
When clusters from the vine depend;*   hang
The snails looks round on flow'r and tree,
20 And cries, all these were made for me!

 What dignity's in human nature,
Says Man, the most conceited creature,

As from a cliff he cast his eye,
And viewed the sea and arched sky!
25 The sun was sunk beneath the main,
The moon, and all the starry train
Hung the vast vault of heav'n. The Man
His contemplation thus began.
    When I behold this glorious show,
30 And the wide watry world below,
The scaly people* of the main,   fish
The beasts that range the wood or plain,
The wing'd inhabitants of air,
The day, the night, the various year,
35 And know all these by heav'n design'd
As gifts to pleasure human kind,
I cannot raise my worth too high;
Of what vast consequence am I!
    Not of th'importance you suppose,
40 Replies a Flea upon his nose:
Be humble, learn thyself to scan;
Know, pride was never made for man.
'Tis vanity that swells thy mind.
What, heav'n and earth for thee design'd!
45 For thee! made only for our need;
That more important Fleas might feed.

MARY BARBER (1690?–1757)
From *Poems on Several Occasions* (1734)

Wife of a Dublin clothing merchant, Barber attracted the attention of Jonathan Swift through her anonymous poem petitioning for relief for an officer's widow with a blind child. Swift, who called her 'Sapphira', was Barber's mentor and champion. Her first publication, *A Tale* (1728), printed in Dublin and slightly modified for the later collection, was an addition to Gay's *Fables*. It recounts the 'vast Pleasure' of this mother 'in forming of her Children's Minds', and particularly her son's delight with Gay's tales. Ironically, since she was always pressed for funds, the poem depicts Barber as a queen bestowing a lavish pension on Gay. *Poems on Several Occasions* (1734), which went through three editions by 1736, was published in London by subscription; Barber's supporters included the nobility and literary elite. Selections were also featured in *Poems by Eminent Ladies* (1755), in which Barber occupied first place. Barber began writing to instruct her own children; among the most charming pieces are monologues she wrote for her son Constantine (b. 1713), who later was President of the Dublin College of Physicians. As a schoolboy 'Con' was regaled with his mother's account of his reaction to the change from a frock to short pants ('breeches') and her concern about the practicality of his education. The mock serious tone of these ventriloquized monologues barely conceals Barber's wit. The verse letter addressed to Henry Rose is not as utilitarian as it first sounds, for the ironic flip of the conclusion puts a valuable premium on learning that embellishes the mind.

Written for My son, and Spoken by Him at His First Putting on Breeches

What is it our mamma's bewitches,
To plague us little boys with Breeches?
To Tyrant *Custom* we must yield
Whilst vanquish'd *Reason* flies the field.
5 Our legs must suffer by Ligation,*   binding
To keep the Blood from Circulation;
And then our Feet, tho' young and tender,
We to the Shoemaker surrender,
Who often makes our Shoes so strait
10 Our growing Feet they cramp and fret;
Whilst, with Contrivance most profound,
Across our Insteps we are bound;
Which is the Cause, I make no Doubt,
Why thousands suffer in the gout.*   painful inflammation of joints,
                                       especially the great toe
15 Our wiser Ancestors wore Brogues,
Before the Surgeons bribed these Rogues,
With narrow Toes, and Heels like Pegs,
To help to make us break our Legs.

Then, ere we know to use our Fists,
20 Our Mothers closely bind our wrists;
And never think our cloaths are neat,
Till they're so tight we cannot eat.
And, to increase our other Pains,
The Hat-band helps to cramp our Brains.
25 The Cravat finishes the Work,
Like Bowstring sent from the *Grand Turk*.

Thus Dress, that should prolong our Date,
Is made to hasten on our Fate.
Fair Privilege of nobler Natures,
30 To be more plagu'd than other Creatures!
The wild Inhabitants of Air
Are cloath'd by Heav'n with wondrous care;
Their beauteous, well-compacted Feathers
Are Coats of Mail against all Weathers;
35 Enamell'd, to delight the Eye,
Gay, as the Bow that decks the Sky.
The Beasts are cloath'd with beauteous skins;
The Fishes armed with Scales and Fins,
Whose Lustre lends the Sailor Light,
40 When all the Stars are hid in Night.

O were our Dress contriv'd like these,
For Use, for Ornament and, Ease!
Man only seems to Sorrow born,
Naked, defenceless and forlorn.

45 Yet we have *Reason*, to supply
What Nature did to Man deny:
Weak Viceroy! Who thy Pow'r will own,
When *Custom* has usurp'd thy Throne?
In vain did I appeal to thee,
50 Ere I would wear his Livery;
Who, in Defiance to thy Rules,
Delights to make us act like Fools.
O'er human Race the Tyrant reigns,
And binds them in eternal Chains.
55 We yield to his despotic Sway,
The only Monarch all obey.

A Letter for My Son to One of His School-Fellows, Son to *Henry Rose*, Esq.

Dear *Rose*, as I lately was writing some Verse,
Which I next Day intended in School to rehearse,
My Mother came in, and I though she'd run wild:
5 'This Mr. *Macmullen* has ruin'd my Child:
He uses me ill, and the World shall know it;
I sent you to *Latin*, he makes you a Poet:
A fine Way of training a Shop-keeper's son!
'Twould better become him to teach you to dun:*   demand payment for debt
10 Let him teach both his Wit, and his Rhyming, to *Rose*;
And give you some Lessons, to help to sell Cloaths:
He'll have an Estate, and 'twill do very well,
That he, like his Father, in Arts should excel:
But for *you*, if your Father will take my Advice,
15 He'll send you no more, till he lowers his Price:
A Guinea* a Quarter! 'tis monstrously dear!   ordinary unit for
You might learn to *dance* for four Guineas a year: professional fee: 21 shillings
Then, Sir, tell your Master, That these are hard Times;
And Paper's too dear to be wasted in Rhymes:
20 I'll teach you a Way of employing it better,
As, 'July *the fifteenth*, Lord Levington *Debtor*':
You may rhyme till you're blind, what arises from thence?
But *Debtor* and *Creditor* brings in the Pence:
Those beggarly Muses but come for a Curse;
But give me the Wit, that puts Gold in the Purse':

25   From what she then told me, I plainly discern,
What different Lessons we Scholars must learn.
You're happy, dear *Rose*; for, as far as I find,
You've nothing to do, but embellish your Mind.
What different Tasks are assign'd us by Fate!
30 'Tis yours to *become*, mine to *get* an Estate.
Then, *Rose*, mind your Learning, whatever you do;
For I have the easier Task of the two.

4. CHAPBOOKS AND PENNY HISTORIES

Sunday 10 July 1763
Some days ago I went to the old printing-office in Bow Church-yard kept by
Dicey, whose family have kept it fourscore years. There are ushered into the world
of literature Jack and the Giants, The Seven Wise Masters of Gotham *and*
other story-books which in my dawning years amused me as much as Rasselas
does now. I saw the whole scheme with a kind of romantic feeling to find myself
really where all my old darlings were printed.

—*James Boswell*, London Journal 1762–3

By the end of the seventeenth century children were not only borrowing from 'serious' adult literature, they were also indulging in the growing market of popular booklets. Fairy tales, medieval romances, fables, and ballads—often related in local speech and crude formulae, and catering for appetites for stupendous feats, exotic settings, curious riddles, and fortune telling—exerted a lifelong hold on the reader's imagination.

Recollections of this early reading can range from penitent to nostalgic. As he confessed in *Sighs from Hell* (1666), Bunyan lamented his reading of cheap print as a childhood sin, but he did capture the sense of fascination:

> *Give me a ballad, a news-book, George on*
> *Horseback or Bevis of Southampton, give*
> *me some book that teaches curious arts,*
> *that tells of old fables; but for the Holy*
> *Scriptures, I cared not. And as it was with*
> *me then, so it is with my brethren now.*

Although Bunyan reveals his past to lecture backsliders in the present, other recollections are more affectionate. In addition to Boswell's memories of 'old darlings', Sterne's Uncle Toby, in *Tristram Shandy*, remembers 'when Guy, Earl of Warwick, and . . . Valentine and Orson and the Seven Champions of England, were handed round at school', and observes that they were 'all purchased with [his] pocket money' (Bk VI, chap. 32). Jane Porter's introduction to her *The Two Princes of Persia. Addressed to Youth* (1801) recreates her own youth when 'the nurse's story of the tripping fairy, the witch riding her broomstick, the turban'd giant, and the sheeted ghost, were the earliest accounts of the universe which were offered to an infant's mind.' She remembers these tales, 'gemmed with ten thousand glittering meteors', as arousing her imagination: 'infant credulity mistook them for stars : and for a time the delusion was enchanting.'

Whether it was remembered fondly or guiltily, the widespread popularity of these early reading practices was fostered in a particular set of cultural conditions. The lapse of the Licensing Act in 1695 contributed to the expansion of the press and the lessening of controls over registering material with the Stationers Company. The press had been licensed since the time of Henry VIII, and the monopoly of the Stationers Company had been established in Elizabeth's reign. However, as John Brewer remarks, during the turbulent decades of the mid-seventeenth century, when new print shops appeared and the number of presses almost trebled, the demand for ephemeral literature increased enormously. Despite such warnings as Thomas White's injunction to his young readers, 'When thou canst read, read no Ballads or foolish Books,' in his *A Little Book for Little Children* (1660), whose stories of holy children became the prototype of the longstanding obituary and martyrology

tradition, other voices were supplanting this strictly catechetical emphasis. Prominent among them was John Locke, who considered children 'rational creatures' to be allowed 'liberties and freedom suitable to their ages'. His *Some Thoughts Concerning Education* (1693), influential throughout the eighteenth century, argued that children should not 'be hindered from being children, nor from playing and doing as children. . . . They love to be busy, change and variety are what they delight in; curiosity is but an appetite for knowledge, the instrument nature has provided to remove ignorance' (Section 118). As Neil McKendrick and others have noted, shrewd printers, booksellers, and hawkers realized that one way of feeding this appetite was to appeal to the fantasies and aspirations of an emerging consumer society.

Among the first entrepreneurs to take advantage of these developments was a group of low-class itinerant salesmen, known as chapmen. As the songs of Shakespeare's Autolycus urging folk to 'come buy' (*The Winter's Tale*, 4. 4. 230) confirm, they had been peddling pins, needles, and ballads for over a century. Now they added to their wares small paperbound books supplied by publishers. The compilers of these chapbooks—or penny histories, as many were called—borrowed from jestbooks, broadsides, and romances in offering stories of Guy of Warwick and Bevis of Southampton, Dick Whittington and Tom Thumb, Jack Horner and Cock Robin; such legends as that of Faust in *Fortunatus*, abridged from medieval romance; and native English folklore, popularizing the prophecies of Mother Shipton, the feats of Mother Bunch and Tom Hickathrift, and the daring of Robin Hood. Children and adults devoured the chapmen's fare voraciously.

Chapbooks (the term is possibly derived from the Anglo-Saxon *ceap*, meaning 'trade') were all the more successful because they were inexpensive, attractive, and small. They could be purchased for as little as a penny, although the price rose slightly in the nineteenth century with improved bindings, leather covers, and hand-coloured copperplate illustrations. Originally they were paper-covered booklets, produced by folding a single sheet several times. They often consisted of twenty-four uncut pages, though lengths of eight and sixteen pages were also common, and they were adorned with woodcut illustrations on the title-page and throughout the text.

While few chapbooks could make claims to literary value, they have enduring importance in the history of children's literature. Satisfying the human desire for stories, conducting readers into the realm of fancy, celebrating heroes, they created and pleased a new market for books. For generations of children to whom little else was available they provided their first, and therefore formative, reading matter, and as a result contributed to the spread of literacy. Chapbooks were also an archive of fairy mythology that might have been lost if these publications had not existed. Finally, the popularity of chapbooks drew to the attention of serious writers the fact that there was a specific audience, young and keen, waiting to be introduced to new works of the imagination.

An Elegy on the Death and Burial of Cock Robin

The first four verses of 'Cock Robin' appeared in *Tommy Thumb's Pretty Song-Book* (1744); by the 1780s the entire rhyme had been published. In *The Oxford Dictionary of Nursery Rhymes* Iona and Peter Opie present two theories about its origin. It may describe the 'intrigues attending the downfall of Robert Walpole's ministry (1742)'; or it may be of much earlier provenance, possibly deriving from the Norse tale of the death of Balder. These two theories are not incompatible. It could have been an old rhyme rewritten to fit the political situation in Walpole's day. The long ministry of Sir Robert Walpole (1675–1745) is a tale of political intrigue. He suffered from gout and the stone through all his attempts to outwit the Whig opposition, led by the Prince of Wales, who in the early 1740s were petitioning for his removal from office. Walpole retired as prime minister in February 1742—much to the distress of King George II. He was created the first Earl of Orford and continued to influence national policy from the sidelines and the House of Lords, until illness debilitated him completely. Known for the remarkable collection of paintings with which he decorated his London residences at Downing Street, Grosvenor Street, and the Chelsea retreat, Walpole was generous toward Congreve and Gay (who satirized him as 'Bob Booty' in *The Beggar's Opera*), and on friendly terms with Addison, Steele, and Pope.

COCK ROBIN.

WHO kill'd Cock Robin?
  I, says the Sparrow,
    With my bow and arrow,
And I kill'd Cock Robin.

This is the Sparrow,
With his bow and arrow.

5

Who saw him die?
  I, said the Fly,
    With my little eye,
And I saw him die.

This is the Fly,
With his little eye.

6

Who caught his blood?
1, said the Fish,
With my little dish,
And I caught his blood.

This is the Fish,
That held the dish.

7

Who made his shroud?
I, said the Beetle,
With my little needle,
And I made his shroud.

This is the Beetle,
With his thread and needle.

8

Who shall dig the grave?
I, said the Owl,
With my spade and shov'l,
And I'll dig his grave.

This is the Owl so brave,
That dug Cock Robin's grave.

9

Who will be the Parson?
I, said the Rook,
With my little book,
And I will be the Parson.

Here's parson Rook,
A reading his book.

10

Who will be the clerk ?
    I, said the Lark,
    If 'tis not in the dark,
And I will be the clerk.

Behold how the Lark,
Says Amen, like a clerk.

11

Who'll carry him to the grave?
    I, said the Kite,
    If 'tis not in the night,
And I'll carry him to the grave.

Behold now the Kite,
How he takes his flight.

Who will carry the link,
  I, said the Linnet,
  I'll fetch it in a minute,
And I'll carry the link.

Here's the Linnet with a light
Altho' 'tis not night.

Who'll be the chief mourner?
  I, said the Dove,
  For I mourn for my love,
And I'll be the chief mourner.

Here's a pretty Dove,
That mourns for her love.

14

Who'll bear the pall?
　We, says the Wrens,
　　Both the cock and the hen,
And we,ll bear the pall.

See the Wrens so small,
Who bore Cock Robin's pall.

15

Who'll sing a psalm?
　I, says the Thrush,
As he sat in a bush,
　And I'll sing a psalm.

Here's a fine Thrush,
Singing psalms in a bush.

16

Who'll toll the bell?
I, says the Bull,
Because I can pull,
So Cock Robin farewell.

All the birds in the air,
Fell a sighing and sobbing,
When they heard the bell toll
For poor Cock Robin.

The Interesting Story of the Children in the Wood

Also known as *The Babes in the Wood*, this story appeared in book form as early as 1595. An affecting combination of parental concern, brotherly betrayal, and childhood abandonment, it was a favourite ballad with minstrels. Mrs Trimmer recalled reading a chapbook version in her childhood in the 1740s.

The Children in the Wood

Now ponder well, ye parents dear,
  The words which I shall write,
A dismal story you shall hear,
  In time brought forth to light.

5 A merchant of no small account,
  In England dwelt of late,
Who did in riches far surmount
  Most men of his estate.

Yet sickness came, and he must die,
10   No help his life could save;
In anguish too his wife did lie,
      Death sent them to the grave.

No love between this pair was lost,
      For each was mild and kind;
15 Together they gave up the ghost,
      And left two babes behind.

The one a fine and pretty boy,
      Not passing six years old;
A girl the next, the mother's joy,
20   And cast in beauty's mould.

The father left his little son,
      As it was made appear,
When at the age of twenty-one,
      Three hundred pounds a year.

25 And to his daughter, we are told,
      Six hundred pounds to pay,
In value full of English gold,
      Upon her wedding day.

But if these children chanced to die,
30   As death might soon come on,
The uncle then (none can deny)
      Made all the wealth his own.

Pisarius call'd his brother near,
      As on his bed he lay:
35 Remember, oh! my brother dear,
      Remember what I say?

This life I quit, and to your care
      My little babes commend:
Their youth in hopeful virtue rear;
40   Their guardian, uncle, friend.

Their parents both you must supply,
      They do not know their loss,
And when you see the tear-swoln eye,
      For pity be not cross:

45 'Tis in your power (now alone)
    Their greatest friend to be;
    To give them, when we're dead & gone,
      Or bliss, or misery.

    If you direct their steps aright,
50   From God expect reward;
    All actions are within His sight,
      Of which He takes regard.

    With clay-cold lips the babes they kiss'd,
      And gave their last adieu!
55 A heart of stone would melt, I wist,
      So sad a scene to view.

    With tears, Androgus did reply—
      Dear brother, do not fear;
    Their ev'ry wish I will supply,
60   And be their uncle dear.

    God never prosper me nor mine,
      In whatsoe'er I have,
    If e'er I hurt them with design,
      When you are in the grave!

65 The parents being dead and gone,
      The children home he takes,
    And seems to soften all their moan,
      So much of them he makes:

    But had not kept the little souls
70   A twelvemonth and a day,
    But in his breast a scheme there rolls,
      To take their lives away.

He bargain'd with two ruffians strong,
    Who were of furious mood,
75 To take away these children young,
    And slay them in a wood.

Then gave it out both far and near,
    That he them both did send
To town for education there,
80   To one who was their friend.

Away the little babes were sent,
    Rejoicing with much pride;
It gave them both no small content,
    On horseback for to ride:

85 They prate and prattle pleasantly,
    As they ride on the way,
To those who should their butchers be,
    And work their lives decay.

The pretty speeches which they said,
90   Made one rogue's heart relent;
For though he undertook the deed,
    He sorely did repent.

The other still more hard of heart,
    Was not at all aggrieved,
95 And vow'd that he would do his part,
    For what he had received.

The other wont thereto agree,
    Which caused no little strife;
To fight they go right suddenly,
100   About the children's life.

And he that was in mildest mood,
    Did slay the other there,
Within an unfrequented wood,
    The babes did quake with fear.

105 He took the children by the hand,
    While tears were in their eyes;
And for a scheme which he had planned,
    He bid them make no noise:

Then two long miles he did them lead,
110   Of hunger they complain
Stay here, says he, I'll bring you bread,
    And soon be back again.

Then hand in hand they took their way,
    And wandered up and down;
115 But never more did they survey
    The man come from the town.

Their pretty lips with blackberries
    Were all besmeared and dy'd,
And when the shades of night arose,
120   They sat them down and cry'd.

These pretty babes thus wandered long,
    Without the least relief,
The woods, the briers, and thorns among,
    Till death did end their grief.

125 These pretty babes from any man,
    No funeral rite receives;
But Robin Redbreast forms the plan,
    To cover them with leaves.

And now the heavy wrath of God
130   Upon their uncle fell;
The furies haunt his curst abode,
    And peace bade him farewell.

His barns consum'd, his house was fired,
    His lands were barren made,
135 His cattle in the fields expired,
    And nothing with him staid.

His ships, which both were gone to sea
   Were on their voyage lost,
And fate did order him to be
140   With wants and sorrows crost.

His lands or sold or mortgag'd were,
   Ere seven years were past,
Attend, and you shall quickly hear
   How prosper'd guilt at last.

145 The fellow who did take in hand
   The children both to kill,
To die was judged by the land,
   For murder—by God's will.

The guilty secret in his breast
150   He could no more contain:
So all the truth he then confess'd,
   To ease him of his pain.

The uncle did in prison die,
   Unpitied was his fate:
155 Ye guardians, warning take hereby,
   And never prove ingrate.

To helpless infants still be kind,
   And give to each his right;
For, if you do not, soon you'll find
160   God will your deeds requite.

From *The Life and Death of Tom Thumb*

The adventures of a miniature man are part of international folklore. The earliest known text of the story in English (1621) is attributed to Richard Johnson (1573–1659?). The English versions of the tale, in both prose and verse, have such details as Tom's finding favour with the Fairy Queen and performing service in King Arthur's court.

This version is from a chapbook in the collection of the politician and uninhibited diarist, Samuel Pepys (1663–1703), which he called 'Penny Merriments'. An alert connoisseur of popular culture, Pepys himself rose from humble origins (a tailor's son) to become Clerk of the Privy Seal and Secretary of the Admiralty; however, with the Glorious Revolution of 1688 and the coronation of William III in 1689, Pepys's Stuart sympathies forced him into bookish retirement.

Of the Birth, Name, and bringing up of Tom Thumb, with the merry Pranks he played in his Child-hood.

In Arthurs Court Tom Thumb did live,
   a man of mickle might,
The best of all the Table round,
   and eke a doughty Knight!
5 In stature but an inch in height,
   or quarter of a span,
Then think you not this worthy Knight,
   was proved a valiant man.

His Father was a Plow-man plain,
10 his mother milkt the Cow,
And yet a way to get a Son,
   these couple knew not how;
Until such time the good old man
   to learned Merlin goes,
15 And there to him in deep distress,
   in secret manner show.

How in his heart he wisht to have
   a Child in time to come,
To be his heir, though it might be,
20 no bigger then his Thumb:
Of which Old Merlin was foretold,
   that he his wish should have,
And so his Son of Stature small,
   the Charmer to him gave.

25 No blood nor bones in him should be,
   in shape, and being such,
That he should hear him speak, but not
   his wandring shaddow touch,
But so unseen to go or come,
30 whereas it pleas'd him well,
Begot and born in half an hour,
   to fit his Fathers will.

And in four minutes grew so fast,
   that he became so tall,
35 As was the Plow-mans Thumb in length,
   and so she did him call:
Tom Thumb, the which the Fairy Queen,
   there gave him to his name,
Whom with her train of Goblins grim,
40 unto the Christening came.

Whereas she cloath'd him richly brave,
    in Garments richly fair,
The which did serve him many years
    in seemly sort to wear:
45 His hat made of an Oaken leaf,
    his Shirt a Spiders web,
Both light and soft for these his limbs,
    which was so smally bred.

His hose and Doublet thistle down,
50   together weav'd full fine,
His Stockins of an apple green,
    made of the outward Rhine: *   fine hemp
His Garters were two little hairs,
    pluckt from his Mothers eye,
55 His Shooes made of a Mouses skin,
    and tann'd most curiously.

Thus like a valiant gallant he,
    adventures forth to go,
With other Children in the streets,
60   his pretty tricks to show;
Where he for Counters, Pins and Points,*   ribbons
    and cherry-stones did play,
Till he amongst those Gamesters young,
    had lost his stock away.

65 Yet he could soon renew the same,
    when as most nimbly he,
Would dive into the cherry bags,
    and there partaker be:
Unseen or felt of any one,
70   until a Schollar shut,
This nimble youth into a box,
    wherein his Pins were put.

Of whom to be reveng'd, he took,
    in mirth and pleasant game,
75 Black pots and Glasses, which he hung
    upon a bright Sun beam,
The other Boys to do the same;
    in pieces broke them quite,
For which they were most soundly whipt,
80   whereat he laught out-right.

From *The Pleasant History of Thomas Hickathrift*

Tom Hickathrift is only one English example of the type of the invulnerable muscleman, another being the Lincolnshire folk hero William of Lindholme. Whether killing a giant, kicking a football, or out-witting highwaymen, Tom combines physical strength and strategic cunning. Like the *Tom Thumb*, the following is taken from a chapbook in Pepys's collection, *Penny Merriments*.

How Tom kept a pack of Hounds; and kickt a Foot-ball quite away; and how he had like to have been robbed by Four Thieves, and how he escaped.

Tom having so much about him and not used to it could hardly tell how for to dispose of it, but yet he did use a means to do it, for he kept a pack of hounds and men to hunt with him, and who but Tom then. So he took such delight in sport that he would go far and near to any meetings, as cudgel-play, bear-baiting, football play, and the like. But as Tom was riding one day, he seeing a company at football play, he lighted off his horse to see that rare sport, for they were playing for a wager; but Tom was a stranger there and none did know him there; but Tom soon spoiled their sport, for he meeting the football took it such a kick that they never found their ball no more; they could see it fly, but whither none could tell, nor to what place; they all wondered at it, and began to quarrel with Tom, but some of them got nothing by it, for Tom gets a spar which belonged to a house that was blown down and all that stood in his way he either killed or knocked down, so that all the country was up in arms to take Tom, but all in vain, for he manfully made way wherever he came. So when he was gone from them and was going homeward, he chanced to be somewhat late in the evening. On the road there met him four lusty rogues that had been robbing of passengers that way, and none could escape them, for they robbed all they met, both rich and poor. They thought when they met Tom they should get a good prize, they perceiving he was alone, made them cocksure of his money, but they were mistaken, for he got a prize by them. When they met with Tom they straight bid him stand and deliver. What, said Tom, what should I deliver? Your money, sir-rah, said they. But, said Tom, you shall give me better words for it first, and be better armed too. Come, come, said they, we do not hither to prate, but we come for money, and money we shall have before you stir from this place. I, said Tom, is it so? Nay then, said he, get it and take it.

So one of them made at him, but he presently unarmed him, and took away his sword which was made of good trusty steel, and smote so hard at the others that they began to set spurs to their horses and begone, but he soon stayed their journey, one of them having a portmantle behind him, Tom perceiving it to be money, fought with more courage than he did before, till at the last he had killed two of the four, and the other two he wounded most grievously that they cryed for a quarter. So with much intreating he gave them quarter, but he took all their money which was two hundred pounds to bear his charges home. So when Tom came home he told them how he had served the football players and the four thieves which caused a laugh from his old mother.

The Trial of an Ox, for Killing a Man (late eighteenth century)

The animal court is a common scene in many fables. In this profusely illustrated, frequently produced late eighteenth-century chapbook, the version of 'The Trial of an Ox' contrasts strikingly with the less lenient and more dishonest court depicted by La Fontaine in 'Les Animaux malades de la peste'(The Animals Sick of the Plague) [*Fables*, Book VII. 1].

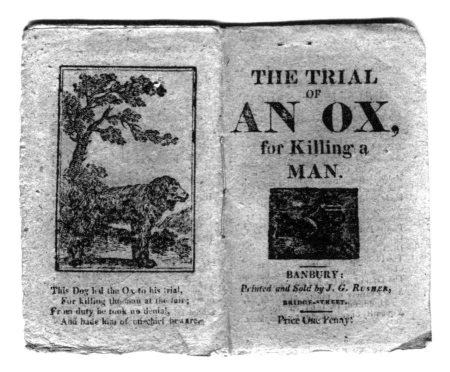

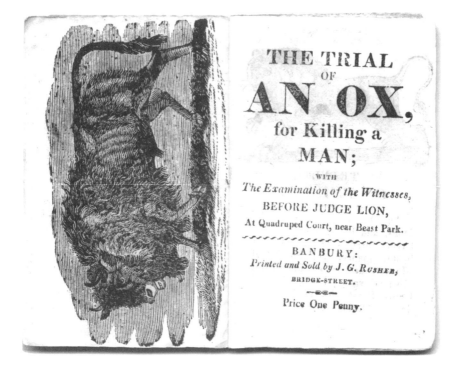

THE TRIAL

OF

AN OX,

for Killing a

MAN;

WITH

The Examination of the Witnesses,

BEFORE JUDGE LION,

At Quadruped Court, near Beast Park.

BANBURY:

Printed and Sold by J. G. RUSHER,

BRIDGE-STREET.

Price One Penny.

THE FOLLOWING PENNY BOOKS,

and many others,

Adorned with a great number of Cuts,

Are just Printed and Sold by

J. G. RUSHER, BANBURY.

History of a Banbury Cake
History of John Gilpin
Good Farmer, or History of T. Wiseman
Galloping Guide to the A B C
Adventures of Sir Richard Whittington
    and his Cat
Riddler's Riddle Book, by Peter Puzzlecap
The New House that Jack Built
Short Stories, or Treasures of Truth
Anecdotes for Good Children
Adventures of a Birmingham Halfpenny
Pretty Poems for young Folks
Dr. Watts's Divine Songs
Dr. Watts's Moral Songs
The Children in the Wood, in verse
Children in the Wood Restored, in prose
The Trial of an Ox for killing a Man

Also a variety of others, at ½, 1d, 2d,
    3d, 4d, 6d, 1s, 1s 6d, &c. for Sale.
A quantity of entertaining 6d Pamphlets.

Now each lad and each lass,
    Both sister and brother,
May have books for each class,
    For Father, or Mother.

And when, with much pleasure,
    You've read 'em all o'er,
Then hasten to RUSHER's,
    He's printing some more.

Where each daughter and son,
    And each nephew and niece;
Each good child may have one,
    For a penny a piece.

707065

TRIAL
OF THE OX.

An Ox was seized by the Dogs, and brought to trial, for having gored his Driver in such a brutal manner, in Smithfield Market, as caused his death. His trial was held at Quadruped Court, Beast Park, near the Pedestrian Hotel. The Lion sat as

Judge. The Dogs offered themselves as witnesses, which the Judge refused, as they were thieftakers, and interested. Here the council too began to arrangue, which the Judge would not admit of; he told them, indeed, if a point of law should arise, they might speak to it, but he would have no witness brow-beaten or misled in that court.

The Horse and Ass were then called up; who deposed, that they saw the Ox go to a Man and gore him, near Smithfield, and that his life was despaired of.

To this the Ox pleaded ignorance, and said, that he had been ill-used and deprived of his senses, and knew not what happened in consequence thereof; but, provided that were not the case, he certainly would have lost his life

by the murdering Butcher, who deals death and destruction to our race, to procure subsistence for himself and family, by the sale of our carcases. So now, my lord, I stand here, arraigned for the accidental offence of goring an inhuman drover, whose only business it was to dispose of me to the keeper of the slaughter house.

10   TRIAL OF AN OX,

A Bee, that had been perched on the Oxes head, offered his evidence,—and deposed, that he had been an eye witness of the whole affair.

"This poor Ox, my Lord," says he, "was taken from his friends and relations in the country, where he led a peaceful innocent life, and put under the care of a cruel and inhuman drover, who pricked him all the way to London, with a nail at the end of a pole; and when he was lame, and unable to walk so

FOR KILLING THE DROVER. 11

fast as the savage driver designed, he beat him about the legs, with a stick, with a great knob at the end of it, which still made him more lame. When he came to Smithfield, he stood, with his head tied on the rails, from 4 o'clock on Monday morning, till 8 on Monday night, which was sixteen hours, when the anguish he was in affected his head so much, that he lost his senses, and

12   TRIAL OF THE OX,

committed the act for which he stands indicted. Who is to blame, my Lord? It is true, the Man lost his life, but the innocent Ox is not to suffer for it: because from ill treatment the Ox had lost his senses, and therefore could not be accountable for his actions. Those are too blame, my Lord, who encourage drivers in such acts of inhumanity; and suffer a market for wild and mad beasts, to be held in the middle of a large and opulent city; do you

FOR KILLING A MAN. 13

think the queen of my hive would suffer us to bring home what we make boot upon? No, in order to prevent mischief and confusion, we prepare our meat before we are let into the city, and so would these people, had they half the sense they pretend to have!"

Then the Judge interrogated several other witnesses, who corroborated the fact of the former, and the Bear, as counsel, cross-

14   TRIAL OF THE OX,

FOR KILLING A MAN.   15

examined them, in a mild and friendly manner, so as not to confuse their evidence.

Then the Tiger arose, and having commanded silence, spoke as follows:

"*Gentlemen of the Jury,*

You hear what a distinct and clear evidence the Bee has given, in behalf of the prisoner, and you seem sensible of the truth of it. 'Tis amazing that mankind should complain of cruelty in animals, when their own minds are productive of such scenes of inhumanity: Are not the Ox and other creatures murdered for their emolument? Are not we hunted to death for their amusement, as well as the Stag and the Hare? Are not the Bees burnt, and their houses plundered for their use?

16   TRIAL OF THE OX,

FOR KILLING A MAN.   17

What have you Mr. Horse, for carrying the boobies on your back, but stripes and ill treatment? And what have you, Mr. Ass, who are their nurse and doctor, but lashes and ill language? Man, the two legged Tiger man, is the most ungrateful of beasts."

Then the Judge recapitulated the evidence, which appeared too clear to admit of a doubt, that the poor Ox was pricked and beaten in a most inhuman manner, by the drover, and that being driven to desparation by the cruel treatment, he turned suddenly round, and gored the heard-hearted Drover. Upon which, the Jury returned a *Verdict of Manslaughter,* and the Judge *Fined him a Blade of Grass,* ordered him to be *Imprisoned an Hour,* and then *Discharged him,* amid general acclamations.

18   TRIAL OF THE OX.

Upon which, the Cock clapped
his wings, and crowed applause
to the verdict ; and the spectators
departed, perfectly satisfied with
the sentence.

THE END.

From *The Riddle Book; or, Fireside Amusements,* printed by and for
Thomas Richardson, Derby (late eighteenth century).

> My face is smooth and wondrous bright,
> Which mostly I keep out of sight
> Within my house; how that is made
> Shall with much brevity be said:
> 5 Compos'd with timber and with skin,
> Cover' d with blankets warm within:
> Here I lie snug, unless in anger,
> I look out sharp suspecting danger;
> For I'm a blade of mighty wrath,
> 10 Whene'er provok'd I sally forth;
> Yet quarrels frequently decide,
> But n'er am known to change my side,
> Tho e'er so much our party vary,
> In all disputes my point I carry.
> 15 Thousands by me are daily fed,
> As many laid among the dead.

I travel into foreign parts;
But not in coach convey'd, or carts.
Ladies, for you I often war,
20 Then in return my name declare.

7. A SWORD.

With words unnumber'd I abound,
In me mankind take much delight,
In me great store of learning's found,
Yet I can neither read nor write.

10. A BOOK.

In places where mirth and good-humour abound,
Who so welcome as I, or so commonly found?
If I get among gamblers, I never am winner;
Eat nothing, yet who can afford better dinner.
5 At church of my privilege n'er bate an ace;
Not e'en to churchwarden or parson give place.
In verse or in prose, there are few who indite,
But to me they apply e'er they venture to write.
In council I'm present, nor absent at sea,
10 Nymphs who're courted by all, come and pay court to me.
Then seek out my title, each spirit lover,
Who dares such a favourite rival discover:
If I move not on four, as I usually do,
You may find me on one leg, but never on two.

13. A TABLE.

Ever eating, never cloying,
All devouring, all destroying,
Never finding full repast
'Till I eat the world at last

14. TIME.

Conundrums

Q. Why is a good tragedy like a good onion?
A. Because it will make you cry.
Q. Why is a barber like a pepper-box?
A. Because he often takes people by the nose.
Q. Why is a bad woman like a good epigram?
A. Because she carries a sting in her tail.
Q. Why is a large wig like a fierce engagement?
A. Because it consumes much powder.
Q. Why are submissive husbands like barleycorns given to poultry?
A. Because they are hen-pecked.
Q. Why is a diverting novel like a canister of tea?
A. Because the leaves afford pleasure to the ladies.
Q. Why is ink like scandal?
A. Because it blackens the fairest things.

Delectando monemus
Instruction with Delight

5. BOREMAN, COOPER, AND NEWBERY: 'INSTRUCTION WITH DELIGHT'

Too rigid precepts often fail,
Where short amusing tales prevail.
That author, doubtless, aims aright,
Who joins instruction with delight.

—*Thomas Boreman,*
Curiosities in the Tower of London (1741)

The 1740s was a transformative decade of firsts for the history of children's literature. It signalled the first mention of 'delight' as an aim, the appearance of the first printed books expressly catering for juvenile readers, and the first genuinely popular publications, sized to be held by a child. These developments focused on childhood and combined an insightful awareness of children's appetites and the attitudes of middle class purchasers. The innovators were Thomas Boreman, Mrs Mary Cooper, and John Newbery. Although Boreman and Cooper virtually fade from view with the arrival of Newbery, their innovations—

products of ideal timing, business acumen, and market forces—need to be examined together.

Boreman (*fl.* 1730–43) was the first publisher to cater primarily for juvenile readers, thereby antedating the work of Newbery in London and Isaiah Thomas in Boston and Worcester, Massachusetts. Information about Boreman resides only in his publications; he maintained bookstalls at several different London locations: the corner of St Clement's Lane without Temple-Bar, Ludgate Hill, near Child's coffeehouse in St Paul's Churchyard, and near the Guildhall. Co-published with Richard

Ware and Thomas Game in 1730, Boreman's *A Description of Three Hundred Animals* was, as Arthur Lisney observes, the first work on natural history written for children. His address to the reader makes clear his intention to 'entertain' rather than 'cloy' young readers, 'with short descriptions of animals, and pictures fairly drawn (which last Experience shews them to be much delighted with) to engage their attention.' Adapted from Topsell's *Histories*, the text proved so popular that Boreman alone produced two supplements: *A Description of a Great Variety of Animals* (1736) and *A Description of Some Curious and Uncommon Creatures* (1739). *A Description of Three Hundred Animals*, which had gone through thirty-eight editions by the end of the nineteenth century, influenced Buffon's thirty-six-volume *Histoire naturelle* (1749–88) and the engravings of Thomas Bewick. In addition to the precise detail of the illustrations, Boreman's *Description* contained such exotic features as a triple-page fold-out depiction of the Greenland Whale fishery, along with some spirited disagreement that Jonah could possibly have been swallowed by a whale, 'whose throat can hardly take in the arm of a man.'

The ten miniature volumes comprising his *Gigantick Histories of the Curiosities of London* (1740–3), with formats measuring 2.5 by 1.8 inches, define Boreman?s innovations in the embryonic field of publishing for children. Each tiny illustrated volume of more than 100 pages of verse and prose, bound in Dutch flowery embossed paper, published a list of juvenile subscribers. In the miniature format previously associated only with biblical material, as in John Weever's *Agnus Dei* (1601) and John Taylor's *Verbum Sempiternum* (1614), Boreman engaged an eager urban readership and solicited their involvement in the continued success of the series. The initial two volumes, *The Curiosities in the Tower*

of London, include the Guildhall giants Gogmagog and Corineus as subscribers along with such prominent London youth as the son of the Lord Mayor, Thomas Abney (also Isaac Watts's patron), and children from Portugal, East India, and America, among them the grandson of Cotton Mather and the nieces and nephews of the Governor of Massachusetts Bay, Thomas Hutchinson.

Narrating the curious histories of the Guildhall giants, the Tower of London, St Paul's Cathedral, Westminster Abbey, and the contemporary Swedish giant Cajanus, Boreman was adept at puffery and promotion. Not only did he refer to himself as Master Tommy, he also ghost-wrote the praise of the 'well-wisher A.Z.', prefacing *Curiosities in the Tower of London*, disparaging the 'artless lyes' of Tom Thumb and Jack the Giant Killer in favour of Boreman's *Gigantick* works that offer 'something to please and form the mind.' He also informed by inculcating obedience to authority. In *The Gigantick History of the Two Famous Giants* the 'crimes which 'prentice boys commit' lead to their confinement in 'that terrible place call'd Little Ease', a prison in the basement of the Guildhall, 'among rats, mice, and other vermin'. Boreman's warning is blunt and monosyllabic: 'so take great heed that you keep out.' After the opening of Newbery's bookshop in 1744, no record of him exists.

A printer's widow, Mrs Cooper produced the first collections of nursery rhymes in *Tommy Thumb's Song-Book* and *Tommy Thumb's Pretty Song-Book* (1744), which, as noted in the previous chapter, contained the first published version of 'Cock Robin'. She was the first user of the extremely popular pseudonym Nurse Lovechild. Cooper's understanding of the market was every bit as informed as Boreman's and Newbery's. Her *The Child's New Play-Thing: Being a Spelling Book Intended to Make the Learning to Read, a*

Diversion instead of a Task (1745), housed now in the Opie Collection in the Bodleian Library, was shrewd enough to include 'Moral Precepts proper for Children and Religious Precepts proper for Children' along with the stories of Guy of Warwick and Fortunatus. Cooper also responded to the growing popularity of games for children by announcing 'a new-invented Alphabet for Children to play with' consisting of a fold-out endpiece from which imprinted squares could be cut and, as suggested, 'put in a hat-box and drawn out at random'. On one side of the piece of paper was a proper noun, usually the name of a biblical figure like 'Abraham' and 'Balaam', while the verso had a common noun from the world of everyday activities and objects like 'apple' and 'bread'.

Enter the entrepreneur, John Newbery, a London businessman with the ability to synthesize these forces. Knowledgeable as well as solvent, Newbery had the happy fortune to be in the publishing business at the right time. On 18 June 1744 this seemingly inauspicious advertisement appeared in the *London Penny Advertiser*:

A LITTLE PRETTY POCKET-BOOK, intended for the Instruction and Amusement of little Master Tommy and pretty Miss Polly; with an agreeable Letter to each from Jack the Giant-Killer; as also a Ball and Pincushion, the Use of which will infallibly make Tommy a good Boy and Polly a good Girl.

The book stands today as a landmark in children's literature. Its explicit pronouncement regarding the 'amusement' of Master Tommy and Miss Polly, and its success in fulfilling that aim, have made it the embodiment of the enlightened eighteenth-century view of literature for the young.

A Little Pretty Pocket-Book boldly asserted the motto 'Delectando Monemus: Instruction with Delight'. Newbery, of course, was not blind to the opposition such a book might encounter, and he introduced it with calculated caution. First he lectured parents, guardians, and nurses on the ways to make a child 'strong, hardy, healthy, virtuous, wise and happy' in the acquisition of a 'method of reasoning'—echoing Locke's educational theories. Then, casting aside this role as parental advisor, he became a salesman in the guise of a sanitized Jack the Giant-Killer, addressing Master Tommy and Miss Polly about the toys that could be purchased to accompany his book: a ball for the boy and a pincushion for the girl, both red-and-black, in both of which pins could be stuck to record good and bad behaviour. The book cost sixpence, and each toy tuppence.

The Pocket-Book is an illustrated catalogue of children's amusements based on the alphabet. Newbery (or a hack writer employed by him) begins instructively, attaching a 'moral' or a 'rule of life' to the homely rhymes; but he soon indulges in some fun:

Here's great K, and L,
Pray Dame can you tell,
Who put the Pig-Hog
Down into the Well?

and introduces a few fables, an illustrated 'catalogue' of the actions of good children, a 'Poetical Description of the Four Seasons', and 'Select Proverbs for the Use of Children'. Even when the verses are pre-eminently didactic, they are all composed with a light touch. Furthermore, *The Little Pretty Pocket-Book*, which was published in a facsimile edition in 1966, *is* pretty, with original woodcuts and a handsomely designed small-page layout. It was intended for middle class children who said their prayers, sought their parents' blessing, learned their lessons, and bestowed charity—and whose parents could afford to buy it.

Newbery's next major venture, *The Lilliputian Magazine* (1751–52), was, as Janis Dawson explains, a very ambitious attempt to capitalize on Boreman's juvenile subscription idea and the popularity of Swift's *Gulliver's Travels* (1726). Although Newbery appealed to the child as consumer and featured narratives that promoted praise (rather than terror or denigration) as a way of learning, this periodical experiment was not as successful as he had anticipated—possibly because he had stressed the notion of child ownership and underplayed the role of parents.

The composition of his audience had changed little in 1755 when Newbery offered them *Nurse Truelove's New Year's Gift; or, The Book of Books for Children*. This time he had sharpened his skills as an advertiser, perfecting the formula which Andrew O'Malley identifies as 'combining plebeian chapbook characters and narrative elements with the middle class values that furthered his own success.' This gift book cost only tuppence ('for the Binding') and was 'designed for a present to every little Boy who would become a great Man, and ride upon a fine horse, and to every little Girl who would become a fine Woman, and ride in a Governour's gilt coach'. Accordingly, the first story recounted the successes of Miss Polly Friendly in childhood and young womanhood. The ease with which the innocent cook-maid is accused of breaking the china and the gift that promptly rewards Polly's delayed confession underscore the focus on the middle class and their ideology; the working poor, if not invisible, are mute. In marrying Mr Alderman Foresight, 'who was always of the opinion that virtue and industry was the best portion with a wife', Polly illustrates that virtue is more than its own reward; in most of Newbery's stories, it usually netted some recognizable, value-laden social gain as well. Copiously illustrated, the *New Year's Gift* marked the first

appearance of the cumulative rhyme, 'The House that Jack Built'.

The book most often associated with Newbery's name is *The History of Little Goody Two-Shoes* (1765). As with most of Newbery's children's books, its authorship remains uncertain; the publisher himself may have had a hand in it, but unsubstantiated attributions to Oliver Goldsmith and Giles Jones are still current. Ornamented with thirteen woodcuts, which the title page attributed to 'Michael Angelo', it charts the rise to renown and fortune of the ever-virtuous Margery Meanwell, more popularly known as Goody Two-Shoes. Proper names label the story's personified abstractions of evil and good. Little Margery, possessing only one shoe, and her fully shod brother Tommy were orphaned at an early age. Their father had succumbed to a 'violent Fever' because, alas, the Meanwells lived in an area 'where Dr James's Powder was not to be had' (a puff for Dr Robert James's product sold by Newbery, which helped to make much of his fortune). Satire directed against idle landed gentry, avaricious farmers, and the movement to consolidate and enclose farms was scarcely concealed. The landowner was Sir Timothy Gripe; the 'overgrown farmer', Mr Graspall. Although Newbery dedicated the book 'to all young Gentlemen and Ladies, who are good, or intend to be good,' he hoped his burlesque of adult foibles would appeal to 'Children of six Feet high, of which . . . there are many millions in the Kingdom,' and he addressed his introduction to them.

The pace of this lengthy (140 pp.) story is mercifully rapid. Little in the way of obstacles is allowed to interfere with Margery's sure and steady rise, with the result that there is a minimum of conflict and suspense. When Margery's first benefactors, the Smiths, under threat of seizure by the nefarious Sir Timothy, send her away, the girl does not mope but promptly teaches herself to read, and because of her great natural abilities helps others to learn too. Just as her goodness prompts the Smiths to order a pair of shoes for Margery, her aptitude as an instructor ensures her success as a travelling tutor. She acquires a reputation among old and young as both 'a cunning little Baggage' and 'a sensible Hussey'. She allays fears of ghosts and, true to the beliefs of her publisher, censoriously deflates the importance of fairies, 'for the Tales of Ghosts, Witches, and Fairies, are the Frolicks of a distempered Brain'. In Part Two she presides over ABC College, teaches a devoted menagerie many strange tricks, escapes charges of witchcraft, is reunited with her brother, marries Sir Charles Jones, and survives as his widow, the esteemed 'benefactress' of the Manor of Mouldwell. While Sir Timothy and Graspall are suitably mortified, the now-wealthy Lady Margery becomes the patron of the poor, making provision for the annual planting of potatoes 'for all the Poor of any Parish who would come and fetch them for the Use of their Families.'

Goody Two-Shoes is often too good to be believed, and the story's picture of an idealized rural life is an utter illusion. Nevertheless her adventure-filled (but always didactic) story was one of the most successful Newbery publications. Though prolix and repetitive, it is one of the first full-length English stories written expressly for the amusement of children.

Newbery is a pivotal figure in this anthology for several reasons. With a businessman's sense of capitalizing on the successes of competitors like Boreman and Cooper, he published and marketed dozens of titles, doing more than any other single publisher of his day to encourage the production of books for children. Thanks to his example, the presses of John Marshall, John Harris, and Benjamin Tabart—all catering to juvenile readers— came into existence, thereby increasing the production of children's books a hundredfold. In the century that followed the establishment of his shop at the Bible and Crown, many writers of widely differing philosophies and talents began to focus on the market Newbery had uncovered. His name and importance have been commemorated by the American Library Association, whose Newbery Medal is awarded annually to the outstanding juvenile book published in the United States.

Joining the accelerated publishing activity that Newbery started were at least three distinct groups of writers: the Rational Moralists, influenced by Locke and Rousseau; the Sunday School and Evangelical writers; and a number of poets and storytellers whose daring and individuality ushered in the Golden age of children's literature. The following chapters will examine their contributions more closely.

THOMAS BOREMAN (*fl.* 1730–1743)

From *The Gigantick History of the two famous Giants and Other Curiosities in Guildhall, London* (1741)

Boreman succeeds in animating the two carved wooden statues in the Guildhall, providing details of their dimensions and diet. He humanizes and tames Gogmagog and Corineus, to the extent that the young reader learns about the routine for cleaning, dressing, and shaving them (since they 'eat as much hair as victuals'), their vigilance, and their bashfulness. Boreman tips in biblical references as well, indicating the origin of Gogmagog as one of the sons of Noah (Genesis 10. 2), also invoked in a scene of apocalyptic vengeance (Revelation 20. 8), and Corineus, as a descendant of the 'grandson of Japhet, to whom the Germans owe their origin' (53). The grandfathers of Gogmagog and Corineus, 'giants made only of wickerwork and pasteboard', were eaten by rats and mice.

Chapter 1. A description of giant Gogmagog

As soon as you enter the great door of Guildhall, look up, right before you, there you will see those huge giants, one standing on each side of the balcony, about twenty six feet from the floor of the hall, their heads reaching near forty feet.

The old giant we shall call Gogmagog, the young one Corineus, for reasons which we shall tell by and by.

Gogmagog is in height fourteen feet, round his body twelve feet, the length of his arm seven, and of his leg and thigh five feet: the calf of his leg is forty two inches in compass, and his wrist twenty four inches: his middle finger is sixteen inches long, and his great toe twelve.

His nose is twelve inches long; his eyes of the size of tea sawcers, and his mouth, when he opens it, big enough to take in a half-peck loaf; and so in proportion for the rest of his parts.

In his right hand he holds a staff seventeen feet long, with a grabling ball at the end of it; being such an instrument of war as is used by the pioneers, when they march at the head of the artillery company, &c. to drive the enemy out of their trenches &c.

At his left side he has a sword six feet six inches long, and at his back a bow and quiver of arrows.

His habit is like the ancient Britons, who went with their bodies great part naked; only painted with diverse figures to seem terrible, as they thought, and thereby make themselves more formidable to the people against whom they design'd to make war. His hair is long, like that of the Druids (a sort of priests) of old; that of his beard has a snakie hue, appearing like a number of that vermin interwoven with each other.

He was a giant strong and valiant in his time, therefore his head is crown'd with laurel; and he was of a fierce temper, but at the same time cunning and full of subtilty.

Chap. II. A description of giant Corineus

This giant appears much younger than Gogmagog, but of the same stature, only in the compass of his body and limbs much lesser, being every way made more proportionable.

His dress is like that of an ancient Roman warrior, and his body fenced with exceeding strong armour, as are likewise his legs, arms, and wrists.

In his right hand he holds a halbert of a gigantick size, instead of the battle-ax, with which Corineus was wont to fight, and to do great execution; and in his left hand the black spread eagle painted on a shield, being the arms of the German empire; which denotes him of that extraction.

The hair of this giant's head and beard is black and short; upon his head he has a strong helmet, or cap, like that of an ancient Roman soldier, and upon his cap a crown of laurel.

He was a hail, robust, strong, bold warrior; of a lively spirit; but, by reason of his great strength, fierce, proud and haughty.

Chap. V. A vindication of the giants reputation and good behaviour

The two ancient giants, the grand fathers of the present, having been reclaimed from their savage and brutal way of living, became so far civilized, that they were deservedly promoted to those high places in Guildhall, which they continued in for many years, time out of mind, even to the day of their deaths.

And when those two worthy old giants had ended their days, these their two grandsons, being the only surviving heirs that were left of the whole giant race, laid claim to their grandfathers inheritance, which the city soon put them in possession of and which they have remain'd in for upwards of thirty years, during which time they have enjoyed an uninterrupted tranquility, behaving peaceably to all mankind; nor do they ever quit their stations, but are always constant and watchful in that great trust committed to their care.

Indeed, 'tis said, that when the giants hear the clock at noon strike twelve, they strait step down from off the shelve they stand upon, to eat their dinners, and when they hear the clock at one, they step from whence they come. Tho' this may seem very strange, yet 'tis well known that several gaping fellows have come to Guildhall on purpose to see 'em walk down to dinner; but were always disappointed, for either they happen'd to come on a fast-day, or the giants growing older, are more shy of company, and will sooner go without their meat, than be star'd and yawn'd at while they are eating it.

JOHN NEWBERY From *A Little Pretty Pocket-Book* (1744)

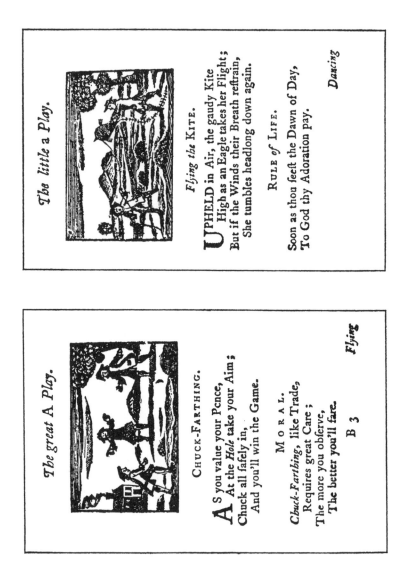

The little a Play.

Flying the KITE.

UPHELD in Air, the gaudy Kite
High as an Eagle takes her Flight;
But if the Winds their Breath refrain,
She tumbles headlong down again.

RULE *of* LIFE.

Soon as thou feeſt the Dawn of Day,
To God thy Adoration pay.

Dancing

The great A Play.

CHUCK-FARTHING.

AS you value your Pence,
At the *Hole* take your Aim;
Chuck all ſafely in,
And you'll win the Game.

M O R A L.

Chuck-Farthing, like Trade,
Requires great Care;
The more you obſerve,
The better you'll fare.

B 3

Flying

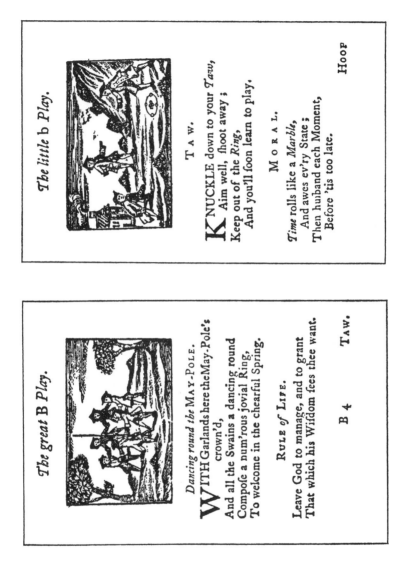

The little b Play.

T A W.

KNUCKLE down to your *Taw*,
   Aim well, fhoot away;
Keep out of the *Ring*,
   And you'll foon learn to play.

M O R A L.

Time rolls like a *Marble*,
   And awes ev'ry State;
Then hufband each Moment,
   Before 'tis too late.

HOOP

The great B Play.

Dancing round the MAY-POLE.

WITH Garlands here theMay-Pole's
    crown'd,
And all the Swains a dancing round
Compofe a num'rous jovial Ring,
To welcome in the chearful Spring.

RULE *of* LIFE.

Leave God to manage, and to grant
That which his Wifdom fees thee want.

B 4   TAW.

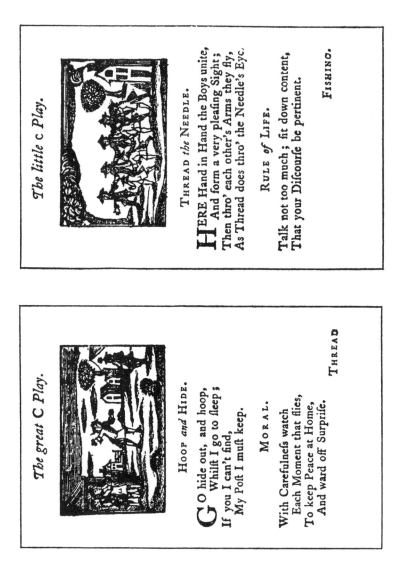

The little c Play.

THREAD *the* NEEDLE.

HERE Hand in Hand the Boys unite,
 And form a very pleaſing Sight;
Then thro' each other's Arms they fly,
As Thread does thro' the Needle's Eye.

RULE *of* LIFE.

Talk not too much; ſit down content,
That your Diſcourſe be pertinent.

FISHING.

The great C Play.

HOOP *and* HIDE.

GO hide out, and hoop,
 Whilſt I go to ſleep;
If you I can't find,
My Poſt I muſt keep.

MORAL.

With Carefulneſs watch
 Each Moment that flies,
To keep Peace at Home,
And ward off Surpriſe.

THREAD

The great D Play.

FISHING.

THE artful Angler baits his Hook,
  and throws it gently in the Brook;
Which the Fish view with greedy Eyes,
And soon are taken by Surprise.

RULE *of* LIFE.

Learn well the Motions of the Mind;
Why you are made, for what design'd.

BLIND-

The little d Play.

BLINDMAN's BUFF.

BEREFT of all Light,
  I stumble alone;
But, if I catch you,
  My Doom is your own.

MORAL.

How blind is that Man,
  Who scorns the Advice
Of Friends, who intend
  To make him more wise!

SHUTTLE-

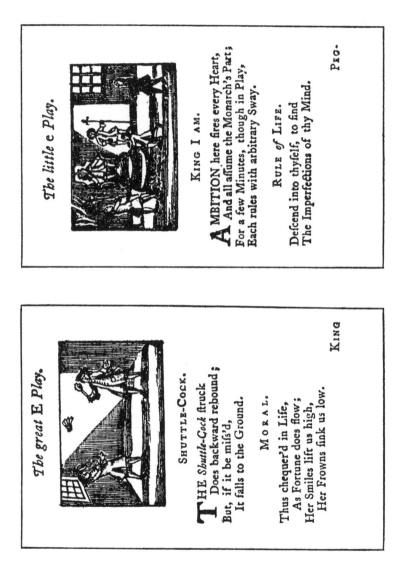

The little e Play.

KING I AM.

AMBITION here fires every Heart,
And all affume the Monarch's Part;
For a few Minutes, though in Play,
Each rules with arbitrary Sway.

RULE *of* LIFE.

Defcend into thyfelf, to find
The Imperfections of thy Mind.

Pro-

The great E Play.

SHUTTLE-COCK.

THE *Shuttle-Cock* ftruck
Does backward rebound;
But, if it be mifs'd,
It falls to the Ground.

MORAL.

Thus chequer'd in Life,
As Fortune does flow;
Her Smiles lift us high,
Her Frowns fink us low.

KING

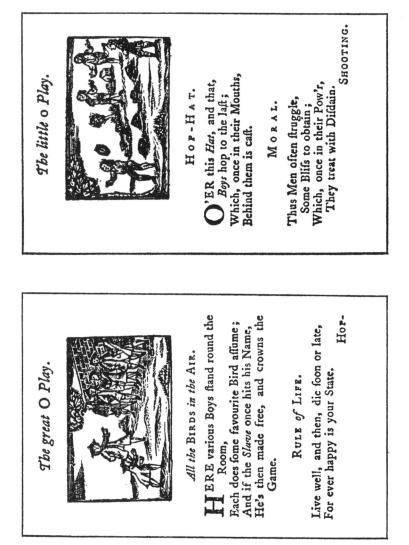

The great O Play.

All the BIRDS *in the* AIR.

H ERE various Boys ſtand round the Room,
Each does ſome favourite Bird aſſume;
And if the *Slave* once hits his Name,
He's then made free, and crowns the Game.

RULE *of* LIFE.

Live well, and then, die ſoon or late,
For ever happy is your State.　　Hor-

The little o Play.

HOP-HAT.

O'ER this *Hat,* and that,
Boys hop to the laſt;
Which, once in their Mouths,
Behind them is caſt.

MORAL.

Thus Men often ſtruggle,
Some Bliſs to obtain;
Which, once in their Pow'r,
They treat with Diſdain.

SHOOTING.

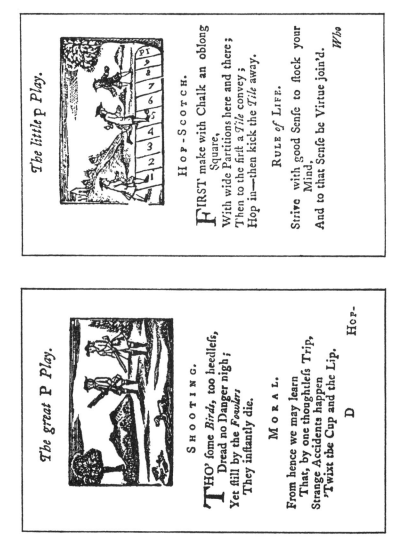

The great P Play.

SHOOTING.

THO' some *Birds*, too heedless,
    Dread no Danger nigh;
Yet still by the *Fowlers*
    They instantly die.

MORAL.

From hence we may learn
    That, by one thoughtless Trip,
Strange Accidents happen
    'Twixt the Cup and the Lip.

D   Hop-

The little p Play.

HOP-SCOTCH.

FIRST make with Chalk an oblong
    Square,
With wide Partitions here and there;
Then to the first a *Tile* convey;
Hop in—then kick the *Tile* away.

RULE of LIFE.

Strive with good Sense to stock your
    Mind,
And to that Sense be Virtue join'd.

Who

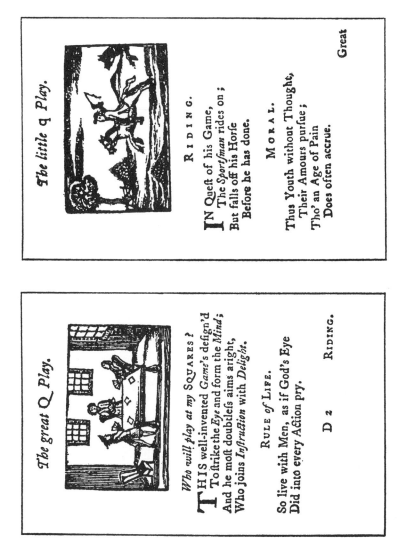

The little q Play.

RIDING.

IN Quest of his Game,
  The *Sportman* rides on ;
But falls off his Horse
  Before he has done.

MORAL.

Thus Youth without Thought,
  Their Amours pursue ;
Tho' an Age of Pain
  Does often accrue.

Great

The great Q Play.

Who will play at my SQUARES ?

THIS well-invented *Game's* defign'd
  To ftrike the *Eye* and form the *Mind* ;
And he moft doubtlefs aims aright,
  Who joins *Inftruction* with *Delight.*

RULE *of* LIFE.

So live with Men, as if God's Eye
Did into every Action pry.

D 2   RIDING.

From *Nurse Truelove's New-Year's Gift: or, The Book of Books for Children.*

Designed for a Present to every little Boy who would become a great Man, and ride upon a fine Horse; and to every little Girl who would become a great Woman, and ride in a Governour's gilt Coach. (1755)

The History of Miss Polly Friendly

You may remember, my dear, to have read at the end of my Christmas Box, the history of Master *Friendly*; and this is the history of Miss *Polly*, his Sister, who you must know was altogether as good as her brother; for indeed she imitated him in everything. She was dutiful to her Papa and Mamma, loving to her brothers and sisters, kind to her play-mates, and very complaisant and obliging to everybody. Then she never miss'd saying her prayers morning and evening, as some naughty girls do.—No, no! She always remembered her Creator in the days of her Youth; and asked a blessing of her Papa and Mamma every morning and night. Then she was so fond of going to church and to school; so ready and willing to do as she was bid, and so ready at her work, that I think she was the best little girl I ever knew; and everybody lov'd her. Then she never told a lie in her life. No, no! She knew that was a naughty pau-pau trick. Why I remember once she by accident, poor girl, broke a whole set of the finest China I ever saw; and for fear her Mamma should be angry, truly she hid the pieces in the coal-hole. All the servants were called to account for it, and they all affirmed they were innocent; so the fault laid upon No-body; for there is an old imaginary fellow of that name in every family, who generally does a great deal of mischief. However, to make short of my story, the broken pieces were found two days afterwards in the coal-hole in the kitchen; and that being the province of Dolly the cook-maid, the poor girl was again taxed with the crime, and threaten'd to be turned away, when in comes Miss Polly with tears in her eyes, and falling on her knees to her Mamma, begged she would not be angry with Dolly the cook, or any body else; for 'twas she that broke the China, and hid it there, to avoid her displeasure. Her Mamma was so pleased with her open and generous confession, that she took her up in her arms, and kissed her a thousand times. 'Now, my dear, says she, I love you better than ever I did, because you would not tell me a lie nor suffer your own faults to be laid upon another; and as a reward for your honesty and love of truth, here, d'ye see I will give you this fine watch.' Little Polly took the watch indeed, and thanked her Mamma, with a curtsey down to the ground, but would not wear it: 'For, says she, as none of the other children at school have watches, Mamma, they may think I am proud; and you know, Mamma, you always told me it was a very naughty thing to be proud.'

As she grew up she made it her business to visit the poor, and to make every body happy in the neighbourhood; by which means she obtained such a good character, and was so esteemed, that a great many gentlemen made their addresses to her, though her fortune was but small; and among the rest of her admirers came Mr Alderman Foresight, who was always of opinion, that virtue and industry was the best portion with a wife. He therefore married Miss Polly, who made him a dutiful, obedient and loving wife; and he in return proved to her a kind, indulgent and affectionate husband. Soon after the wedding Mr Alderman was chosen Lord-Mayor; and now she is the great Lady-Mayoress, and rides in the grand gilt coach which you have seen drawn by fine prancing horses.

The House That Jack Built

This is the house that Jack built.

This is the malt
That lay in the house that Jack built.

This is the rat,
That ate the malt
That lay in the house that Jack built.

This is the cat,
That killed the rat,
That ate the malt
That lay in the house that Jack built.

This is the dog,
That worried the cat,
That killed the rat,
That ate the malt
That lay in the house that Jack built.

This is the cow with the crumpled horn,
That tossed the dog,
That worried the cat,
That killed the rat,
That ate the malt
That lay in the house that Jack built.

This is the maiden all forlorn,
That milked the cow with the crumpled horn,
That tossed the dog,
That worried the cat,
That killed the rat,
That ate the malt
That lay in the house that Jack built.

This is the man all tattered and torn,
That kissed the maiden all forlorn,
That milked the cow with the crumpled horn,
That tossed the dog,
That worried the cat,
That killed the rat,
That ate the malt
That lay in the house that Jack built.

This is the priest all shaven and shorn,
That married the man all tattered and torn,
That kissed the maiden all forlorn,
That milked the cow with the crumpled horn,
That tossed the dog,
That worried the cat,
That killed the rat,
That ate the malt
That lay in the house that Jack built.

This is the cock that crowed in the morn,
That waked the priest all shaven and shorn,
That married the man all tattered and torn,
That kissed the maiden all forlorn,
That milked the cow with the crumpled horn,
That tossed the dog,
That worried the cat,
That killed the rat,
That ate the malt
That lay in the house that Jack built.*

---

* Iona and Peter Opie note that 'The House that Jack Built' may have originated in the Hebrew chant, 'Had Gaddyo', from an early Prague edition of the *Haggadah*.

From Part I of *The History of Little Goody Two-Shoes; Otherwise called Mrs Margery Two-Shoes* (1765)

Chapter IV

How Little Margery learned to read, and by Degrees taught others.

Little *Margery* saw how good, and how wise Mr Smith was, and concluded, that this was owing to his great Learning, therefore she wanted of all Things to learn to read. For this Purpose she used to meet the little Boys and Girls as they came from School, borrow their Books, and sit down and read till they returned; By this Means she soon got more Learning than any of her Playmates, and laid the following Scheme for instructing those who were more ignorant than herself. She found, that only the following Letters were required to spell all the Words in the World; but as some of these Letters are large and some small, she with her Knife cut out of several Pieces of Wood ten Setts of each of these:

a b c d e f g h i j k l m n o p q r s
t u v w x y z.

And six Setts of these:

A B C D E F G H I J K L M N O P Q R S T
U V W X Y Z.

And having got an old Spelling-Book, she made her Companions set up all the Words they wanted to spell, and after that she taught them to compose Sentences. You know what a Sentence is, my Dear, *I will be good*, is a Sentence; and is made up, as you see, of several Words.

The usual Manner of Spelling, or carrying on the Game, as they called it, was this: Suppose the Word to be spelt was Plumb Pudding (and who can suppose a better) the Children were placed in a Circle, and the first brought the Letter *P*, the next *l*, the next *u*, the next *m*, and so on till the Whole was spelt; and if any one brought a wrong Letter, he was to pay a Fine, or play no more. This was at their Play; and every Morning she used to go round to teach the Children with these Rattle-traps in a Basket, as you see in the Print. I once went her Rounds with her, and was highly diverted, as you may be, if you please to look into the next Chapter.

Chapter V

How Little Two-Shoes became a trotting Tutoress, and how she taught her young pupils.

It was about seven o'Clock in the Morning when we set out on this important Business, and the first House we came to was Farmer Wilson's. See here it is. Here Margery stopped, and ran up to the Door, *Tap, tap, tap*. Who's there? Only little goody Two-Shoes, answered Margery, come to teach Billy. Oh Little Goody, says Mrs. Wilson, with Pleasure in her Face, I am glad to see you, Billy wants you sadly, for he has learned all his Lesson. Then out came the little Boy. *How do doody Two-Shoes*, says he, not able to speak plain. Yet this little Boy had learned all his Letters; for she threw down this Alphabet mixed together thus:

b d f h k m o q s u w y z
a c e g i l n p r t v x j

and he picked them up, called them by their right Names, and put them all in order thus:

a b c d e f g h i j k l m n o
p q r s t u v w x y z

She then threw down the Alphabet of Capital Letters in the Manner you here see them.

B D F H K M O Q S U W Y Z
A C E G I L N P R T V X J

and he picked them all up, and having told their Names, placed them thus:

A B C D E F G H I J K L M N O
P Q R S T U V W X Y Z

Now, pray little Reader, take this Bodkin, and see if you can point out the Letters from these mixed Alphabets, and tell how they should be placed as well as little Boy *Billy*.

From Part II of *The Renowned History of Mrs Margery Two-Shoes* (1765)

Chapter V

The whole History of the Considering Cap, set forth at large for the Benefit of all whom it may concern.

The great Reputation Mrs *Margery* acquired by composing Differences in Families, and especially, between Man and Wife, induced her to cultivate that Part of her System of Morality and Economy, in order to render it more extensively useful. For this Purpose, she contrived what she called a Charm for the Passions; which was a considering Cap, almost as large as a Grenadier's, but of three equal Sides; on the first of which was written, I MAY BE WRONG; on the second, IT IS FIFTY TO ONE BUT YOU ARE; and on the third, I'LL CONSIDER OF IT. The other Parts on the out-side, were filled with odd Characters, as unintelligible as the Writings of the old *Egyptians*; but within Side there was a Direction for its Use, of the utmost Consequence; for it strictly enjoined the Possessor to put on the Cap, whenever he found his Passions begin to grow turbulent, and not to deliver a Word whilst it was on, but with great Coolness and Moderation. As this Cap was an universal Cure for Wrong-headedness, and prevented numberless Disputes and Quarrels, it greatly hurt the Trade of the poor Lawyers, but was of the utmost Service to the rest of the Community. They were bought by Husbands and Wives, who had themselves frequent Occasion for them, and sometimes lent them to their Children: They were also purchased in large Quantities by Masters and Servants; by young Folks, who were intent on Matrimony, by Judges, Jurymen, and even Physicians and Divines; nay, if we may believe History, the Legislators of the Land did not disdain the Use of them; and we are told, that when any important Debate arose, *Cap, was the word*, and each House looked like a grand Synod of *Egyptian* Priests. Nor was this Cap of less Use to Partners in Trade, for with these, as well as with Husband and Wife, if one was out of Humour, the other threw him the Cap, and he was obliged to put it on, and keep it till all was quiet. I myself saw thirteen Caps worn at a Time in one Family, which could not have subsisted an Hour without them; and I was particularly pleased at Sir *Humphry Huffum's*, to hear a little Girl, when her Father was out of Humour, ask her Mamma, *if she should reach down the Cap?* These Caps, indeed, were of such Utility, that People of Sense never went without them; and it was common in the Country, when a

Booby made his Appearance, and talked Nonsense, to say, *he had no Cap in his Pocket.*

What was *Fortunatus's* Wishing Cap, when compared to this? That Cap, is said to have conveyed People instantly from one Place to another; but, as the Change of Place does not change the Temper and Disposition of the Mind, little Benefit can be expected from it; nor indeed is much to be hoped from his famous Purse'. That Purse, it is said, was never empty, and such a Purse, may be sometimes convenient; but as Money will not purchase Peace, it is not necessary for a Man to encumber himself with a great deal of it. Peace and Happiness depend so much upon the State of a Man's own Mind, and upon the Use of the considering Cap, that it is generally his own Fault, if he is miserable. One of these Caps will last a Man his whole Life, and is a Discovery of much greater Importance to the Public than the Philosopher's Stone. Remember what was said by my Brazen Head, *Time is, Time was, Time is past.* Now the *Time is,* therefore buy the Cap immediately, and make a proper Use of it, and be happy before the *Time is past.*

Yours, ROGER BACON.

6. RATIONAL MORALISTS

It will perhaps be wondered that I mention Reasoning *with Children: And yet I cannot but think that the true Way of Dealing with them. They understand it as early as they do Language; and, if I misobserve not, they love to be treated as Rational Creatures sooner than is imagined. 'Tis a Pride should be cherished in them, and, as much as can be, made the great Instrument to turn them by.*

—*John Locke*, Some Thoughts Concerning Education (Section 81)

Their published observations on learning inspired schools of followers; however, John Locke (1632–1704) and Jean Jacques Rousseau (1712–78) refused to think of education as primarily textual. For them it was not a series of imposed dictates but a process of discovery whose main instrument was the tutor or preceptor, who stimulated the exercise of innate perceptions and judgements. Such beliefs may appear commonplace today, yet in their time Locke's *Some Thoughts Concerning Education* (1693) and Rousseau's *Émile; ou de l'éducation* (1762) caused a considerable stir.

Locke's work, which had more than twelve editions before the middle of the eighteenth century, was the less controversial of the two. Oxford don and medical practitioner, philosopher and essayist, Locke was a well-travelled and respected intellectual who had served as both private tutor and travelling 'governor' to sons of the nobility. Hence, this bachelor brought to his educational treatise direct experience of children and an impressive knowledge of books and men. Like Montaigne before him, he was most concerned with the complete education of young gentlemen, which should have both rigorous and sympathetic aspects. He did not want to turn his charges into 'low spirited, moap'd Creatures[s]' or 'tame, unactive Children' (Section 51). For Locke anyone who has 'a Sound Mind in a sound Body . . . has little more to wish for' (Section 1). *Some Thoughts Concerning Education* opens with a long disquisition about the ways to obtain a sound body; a plain, sugarless diet, fresh air, swimming, cold foot-baths, and shoes 'that let in water' were prominent in the hardening regimen he advocated. Placing little importance on works of imaginative literature, Locke's curriculum was eminently sensible, beginning with the learning of the alphabet as a 'sport', recreational literature that was also instructional (Aesop, Reynard the Fox, some Old Testament stories), and graduating to calligraphy, drawing, composition, French and Latin, and the sciences. Crucial to the educational process was one person to act as an unassertive, all-wise guide and counsellor—a hired tutor chosen for his 'Sobriety, Temperance, Tenderness, Diligence, and Discretion' (Section 90). This paragon set the stamp of 'good Breeding' on his pupil, without which the learner's 'other Accomplishments make him pass but for proud, conceited, vain or foolish.' Locke's system was fundamentally one of character formation, to which health, knowledge, and habits of mind that are rational, moral, and just, all contributed.

Locke's pronouncements, buttressed with a wealth of classical examples, have a more theoretical cast than Rousseau's text, which is much more personal, approachable—and polemical. An unsuccessful apprentice and self-educated wanderer, Rousseau as a child had been an omnivorous reader and an attentive listener to adult conversation. Disapproving in retrospect of this uncritical and indiscriminate introduction to books, he advocated keeping his hypothetical pupil, Émile, illiterate until the age of twelve, to protect him from the negative and corrupting effects of adults' received opinions; in contrast to Rousseau's own unsupervised childhood, Émile's was constantly monitored by a dedicated tutor (*maître*). Judicious tutelage, not doctrinal proscriptions, was to guide the pupil's activities and intellectual development, and this was to be undertaken (until the age of twenty!) apart from the possibly restrictive influences of family, and protected from the negative influences of society and books—of civilization in general. Respect for the nature of the child, as Rousseau understood it, meant introducing nothing that would alter his primitive innocence. His goal in *Émile* was to recreate the natural man.

Rousseau's concept of the 'natural' being was vastly different from that of Benjamin Keach a generation or two before (see chapter two). Rousseau's own early experiments with natural behaviour were sources of regret; in both *Confessions* (Book 12) and *Émile* (Book 1) he mentions apologetically the fact that he abandoned all five of his natural (illegitimate) children. However shocking the disclosure might be for us today, we should remember, as John Boswell's study notes, that in the second half of the eighteenth century one of every three or four children was abandoned in French, Italian, and Spanish cities. Another aspect of Rousseau's theorizing that may perplex us is his treatment of the education of girls. While Locke ignored the topic, Rousseau devoted the fifth book of his treatise to Émile's helpmeet, Sophie, who was properly docile, restrained, and ornamental—a competent embroiderer, lacemaker, singer, and dancer—whose 'mind knows little, but is trained to learn; it is well-tilled soil ready for the sower [her husband].'

Émile was a radical antidote for the ills of what its revolutionary author saw as a degenerating society. He had intended it as an introduction to *The Social Contract*, also published in 1762, though separate publication by two rival firms destroyed this interdependence. Both books were written in opposition to all doctrinaire influences, and advocated a new liberating basis for human development and for society: a new social contract. They so scandalized his native city of Geneva, as well as his adopted country, France, that Rousseau was banished from both. The Sorbonne condemned them; sales were forbidden; and copies were burned in the public squares of Geneva and Paris.

Cultivating rational thought and moral judgements along the general lines proposed by Locke and Rousseau was the paramount concern of a large group of authors who wrote improving books for children between 1750 and 1850. Their work was published by a range of printers—from the successors of Newbery, John Marshall, John Harris, and Benjamin Tabart, to the Quaker William Darton and the radical Joseph Johnson—whose establishments and juvenile lists represented the commercial prosperity of the field. These writers were keen believers in the power of carefully designed narratives and of positive as well as negative examples to shape children's understanding. All emphasized tutelage: most of their stories feature a hired tutor, but sometimes a parent is the dispenser of information. The purpose remains the same whoever the instructor: to make learning an active, engaging pursuit.

In the books here excerpted by Sarah Fielding, Thomas Day, and Mary Wollstonecraft, the tutor, who aims to instill a sense of rational agency and self-command, is all-important. Fielding's Mrs Teachum runs her 'little female academy' with strictness and common sense; her response to a quarrel among the girls that breaks out in her absence is both consistent and humane. Day's omnipresent Mr Barlow—patient but loquaciously instructive—superintends the learning of plucky Harry

Sandford and cosseted Tommy Merton. Mary Wollstonecraft's Mrs Mason lucidly directs the girls' attention away from ornamental displays to an awareness of 'conscious worth', 'simple elegance', and 'a most excellent understanding and feeling heart'.

Among writers who give parents, especially mothers, the formative role in their children's early education, Lady Fenn dedicates her simple dialogues to fond mothers who, in the nursery, teach children 'the first rudiments of knowledge'. The mother's voice both in Jane Cave's poem cautioning against the torture of animals and Nancy Livingstone's pointers for her infant daughter's education resonates with Lockean principles. In Jane Marcet's story, Mary's mother is as keen to demystify the grammatical complexities of nouns for her daughter as is Janetta's mother, in Barbara Hofland's tale, to show Janetta the errors of her admirable generosity. The prize for terrifying modes of instruction must go to Henry Horsley's 'affectionate parent'. Having announced his intention to promote 'temporal Prosperity and eternal Happiness' in his two sons, a father provides cautionary examples by conducting visits to Newgate Prison and a 'Lunatic Asylum'.

Instruction, of course, was the primary aim of these Rational Moralists, not instruction with delight. But some of their books have modest though effective literary qualities (obscured, at times, by their open didacticism), for the authors were anxious to enliven information and moral principles to hold young readers' attention. They reveal varying degrees of skill in the handling of narrative, dialogue, characterization, and incident. Mary Ann Kilner crafts a two-volume narrative from the point of view of a pincushion. Dorothy Kilner does not stint on melodrama in a tale about bullying and its unexpected consequences. In the family conversations that she makes her narrative medium, Priscilla Wakefield folds in scientific fact about the manufacture of sugar with abolitionist rhetoric about the slave trade. The most skilful writer in this section is Maria Edgeworth, the author of 'The Purple Jar'. Edgeworth's characterization of her autobiographical protagonist, Rosamond, captures all the conversational tics and impulsive curiosity of a child on a shopping trip. Thomas Day's Tommy Merton, a wonderfully reluctant pupil who is almost impervious to Mr Barlow's moralizing, articulates his selfish desires confidently. Sarah Fielding describes the fray in which Mrs Teachum's female pupils 'pull one another to pieces for a sorry Apple' with fast-paced action and spirited dialogue. And the anguished soliloquy that is the climax of Miss Sukey's realization of her guilt is an effective emotional outburst that clears the way for the concluding reconciliation.

One thing that strikes the modern reader about these books is that they seem to have been written for adults. It is worth noting that many of the authors represented—Sarah Fielding, Mary Wollstonecraft, Maria Edgeworth, Catharine Parr Traill, and Barbara Hofland, among them—enjoyed equally successful careers writing for adult readers. The diction in these stories of Rational Moralists is, for the most part, uncompromisingly elevated. The interests and activities of children, who soberly enter into discussion with their seniors, are coloured by adult emotions and viewpoints. Parenthood was not a criterion for juvenile writing or theorizing, as the examples of Locke, Fenn, Kilner, and Edgeworth attest. Their work, however, appealed to well-intentioned parents, who pressed them on their offspring. They, poor lambs, were conditioned to accept and profit by such gifts. Like the hellfire tales of the Puritans, these books of the Rational Moralists tell us more about their authors and other like-minded adults than about the true interests of the youngsters for whom they were written.

SARAH FIELDING (1710–68)
From *The Governess; or, Little Female Academy* (1749)

Sister and devoted admirer of the novelist Henry Fielding, Sarah published her first novel, *The Adventures of David Simple in Search of a Faithful Friend*, in 1744; her preface identifies 'Distress in her Circumstances' as the 'Excuse . . . for a Woman's venturing to write at all.' Since she and her three sisters had been sent to Mrs Rooke's boarding school in The Close, Salisbury, where they acquired a gentlewoman's knowledge of reading, writing, dancing, and French conversation, she could write about a 'little Female academy' from personal experience. Fielding's governess is Mrs Teachum in this first full-length original story for children in English. Relating the direct and indirect ways through which Mrs Teachum, a widow in reduced circumstances whose two children have died,

instructs her nine girls over a period of nine days, *The Governess* is an appealing mixture of realism and romance. On the first day the girls engage in a pitched battle over an apple. Fielding manages the battle and the reconciliation with a psychological acuteness quite unique in children's stories of the mid-eighteenth century. It is worth noting that she does not make the teacher an omnipresent character; instead, the girls themselves often teach one another, as in the following example of the intervention of the oldest pupil, Jenny Peace. After concord is assured, Miss Jenny, the prefect, is permitted to regale the others with an entertaining tale about the 'cruel giant Barbarico' and the 'good giant Benefico'— a diversion Mrs Teachum allows because of its 'very good moral'.

An Account of a Fray

Begun and carried on for the sake of an Apple: In which are shewn the sad Effects of Rage and Anger.

It was on a fine Summer's Evening, when the School-hours were at an End, and the young Ladies were admitted to divert themselves for some time as they thought proper, in a pleasant Garden adjoining to the House, that their Governess, who delighted in pleasing them, brought out a little Basket of Apples, which were intended to be divided equally amongst them: But Mrs *Teachum* being hastily called away (one of her poor Neighbours having had an Accident which wanted her Assistance), she left the Fruit in the Hands of Miss *Jenny Peace*, the eldest of her Scholars, with a strict Charge to see that every one had an equal Share of her Gift.

But here a perverse Accident turned good Mrs *Teachum's* Design of giving them Pleasure into their Sorrow, and raised in their little Hearts nothing but Strife and Anger: For, alas! there happened to be one Apple something larger than the rest, on which the whole Company immediately placed their desiring Eyes, and all at once cried out, 'Pray, Miss *Jenny*, give me that 'Apple.' Each gave her Reasons why she had the best Title to it: The youngest pleaded her Youth, and the eldest her Age; one insisted on her Goodness, another from her Meekness claimed a Title to Preference; and one, in confidence of her Strength, said positively, she would have it; but all speaking together, it was difficult to distinguish who said this, or who said that.

Miss *Jenny* begged them all to be quiet: But in vain: For she could not be heard: They had all set their Hearts on that fine Apple, looking upon those she had given them as nothing. She told them, they had better be contented with what they had, than be thus seeking what it was impossible for her to give to them all. She offered to divide it into Eight Parts, or to do any-thing to satisfy them: But she might as well have been silent; for they were all talking, and had no Time to hear. At last, as a Means to quiet the Disturbance, she threw this Apple, the Cause of their Contention, with her utmost Force, over a Hedge into another Garden, where they could not come at it.

At first they were all silent, as if they were struck dumb with Astonishment with the Loss of this one poor Apple, tho' at the same time they had Plenty before them.

But this did not bring to pass Miss *Jenny's* Design: For now they all began again to quarrel which had the most Right of it, and which *ought* to have had it, with as much Vehemence as they had before contended for the Possession of it; And their Anger by degrees became so high, that Words could not vent half their Rage; and they fell to pulling of Caps, tearing of Hair, and dragging the Cloaths off one another's Backs. Tho' they did not so much strike, as endeavour to scratch and pinch their Enemies.

Miss *Dolly Friendly* as yet was not engaged in the Battle: But on hearing her Friend Miss *Nancy Spruce* scream out, that she was hurt by a sly Pinch from one of the Girls, she flew on this sly Pincher, as she called her, like an enraged Lion on its Prey; and not content only to return the Harm her Friend had received, she struck with such Force, as felled her Enemy to the Ground. And now they could not distinguish between Friend and Enemy; but fought, scratch'd, and tore, like so many Cats, when they extended their Claws to fix them in their Rival's Heart.

Miss *Jenny* was employed in endeavouring to part them.

In the Midst of this Confusion, Mrs *Teachum*, who was returning in Hopes to see them happy with the Fruit she had given them, appeared: But she was some time there before either her Voice or Presence could awaken them from their Attention to the Fight; when on a sudden they all faced her, and Fear of Punishment began now a little to abate their Rage. Each of the Misses held in her Right-hand, fast clenched, some Marks of Victory; for they were beat and beaten by Turns. One of them held a little Lock of Hair, torn from the Head of her Enemy: Another grasped a Piece of a Cap, which, in aiming at her Rival's Hair, had deceived her Hand, and was all the Spoils she could gain: A third clenched a Piece of an Apron; a fourth, of a Frock. In short, every one unfortunately held in her Hand a Proof of having been engaged in the Battle. And the Ground was spread with Rags and Tatters, torn from the Backs of the little inveterate Combatants.

Mrs *Teachum* stood for some time astonished at the Sight: But at last she required Miss *Jenny Peace*, who was the only Person disengaged, to tell her the Truth, and to inform her of the Cause of all this Confusion. Miss *Jenny* was obliged to obey the Commands of her Governess; tho' she was so good-natured, that she did it in the mildest Terms; and endeavoured all she could to lessen, rather than increase, Mrs *Teachum's* Anger. The guilty Persons now began all to excuse themselves as fast as Tears and Sobs would permit them.

One said, 'Indeed, Madam, it was none of my Fault; for I did not begin; for Miss *Sukey Jennett*, without any Cause in the World (for I did nothing to provoke her), hit me a great Slap in the Face, and made my Tooth ache; The Pain *did* make me angry; and then, indeed, I hit her a little Tap; but it was on her Back; and I am sure it was the smallest Tap in the World; and could not possibly hurt her half so much as her great Blow did me.'

'Law, Miss! replied Miss *Jennett*, How can you say so? when you know that you struck me first, and that yours was the great Blow, and mine the little Tap; for I only went to defend myself from your monstrous Blows.'

Such like Defences they would all have made for themselves, each insisting on not being in Fault, and throwing the Blame on her Companion: But Mrs *Teachum* silenced them by a positive Command; and told them, that she saw they were all equally guilty, and as such would treat them.

Mrs *Teachum's* Method of punishing I never could find out. But this is certain, the most severe Punishment she had ever inflicted on any Misses, since she had kept a School, was now laid on these wicked Girls, who had been thus fighting, and pulling one another to Pieces, for a sorry Apple.

The first thing she did, was to take away all the Apples; telling them, that before they had any more Instances of like Kindness from her, they should give her Proofs of better deserving them. And when she had punished them as much as she thought proper, she made them all embrace one another, and promise to be Friends for the future; which, in Obedience to her Commands, they were forced to comply with, tho' there remained a Grudge and Ill-will in their Bosoms; every one thinking she was punished most, altho she would have it, that she deserved to be punished least; and they contrived all the sly Tricks they could think on to vex and teaze each other.

A Dialogue between Miss Jenny Peace, *and Miss* Sukey Jennett; *wherein the latter is at last convinced of her own Folly in being so quarrelsome; and, by her Example, all her companions are brought to see and confess their Fault.*

The next Morning Miss *Jenny Peace* used her utmost Endeavours to bring her School-fellows to be heartily reconciled; but in vain: For they all insisted on it, that they were not to blame; but that the whole Quarrel arose from the Faults of others. At last ensued the following Dialogue between Miss *Jenny Peace* and Miss *Sukey Jennett*, which brought about Miss *Jenny's* Designs; and which we recommend to the Consideration of all our young Readers.

Miss Jenny. Now pray, Miss *Sukey*, tell me. What did you get by your Contention and Quarrel about that foolish Apple?

Miss Sukey. Indeed, Ma'am, I shall not answer you. I know that you only want to prove, that you are wiser than me, because you are older. But I don't know but some People may understand as much at Eleven Years old, as others at Thirteen: But, because you are the oldest in the School, you always want to be tutoring and governing. I don't like to have more than one Governess; and if I obey my Mistress, I think that is enough.

Miss Jenny. Indeed, my dear, I don't want to govern you, nor to prove myself wiser than you: I only want, that, instead of quarrelling, and making yourself miserable, you should live at peace, and be happy. Therefore, pray do answer my Question. Whether you got any-thing by your Quarrel?

Miss Sukey. No! I cannot say I got anything by it: For my Mistress was angry, and punished me; and my Hair was pulled off, and my Cloaths torn in the Scuffle: Neither did I value the Apple: But yet I have too much Spirit to be imposed on. I am sure I had as good a Right to it, as any of the others: And I would not give up my Right to any one.

Miss Jenny. But don't you know, Miss *Sukey*, it would have shewn much more Spirit to have yielded the Apple to another, then to have fought about it? Then, indeed, you would have proved your Sense; for you would have shewn, that you had too much Understanding to fight about a Trifle. Then your Cloaths had been whole, your Hair not torn from your Head, your Mistress had not been angry, nor had your Fruit been taken away from you.

Miss Sukey. And so, Miss, you would fain prove, that it is wisest to submit to every-body that would impose upon one? But I will not believe it, say what you will.

Miss Jenny. But is not what I say true? If you had not been in the Battle, would not your Cloaths have been whole, your Hair not torn, your Mistress pleased with you, and your Apples your own?

Here Miss *Sukey* paused for some time: For as Miss *Jenny* was in the Right, and had Truth on her Side, it was difficult for Miss *Sukey* to know what to answer. For it is impossible, without being very silly, to contradict Truth: And yet Miss *Sukey* was so foolish, that she did not care to own herself in the Wrong; tho' nothing could have been so great a Sign of her Understanding.

When Miss *Jenny* saw her thus at a Loss for an Answer, she was in Hopes she should make her Companion happy; for, as she had as much Good-nature as Understanding, that was her Design. She therefore pursued her Discourse in the following Manner:

Miss Jenny. Pray, Miss *Sukey*, do, answer me one Question more. Don't you lie awake at Nights, and fret and vex yourself, because you are angry with your School-fellows? Are not you restless and uneasy because you cannot find a safe Method to be revenged on them, without being punished yourself? Do, tell me truly, Is not this your Case?

Miss Sukey. Yes, it is. For if I could but hurt my Enemies, without being hurt myself, it would be the greatest Pleasure I could have in the World.

Miss Jenny. Oh fy, Miss *Sukey*! What you have now said is wicked. Don't you consider what you say every Day in your Prayers? And this Way of thinking will make you lead a very uneasy Life. If you would hearken to me, I could put you into a Method of being very happy, and making all those Misses you call your Enemies become your Friends.

Miss Sukey. You could tell me a Method, Miss! Do you think I don't know as well as you what is fit to be done? I believe I am as capable of finding the Way to be happy, as you are of teaching me.

Here Miss *Sukey* burst into Tears, that any-body should presume to tell her the Way to be happy.

Miss Jenny. Upon my Word, my Dear, I don't mean to vex you; but only, instead of tormenting yourself all Night in laying Plots to revenge yourself, I would have you employ this one Night in thinking of what I have said. Nothing will shew your Sense so much, as to own that you have been in the Wrong: Nor will any-thing prove a right Spirit so much, as to confess your Fault. All the Misses will be your Friends, and perhaps follow your Example. Then you will have the Pleasure of having caused the Quiet of the whole School; your Governess will love you; and you will be at Peace in your Mind, and never have any more foolish Quarrels, in which you all get nothing but Blows and Uneasiness.

Miss *Sukey* began now to find, that Miss *Jenny* was in the Right, and she her-self in the Wrong; but yet she was so proud she would not own it. Nothing could be so foolish as this Pride; because it would have been both good and wise in her to confess the Truth the Moment she saw it. However, Miss *Jenny* was so discreet, as not to press her any farther that Night; but begged her to consider seriously on what she had said, and to let her know her Thoughts the next Morning. And then left her.

When Miss *Sukey* was alone, she stood some time in great Confusion. She could not help feeling how much hitherto she had been in the Wrong; and that Thought stung her to the Heart. She cried, stamped, and was in as great an Agony as if some sad Misfortune had befallen her. At last, when she had some-what vented her Passion by Tears, she burst forth into the following Speech:

'It is very true what Miss *Jenny Peace* says; for I am always uneasy. I don't sleep in Quiet; because I am always thinking, either that I have not my Share of what is given us, or that I cannot be revenged on any of the Girls that offend me. And when I quarrel with them, I am scratched and bruised, or reproached. And what do I get by all this? Why, I scratch, bruise, and reproach them in my Turn. Is not that Gain enough? I warrant I hurt them as much as they hurt me. But then indeed, as Miss *Jenny* says, if I could make these Girls my Friends, and did not wish to hurt them, I certainly might live a quieter, and perhaps a happier Life.— But what, then, have I been always in the Wrong all my Life-time? for I always quarrelled and hated everyone who had offended me.—Oh! I cannot bear that Thought! It is enough to make me mad! when I imagined myself so wise and so sensible, to find out that I have been always a Fool. If I think a Moment longer about it, I shall die with Grief and Shame. I must think myself in the Right; and I will too.—But, as Miss *Jenny* says, I really am unhappy; for I hate all my School-fellows: And yet I dare not do them any Mischief; for my Mistress will punish me severely if I do. I should not so much mind that neither: But then those I intend to hurt will triumph over me, to see me punished for their sakes. In short, the more I reflect, the more I am afraid Miss *Jenny* is in the Right; and yet it breaks my Heart to think so.'

Here the poor Girl wept so bitterly, and was so heartily grieved, that she could not utter one Word more; but sat herself down, reclining her Head upon her Hand, in the most melancholy Posture that could be: Nor could she close her Eyes all Night; but lay tossing and raving with the Thought how she should act, and what she should say to Miss *Jenny* the next Day.

When the Morning came, Miss *Sukey* dreaded every Moment, as the Time drew nearer when she must meet Miss *Jenny*. She knew it would not be possible to resist her Arguments; and yet Shame for having been in Fault overcame her.

As soon as Miss *Jenny* saw Miss *Sukey* with her Eyes cast down, and confessing, by a Look of Sorrow, that she would take her Advice, she embraced her kindly; and, without giving her the Trouble to speak, took it for granted, that she would leave off quarrelling, be reconciled to her School-fellows and make herself happy.

Miss *Sukey* did indeed stammer out some Words, which implied a Confession of her Fault; but they were spoke so low they could hardly be heard: Only Miss *Jenny*, who always chose to look at the fairest Side of her Companions' Actions, by Miss *Sukey's* Look and Manner, guessed her Meaning.

In the same manner did this good Girl, *Jenny*, persuade, one by one, all her School-fellows to be reconciled to each other with Sincerity and Love.

Miss *Dolly Friendly*, who had too much Sense to engage in the Battle for the sake of an Apple, and who only was provoked to strike a Blow for Friendship's Cause, easily saw the Truth of what Miss *Jenny* said; and was therefore presently convinced that the best Part she could have acted for her Friend, would have been to have withdrawn her from the Scuffle.

MARY ANN KILNER (1753–1831)

From *The Adventures of a Pincushion designed chiefly for the Use of Young Ladies* (two volumes, *c.* 1780)

The Kilners, Mary Ann Maze and Dorothy, were sisters-in-law, both of whom wrote improving stories for children at approximately the same time. Each used a pseudonymn: Mary Ann adopted S.S. ('Sarah Slinn'), and Dorothy, M.P. ('Mary Pelham'). In addition to the tale of the Pincushion, Mary Ann's best-known stories are *Jemima Placid; or, The Advantage of Good-Nature* (*c.* 1783) and *William Sedley; or, The Evil Day Deferred* (1783). Master Sedley's 'evil day' actually marks his return to school; by contrast, Jemima, a paragon of agreeableness, extols the advantages of docility to her fretful cousins, at one point versifying '*Tho' the elements will not resign to my sway, / My own temper, I trust, reason's voice will obey.*' In her earliest story Kilner succeeds in animating the first-person narration of the Pincushion as 'an Historian or Biographer', who speaks for himself and tells readers what he 'saw and heard in the character of a Pincushion'. The extract that follows from the first volume neatly traces the differences between the two Airy sisters, from the Pincushion's perspective. Kind, capable, organized Martha is constantly running to the rescue of the indulgent, peremptory, but imaginative Charlotte. It is clear that Mrs Airy is educating her daughters to be productive and thrifty. Remarkably the Pincushion's counsel highlights the instruction, in commenting on the girls' different temperaments and on the importance of a seemingly inconsequential pin to a presentable appearance.

From *The Adventures of a Pincushion designed chiefly for the Use of Young Ladies*

After the young ladies had amused themselves a great while with the pieces of silk I have so often had occasion to mention, and Miss Martha had completed me to her entire satisfaction; she took all the pins out of an old green one, which was originally in the shape of a heart, but had, by losing a great part of its inside, through various little holes, quite lost its form: and which, that she might find those pins which had gone through the silk, she cut open an old news-paper, and then stuck all she could find upon my sides in the shape of letters, which she afterwards changed to flowers, and a third time altered to stars and circles; which afforded her full amusement till bed-time. Miss Charlotte, though her mamma had given her as much silk as her sister, had only cut it into waste; while Martha, after she had furnished me, had saved the rest towards making a housewife for her doll.

I could not help reflecting when I saw all Charlotte's little shreds and slips littering the room, what a simple method many little girls are apt to get into, of wasting every thing which their friends are so kind as to give them, and which properly employed, might make them many useful ornaments for their dolls, and sometimes pretty trifles for themselves. Charlotte Airy, as such children usually are, was desirous of having every thing she saw; so that her drawers were always filled with bits of ribbon, pieces of silk, cuttings of gauze, catgut, and muslin: and if she wanted to find her gloves, tippet, tuckers, or any part of her dress, she was obliged to search for them in twenty different places, and frequently to go without what she was looking for. Martha, on the contrary, by taking care of what might be of use, and laying it by in a proper place, always knew where to find what she had occasion for directly. So that it frequently happened that she went out with her mamma, when her sister was forced to stay at home; because she had lost something which had delayed her so long to look for, that she could not get ready in time.

This very circumstance happened the day after I became acquainted with her, to her no small mortification. Mrs Airy was going to see the exhibition of pictures at the Royal Academy, and told her daughters that if they behaved well they should accompany her; as Mrs Gardner and her niece Miss Lounge would call at one o'clock. After breakfast, Charlotte, who had found the mould of an old button in one of her papa's waistcoat pockets which she had been rummaging, had cut to pieces an axle-tree of a little cart, which belonged to her brother, to make a spindle, in order to convert it into a tea-totum [a top twirled by the fingers]; with which she was so much entertained, that she was very unwilling to leave it to go to work, though her mamma repeatedly told her, she would not be ready against Mr Gardner's coach came. 'Yes, I shall, Madam!' said she, and played on. 'Do pray go to work, Charlotte!' 'Presently, madam.' But still she thought she would give it another twirl. 'You shall not go if you have not finished your morning business!' 'In a minute I will!' And so she simply idled away her time, without heeding her mamma's admonition, till nearly an hour beyond her usual time of beginning. This put her into such a hurry to finish when she found it was so late, that she stitched some wristbands she was about, and which were intended for her grand-papa, so very badly, they were obliged to be undone; which made her so cross, that in pulling out the work, she broke the threads of the cloth, and entirely spoiled it.

Charlotte was a very fair complexioned pretty girl; but you cannot imagine how ugly her ill-humour made her appear; nor how much more agreeable her sister looked, who was much browner, was pitted with the small-pox, and a much plainer child. I surveyed them both as I lay on the table, where my mistress had placed me to stick her pins as she took out of the shirt collar which she was putting on; Martha looked so placid and cheerful, and seemed to speak so kindly when she asked a question, that it made her really charming; while Charlotte, who had a very pretty mouth, and very regular features, stuck out her lips in a manner so unbecoming, and tossed about her head with such illiberal jerks that she lost all natural advantages in her wilful ill-humour.

A person happening to call on Mrs Airy, to speak about some particular business, she left the children to attend him; and Martha who pitied her sister's distress, and saw the impossibility of her finishing the task she was ordered to do, very kindly offered to assist her, without which, she never could have accomplished it. But their mamma, at her return, immediately suspected the case to be as I have told you, and inquired what help Charlotte had received in her absence? They were both girls of too much honour to deny the truth, and in consequence of her frankly owing her sister's kindness, Mrs Airy permitted her to retire, in order to prepare for the intended expedition; but alas! poor Charlotte, who was not always so good as she ought to have been, was not to go that morning, although her mamma had consented to it. Betty, who came to put on her frock, was not very fond of her, for she was sometimes apt, when her mamma was not in the way, to speak very haughtily, and in a manner quite unbecoming a young lady. Unfortunately she forgot herself on the present occasion, and very rudely said, 'You must come and dress me, and you must make haste, or I shall not be ready.' 'Must I?' replied Betty, 'That is if I please, Miss Charlotte, though you forgot to put that in: and unless you speak in a prettier way, I will not help you at all.' 'Then you may let it alone, for I will not ask you any otherwise,' and away she went, banging the door after her, to call her sister, who was ready and waiting for the coach in her mamma's room. Martha ran directly, and began to pin her frock as she desired. But a new distress arose, for as she was too careless ever to retain any of my fellow-servants (commonly called a Pincushion) in her service, so she had not one pin to proceed with after three, which had stuck at one end of me, had been employed. Neither of them chose to apply to Betty, because they were sure from Charlotte's ill-behaviour to be denied: and she would not permit her sister to ask her mamma, for fear of an inquiry which might not turn out to her credit. So, in short, they both traversed the room backwards and forwards, and were quite overjoyed when they found two, (one of which proved to be crooked) between the joining of the floor. Then they each returned and took me up repeatedly, and examined me over and over, though they were convinced I had been empty long ago. At last a loud rap at the door announced Mrs Gardner's arrival. The ladies were called, and Martha obeyed, though with reluctance to leave her sister: and Charlotte, with conscious shame and remorse for her past conduct, and heart-heaving sobs of disappointment, saw them drive away without her.

I was left upon the table in the hurry of my mistress's departure, and Charlotte took me up, and earnestly wished she had had a Pincushion of her own: and so I should think would any one, who had experienced the want of such an useful companion; though unless well furnished with pins, it is in itself but of little assistance, as she had but too unfortunately found. The slatternly appearance, and real inconvenience, which many ladies suffer from neglecting to provide themselves with, and retaining a few such necessary implements of female œconomy about them is really inconceivable by any person accustomed to a proper degree of attention. Trifles are frequently regarded by the giddy and thoughtless as of no moment, when essentials are taken care of: but it is the repetition of trifles which constitutes the chief business of our existence. In other words, people form their opinion of a young lady from her personal appearance; and if, because she is at work, and in want of pins, and destitute of a Pincushion, she has quite undressed herself, and her clothes are dropping off, she will be thought a negligent slattern; which, I suppose, is what no one would chuse to be esteemed: so, when children accustom themselves to loll their elbows, stoop their heads, stand upon one foot, bite their nails, or any other ungraceful actions, it makes them disagreeable, and the object of dislike to all their friends, and every one who is acquainted with them. And it is very foolish to imagine, that because they are not in company with strangers it does not signify; for ill habits, when once they are acquired, are very difficult to leave off; and by being used to do an unpolite action frequently, they will do it without recollecting the impropriety; when if they thought, perhaps, they would have on no account been guilty of it.

JANE CAVE (*c.* 1754–1813)
From *Poems on Various Subjects, Entertaining, Elegiac and Religious* (1783)

Daughter of an English exciseman, Jane Cave (later Winscom) was born and raised in South Wales. Her single volume of verse, *Poems on Various Subjects*, published by subscription, had four editions between 1783 and 1794. The following poem, which appeared in all editions, testifies to the extent of Locke's influence. Cave's iambic quatrains versify Locke's contention that the tormenting and killing of beasts harden the mind toward humankind: *'they who delight in the suffering and destruction of inferiour Creatures, will not be apt to be very compassionate or benigne to those of their own kind'* (Section 116). Cave married an exciseman in 1783 and bore two sons. She lived for a period in Bristol and Winchester, and died in Newport, Gwent.

A Poem for Children. On Cruelty to the Irrational Creation.

<blockquote>

Oh! What a cruel wicked thing,
For me who am a little King,
To give my hapless subjects pain,
And make them groan beneath my reign.

5 Were I a chafer, and could fly,
Ah! should I not with anguish cry,
Should naughty children take a pin,
And run me through to make me spin?

</blockquote>

Were I a bird, took from my nest,
10 Should I not think myself opprest,
If toss'd about in wanton play,
'Till maim'd and faint I die away?

Now, and when I'm a bigger boy,
Let cruelty my heart annoy,
15 Because it is a dreadful evil,
That only fits me for the Devil.

If I must ought of life deprive,
The quickest way I will contrive,
To stop the tremb'ling victim's breath,
20 And give it little pain in death.

I'll not torment a dog or cat,
A toad, a viper, or a rat;
They're form'd by an Almighty hand,
And sprung to life at his command.

25 A bull, a horse, yea every creature,
Of the most mild or savage nature,
Were kindly given for my use,
But never meant for my abuse.

Good men, thy holy word attests,
30 Are kind and tender to their beasts;
May I be merciful and kind,
That I with thee may mercy find.

ANNE 'NANCY' SHIPPEN LIVINGSTON (1763–1841)
From *Nancy Shippen: Her Journal Book* (1783)

Anne ('Nancy') Shippen's *Journal Book* provides an intimate glimpse of privileged family life in Philadelphia in the last quarter of the eighteenth century. At eighteen Nancy Shippen fell in love with Louis Guillaume Otto, who was attaché of the French Legation in Philadelphia and later chargé d'affaires of France in the United States, but her father, Dr William Shippen, director general of the military hospitals of the Continental Army, would not permit her to marry him. Her arranged marriage to Lieutenant Colonel Henry Beekman Livingston was unhappy. They separated during her pregnancy, and no reconciliation was possible. Divorce was impossible too because Livingston insisted on sole custody of their child, Margaret, as the main condition. Shippen Livingston devoted her life to the care and happiness of 'Sweet Peggy', who was seventeen months old at the beginning of the *Journal*. With her concern to sow the 'seeds of reason' and monitor the judgement of her infant daughter, Nancy Shippen Livingston fulfils the role of a true Lockean tutor.

Some Directions Concerning a Daughters Education

1st.   Study well her constitution and genious.
2d.   Follow nature & proceed patiently.
3d.   Suffer not Servants to terrify her with stories of Ghosts & Goblins.
4th.   Give her a fine pleasing idea of Good, & an ugly frightful one of Evil.
5th.   Keep her to a good & natural regimen of diet.
6th.   Observe strictly the little seeds of reason in her, & cultivate the first appearance of it diligently.
7th.   Watch over her childish Passions and prejudices, & labour sweetly to cure her of them.
8th.   Never use any little dissembling arts, either to pacify her or to persuade her to anything.
9th.   Win her to be in love with openness, in all her acts, & words.
10th.   Fail not to instill into her an abhorance of all 'serpentine' wit.
11th.   If she be a brisk witty child do not applaud her too much.
12th.   If she be a dul heavy child, do not discourage her at all.
13th.   Seem not to admire her wit, but rather study to rectify her judgment.
14th.   Use her to put little questions, & give her ready & short answers.
15th.   Insinuate into her the principles of politeness & true modesty, & christian humility.
16th.   Inculcate upon her that most honorable duty & virtue sincerity.
17th.   Be sure to possess her with the baseness of telling a Lye on any account.
18th.   Shew her the deformity of Rage & Anger.
19th.   Never let her converse with servants.
20th.   Acquaint her in the most pleasant & insinuating manner, with the sacred History, nor let it seem her lesson, but her recreation.

21st.   Set before her the gospel in its simplicity & purity, & the great Examples of antiquity unsophisticated.

22d.   Explain to her the nature of the baptismal san[c]tion.

23d.   Prepare her in the best manner for confirmation.

24th.   Animate, and instruct her for the holy communion.

25th.   Particularly inform her in the duties of a single & married state.

26th.   Let her be prepared for the duties & employment of a city life, if her lot should be among citizens.

27th.   See she be inform'd in all that belongs to a country life.

28th.   Discreetly check her desires after things pleasant, & use* her to frequent disappointments *Ro[u]sseau.

29th.   Let her be instructed to do every thing seasonably & in order, & what ever she is set to do let her study to do it well, & peaceably.

30th.   Teach her to improve everything that nothing may be lost or wasted, nor let her hurry herself about any thing.

31st.   Let her always be employ'd about what is profitable or necessary.

32d.   Let nothing of what is committed to her care be spoil'd by her neglect.

33d.   Let her eat deliberately, chew well, & drink in moderate proportions.

34th.   Let her use exercise in the morning.

35th.   Use her to rise betimes in the morning, & set before her in the most winning manner an order for the whole day.

THOMAS DAY (1748–89)
From *The History of Sandford and Merton* (1783)

Although admitted to the Middle Temple and called to the bar, Day was interested more in experimental farming than in the law. A fervent promoter of Rousseau and a disciple of his primitivism, he tailored his two works for children—*The History of Sandford and Merton* (three volumes, 1783, 1786, 1789) and *The History of Little Jack* (1788)—to conform to the philosophy of his master. Harry Sandford, a farmer's son, is a sensible, informed lad (although to the modern reader he is an insufferable, priggish know-it-all); Tommy Merton, from a wealthy family, is coddled, illiterate and high-handed. After Harry rescues Tommy from a snake, the two boys become friends and fellow-pupils of the sententious Mr Barlow. Harry is entirely tractable, whereas Master Merton often presents an uproarious challenge to Mr Barlow's attempts to improve him. Day never misses an opportunity to use the contrasts between the boys to praise the industrious poor and denigrate the idle rich. The narrative line of *Sandford and Merton* is almost non-existent; it is an array of uplifting stories recounted by each of the protagonists. In the extract that follows, Tommy tells a story borrowed from La Fontaine ('Education', Book VIII, No. 24).

Tommy Learns to Read

From this time forward Mr Barlow and his two young pupils used constantly to work in their garden every morning; and when they were fatigued they retired to the summerhouse, where little Harry, who improved every day in reading, used to entertain them with some pleasant story or other, which Tommy always listened to with the greatest pleasure. But Harry going home for a week, Tommy and Mr Barlow were left alone.

The next day, after they had done work, and had retired to the summerhouse as usual, Tommy expected Mr Barlow would read to him, but, to his great disappointment, found that he was busy, and could not. The next day the same accident was renewed, and the day after that. At this Tommy lost all patience and said to himself—'Now, if I could but read like Harry Sandford, I should not need to ask anybody to do it for me, and then I could divert myself: and why (thinks he) may not I do what another has done? To be sure little Harry is very clever; but he could not have read if he had not been taught; and if I am taught, I daresay I shall learn to read as well as he. Well, as soon as ever he comes home, I am determined to ask him about it.'

The next day Harry returned; and as soon as Tommy had an opportunity of being alone with him—'Pray, Harry,' said Tommy, 'how came you to be able to read?'

Harry. Why, Mr Barlow taught me my letters, and then spelling; and then, by putting syllables together, I learned to read.

Tommy. And could not you show me my letters?

Harry. Yes, very willingly.

Harry then took up a book; and Tommy was so eager and attentive, that at the very first lesson he learned the whole alphabet. He was infinitely pleased with his first experiment, and could scarcely forbear running to Mr Barlow to let him know the improvement he had made; but he thought he should surprise him more if he said nothing about the matter till he was able to read a whole story. He therefore applied himself with such diligence, and little Harry, who spared no pains to assist his friend, was so good a master, that in about two months he determined to surprise Mr Barlow with a display of his talents. Accordingly one day, when they were all assembled in the summerhouse, and the book was given to Harry, Tommy stood and said that, if Mr Barlow pleased, he would try to read.—'Oh, very willingly,' said Mr Barlow; 'but I should as soon expect you to fly as to read!' Tommy smiled with a consciousness of his own proficiency, and, taking up the book, read with fluency—

The History of the Two Dogs

In a part of the world, where there are many strong and fierce wild beasts, a poor man happened to bring up two puppies of that kind which is most valued for size and courage. As they appeared to possess more than common strength and agility, he thought that he should make an acceptable present to his landlord, who was a rich man living in a great city, by giving him one of them, called Jowler; while he brought up the other, named Keeper, to guard his own flocks.

From this time the manner of living was entirely altered between the brother whelps. Jowler was sent into a plentiful kitchen, where he quickly became the favourite of all the servants, who diverted themselves with his little tricks and wanton gambols, and rewarded him with great quantities of pot-liquor and broken victuals; by which means, as he was stuffing from morning till night, he increased considerably in size, and grew sleek and comely. He was, indeed, rather unwieldy, and so cowardly that he would run away from a dog only half as big as himself. He was also much addicted to gluttony, and was often beaten for the thefts he committed in the pantry; but as he had learned to fawn upon the footmen, and would stand upon his hind legs to beg when he was ordered, and besides this, would fetch and carry, he was much caressed by all the neighbourhood.

Keeper, in the meantime, who lived at a cottage in the country, neither fared so well, looked so plump, nor had learned all these pretty little tricks to recommend him: but as his master was too poor to maintain anything that was not useful, and was obliged to be always in the air, subject to all sorts of weather, and labouring hard for a livelihood, Keeper grew hardy, active, and diligent. He was also exposed to incessant danger from the wolves, from whom he had received many a severe bite while guarding the flocks. These continual combats gave him such intrepidity, that no enemy could make him turn his back. His care and assiduity so well defended the sheep of his master, that not one had ever been missing since they were placed under his protection. His honesty too was so great, that no temptation could overpower it; and though he was left alone in the kitchen while the meat was roasting, he never attempted to taste it, but received with thankfulness whatever his master chose to give him. From living always in the air he had become so hardy, that no tempest could drive him to shelter when he ought to be employed in watching the flocks; and he would plunge into the most rapid river in the coldest weather of the winter at the slightest sign from his master.

About this time it happened that the landlord of the poor man went to examine his estate in the country, and brought Jowler with him to the place of his birth. On his arrival there, he could not help viewing with great contempt the rough, ragged appearance of Keeper, and his awkward look, which discovered nothing of the address he so much admired in Jowler. This opinion, however, was altered by means of an accident which happened to him. As he was one day walking in a thick wood, with no other company than the two dogs, a hungry wolf, with eyes that sparkled like fire, bristling hair, and a horrid snarl that made the gentleman tremble, rushed out of a neighbouring thicket, and seemed ready to devour him. The unfortunate man gave himself over for lost, especially when he saw that his faithful Jowler, instead of coming to his assistance, ran sneaking away, with his tail between his legs, howling with fear. But in this moment of despair the undaunted Keeper, who had followed him humbly and unobserved at a distance, flew to his assistance, and attacked the wolf with so much courage and skill, that he was compelled to exert all his strength in his own defence. The battle was long and bloody; but in the end Keeper laid the wolf dead at his feet, though not without receiving several severe wounds himself, and presenting a bloody and mangled spectacle to the eyes of his master, who came up at that instant. The gentleman was filled with joy for his escape, and gratitude to his valiant deliverer; having learned by his own experience that appearances are not always to be trusted, and that great virtues and good dispositions may sometimes be found in cottages, while they may be totally wanting among the great.

'Very well, indeed,' said Mr Barlow; 'I find that when young gentlemen choose to take pains, they can do things almost, perhaps quite, as well as other people. But what do you say to the story you have been reading, Tommy? Would you rather have owned the genteel dog that left his master to be devoured, or the poor, rough, ragged, meagre, neglected cur, that exposed his own life in his defence?'—'Indeed, sir,' said Tommy, 'I would rather have had Keeper; but then I would have fed him, and washed him, and combed him, till he had looked as well as Jowler.'—'But, then, perhaps, he would have grown idle, and fat, and cowardly, like him,' said Mr Barlow: 'but here is some more of it; let us read to the end of the story.' Tommy then went on thus:—

The gentleman was so pleased with the noble behaviour of Keeper, that he requested the poor man to make him a present of the dog. With this request, though with some reluctance, the farmer complied. Keeper was therefore taken to the city, where he was caressed and fed by everybody; and the disgraced Jowler was left at the cottage, with strict injunctions to the man to hang him up as a worthless, unprofitable cur.

As soon as the gentleman had departed, the poor man was going to execute his commission; but considering the noble size and comely look of the dog, and, above all, being moved with pity for the poor animal, who wagged his tail and licked his new master's feet just as he was putting the cord about his neck, he determined to spare his life, and see whether a different treatment might not produce different manners. From this day Jowler was in every respect treated as his brother Keeper had been before. He was fed but scantily; and, from this spare diet, he soon grew more active and fond of exercise. The first shower he was in he ran away, as he had been accustomed to do, and sneaked to the fireside; but the farmer's wife soon drove him out of doors, and compelled him to bear the rigour of the weather. In consequence of this, he daily became more vigorous and hardy, and in a few months regarded cold and rain no more than though he had been brought up in the country.

Changed as he already was in many respects for the better, he still retained an insurmountable dread of wild beasts; till one day, as he was wandering through a wood alone, he was attacked by a large and fierce wolf, who, jumping out of a thicket, seized him by the neck with fury. Jowler would fain have run, but his enemy was too swift and violent to suffer him to escape. Necessity makes even cowards brave. Jowler, being thus stopped in his retreat, turned upon his enemy, and, very luckily seizing him by the throat, strangled him in an instant. His master then coming up, and having witnessed his exploit, praised him, and stroked him with a degree of fondness he had never done before. Animated by this victory, and by the approbation of his master, Jowler, from that time, became as brave as he had before been pusillanimous; and there was very soon no dog in the country who was so great a terror to beasts of prey.

In the meantime, Keeper, instead of hunting wild beasts or looking after sheep, did nothing but eat and sleep, which he was permitted to do from a remembrance of his past services. As all qualities both of mind and body are lost, if not continually exercised, he soon ceased to be that hardy, courageous animal he was before; and he acquired all the faults which are the consequences of idleness and gluttony.

About this time the gentleman went again into the country, and taking his dog with him, was willing that he should exercise his prowess once more against his ancient enemies the wolves. Accordingly, the country-people having quickly found one in a neighbouring wood, the gentleman went thither with Keeper, expecting to see him behave as he had done the year before. But how great was his surprise when, at the first onset, he saw his beloved dog run away with every mark of timidity! At this moment another dog sprang forward, and seizing the wolf with the greatest intrepidity, after a bloody contest left him dead upon the ground. The gentleman could not help lamenting the cowardice of his favourite, and admiring the noble spirit of the other dog, whom, to his infinite surprise, he found to be the same Jowler that he had discarded the year before. 'I now see', said he to the farmer, 'that it is vain to expect courage in those who live a life of indolence and repose; and that constant exercise and proper discipline are frequently able to change contemptible characters into good ones.'

'Indeed,' said Mr Barlow, when the story was ended, 'I am sincerely glad to find that Tommy has made this acquisition. He will now depend upon nobody, but be able to divert himself whenever he pleases. All that has ever been written in our own language will be from this time in his power; whether he may choose to read little entertaining stories such as we have heard today, or to learn the actions of great and good men in history, or to make himself acquainted with the nature of wild beasts and birds which are found in other countries, and have been described in books. In short, I hardly know of anything that from this moment will not be in his power; and I do not despair of one day seeing him a very sensible man, capable of teaching and instructing others.'

'Yes,' said Tommy, something elated by all this praise, 'I am determined now to make myself as clever as anybody; and I don't doubt, though I am such a little fellow, that I know more already than many grown-up people; and I am sure, though there are now fewer than six blacks in our house, there is not one of them who can read a story as I can.' Mr Barlow looked a little grave at this sudden display of vanity; and said rather coolly, 'Pray, who has attempted to teach them anything?'—'Nobody, I believe,' said Tommy. 'Where is the great wonder, then, if they are ignorant?' replied Mr Barlow; 'you would probably have never known anything had you not been assisted; and even now, you know very little.'

In this manner did Mr Barlow begin the education of Tommy Merton, who had naturally very good dispositions, although he had been suffered to acquire many bad habits, which sometimes prevented them from appearing.

LADY ELEANOR FENN (1743–1813)
From *Cobwebs to Catch Flies; or, Dialogues in Short Sentences, Adapted to Children From the Age of Three to Eight Years* (Two volumes, *c.* 1783)

Lady Fenn's dialogues are 'in words of three, four, five, and six letters' for 'children from three to five years of age' in volume one, and 'in words of one, two, three, and four syllables' for children from five to eight in volume two. In the Dedication Lady Fenn describes herself as 'mistress of the infantine language', and as one who did not 'blush to supply prattle for infants'. She dedicated the book to 'fond mothers', and hoped that 'the mother who herself watches the dawn of reason in her babe, who teaches him the first rudiments of knowledge, who infuses the first ideas in his mind, will approve my *Cobwebs.'* Although Lady Fenn and her antiquarian husband, the first editor of the *Paston* *Letters*, were childless, she wrote grammars and miscellanies for the young, in addition to this gently instructive reader .

The Stubborn Child (Volume II)

Mr Steady was walking with his little son, when he met a boy with a satchel on his shoulder crying and sobbing dismally. Mr Steady accosted him, kindly inquiring what was the matter.

Mr Steady. Why do you cry?

Boy. They send me to school, and I do not like it.

Mr Steady. You are a silly boy; what! would you play all day?

Boy. Yes, I would.

Mr Steady. None but babies do that; your friends are very kind to you. If they have not time to teach you themselves, then it is their duty to send you where you may be taught, but you must take pains yourself, else you will be a dunce.

Little Steady. Pray, may I give him my book of fables out of my pocket?

Mr Steady. Do, my dear.

Little Steady. Here it is—it will teach you to do as you are bid—I am never happy when I have been naughty; are you happy?

Boy. I cannot be happy; no person loves me.

Little Steady. Why?

Mr Steady. I can tell you why; because he is not good.

Boy. I wish I was good.

Mr Steady. Then try to be so; it is easy; you have only to do as your parents and friends desire you.

Boy. But why should I go to school?

Mr Steady. Good children ask for no reasons—a wise child knows that his parents can best judge what is proper; and unless they choose to explain the reason of their orders, he trusts that they have a good one; and he obeys without inquiry.

Little Steady. I will not say Why, again, when I am told what to do; but I will always do as I am bid directly.—Pray, sir, tell the story of Miss Wilful.

Mr Steady. Miss Wilful came to stay a few days with me. Now she knew that I always would have children obey me; so she did as I bade her; but she did not always do a thing as soon as she was spoken to, but would often whine out, Why? That always seems to me like saying, I think I am as wise as you are; and I would disobey you if I durst.

One day I saw Miss Wilful going to play with a dog, with which I knew it was not proper for her to meddle: and I said, Let that dog alone. Why? said Miss. I play with Wag, and I play with Phillis, and why may I not play with Pompey?

I made her no answer; but thought she might feel the reason soon.

Now the dog had been ill-used by a girl who was so naughty as to make a sport of holding meat to his mouth, and snatching it away again: which made him take meat roughly, and always be surly to girls.

Soon after, Miss stole to the dog, held out her hand as if she had meat for him, and then snatched it away again. The creature resented this treatment, and snapped at her fingers.—When I met her crying, with her hand wrapped in a napkin, So, said I, you have been meddling with the dog. Now you know why I bade you let Pompey alone.

Little Steady. Did she not think you were unkind not to pity her? I thought (do not be displeased, papa) but I thought it was strange that you did not comfort her.

Mr Steady. You know that her hand was not very much hurt, and the wound had been dressed when I met her.

Little Steady. Yes, papa, but she was so sorry.

Mr Steady. She was not so sorry for her fault as for its consequences.

Little Steady. Papa!

Mr Steady. Her concern was for the pain which she felt in her fingers not for the fault which had occasioned it.

Little Steady. She was very naughty, I know, for she said that she would get a pair of thick gloves, and then she would tease Pompey.

Mr Steady. Naughty girl! how ill-disposed! Then my lecture was lost upon her. I bade her, whilst she felt the smart, resolve to profit by Pompey's lesson; and learn to believe, that her friends might have good reason for their orders, though they did not think it proper always to acquaint her with them.

Little Steady. I once cut myself with a knife which I had not leave to take, and when I see the scar, I always consider that I ought not to have taken the knife.

Mr Steady. That, I think, is the school-house; now go in, and be good.

MARY WOLLSTONECRAFT (1759–97)
From *Original Stories from Real Life* (1788)

In the same year as the publication of Wollstonecraft's *Mary: A Fiction* her radical publisher, Joseph Johnson, issued the book for children he had commissioned her to write: *Original Stories from Real Life*. This was two years before the appearance of her

Vindication of the Rights of Men (1790), and four years earlier than her famous feminist manifesto, *A Vindication of the Rights of Woman* (1792). Wollstonecraft, even at this early stage of her writing, made a compelling case for the exercise of reason in the upbringing of children. According to her Preface, 'the author attempts to cure those faults by reason which ought never to have taken root in the infant mind.' Wollstonecraft's aesthetic was always purposeful; as she remarked in a letter about this time, 'intellectual and moral improvement seem to me so connected I cannot, even in thought, separate them.' The influence of Locke and Rousseau is vital to her concept of improvement. As a reformist through education, Wollstonecraft believed that 'knowledge should be gradually imparted, and flow more from example than teaching: example directly addresses the senses, the first inlet to the heart, the object education should have constantly in view and over which we have most power.' Her rational dame in *Original Stories* is Mrs Mason, a widow whose only child, a daughter, is dead. In 'fix[ing] principles of truth and humanity' for her two charges, Caroline and Mary, Mrs Mason does not coddle, but makes every incident informative. Coming upon two wounded birds, she promptly draws the girls' attention to the fact that these animals are suffering more than her charges did when they had smallpox, decides that one bird can be helped, and abruptly turns her heel on the other's head to 'put it out of pain'. In his illustration for the 1791 edition, Blake depicted Mrs Mason in a cruciform pose, which also suggested the protective shadow of her wings (Psalms 36. 7). Later in her life, as the mother of two daughters (one of them the future Mary Shelley), Wollstonecraft—like Mrs Mason—continued in her fiction of ideas to adhere to the preeminence of virtue in the moral hierarchy.

Chapter VII

Virtue the Soul of Beauty—The Tulip and the Rose—The Nightingale—
External Ornaments—Characters

The next morning Mrs Mason met them first in the garden; and she desired Caroline to look at a bed of tulips, that were then in their highest state of perfection. I, added she, choose to have every kind of flower in my garden, as the succession enables me to vary my daily prospect, and gives it the charm of variety; yet these tulips afford me less pleasure than most others I cultivate—and I will tell you why—they are only beautiful. Listen to my distinctions;—good features, and a fine complexion, I term *bodily* beauty. Like the streaks of the tulips they please the eye for a moment; but this uniformity soon tires, and the active mind flies off to something else. The soul of beauty, my dear children, consists in the body gracefully exhibiting the emotions and variations of the informing mind. If truth, humanity, and knowledge inhabit the breast, the eyes will beam with a mild lustre, modesty will suffuse the cheeks; and smiles of innocent joy play over all the features. At first sight regularity and color will attract, and have the advantage; because the hidden springs are not directly set in motion; but when internal goodness is reflected, every other kind of beauty, the shadow of it, withers away before it—as the sun obscures a lamp.

You are certainly handsome, Caroline: I mean, have good features; but you must improve your mind to give them a pleasing expression, or they will only serve to lead your understanding astray. I have seen some foolish people take great pains to decorate the outside of their houses, to attract the notice of strangers, who gazed, and passed on; while the inside, where they were to receive their friends, was dark and inconvenient. Apply this observation to mere personal attractions; they may, for a few years, charm the superficial part of your acquaintance, whose notions of beauty are not built on any principles. Such persons might look at you, as they would glance their eye over these tulips, and feel for a moment, the same pleasure that a view of the variegated rays of light would convey to an uninformed mind. The lower class of mankind, and children, are fond of finery; gaudy, dazzling appearances catch their attention; but the discriminating judgment of a person of sense, requires, besides color, order, proportion, grace and usefulness, to render the idea of beauty complete.

Observe the rose, it has all the perfections I speak of; color, grace, and sweetness—and even when the fine tints fade, the smell is grateful to those who have before contemplated its beauties. I have only one bed of tulips, though my garden is large, but, in every part of it, roses catch your sight.

You have seen Mrs B, and think her a very fine woman; yet her complexion has only the clearness that temperance gives; and her features, strictly speaking, are not regular: Betty, the house-maid, has, in both these respects, much the superiority over her. But, though you cannot at once define in what her beauty consists, your eye follows her whenever she moves; and every person of taste listens for the modulated sounds which proceed out of her mouth, to be improved and pleased. It is conscious worth, *truth*, that gives dignity to her walk, and simple elegance to her conversation. She has, indeed, a most excellent understanding, and a feeling heart; sagacity and tenderness, the result of both, are happily blended in her countenance;

and taste is the polish, which makes them appear to the best advantage. She *is* really beautiful; and you see her varied excellencies again and again, with increasing pleasure. They are not obtruded on you, for knowledge has taught her true humility: she is not like the flaunting tulip, that forces itself forward into notice; but resembles the modest rose, you see yonder, retiring under its elegant foliage.

I have mentioned flowers—the same order is observed in the higher departments of nature. Think of the birds; those that sing best, have not the finest plumage; indeed just the contrary; God divides His gifts, and amongst the feathered race the nightingale (sweetest of warblers, who pours forth her varied strain when sober eve comes on) you would seek in vain in the morning, if you expected that beautiful feathers should point out the songstress: many who incessantly chatter, and are only tolerable in the general concert, would surpass her, and attract your attention.

I knew, some time before you were born, a very fine, a very handsome girl; I saw she had abilities, and I saw with pain that she attended to the most obvious, but least valuable gift of heaven. Her ingenuity slept, while she tried to render her person more alluring. At last she caught the smallpox—her beauty vanished, and she was for a time miserable; but the natural vivacity of youth overcame her unpleasant feelings. In consequence of the disorder, her eyes became so weak that she was obliged to sit in a dark room; to beguile the tedious day she applied to music, and made a surprising proficiency. She even began to think, in her retirement, and when she recovered her sight grew fond of reading.

Large companies did not amuse her, she was no longer the object of admiration, or if she was taken notice of, it was to be pitied, to hear her former self praised, and to hear them lament the depredation that dreadful disease had made in a fine face. Not expecting or wishing to be observed, she lost her affected airs, and attended to the conversation, in which she was soon able to bear a part. In short, the desire of pleasing took a different turn, and as she improved her mind, she discovered that virtue, internal beauty, was valuable on its own account, and not like that of the person, which resembles a toy, that pleases the observer, but does not make the possessor happy.

She found, that in acquiring knowledge, her mind grew tranquil, and the noble desire of acting conformably to the will of God succeeded, and drove out the immoderate vanity which before actuated her, when her equals were the objects she thought most of, and whose approbation she sought with such eagerness. And what had she sought? to be stared at and called handsome. Her beauty, the sight of it did not make others good, or comfort the afflicted; but after she had lost it, she was comfortable herself, and set her friends the most useful example.

The money that formerly she appropriated to ornament her person, now clothed the naked; yet she really appeared better dressed, as she had acquired the habit of employing her time to the best advantage, and could make many things herself. Besides, she did not implicitly follow the reigning fashion, for she had learned to distinguish, and in the most trivial matters acted according to the dictates of good sense.

The children made some comments on this story, but the entrance of a visitor interrupted the conversation, and they ran about the garden, comparing the roses and tulips.

PRISCILLA WAKEFIELD (1751–1832)

From *Mental Improvement; or, The Beauties and Wonders of Nature and Art, conveyed in a series of Instructive Conversations* (1794)

Priscilla Wakefield wrote sixteen books of instructive amusement for children. Many of her popular texts, early manuals of home schooling that combined factual and scientific information with domestic realities, had several editions. The mother of five children (two sons and a daughter surviving to adulthood), Wakefield, a Quaker, turned to writing at age forty; as she admitted in her *Journal*, 'Necessity obliges me to write' (14 October 1799) since her husband's financial gambles continued to jeopardize the family's security. Although she never ventured from home, Wakefield read widely on a range of topics and wrote knowledgeably about Continental, Asian, African, and North American travel. Through the narrative device of family conversations, her natural histories introduced youngsters to classification systems of plants and animals. In *Reflections on the Present Condition of the Female Sex* (1798), Wakefield presented enlightened views about women's education, arguing for economic independence and equal pay for women. The nineteen conversations in *Mental Improvement* (1794, 1797), which take place in the Harcourt home, involve both parents, their two daughters, two sons, and a young visitor; the children's ages range from nine to sixteen. They talk about microscopes, telescopes, and compasses; they are eager to learn—from their parents and one another—about the manufacture of linen, silk, rubber, and chocolate. Such fertile curiosity prompts Ann Shteir to label the book 'a marker in the history of women's popular science writing.' As the following conversation about the sugar industry and the slave trade illustrates, science, politics, and morality are blended together in this improving discourse.

Conversation 10

Henry. May I be allowed to chuse a subject for this evening. I want to know what sugar is made of. I heard Mr Jenkins say it was a salt, and I think he must be mistaken, for I cannot taste the least flavour of salt in it.

Mr Harcourt. Chemically considered, he is in the right. Sugar is a sweet, agreeable, saline juice, expressed from many different kinds of vegetables. Carrots, parsnips, white and red beets yield sugar, but the plant, from which the sugar, that is generally used, is procured, is the sugar-cane; a sort of reed that grows in great plenty, in both the East and West-Indies. Sophia, endeavour to give us a botanical definition of it.

Sophia. It is a genus of the *trianda digynia* class. Its characters are, that it has no empalement; but instead of it, a wooly down longer than the flower that incloses it. The flower is bivalve, the valves are oblong, acute pointed, concave, and chaffy. It has three hairs like stamina, the ends of the valves terminated by oblong summits; and an awl-shaped germen, supporting two rough styles, crowned by single stigmas, the germen becomes an oblong, acute pointed seed, invested by the valves. It is cultivated in both the Indies for its juice, which when boiled, affords that sweet salt which is called sugar.

Mr Harcourt. The canes grow from eight to twenty feet high, they are jointed, and at each joint are placed leaves. They are propagated by cuttings, which are generally taken from the tops of the canes, just below the leaves; a deep soil and light land are most suitable to the sugar-plant, and the rainy season is the proper time for planting it. The ground should be marked out by a line, that the canes may be regularly disposed, and at equal distances. The common method of planting them, is to make a trench with a hoe, which is performed by the hand; into this trench a negro drops the number of cuttings intended to be planted, which are planted by other negroes, who follow him: and the earth is drawn about the hills with a hoe.

Charles. I fancy agriculture is not so well understood in the Indies, as it is in Europe: or they would make use of the plough in these operations; as it would perform the work both more expeditiously, and in a completer manner, than can be done by the hand. What length of time and what multitudes of hands, would it occupy, to hoe up all the land of England, that is to be sowed with corn every season!

Mr Harcourt. Horses are very scarce in the West-Indies especially, and almost all laborious operations are performed by the hands of negro slaves.

Augusta. Are those countries inhabited by negroes? I understood that they were the natives of Africa.

Mr Harcourt. You were rightly informed, my dear, they are indeed natives of Africa, but snatched from their own country, friends, and connections, by the hand of violence, and power. I am ashamed to confess that many ships are annually sent from different parts of England, particularly Bristol and Liverpool, to the coast of Guinea, to procure slaves from that unhappy country, for the use of our West-India islands, where they are sold to the planters of sugar-plantations, in an open market like cattle, and afterwards employed in the most laborious and servile occupations, and pass the rest of their lives in an involuntary and wretched slavery.

Sophia. How much my heart feels for them! How terrible must it be to be separated from one's near relations! Parents perhaps divided from their children for ever; husbands from their wives; brothers and sisters obliged to take an eternal farewell. Why do the kings of the African states suffer their subjects to be so cruelly treated?

Mrs Harcourt. Many causes have operated to induce the African princes to become assistants in this infamous traffic, and instead of being the defenders of their harmless people, they have frequently betrayed them to their cruellest enemies. The Europeans have found the means of corrupting these ignorant rulers, with bribes of rum and other spirituous liquors, of which they are immoderately fond. At other times they have fomented jealousies, and excited wars between them, merely for the sake of obtaining the prisoners of war for slaves. Frequently they use no ceremony, but go on shore in the night, set fire to a neighbouring village and seize upon all the unhappy victims, who run out to escape the flames.

Cecilia. What hardened hearts must the captains of those ships have! They must have become extremely cruel before they would undertake such an employment.

Mrs Harcourt. It is much to be feared that most of them, by the habits of such a life, are become deaf to the voice of pity; but we must compassionate the situation of those, whose parents have early bred them to this profession, before they were of an age to chuse a different employment. But to resume the subject of the negroes. What I have related is only the beginning of their sorrows. When they are put on board the ships, they are crowded together in the hold, where many of them mostly die from want of air and room. There have been frequent instances of their throwing themselves into the sea, when they could find an opportunity, and seeking a refuge from their misfortunes in death. As soon as they arrive in the West-Indies, they are carried to a public market, where they are sold to the best bidder, like horses at our fairs. Their future lot depends much upon the disposition of the master, into whose hands they happen to fall, for among the overseers of sugar plantations there are some men of feeling and humanity; but too generally their treatment is very severe. Accustomed to an inactive indolent life, in the luxurious and plentiful country of Africa, they find great hardship from the transition to a life of severe labour, without any mixture of indulgence to soften it. Deprived of hope of amending their condition, by any course of conduct they can pursue, they frequently abandon themselves to despair, and die, in what is called the seasoning, which is becoming inured by length of time to their situation. Those who have less sensibility and stronger constitutions, survive their complicated misery but a few years: for it is generally acknowledged that they seldom attain the full period of human life.

Augusta. Humanity shudders at your account; but I have heard a gentleman, that had lived many years abroad, say, that negroes were not much superior to the brutes, and that they were so stupid and stubborn, that nothing but stripes and severity could have any influence over them.

Mr Harcourt. That gentleman was most probably interested in misleading those with whom he conversed. People, who argue in that manner, do not consider the disadvantages the poor negroes suffer from want of cultivation. Leading an ignorant savage life in their own country, they can have acquired no previous information: and when they fall into the hands of their cruel oppressors, a life of laborious servitude, which scarcely affords them sufficient time for sleep, deprives them of every opportunity of improving their minds. There is no reason to suppose that they differ from us in anything but colour, which distinction arises from the intense heat of their climate. There have been instances of a few, whose situation has been favourable to improvement, that have shewn no inferiority of capacity: and those masters, who neglect the religious and moral instruction of their slaves, add a heavy load of guilt to that already incurred, by their share in this unjust and inhuman traffic.

Charles. My indignation arises at this recital. Why does not the British parliament exert its power, to avenge the wrongs of these oppressed Africans? What can prevent an act being passed to forbid Englishmen from buying and selling slaves?

Mr Harcourt. Mr Wilberforce,* a name that does honour to his humanity, has made several fruitless efforts to obtain an act for the abolition of this trade. Men, interested in its continuance, have hitherto frustrated his noble design; but we may rely upon the goodness of that Divine Providence, that careth for all creatures, that the day will come, that their rights will be considered and there is great reason to hope, from the light already cast upon the subject, that the rising generation will prefer justice and mercy, to interest and policy: and will free themselves from the odium we at present suffer, of treating our fellow-creatures in a manner unworthy of them, and of ourselves.* [Leader of the abolitionist forces in parliament, Wilberforce shepherded passage of the bill for gradual abolition of the slave trade, which received royal assent in 1807.]

Mrs Harcourt. Henry, repeat that beautiful apostrophe to a negro woman, which you learned the other day out of Mrs Barbauld's *Hymns.** [see chapter 7]

Henry. 'Negro woman, who sittest pining in captivity, and weepest over thy sick child, though no one seeth thee, God seeth thee, though no one pitieth thee, God pitieth thee. Raise thy voice, forlorn, and abandoned one; call upon him from amidst thy bonds, for assuredly he will hear thee.'

Cecilia. I think no riches could tempt me to have any share in the slave-trade. I could never enjoy peace of mind, whilst I thought I contributed to the woes of my fellow-creatures.

Mr Harcourt. But Cecilia, to put your compassion to the proof; are you willing to debar yourself of the many indulgences that we enjoy, that are the fruit of their labour? Sugar, coffee, rice, calico, rum, and many other things, are procured by the sweat of their brow.

Cecilia. I would forego any indulgence to alleviate their sufferings.

The rest of the Children together. We are all of the same mind.

Mrs Harcourt. I admire the sensibility of your uncorrupted hearts, my dear children. It is the voice of nature and virtue. Listen to is on all occasions, and bring it home to your bosoms, and your daily practice. The same principle of benevolence, which excites your just indignation at the oppression of the negroes, will lead you to be gentle towards your inferiors, kind and obliging to your equals, and in a particular manner condescending and considerate towards your domestics; requiring no more of them, than you would be willing to perform in their situation; instructing them when you have opportunity; sympathizing in their afflictions, and promoting their best interests when in your power.

DOROTHY KILNER (1755–1836)

From *The Village School; or, a Collection of Entertaining Histories for the Instruction and Amusement of all Good Children* (two volumes, c. 1795)

Sister-in-law of Mary Ann Kilner, Dorothy Kilner adopted the pseudonym of Mary Pelham, or occasionally M. P. (for the village of Maryland Point, near Stratford, in Essex, where she lived). Kilner was adept at injecting elements of pathos into her tales. The popular two-volume *Life and Perambulation of a Mouse* (1783–4), told from the point of view of a venturesome mouse narrator, comments on human tortures of mice, among other foibles; the tale begins with the death in a mousetrap of one of the narrator's brothers. Kilner admits that she 'never heard a mouse speak', yet she created these voices 'as being far more entertaining, and not less instructive, than [her] own life would have been.' Kilner was also a fine ironist. One of her most believable children is Maria, who is supposed to be instructed by Mamma in *First Principles of Religion* (1795); no model of docile submission, this child asks the questions and often backs her mother into a corner. A similar blend of improvement and diversion is evident in *The Village School*, although here Kilner's characters are little more than cardboard personifications of their names or social stations. In Mrs Bell's school in the village of Rose Green, she teaches boys and girls to read. Her pupils are not paragons, but every one of their indiscretions—including the gruesomeness of accidental death—is an object lesson. Kilner clearly enjoyed histrionics: at the close of volume two, Mrs Bell herself goes up in flames, when the shirt she is making for a sick neighbour whom she visits catches a spark from her candle, with the result that the neighbour's wooden house and thatched roof are instantly ablaze.

Chapter VII.

A little before two o'clock, Mrs *Bell's* scholars all set off from their different homes to return to school, and as most of them lived pretty near together, they generally met in the way to school.

At one end of the village which they were to pass before they got to Mrs *Bell's*, there was a well, bricked round about as high as a stool; but though there certainly ought to have been a cover to the top of the well, there was not; yet, though it was so dangerous a place as you shall hear it proved, the children used very often to sit down to play, or rest themselves there. As they were going along, *Jemmy Flint*, a boy about three or four years old, got some stones in his shoes, and he ran first to sit upon the side of the well to take his shoes off, and shake the stones out. *Roger Riot*, who saw him sitting, ran to him with a design of frightening him, by making him believe he would put him down; but happening to run against him, and push him harder than he intended, he did throw him down in earnest, and into the well poor little *Jemmy* tumbled. All the children ran as fast as they could when they saw him fall, in hope of being able to help him up again; but the water was low, and they could not possibly reach him, though they saw the poor little fellow struggling and wanting assistance. They then ran back again to their houses calling for somebody to come and help *Jemmy*! Come and help little *Jemmy*!

Poor Mrs *Flint* and all the neighbours made as much haste as they possibly could to the well, but before they got there, the child was sunk to the bottom, and when at last they got him up, he was quite dead. His mother took him in her arms, and kissed his cold little wet face, whilst her tears dropped upon him. Just as she had carried him in doors, his sister, a little girl about seven years old, returned from an errand she had been sent upon. When she saw her brother in her mother's arms looking so pale, she inquired what was the matter with him? 'Our dear little *Jemmy*, said her mother, tumbled down the well, and is drowned, and he will never speak to us any more.' Upon hearing which *Patty*, who was so very fond of her brother, burst into tears, and said, Oh! What shall I do for my *Jemmy*! She then ran to him, as her mother laid him on the bed, and kissing his wet cheeks, called out *Jemmy*! brother! wake, and open your eyes! What shall I do without you? I love you dearly, and want you to talk to me, to play and run about with me. Oh! my dear, said her mother, he will never talk or run about with you again, for he is dead. But perhaps, said *Patty*, if he were to be wiped dry and warmed, he would come to life; so she pulled off his cloaths, and warmed his night shift and night cap, and put them on, and covered him with the bed-cloaths; but all her care was of no service, as he was quite dead before they got him out of the well.

The next evening Mr *Right* buried him, and all the children of the village were at the funeral. *Roger Riot*, who was amongst them, cried very much, as well he might when he thought of the mischief he had done, and the sorrow he had occasioned poor Mrs *Flint* and her daughter *Patty*, who loved *Jemmy* dearly, because he was a good boy, and they therefore did not like to part from him.

After he was buried, Mr *Right* took *Roger Riot* by the hand, and talked a great deal to him. 'Do not you remember, said he, when you ran after the girls in my field, that I told you how naughty it was to try to tease people, and that you should never do anything without thinking whether what you are going to do is right? And now, by not minding my advice, you have killed one of your play-fellows. Do you consider how wicked it is to kill people? And that those who do so must be hanged? Should you like to be hanged?' Indeed, indeed, Sir, I did not do it for the purpose, replied *Roger*, I always loved *Jemmy Flint*, and would not have hurt him upon any account, if I could have helped it. I am sure I did not mean to drown him.'

'What then did you mean to do?' said Mr *Right*. 'Only to play with, and frighten him,' answered *Roger*. 'And do you like to be frightened? replied Mr *Right*. Do you think that was pretty play, to wish to tease and terrify a poor little boy less than yourself? It is a foolish ill-natured, very wrong thing, to try to frighten any body; you do not know what mischief it may do; sometimes it makes people so sick, that they never get well as long as they live; sometimes it quite kills them; but if it happens not to do so much harm, it is still very *disagreeable*, and we should never do anything that is disagreeable to any body; but should take particular care not to do anything that may make people uneasy or hurt them; and had you minded these rules you would not have knocked poor little *Jemmy* into the well.'

Roger Riot stood very quietly to hear all that Mr *Right* said to him, and then promising to be more careful of his behaviour for the future, walked home very gravely, where he staid the rest of the evening without playing; for he thought so much about little *Jemmy*, that he had no inclination to play or talk. I hope this will be a warning to all children, neither to go too near the water, nor to push or drive one another about without seeing whither they are going, or how much they may hurt one another.

View of M.ʳˢ Bell's School-Houſe at
Roſe - Green.

MARIA EDGEWORTH (1768–1849)
'The Purple Jar' from *Early Lessons* (1801)

Author of over thirty books, including many triple-deckers, Maria Edgeworth was, in Marilyn Butler's estimate, 'the most celebrated and successful of practising English novelists' in the early nineteenth century. Though born in England, the eldest daughter of Richard Lovell Edgeworth, she spent most of her long life in Ireland, as accountant of her father's land holdings at Edgeworthtown, County Longford, as teacher to many younger siblings (eighteen of Richard Lovell's twenty-two children from his four marriages survived to adulthood), and as amanuensis to her father. Ireland is the setting of her first novel, the comic masterpiece, *Castle Rackrent* (1800), and *The Absentee* (1812) and *Ormond* (1817). Although Edgeworth's comfort-

able circumstances meant that she was not forced to earn a living through writing, she was immensely popular. Sir Walter Scott, who admired her as the originator of the regional historical novel, hailed her as 'the great Maria'. Her writing for children and for adults showed a real attentiveness to the nuances of conversation, in the comedies of manners of her 'moral' novels (*Belinda* [1801], *Leonora* [1806], *Patronage* [1814], and *Helen* [1834]), in her many volumes of tales for children, and in her drama collection, *Little Plays for Young People, Warranted Harmless* (1827). 'The Purple Jar', with its autobiographical protagonist, first appeared in a collection of 'Moral Tales', in *The Parent's Assistant* (1796); Edgeworth's Preface drew the line separating fairy and giant stories and practical understanding in this question, 'why should the mind be filled with fantastic visions instead of useful knowledge?' Yet she was not unaware of the need to enliven moral precepts by making 'the stories in which they are introduced in some measure dramatic'. A skilful raconteur, Edgeworth often revealed features of her own personality in the characters of her stories; it is comforting to think that she herself might have been as impulsive as Rosamond. She pleased her young readers so much that she wrote several sequels to the 'lessons' provided by her endearingly real characters Rosamond, Harry, Lucy, and Frank. Her practical stories are grounded in the everyday experience of child minds and child nature. Mitzi Myers has labelled the Rosamond stories 'a coherent blueprint for forming a Georgian girl's mind so that she can cope with the exigencies of her culture.'

On this general theme Maria Edgeworth also wrote *Practical Education* (1798), a collaborative effort with her father; *A Rational Primer* (1799); *Moral Tales for Young People* (5 vols, 1801); and *Popular Tales* (3 vols, 1805).

The Purple Jar

Rosamond, a little girl about seven years old, was walking with her mother in the streets of London. As she passed along, she looked in at the windows of several shops, and saw a great variety of different sorts of things, of which she did not know the use, or even the names. She wished to stop to look at them, but there was a great number of people in the streets, and a great many carts, carriages, and wheelbarrows, and she was afraid to let go her mother's hand.

'O, mother; how happy I should be,' she said as she passed a toy shop, 'if I had all these pretty things!'

'What, all! Do you wish for them all, Rosamond?'

'Yes, mamma, all.'

As she spoke, they came to a milliner's shop, the windows of which were decorated with ribands and lace, and festoons of artificial flowers.

'Oh mamma, what beautiful roses! Won't you buy some of them?'

'No, my dear.'

'Why?'

'Because I don't want them, my dear.'

They went a little further, and came to another shop, which caught Rosamond's eye. It was a jeweller's shop, and in it were a great many pretty baubles, ranged in drawers behind glass.

'Mamma, will you buy some of these?'

'Which of them, Rosamond?'

'Which? I don't know which; any of them will do, for they are all pretty.'

'Yes, they are all pretty; but of what use would they be to me?'

'Use! Oh, I'm sure you could find some use or other for them if you would only buy them first.'

'But I would rather find out the use first.'

'Well, then, mamma, there are buckles; you know that buckles are useful things, very useful things.'

'I have a pair of buckles, I don't want another pair,' said her mother, and walked on. Rosamond was very sorry that her mother wanted nothing. Presently, however, they came to a shop which appeared to her far more beautiful than the rest.

It was a chemist's shop, but she did not know that.

'Oh, mother, oh!' cried she, pulling her mother's hand, 'look, look! blue, green, red, yellow, and purple! Oh, mamma, what beautiful things! Won't you buy some of these?'

Still her mother answered as before, 'Of what use would they be to me, Rosamond?'

'You might put flowers in them, mamma, and they would look so pretty on the chimney-piece. I wish I had one of them.'

'You have a flower-pot,' said her mother, 'and that is not a flower-pot.'

'But I could use it for a flower-pot, mamma, you know.'

'Perhaps, if you were to see it nearer, if you were to examine it, you might be disappointed.'

'No, indeed. I'm sure I should not; I should like it exceedingly.'

Rosamond kept her head turned to look at the purple vase, till she could see it no longer.

'Then, mother,' said she, after a pause, 'perhaps you have no money.'

'Yes, I have.'

'Dear me, if I had money I would buy roses, and boxes, and buckles, and purple flower-pots, and everything.' Rosamond was obliged to pause in the midst of her speech.

'O mamma, would you stop a minute for me? I have got a stone in my shoe, it hurts me very much.'

'How comes there to be a stone in your shoe?'

'Because of this great hole, mamma—it comes in there: my shoes are quite worn out. I wish you would be so very good as to give me another pair.'

'Nay, Rosamond, but I have not money enough to buy shoes, and flower-pots, and buckles, and boxes, and everything.'

Rosamond thought that was a great pity. But now her foot, which had been hurt by the stone, began to give her so much pain that she was obliged to hop every other step, and she could think of nothing else. They came to a shoe-maker's shop soon afterwards.

'There, there! mamma, there are shoes; there are little shoes that would just fit me, and you know shoes would be really of use to me.'

'Yes, so they would, Rosamond. Come in.' She followed her mother into the shop.

Mr Sole, the shoemaker, had a great many customers, and his shop was full, so they were obliged to wait.

'Well, Rosamond,' said her mother, 'you don't think this shop so pretty as the rest?'

'No, not nearly; it is black and dark, and there are nothing but shoes all round; and, besides, there's a very disagreeable smell.'

'That smell is the smell of new leather.'

'Is it? Oh!' said Rosamond, looking round, 'there is a pair of little shoes; they'll just fit me, I'm sure.'

'Perhaps they might; but you cannot be sure till you have tried them on, any more than you can be quite sure that you should like the purple vase *exceedingly*, till you have examined it more attentively.'

'Why, I don't know about the shoes, certainly, till I have tried; but, mamma, I am quite sure that I should like the flower-pot.'

'Well, which would you rather have, that jar, or a pair of shoes? I will buy either for you.'

'Dear mamma, thank you—but if you could buy both?'

'No, not both.'

'Then the jar, if you please.'

'But I should tell you, that in that case I shall not give you another pair of shoes this month.'

"This month! that's a very long time indeed! You can't think how these hurt me; I believe I'd better have the new shoes. Yet, that purple flower-pot. Oh, indeed, mamma, these shoes are not so very, very bad! I think I might wear them a little longer, and the month will soon be over. I can make them last till the end of the month, can't I? Don't you think so, mamma?'

'Nay, my dear, I want you to think for yourself; you will have time enough to consider the matter, whilst I speak to Mr Sole about my clogs.'

Mr Sole was by this time at leisure, and whilst her mother was speaking to him, Rosamond stood in profound meditation, with one shoe on, and the other in her hand.

'Well, my dear, have you decided?"

'Mamma!—yes,—I believe I have. If you please, I should like to have the flower-pot; that is, if you won't think me very silly, mamma.'

'Why, as to that, I can't promise you, Rosamond; but, when you have to judge for yourself, you should choose what will make you happy, and then it would not signify who thought you silly.'

'Then, mamma, if that's all, I'm sure the flower-pot would make me happy,' said she, putting on her old shoe again; 'so I choose the flower-pot.'

'Very well, you shall have it; clasp your shoe and come home.'

Rosamond clasped her shoe, and ran after her mother. It was not long before the shoe came down at the heel, and many times she was obliged to stop to take the stones out of it, and she often limped with pain; but still the thoughts of the purple flower-pot prevailed, and she persisted in her choice.

When they came to the shop with the large window, Rosamond felt much pleasure upon hearing her mother desire the servant, who was with them, to buy the purple jar, and bring it home. He had other commissions, so he did not return with them. Rosamond, as soon as she got it, ran to gather all her own flowers, which she kept in a corner of her mother's garden.

'I am afraid they'll be dead before the flower-pot comes, Rosamond,' said her mother to her, as she came in with the flowers in her lap.

'No, indeed, mamma, it will come home very soon, I dare say. I shall be very happy putting them into the purple flower-pot.'

'I hope so, my dear.'

The servant was much longer returning home than Rosamond had expected; but at length he came, and brought with him the long-wished-for jar. The moment it was set down upon the table, Rosamond ran up to it with an exclamation of joy: 'I may have it now, mamma?' 'Yes, my dear, it is yours.' Rosamond poured the flowers from her lap upon the carpet, and seized the purple flower-pot.

'Oh, dear mother!' cried she, as soon as she had taken off the top, 'But there's something dark in it which smells very disagreeably. What is it? I didn't want this black stuff.'

'Nor I, my dear.'

'But what shall I do with it, mamma?'

'That I cannot tell.'

'It will be of no use to me, mamma.'

'That I cannot help.'

'But I must pour it out, and fill the flower-pot with water.'

'As you please, my dear.'

'Will you lend me a bowl to pour it into, mamma?'

'That was more than I promised you, my dear; but I will lend you a bowl.'

The bowl was produced, and Rosamond proceeded to empty the purple vase. But she experienced much surprise and disappointment on finding, when it was entirely empty, that it was no longer a purple vase. It was a plain white glass jar, which had appeared to have that beautiful colour merely from the liquor with which it had been filled.

Little Rosamond burst into tears.

'Why should you cry, my dear?' said her mother; 'it will be of as much use to you now as ever, for a flower-pot.'

'But it won't look so pretty on the chimney-piece. I am sure, if I had known that it was not really purple, I should not have wished to have it so much.'

'But didn't I tell you that you had not examined it; and that perhaps you would be disappointed?'

'And so I am disappointed, indeed. I wish I had believed you at once. Now I had much rather have the shoes for I shall not be able to walk all this month; even walking home that little way hurt me exceedingly. Mamma, I will give you the flower-pot back again, and that purple stuff and all, if you'll only give me the shoes.'

'No, Rosamond, you must abide by your own choice, and now the best thing you can possibly do is to bear your disappointment with good humour.'

'I will bear it as well as I can,' said Rosamond, wiping her eyes, and she began slowly and sorrowfully to fill the vase with flowers.

But Rosamond's disappointment did not end here. Many were the difficulties and distresses into which her imprudent choice brought her, before the end of the month. Every day her shoes grew worse and worse, till at last she could neither run, dance, jump, or walk in them.

Whenever Rosamond was called to see anything, she was detained pulling her shoes up at the heels, and was sure to be too late. Whenever her mother was going out to walk, she could not take Rosamond with her, for Rosamond had no soles to her shoes, and at length, on the very last day of the month, it happened that her father proposed to take her with her brother to a glasshouse, which she had long wished to see. She was very happy; but, when she was quite ready, had her hat and gloves on, and was making haste down stairs to her brother and father, who were waiting for her at the hall door, the shoe dropped off. She put it on again in a great hurry, but as she was going across the hall, her father turned round. 'Why are you walking slipshod? no one must walk slip-shod with me. Why, Rosamond,' said he, looking at her shoes with disgust, 'I thought that you were always neat; go, I cannot take you with me.'

Rosamond coloured and retired. 'O mamma,' said she, as she took off her hat, 'how I wish that I had chosen the shoes! They would have been of so much more use to me than that jar: however, I am sure—no not quite sure, but I hope I shall be wiser another time.'

CATHARINE PARR TRAILL (1802–1899)
From *The Young Emigrants; or, Pictures of Canada* (1826)

Six years before her marriage to Lieutenant Traill and their emigration to Upper Canada, Catharine Strickland wrote this unique Canadian travelogue for children. It was based on accounts like John Howison's *Sketches of Upper Canada* (1821) and on letters received from friends who had already arrived in Canada. Although the author herself had not yet experienced the new land, *The Young Emigrants* foreshadows her later and famous *Backwoods of Canada* (1836) in its use of the epistolary form, and in its wealth of naturalist's lore.

Financial ruin in England forces the fictitious Clarence family to emigrate to the much-feared 'wild woods of Canada'. They settle close to Lake Ontario, in a farming community about thirty-six miles from York (Toronto). Richard and Agnes Clarence write to their sister, Ellen, who, because of ill health, has remained in England; their letters show that the Clarences, while transplanting names and customs from home, learn to appreciate a rich newness. (So too did Catharine Traill, her brother Samuel Strickland, and her sister Susanna Moodie adjust successfully to unaccustomed hardships in Canada.) As pioneers the Clarence children turn out to be sensible and hardy, informed and observant; their story is unusual as an example of informational children's fiction in which children act as the instructors.

Traill's next and more vigorous book for children, *Canadian Crusoes* (1852), combined first-hand knowledge of landscape, vegetation, and her own children with the borrowed theme of the stranded but self-reliant journeyer. About children lost in the bush who must look after themselves, it is the first distinctly Canadian Robinsonnade.

Letter V: Agnes to Ellen

Roselands, June 22
After a silence of some months, I again sit down to write to my beloved sister, assured that a letter from her absent Agnes will be welcomed with delight. With

what joy should I hail the day that made us once more inmates of the same dwelling. I think I should then be quite happy, and not have a thought or wish beyond the home I now inhabit, which is becoming dearer to me every day.

It is true, I find a great deal more to employ my hands than I have ever been accustomed to; but my labours are light. My health is good, and as my exertions conduce to the general comfort and happiness of my family, I endeavour to perform them with cheerfulness, and with a grateful heart; for how much better am I off, than many who are far more deserving than myself. Ah! dear Ellen, how thankful we ought to be, to that merciful God who has kindly watched over and preserved us from the dangers of crossing the great Atlantic, and has bestowed so many blessings on us; more, indeed, than we could possibly expect. Should we not be most ungrateful to Him, were we at any time to indulge ourselves in discontent and repining, because we cannot possess all those luxuries and enjoyments which I *once* thought so indispensable, but which I find, by experience, are not necessary for our happiness, and can very well be dispensed with.

I remember, I used once to place the utmost importance on the smartness of my dress, the fashion of my bonnet, and the shape of my gown; but now my dress is cut to the most convenient shape; and my chief study in choosing a hat, is to suit it to the different seasons of the year. And, indeed, I am quite as well pleased with my dark stuff and blue cotton gowns, and with my checked or linseywoolsey apron, as I was formerly in wearing the finest muslin or richest silk. I think I see my sister smile at my change of ideas, and hear her exclaim, 'A blue cotton gown and checked apron!' Yes, dearest Ellen, this is my winter's attire, and I am quite reconciled to wearing it. Indeed, were I to do otherwise, I should be laughed at for effecting a singularity of dress. Nor need I be ashamed of appearing in such homely apparel, when I see my neighbours, Jane and Charlotte Hamilton, who have received as good an education as myself, wearing the same. It is a general thing in this country to dress according to your circumstances, and to suit the fashion to the seasons and to your own convenience. The ladies all wear a thick, warm stuff gown, trimmed with fur, for the winter, with a blue or grey cotton for morning. Cloth pelisses are worn only by rich people, and then only in towns or cities. We, who are more humbly situated, are contented with plaids, lined with green, purple, or red baize. We have fur bonnets, tied close to the face; and fur or feather muffs and tippets. Our shoes are also lined with fur or flannel; as, when we travel during the cold season, the warmest clothing is requisite. In spring and summer we cast off our furs and wrappings, and dress as light and thin as possible; the heat being at times insupportable, during the months of July and August.

Among other useful arts, I have learned to make very pretty muffs and tippets, with feathers sewed together: they are greatly admired, and they look quite as handsome as some of the expensive furs. Flora Gordon has taught me to plat straw, and I shall try my skill in platting a cottage-bonnet for little Annie: if I succeed, I shall make a bonnet for mamma, and one for myself, as they will prove very useful to us, every article of dress being very expensive in this country. Even needles are so dear, that I am obliged to be quite miserly over my small stock: you cannot purchase one under a copper (a half-penny.) Every thing else is proportionably dear.

We have had a very pleasant winter. The snow lay, for eight weeks, to the depth of many feet. The fields, the woods, the lakes, every outward object presented the unvaried livery of nature. But though the frost was intense, I felt much less inconvenience from the cold than I had expected: thirty degrees below zero was frequently the temperature of the atmosphere. But, in spite of this cold, it is the most healthful and agreeable season of the year: no colds, no coughs. The air is clear and bracing; and the sky, for many days, continues bright and cloudless. The sun is very powerful, even when the frost is the most intense. We have had a favourable season for sleighing, which is most delightful: you seem actually to glide along over the frozen surface. The bells which are attached to the necks of the horses (to the number of eighteen each) make a pretty jingling noise; and, when accustomed to the sound, you do not like to travel without them. The roads at this season present a lively, bustling scene. You cannot go a mile from home without meeting or passing twenty or thirty sleighs or cutters; parties of gentlemen and ladies skating; and children sliding, with cheeks glowing with exercise and health. The farmers take this opportunity of carrying their corn to the mill, to be ground into flour; and to procure such articles from the more distant towns and settlements, as they cannot meet with near the homesteads (or farm-houses.) You may travel sixty or seventy miles in a sleigh, with one pair of horses, without suffering any fatigue from your journey, or any inconvenience, unless from the cold; but we wrap up so closely in our plaids and furs, leaving only a sufficient part of our faces uncovered to enable us to look about and breathe freely, that we suffer comparatively little to what might be expected.

Andrew and Flora have made many comfortable additions to our travelling attire, by knitting warm mittens and comforters, which we find very useful; for, indeed, you cannot dress too close and thick during the cold weather.

Our fireside presents a scene of equal cheerfulness to that I have described abroad. The hearth is piled with blazing faggots of pine and hickory wood, which fill the room with a delightful warmth, and seem to enliven every face as we gather round the fire. Sometimes we have an agreeable addition to our family-party in the Hamiltons: the evening is then passed in social chat or innocent gaiety. Frank Hamilton plays on the flute to us, or else we sing duets; or one of the party reads aloud, while the rest work, or play at chess, or draw. When the hour of supper arrives, Flora and I lay the cloth, and prepare our frugal meal, which consists of the finest white bread, dried venison, butter, honey, apples, and cranberry-tarts; with birch-wine, warmed in an earthen pipkin over the fire, and sweetened with maple-sugar. Such is our supper, and who would wish for greater delicacies?

In this manner passes our time till the hour of prayer, and then we summon all the household, while papa takes down the great Bible and reads a passage from the Old and New Testament, and explains the subject to us. Do you remember, dear Ellen, Burns's poem of the 'Cotter's Saturday Night?' I always think of those beautiful lines, when I see our dear papa open the sacred volume, and look round upon us with that benevolent and amiable expression that so well becomes his mild and placid features: he seems to regard us all as his children and his equals, though he is superior to us in every respect. At such times, the spirit of peace and truth seems to rest upon us, and every face beams with piety and gratitude to the Almighty, 'who has given us grace, with one accord, to make our common supplications unto him,' and who has assured us, that where two or three are gathered together in His name, there is He in the midst of them. Nor are you, my beloved sister, absent from our prayers. You are *never* forgotten by your parents, or by your own Agnes and Richard; and we never rise from our devotions without first having implored the blessing and protection of the Almighty for our own dear Ellen. Such are the amusements and employments of our winter evenings; but they are varied according to circumstances. Sometimes I spend an hour or two in instructing Flora, and I have already taught little Annie some of her letters: she is quite a pet, and is as lively and playful as a kitten. I love the little creature as though she were my younger sister. She runs after me, repeating my name in her infantine accents, calling me Miss *Annice*, for she cannot say Agnes. Flora takes great pride in her, and already talks of teaching her the use of the knitting-needles, though Annie is little more than two years old; but Flora is very notable, and says, 'Annie must not be idle.'

We are very fortunate in having such faithful and industrious domestics: both father and children seem to vie with each other in attention to our comforts, and endeavour, by every possible means, to show their gratitude for the kindness they received at our hands, when they were in sickness and distress, and without friends or any one to pity and relieve them.

Our spring commences in March; but the early part of this season is far from agreeable, and frequently unhealthy, being cold, rainy, and tempestuous. The melting of the snow is very unpleasant: the roads are then quite impassable, being very slippery and swampy. The air is over-charged with fogs and damps, owing to the exhalations which are drawn up from the earth by the rays of the sun. Towards the end of April, the ground becomes once more firm and dry: the fields begin to wear the livery of spring, though the air is still cold and damp. In May there is little vestige of ice or snow left, excepting in the hollows of the dells and dingles, where it has been sheltered from the effects of the thaw and sun. Towards the middle of May, the air becomes soft and warm; vegetation proceeds with astonishing rapidity; the fields, woods, and banks are covered with an emerald verdure; flowers and buds, of a thousand lovely hues, which have been nourished by the snow, spring up among the turf; the forest-leaves expand, and all nature seems to hail the return of spring.

It is now June, and every thing above, below, and around us, presents a scene of exquisite beauty and freshness to the eye. The fruit-trees are loaded with blossoms, and the woods are waving with an endless variety of green. Cloudless skies and continual sunshine prevail. I wish my dear Ellen were here, to enjoy with me the beauties of this most delightful season of the year.

The wild flowers here are remarkably beautiful: I send you a few sketches from nature, of my chief favourites. I have also commenced a *hortus siccus*** which will be an amusing study for us at some future time.

---

*Hortus siccus, (or, dried garden) an appellation given to a collection of specimens of plants, carefully dried and preserved. Gather handsome specimens of flowers, grasses, or mosses, and spread the leaves and petals of the flowers quite flat between sheets of blotting-paper, laying a flat board over each sheet containing your specimens, on which place a heavy weight; taking care to shift your flowers into fresh sheets of paper, at least once a day.

Perhaps it will amuse my dear Ellen to hear how I pass my time, and what are my employments. I rise in general at five o'clock, and, while Flora is milking the cows, I am in the dairy taking the cream off the milk, and making the cheese; which useful art I learned while staying at Woodley Grange, with my good friend Mrs Hartley; and I have now a dozen specimens of my skill in my cheese room, which will soon be fit for use. Twice a week we churn, and Flora assists me in making the butter. As soon as the business of the dairy is over, I fill my apron with dross corn, and, attended by my little maid Flora, bearing a pitcher of clear water in her hand, I go to my poultry-yard, where I am greeted by fowls of all sorts and sizes, which run and fly to meet me, eager to receive their breakfasts from my hand. I have some favourites among my fowls, especially one chicken with a cross-bill, which attracted my attention on account of the slow progress she made in picking; so I took her under my protection, and now she is so fond of me, she flies into my lap and picks out of my hand, and seems, by her caresses, to be quite sensible of my regard for her. The foxes abound so in the woods, that it is with difficulty I can preserve any of my fowls from their depredations. Last week I had four young broods of nice little chickens, thirty-eight in the whole; and now I have only two little ones left out of that number, those wicked foxes having eaten all the rest. My best old brood-goose hatched twelve little goslings, and I was quite proud of the addition to my poultry-yard; but the foxes came last night, and robbed me of all but four.

Richard found me lamenting over the loss of my poor goslings. He consoled me with his usual kindness, promising he would contrive some means of securing my fowls from any further depredations. He instantly set to work, and, with Andrew for his assistant, began to rail my poultry-yard all round. I watch their progress with much interest, and shall be rejoiced when it is completed; for I cannot bear to see my nice little chickens devoured by those disagreeable foxes; and the wild cats from the woods are quite as bad as the foxes.

Richard has promised to make me some coops for my young broods, some pens for my fatting fowls; and to build a nice house for the accommodation of my old hens, ducks, and geese.

As soon as I have attended to the wants of my poultry, and Flora has collected all the eggs she can find, I give my two weanling calves, Blackberry and Strawberry, their breakfast of warmed milk, which they receive with gratitude from our hands. We then return to the house, and prepare breakfast; for in Canada, my dear Ellen, it is not sufficient to give orders, and look on while the servants work: you must also lend your assistance, and help to do some of the labours of the house.

Once a week we bake. This is my busy day, and I find enough to employ me. The household-bread is made with a mixture of rye and maize-flour, with new milk; and it is far nicer, and more delicate, than the best English bread I ever tasted. My cakes and puddings gain me great credit. I also make all the pastry.

When thoroughly dried and flattened, wash the backs of the leaves, flowers &c. over with a camel's hair pencil, dipped in a solution of gum-tragacanth and spirits of wine; and arrange them, according to class, on the pages of a blank book. If this is carefully done, you will have a good hortus siccus, which, if the specimens are scarce and well chosen, will be of considerable value to those young persons who take pleasure in the study of botany.

I intend preserving a great deal of fruit this summer, such as cranberries, raspberries, and strawberries. This we can do with very little expense, as we have a plentiful store of maple-sugar, having made nearly six hundred weight this spring.

Papa engaged a party of Indians to make the sugar for us, as they far excel the settlers in the art of refining it. The method practised round us, is to top the maples when the sap rises, and place a trough under them; but this is very wasteful, as it kills the tree. The Indian plan is much better: with a hollow knife they scoop out a piece from the trunk of the tree, at a certain distance from the ground; into this incision they insert a spout or tube of elderwood, through which the sap flows into the troughs below. Every day the liquor is collected into one great vessel. A fire is lighted round it, and the sap is kept boiling till the watery particles have evaporated; it is then purified with eggs, and kept stirred with an iron ladle. Two gallons of sap are reckoned to produce one pound of sugar. From two hundred and sixty maple-trees, the Indians produced six hundred weight of sugar, and a quantity of molasses: a goodly stock you will say, for such a small household as ours.

I used often to walk with papa and mamma into the woods, to visit the Indians, while they were making the sugar. Their picturesque figures, dresses, attitudes, and employments, contrasted with the ruddy glare of the fires, and the dark trees of the forest above them, would have formed a subject worthy of the pencil of a West or a Salvator Rosa.

Some of the men were tending the fires stirring the liquor in the boiling kettles, or purifying it: others collecting the fresh sap, tapping the trees, or binding up the wounds in those that had ceased to flow. Here a group of Indian children were seated on their fathers' blankets, round the fires, weaving baskets or mats, or scooping the tubes of elder-wood: there a party were dancing the Indian dance, or singing, in wild, irregular cadence, the songs of their native tribes; while some, more industrious, were employed in collecting wood and supplying the fires with fuel.

Among the Indians there was one old man, for whom I contracted quite a friendship. He used to lift me over the fallen timbers, and place me near the fire at which he was at work, spreading his blanket on a block or trunk of wood, for my accommodation. This old Indian told me he was called Hawk-head by his own people, but that he had been baptized into the Christian church by a white missionary, who came from a distant country and preached the word of God in their village. But this was many years ago, when he was in the pride of his strength; and he had forgotten much of his duty since that time. He said, in excuse for it, 'Young lady! the Hawk-head has grown old, and his memory has faded, and his eyes have waxed dim, since he heard the words of missionary John. He has seen his children, to the third generation, rise up before him, ready to fill his place; and he expects soon to be called away to the land of spirits.'

I was much interested by the conversation of this venerable man, and hoped to improve the good seed that the missionary had sown in his heart. I explained to him many points of faith, of which he was anxious to be informed; and I also mentioned to him my intention of opening an evening school, for the instruction of the children of his tribe in the knowledge of God and of their Saviour. The old man said, 'Hawk-head would be glad to see his children taught that which is right and good;' and he promised to speak to his children on the subject. I found my Indian proselyte a powerful auxiliary, as he possessed great influence over the minds of the tribe of which he was the chief. I have now fourteen Indian children under my tuition, who are making great improvement in their moral conduct. Several Indian mothers came to our school, a short time since, and entreated that they also might be taught what was good, as well as their children.

At first our school opened under very unpromising auspices: few of the labourers would allow their children to attend it, and we had but four little Indians, who had been prevailed upon by my friend the Hawk-head to attend. But, in spite of this disappointment, we resolved not to be discouraged; and in the course of another month we had gained ten more Indians, and several of the children of the Irish peasants. The school has only been established since the beginning of last March, and we have now twenty-five regular scholars; and I am happy to say that a considerable alteration has already taken place in the manners and behaviour of the inhabitants of the village, which, when we first settled here, was a sad, wicked, disorderly place.

Besides our constant attendance at the school, we have some who only come occasionally; (perhaps once a week); but these are idle, and of irregular habits, and do not like to observe the necessary restraints which we are forced to exact. Some few come from motives of curiosity, or to pass away a dull hour; but we do not exclude any. And I trust that not unfrequently it happens, that 'Those who came to scoff remained to pray.'

You do not know, my dear Ellen, what real and heartfelt pleasure we feel in instructing these children in their moral duties, and teaching them the knowledge of God and the advantages of religion.

Jane and Charlotte Hamilton are my assistants in the business of the school. Charlotte returned home last Christmas, to Oakdale. She is as near my own age as possible. I like her much, she is so sprightly and amusing; but I love her sister Jane best, partly because I have known her longer, and partly because I fancy there is a resemblance between her and my own dear Ellen. Charlotte declares she shall love you, and is delighted when I talk to her of you, or read a portion of your letters to her, which I always do when I am so fortunate as to receive one from my Ellen. How happy should I be, could I welcome the beloved writer of those letters to our dwelling; and I trust the time may not be very distant when I shall enjoy that pleasure.

Our garden already begins to look very pretty. I work in it every day, when the weather is not too warm. I have several parterres of beautiful native flowers, besides those plants which we brought from Roselands; and the seeds which you sent to us in the winter have now become strong plants. Every root we put into the ground flourishes, and increases in a wonderful manner, owing to the richness and fertility of the soil. The labours of our hands are repaid in a fourfold degree; and in the course of another year or two, the garden will become a lovely spot. At present all our fruits are confined to the wild sorts, excepting such as we are supplied with by our kind neighbour, whose garden having been under cultivation some years, is now become very productive. The fence which Richard made round the garden last year, has taken root, and is thriving nicely, presenting to the eye a wall of lively green.

We have just finished getting our seed-corn into the ground. The wheat-crops are up, and look beautifully green and fresh. Spring is the busy time of the year, both on the farm and within-doors. Papa has astonished our Canadian neighbours by some of his English improvements; such as building corn-stands, making five-barred gates, English hay-stacks, and sheep-pens.

Our stock has increased considerably since last year. We have a flock of ten young lambs, as white as snow, which feed on the lawn before our door with the old ewes; these are under Andrew's care, and he is very proud of his flock. Flora has a cosset-lamb, which she doats on: it was a very weakly twin when she first took it under her protection. She fed it for a whole fortnight with warm milk out of a teapot, till it grew strong, and learned to drink by itself. It is now so tame, that it runs after her all over the fields. We have also three calves, two of which are weanlings. We have bought another yoke of oxen. We have also fifteen head of swine, which get their living during one half the year in the fields and woods, feeding on the wild nuts and esculent roots, which they find, in vast profusion, under the trees in the forest.

The Canadian farmers live entirely on their own produce. Their chief subsistence consists in pork, mutton, venison, poultry, game, fish, the best bread, cakes of Indian corn, milk, eggs, and sugar. Besides this, they manufacture their own malt, candles, and soap; for which articles they pay no duties. Thus you see, my dear sister, that if we have not the luxuries and superfluities of life, the real, substantial comforts may be easily obtained by industry and forethought.

Taxes are very low; viz. for every acre of cultivated land, the settler pays one penny; waste land, one farthing. Live stock pays a tax of one penny in the pound. Besides this, we have highway-rates to pay, or so many days in the year to labour on the roads, which is very necessary; and it is certainly the interest of every person to improve them as much as possible.

Papa intends making potash this year; likewise building a saw-mill, which can be worked by the little stream of water that flows through our grounds. He will then ship timber for Montreal, which he hopes will answer well.

The settlers who make potash, clear the land by firing the woods, or setting fire to the timber, after they are piled in heaps. You will see twenty or thirty acres, chopped into lengths and heaped together, all blazing at once. Of a night, the effect is very grand. But it is a dangerous practice; for if the weather is dry and warm, there is a great chance of the flames communicating from the woods to the cornfields and fences, and from thence to the out-buildings and the homesteads.

Last summer, the woods near us caught fire, owing to the extreme dryness of the season, and occasioned considerable damage to the farmer on whose land it commenced, scorching up one hundred and twenty acres of meadow land. We had one acre of wheat in the ear destroyed; and we were beginning to entertain great fears for the safety of our corn and cattle, when a very heavy shower of rain falling, (which seemed as if by the interposition of the Almighty himself,) extinguished the flames.

When the forests take fire, which not unfrequently happens, they present a most awful and imposing spectacle. The flames rush to the tops of the trees, roaring, crackling, crashing, and filling the air with glowing sparkles and burning splinters, as the trees sink beneath the wasting effects of the devouring element; wreaths of red and yellow smoke hover and wave above the burning woods, while the surrounding atmosphere becomes tinged with a lurid and angry redness. When the flames are extinguished, the scene presents an appearance of desolation, dreary beyond description. Instead of waving woods of green, once so charming to the eye, you behold only the trunks of black and branchless trees: white ashes (beneath which the fire still lingers) strew the once-verdant and flowery ground: all is dark and dismal, that was lately so fresh and lovely. Such, my dear Ellen, is the appearance of a Canadian forest on fire. But even this (which in many respects might be considered as a calamity) is not without its benefits; the earth being freed, in the course of a few hours, from a superfluity of timber, which would take the settler at least many weeks, or even months, to accomplish; and the wood-ashes which strew his land, render it fruitful to a most astonishing degree. Thus, in nature, we often see that which we at first rashly accounted an evil, become, through the superintending providence of an all-wise and merciful God, a positive blessing and benefit to mankind.

Our kind parents have promised to indulge Richard and me by a view of the falls of the Niagara, (if the winter should prove favourable for travelling,) and also a tour along the coast of the lake Erie; and we anticipate much pleasure from our excursion, especially as our neighbour, Mr Hamilton, has consented to let his son and daughters accompany us in the journey. But as some months must necessarily intervene, we must not permit ourselves to be too sanguine, lest disappointment should follow; for, as the wise writer of the book of Ecclesiastes says, 'There is no new thing under the sun'; so, from our own experience, we may add, 'There is no certain thing under the sun.'

Were it not for the society of the Hamiltons, we should find this place quite a solitude, as our other neighbours consist chiefly of mechanics or labourers, (I mean those in our immediate vicinity,) whose education has unfitted them for the pleasures of intellectual conversation, and we cannot take interest in theirs. But we practise a mutual kindness towards each other, and there is no lack of friendship on either part; each acting on the law of obligation, which forms a great bond of unity between the inhabitants of this country.

Sometimes we are enlivened by an occasional visit from travellers, such as the Canadian merchants, timber-merchants, overseer of the roads, tax-gatherer, or our Indian hunters or fowlers. According to the custom of this country, we entertain all strangers, setting before them the best food the house affords, and taking care of their horses; giving them accommodation for as long a time as our hospitality is required. We then speed them on their journey, wishing them health and prosperity.

Sometimes we chance to meet with an agreeable, sensible person among these wayfaring men; but in general they are very talkative, and inquisitive about the concerns of their neighbours, and very silent and reserved respecting their own.

At this time we are entertaining a very amiable lady, with her son, a young man about five and twenty. They are travelling home, from York (where the lady has a daughter, who is married and settled in that place) to the city of New York; and she has kindly offered to forward any packet we might wish to send to England, by the first packet that sails for Liverpool.

They arrived yesterday morning, and will leave us again this afternoon; so I must hasten to draw this already long letter to a speedy conclusion, as it will take me some little time to pack the flower-sketches I have prepared for you; also, a few Indian toys, which were presented to me by one of my little scholars; and a specimen of my feather-work, which I shall have great pleasure in forwarding to my dear Ellen; assured that a trifle from her Agnes, however insignificant in *real* value, will be prized by her as a remembrance, from her fondly-attached friend and sister,

AGNES CLARENCE

HENRY SHARPE HORSLEY
From *The Affectionate Parent's Gift; and the Good Child's Reward* (1828)

Writing in what he called 'the plain garb of honest sincerity', this versifier, about whom little is known, made liberal use of maudlin, pathetic exempla to further his practical and pious design: 'to lead the tender Mind of Youth in the early Practice of Virtue and Piety, and thereby promote temporal Prosperity and eternal Happiness.' A collection of poems and essays, *The Affectionate Parent's Gift* was also intended to satisfy children's 'thirst after novelty'; however, Horsley thought this appetite 'ought to be kept within the restricted limits of prudence by those who have the control over them, and the culture of their minds entrusted to their care.' His 'affectionate' parent assumes the role of a terrifying monitor, equating ignorance with sin and forecasting threats of imprisonment as the just desserts of stubbornness.

School

Children are sent to school to learn,
    And diligent should be;
Then their improvement will shine forth,
    And all will plainly see,

5 That they are good, and friends will praise;
    Their parents will caress
The child who diligently tries
    Sound learning to possess.

Abundant cause for gratitude
10   Have children, who are taught
At School to read, to spell, and write,
    And are from ign'rance brought.

What is a child, unlearnt, untaught,
    His mind is wild and vague;
15 A book is seal'd—his vacant time
    Is irksome and a plague.

What better than poor Afric's son,
  Or savage of the wood,
Who wildly run thro' deserts, moors,
20   To join the chase of blood?

But learning curbs the wand'ring mind,
  It chases nature's night;
Affords a mental feast, and gives
  A soul-reviving light.

25 Prize, children, prize your book while young,
  Anticipate your school;
When you've a chance to learn, and not,
  You ought to die a fool.

Children who neglect to learn,
30   Give evidence they're bad;
What must a tender parent feel,
  Whose son is such a lad!

Such children must be whipt and scourg'd,
  They don't deserve to eat;
35 For 'tis the diligent alone
  Are worthy of their meat.

Contrast a child that's good, with one
  Who hates his book and school;
What picture does the blockhead give,
40   But that he is a fool?

Then view the diligent and good,
  The child whose willing mind
Is bent on learning—ever tries
  To seek, the prize—he'll find.

A Visit to Newgate

The Father of two little boys,
    Resolved one day to take
A walk through Newgate with the lads,
    Just for example's sake:

5 One of these boys was very good,
    The other the reverse;
A pilfering little petty thief,
    Was stubborn and perverse.

The father's fears would oft pourtray
10   The little rascal's end;
If he was not reclaim'd, and soon,
    And did his conduct mend.

Come, Jack, the father said, you'll see
    What thieving does my lad;
15 This prison's built thus strong to keep
    The wicked and the bad.

The outer door turns on its hinge,
    The massive bars between;
And through the gratings of the cells,
20   The inmates faintly seen.

'Twas here the voice of sorrow struck
    Th' affrighted ear of all;
The clinking chains, the frenzied yell,
    The harden'd culprit's bawl.

25 Confin'd within a grated cell,
    A little boy they spy'-d,
With nothing but a crust to eat,
    All other food denied.

For why this little boy put here?
30   For thieving you must know;
And there are many more beside,
    In lock-ups down below.

The little urchin's meagre face
    Was moisten' d with his tears;
35 The dread of punishment had rous'd
    His keen foreboding fears.

His parents he at first would rob,
    Then after bolder grew;
Stole trifles first, then grasp'd at all,
40   Or anything in view.

Exploring still the vaulted maze,
    Some dismal sobs assail'd
Their nerve-drawn ears—'twas grief, alas!
    Repentance unavail'd.

45 The sighs were shuddering exiles' cast
    To echo 'long the walls,
Repeating chill'd responses hoarse,
    And mock'd the victim's calls.

'Twas some poor men, who, doom'd to die
50   Upon the coming day,
Were venting frantic tears of grief,
    And kneeling down to pray.

This was matur'd full-grown crime,
    Its end, and its reward;
55 Reproaches in full stature stood,
    And death to fainting aw'd.

Come, Children, view the march of crime
    Exploring shun the road;
'Steal not at all,' your Maker says,
60   Such is the law of God.

A Visit to the Lunatic Asylum

Come child with me, a father said,
I often have a visit paid
To yon receptacle of woe,
For Lunatics.—Come, child, and know,
5 And prize the blessing you possess,
And prove the feeling you profess.
Come, shed a tear o'er those devoid
Of what you have through life enjoy'd:
See, in this mansion of distress,

Scared ? ?.
straight

10 The throngs of those who don't possess
Their reason; but with constant moan
Cast ashes on her vacant throne;
Her sceptre cankering in the dust,
Fair reason weeping o'er the rust;
15 Her seat deserted, fallen, decay,
And midnight horrors shade fair day.
Reason, thy grateful cheering light
Entomb'd 'neath ashes, clad in night,
Lays prostrate—where thy being's ceas'd,
20 Thy sons are levell'd with the beast.
    What means that horrid dreadful yell,
Those screeches from yon grated cell;
The frightful clinking of the chain,
And wild effusions of the brain?
25   How madly now he tears his hair,
What wildness mixes with his stare;
With rage he rends his tatter'd clothes,
More vicious and still stronger grows.
What awful wreathings vent in rage,
30 With eye-balls starting, dread presage;
My God! can creature man thus sink,
Plung'd headlong down th' appalling brink.
    Point out the man who grateful shows
That he the worth of reason knows;
35 That he his reason holds from God,
And stays by gratitude the rod
That might afflict—that might chastise—
The man who does the gift despise.
    Were reason's channels choak'd and dried,
40 You of her benefits denied;
Read here what you would surely be,
Your picture in these inmates see.
    Who could withhold a grateful heart,
For the possession of that part
45 Which lifts the mortal from the beast?
Yes, gratitude it claims at least.
    But, oh! possessor ever know,
If gratitude you'd truly show,
Let every reasoning power be given
50 Up to the service of kind Heav'n.

JANE MARCET (1769–1858)

From *Mary's Grammar Interspersed with Stories and Intended for the Use of Children* (1835)

Mother of three children and author of several widely popular informational texts on such topics as chemistry, philosophy, economics, and botany, Jane (Haldimand) Marcet was a real pioneer in the area of girls' scientific education. Like Priscilla Wakefield, she relied on a family-based conversational format. A devoted pedagogue, Mrs Marcet made it clear in her Preface that she had introduced stories in the grammar 'with the view of amusing children during the prosecution of so dry a study.' Amusement, however, plays a secondary role: the stories in *Mary's Grammar* are largely exercises in identifying parts of speech. Thanks to these, to tests, and to the constant dinning of grammatical rules, Mary proceeds to triumph over the mysteries of parsing, participles, and pronouns.

Nouns. Lesson 1

A little girl was sitting one day with a book in her hand, which she was studying with a woe-begone countenance, when her mother came into the room. 'Why, Mary!' said she, 'what is the matter? Your book is not very entertaining, I fear.'

'No, indeed it is not,' replied the child, who could scarcely help crying; 'I never read such a stupid book; and look,' added she, pointing to the pencil marks on the page, 'what a long hard lesson I have to learn! Miss Thompson says, that now I am seven years old, I ought to begin to learn grammar; but I do not want to learn grammar; it is all nonsense; only see what a number of hard words that I cannot understand!'

Her mother took up the book and observed that the lesson marked out for her to learn was not the beginning of the Grammar.

'No, mamma, the beginning is all about the letters of the alphabet, and spelling; but I am sure I know my letters, vowels, and consonants too, and I can spell pretty well: so Miss Thompson said I might begin here,' and she pointed out the place to her mother, who read as follows:— ' "There are in the English language nine sorts of words, or parts of speech: article, noun, pronoun, adjective, verb, adverb, preposition, conjunction, and interjection." '

When she had finished, Mary said, 'Well, mamma, is not all that nonsense?'

'No, my dear; but it is difficult for you to understand, so you may skip over that. Let us see what follows.' Mary seemed much pleased; and her mother continued reading. ' "An article is a word prefixed to nouns to point them out, and show how far their signification extends." '

'Well, mamma, that is as bad as the rest; and if it is not real nonsense, it is nonsense to me at least, for I cannot understand it; so pray let us skip over that too.'

'Let us see if something easier comes next,' said her mother, and she went on reading.

'"A noun is the name of any thing that exists: it is therefore the name of any person, place, or thing." Now Mary, I think you can understand that: what is your brother's name?'

'Charles,' replied Mary.

'Well then, Charles is a noun, because it is a name; it is the name of a person.'

'And am I a noun as well as Charles, mamma?'

'I is not your name,' replied her mother; 'when I call you, I do not say "Come here, I."'

'Oh no; you say; "Come here, Mary."'

'Then *Mary* is a noun, because it is your name.'

'But sometimes you say, "Come here, child;" is child a noun as well as Mary?'

'Yes, because you are called child as well as Mary.'

'And when I am older, mamma, I shall be called a girl, and not a child; and is a girl a noun too?'

'Yes, every name is a noun.'

'Then papa is a noun, and mamma is a noun, and little Sophy is a noun, and baby is her other noun, because it is her other name; and John and George. Oh, what a number of nouns! Well, I think I shall understand nouns at last;' and her countenance began to brighten up.

'There are a number of other nouns,' said her mother. 'Sheep and horses, cats and dogs, in short, the names of all animals, are just as much nouns as the names of persons.'

'But the Grammar does not say so, mamma!'

'It is true,' replied her mother, 'that it does not mention animals; but when it says that a noun is the name of any thing that exists, animals certainly exist, so they are nouns.'

'Well, I think mamma, the Grammar ought to have said persons and animals.'

'Or it might have said animals alone: for persons are animals, you know, Mary.'

'Oh yes, I know that men, women, and children are all animals; and they are nouns, as well as geese and ducks, woodcocks and turkeys: and oh! my pretty canary bird too; and I suppose the names of ugly animals, such as rats and frogs and toads and spiders are nouns also?'

'Certainly,' replied her mother; 'but look, Mary, the Grammar says that the name of a place is also a noun.'

'What place, mamma?'

'All places whatever. A town is the name of a place that people live in.'

'Yes,' said Mary, 'so London, and Hampstead, and York are nouns; but a house is a place people live in too, mamma.'

'Therefore *house* is a noun as well as *town*. What is this place we are now sitting in called, Mary?'

'It is called a room; so *room* is the name of a place to sit in, and *stable* a place to keep horses in, and *dairy* is a place to keep milk and butter in; they are all nouns. And *cupboard* is a noun, mamma, because it is the name of a place to keep sweetmeats in.'

'Certainly,' replied her mother.

'Then the *house* and the *garden*, and the *church* and the *fields*, are nouns? What great nouns!' exclaimed Mary; 'and are little places nouns?'

'Certainly; this little box is a place to hold sugar plums in, therefore box is a noun; and the key-hole of the door is a place to put the key in, so key-hole is a noun.'

'And drawer is a noun, I am quite sure, mamma; for it is a place I keep my toys in. But, mamma, I think the key-hole of the lock, and the box for the sugar plums, are more like things than places?'

'They are both; for things that are made to hold something, such as a drawer and a box, are also places; especially if they are made for the purpose of keeping things safe.'

'Oh yes,' said Mary; 'papa's desk is a place where he keeps his letters and bills so carefully; you know, mamma, I am never allowed to touch any thing in it. Then there is the tea-chest, which is a place and a thing too. It is a very pretty thing and a very safe place; for you know you always keep it locked. Oh, I begin to like nouns, they make me think of so many pretty things.'

'I am glad to hear it, my dear,' said her mother; 'but I think we have had enough of them today. You must not learn too much at once, or you will not be able to remember what you learn. We shall find enough to say on nouns for a second lesson.'

JACOB ABBOTT (1803–79)
'The Reason Why' from *Rollo At School* (1839)

Carefully educated in the classics and religion at Hallowell Academy, Bowdoin College, and Andover Theological Seminary, Jacob Abbott, founder of the Massachusetts girls' school Mount Vernon, exerted a strong influence over American children's literature as a teacher and Congregational minister. He was the sole or joint author of over 200 books. One of his earliest works was *The Young Christian* (1832), essays on prayer, the Bible, confession, and self-improvement. The books most frequently associated with his name are the Rollo series, twenty-eight in all, begun in 1834, with a second series beginning in 1853, cataloguing Rollo's European travels. Some of the titles in the first series—*Rollo Learning to Talk, Rollo Learning to Read, Rollo at Work, Rollo at Play, Rollo at School, Rollo's Vacation*, and *Rollo's Experiments*—provide a descriptive account of growing up. Rollo lives on a New England farm with a kind father, gentle mother, older sister, and troublesome younger brother. Abbott announced, in the Preface to *Rollo at Work* (1837), that he was concerned not merely with advancing 'thinking powers' and 'promoting the progress of children in reading and language', but also with 'cultivating the amiable and gentle qualities of the heart'. That cultivation seems quaintly formal today; without embarrassment, it defers to propriety and authority—as in this account of how and when explanations are dispensed.

The Reason Why

One afternoon, in the recess, Henry was playing with some stones in the walk, near the gate, and Rollo and Dovey and some other children were sitting by, on the grass. Henry was making a well. He had dug a small hole in the walk, and had put little stones all round it inside, as men stone up a well, and then he asked Dovey if she would not go in and get some water to pour into his well.

'No,' said Dovey. 'I can't go very well now; I am tired.'

'Well, Rollo, you go, won't you?'

'Why—no—,' said Rollo. 'I can't go—very well.'

He then asked one or two other children, but nobody seemed inclined to go. 'Oh dear me,' said Henry, with a sigh, 'I wish somebody would go; or else I wish water would come in my well of itself, as it does in men's wells. I don't see why it won't.'

'It is because your well is not deep enough,' said one of the children.

'Then I will dig it deeper,' said Henry; and he took out the stones and began to dig it deeper, with a pointed stick, which served him for a shovel. But after digging until he was tired, his well was as dry as ever.

'I don't see why the water won't come,' said he. 'I mean to ask Miss Mary.'

'No you mustn't ask Miss Mary,' said a little round-faced boy standing there, with a paper windmill in his hand.

'Yes, I shall,' said Henry.

'No, you mustn't; it is wrong to ask why.'

'No, it isn't.'

'Yes, it is,' said George, 'my mother said so.'

'It is not wrong to ask why,' said Rollo; 'my father said it wasn't. It is very right.'

George insisted that it was wrong. His mother knew, he said, as well as any-body, and she said it was wrong. Rollo was, however, not convinced; and the other children took sides, some with George, and some with Rollo; and, finally, after considerable dispute, they all arose, and went off in search of Miss Mary, to refer the question to her.

They entered the school-room, and all crowded up around Miss Mary's desk, Rollo and George at the head.

'Is it wrong, Miss Mary,' said Rollo, 'to ask why?'

'Isn't it, Miss Mary?' said George.

'That depends upon circumstances,' said Miss Mary.

The children did not know what she meant by 'depends upon circumstances,' and they were silent. At length one of the children said.

'George says that his mother told him it was wrong; but Rollo's father said it was right.'

'It is a very important question,' said Miss Mary. 'I will answer it by and by, to the whole school. So you may go out and play for the rest of the recess, but do not talk about it any more among yourselves.'

So the children went out to play until the bell rang to call them in.

At the close of the school, or rather just before the hour of closing it, Miss Mary, having asked the children to put their books away, addressed them as follows:

'Two of the scholars came to me with this question today: whether it was proper for children to ask their parents or teachers the reasons of things. One thought it was, and the other thought it was not. I told them I would consider the question when all the school could hear, and we will accordingly take it up now. George, you may tell us why you thought it was not.'

George was quite a little boy, and he was at first rather intimidated at being called upon before the whole school to state his opinion. So he only answered faintly that his mother told him so.

'When was it, George?'

'Yesterday.'

'Do you recollect what you were doing when she told you, and what she said? Tell us all about it.'

'Why, I was playing with some blocks, and mother said I must go to bed, and I asked her why; she said I was always asking why, and it was wrong to ask her why.'

'Well, Rollo, now let us hear your story.'

'Why, one day I was playing in a tub of water by the pump, and I had a little cake-tin which I was sailing about for a ship, and I had another flat piece of tin for my raft. My ship would sail about very well, but my raft would not sail at all; it would sink directly to the bottom. I could not make it stay up. And so I went in to my father, and I asked why one would sail and the other would not, when they were both tin. And he said he was very glad that I asked him, and that it was right for children to ask why.'

'Very well,' said Miss Mary, as soon as Rollo had finished. 'You have both told your stories very well. For children to ask their parents the reason for anything they see or hear, is sometimes right and sometimes wrong. It depends upon circumstances. In George's case, now, the circumstances were very different from those of Rollo's. Rollo's motive was a desire of knowledge. He wanted to have a difficulty explained, and so he went to his father, at a proper time and under proper circumstances, and asked him. In such cases as this, it is very right to ask the reason why.

'But in George's case it was different. He asked why he must go to bed, not from a desire to learn and understand, but only because he did not want to go. He knew well enough why he must go. It was time. He only asked for the purpose of making delay, and perhaps getting leave to sit up longer.

'This now is a very common case of boys' asking why. They are told to do something, and instead of obeying promptly and at once, they ask why they must do it. It is one kind of disobedience, and it is, of course, always wrong.'

'Then it is always wrong,' said Lucy, 'to ask our father and mother the reason for what they tell us to do?'

'No,' said Miss Mary; 'not unless you make it an excuse for putting off obeying. For instance, if George had gone to bed directly and good humouredly when his mother told him to go, and then, the next day, when he saw that she was at leisure, if he had gone and said to her, "Mother, what is the reason that children are generally sent to bed earlier than grown persons?" I don't think she would have considered it wrong. If he had asked the question in that way, it would have shewn that he really wanted to know; but in the other way he stops to ask about the reason of the command, at the time when he ought to have gone off and obeyed it.'

'My father never lets me ask him the reason for what he tells me to do,' said Henry.

'You mean, I rather think, that he never lets you stop to ask him the reason at the time when you ought to be doing it.'

'No,' said Henry. 'I don't think he would let me ask him at all.'

'Suppose you try the experiment. Next time he gives you any command which you do not understand, go and obey it at once, with alacrity, and then, afterwards, when he is at leisure, go and ask him pleasantly if he will tell you the reason.'

'I will,' said Henry, 'but I know he won't tell me.'

'Well,' said Miss Mary, 'we will now close the school; and I want you all to remember what I have told you. It is right for you to want to understand what you see and hear; and it is even right for you to wish to know the reasons for the commands your parents give you. But you must always do it at a proper time, and with proper motives, and you must never stop to ask why, when the command is given and you ought to be obeying it. And above all, you must never stop to say, "Why must I?" in a repining tone, when you don't really wish to know why, but only to show your unwillingness to obey.'

That night, when Henry went home from school, he had an opportunity to put Miss Mary's opinions to the test, sooner than he had expected. He walked along with Rollo as far as their roads went together, and then he turned down a green lane, which led, after some time, to a pleasant-looking house, with a fine large martin-house upon a tall pole near it. This was where Henry lived. He heard his father at work in the barn, and he went and looked in. His father and a boy were grinding some scythes. He looked at them a few minutes, and then went into the house.

His mother was at work in the kitchen, getting supper. A small table was set in the middle of the room with two plates upon it, for Henry's father and mother. At another table, by the window, there was a large pan of milk, and a bowl full by the side of it.

'Is this my bowl of milk?' said Henry.

'Yes,' said his mother.

So Henry took up his bowl of milk, and carried it carefully out to the door, and put it down on a large stone which was in the back yard, and which made a sort of seat, where he often went to eat his bread and milk. Then he went in and got a spoon and a large piece of bread, and came out and sat down upon the stone and ate his supper. After this his mother told him it was time to go after the cows, and so he put on his cap and walked along.

Henry went through a pair of bars which led to a lane by the side of the barn. He went down this lane for some distance, until he reached the place where the path entered among the trees and bushes. He was just disappearing in the thicket, when his father saw him through the back barn door. He called aloud.

'Henry.'

Henry turned round, saw his father, and answered,

'What, sir?' in a loud voice.

'Are you going after the cows?'

'Yes, sir,' said Henry.

'Well,—don't go over the bridge,—but go round by the stepping-stones,— going and coming.'

Henry was so far off that his father had to call in a loud voice, and to speak very slowly and distinctly, in order to make him hear. After he had done speaking, he paused a moment, in order to observe whether Henry appeared to understand him.

'*Why* mustn't I go over the bridge?'

His father, in reply to this question, only said, 'Obey!'

Henry understood by this that he did not think it proper for him to ask the reason.

'There,' said he to himself, 'I told Miss Mary so. My father never lets me ask why.'

The bridge which his father meant, was only a couple of old logs laid across a brook in the woods, so that they could get over. The cows could not walk upon it, and so they usually came across through the water. They had thus worn a deep place in the brook, both above and below the bridge, and here Henry used to love to stop and play, sailing boats, watching little fishes, skippers, &c. There was another way of going in the pasture, by turning off just before you come to the bridge, through some cedar bushes, until you come to the brook at another place below; and there, there were stepping-stones. The path beyond led on to the pasture, though it came into a little different part of it.

Now Henry preferred to go by the bridge, and he asked his father why he mustn't, not because he really wished to know the reason, but only as a way of begging his father to let him go that way.

Henry, however, obeyed. He left the path which led to the bridge, at the proper place, and went through among the cedars and other trees which grew near the brook, until he came to the stepping-stones. He then went on to the pasture and found the cows. He drove them along towards home, and tried to make them go by the path his father had directed him to take; but they liked the other road better, as well as he, and, notwithstanding all his efforts, they would go into the woods by the path which led to the bridge.

'Now I *must* go by the bridge,' said Henry.

On second thoughts, however, he concluded to obey his orders at all hazards. So he went to the entrance of the woods, where the cows had gone in, and shouted to them some time to make them go on, and then he went himself round the other way.

The cows stopped a few minutes to drink at the brook and accordingly they and Henry came out at the junction of the two paths very nearly together. Henry then drove them along the lane towards the house.

He wondered what the reason could be why his father would not let him take the usual path; and just then he happened to think of the experiment which Miss Mary had advised him to try.

'Here is a fine chance,' said he to himself. 'I will ask my father, but *I know* he won't tell me.'

Accordingly, when he reached the yard, he went to the barn to find his father. It was almost dark, and he was just shutting the great doors. Henry pushed the doors to, for him, and his father fastened them. Then he took hold of his father's hand, and they walked towards the house.

'Father,' said he, in a good natured tone, 'will you be good enough to tell me what the reason was why you were not willing to have me go over the bridge?'

'Oh yes,' said his father. 'We found a great hornet's nest close by the bridge today, and I don't want you to go by that way until we destroy it, for fear you will get stung.'

'A hornet's nest?' said Henry.

'Yes' said his father, 'a monstrous one.'

'How big?' said Henry.

'Oh, as big as your head.'

'As big as my head?' said Henry, with astonishment.

'Yes, cap and all.'

'Do you think the hornets would have stung me?' asked Henry again, after a moment's pause.

'No, I don't think they would.'

'Then why didn't you let me go?'

'Because they *might* have stung you, though probably they would not have done it, if you had let them alone.'

'When are you going to destroy the nest?' said Henry.

'Early to-morrow morning.'

Here they reached the house, and Henry's father went in to his supper. Henry himself sat upon the door step, saying to himself.

'Well, Miss Mary was right, it seems, after all.'

The next day, when Henry came to school, he went to Miss Mary's table, and told her he had tried the plan of asking his father the reason at the proper time.

'And did he tell you?' said Miss Mary.

'Yes,' said Henry smiling; 'he did.'

'I thought he would. Parents are generally willing to give their children reasons, if they ask at a proper time and in a proper manner.'

Miss Mary then asked Henry what it was that he asked his father the reason for, and he told her the whole story. She then asked him if he was willing that she should tell the story to all the scholars, and he said yes; and she accordingly did so.

BARBARA HOFLAND (1770–1844)
'Janetta and her Jujubes' from *Farewell Tales Founded on Facts* (1840)

Poet and widely translated novelist, Barbara (Wreaks) Hofland wrote over sixty books, many of which garnered great acclaim. Her first collection of poems, in 1805, had 2,000 subscribers. Her first novel, *The Clergyman's Widow* (1812), sold 17,000 copies. Among her best known works, loosely based on her own domestic situation, are portraits of the resourceful children of a feckless artist-father, *Son of a Genius* (1812) and *Daughter of a Genius* (1823). A widow who chose a gifted but improvident landscape painter as her second husband, Mrs Hofland wrote not only to instruct the young but to support her family. Necessarily a prolific writer for adults as well as children, she used many family experiences, and those involving the boarding school she established at Harrogate, in her tales for the young. 'Janetta and her Jujubes' illustrates Mrs Hofland's belief that every action should be submitted to prolonged and intense scrutiny. Janetta learns that selfless generosity can be 'foolish and imprudent'.

Janetta and her Jujubes

'Oh, Mamma, what a very large bag of jujubes! I never saw so many together before.'

'Perhaps not, my dear, but they are things that will keep; and you are not the only person in the house that is troubled with a cough: take them, my love, and give them to those who have colds; I am afraid I may want jujubes for myself before long.'

Away went Janetta, happiest of the happy, though a bad cold somewhat depressed her spirits; but she knew some whom she thought worse than herself, and she was eager to administer to their relief; besides, there was some pleasure in exhibiting so large a paper of such very pretty-looking things; for although jujubes are nearly tasteless, they look as if they were delicious, and are more tempting than many much sweeter confections.

Janetta was the only daughter of a lady who had an establishment for twenty little girls, whom she educated with all the tenderness of maternal love, and the wisdom gained by knowledge and experience; being assisted in communicating the accomplishments called for by their rank in life, by her excellent husband, and several judicious teachers. In this situation, it will readily occur to every thinking person, the only daughter of the governess ran no little risk of being spoiled, especially if she was a clever and pretty child, as it was the interest of every person around her, to exhibit her acquirements, and contribute to her attainments—to engage her affections and indulge her wishes, in order that her influence might, in some shape or other, prove beneficial to them, during their residence with her mamma. Perhaps few situations in early life can be found, where a child may be equally important, and, of course, equally surrounded by those temptations likely to injure her temper, awaken her pride, and destroy that simplicity and ingenuousness, which are the best characteristics of her age: her faculties are likely to be prematurely nurtured, but her virtues to be blighted, by that consciousness of power which is so generally injurious to all, even when time and trouble should have taught better things.

Happily for Janetta, the parents she was blest with, influenced by a deep sense of religion, sound understandings, and that actual knowledge of her predicament necessary for her real welfare, guarded her in every point; and whatever might be, and indeed *must* be, their gratification in her progress, never suffered her superiority to induce vanity, much less exultation, over others. She was a child with the rest, subject to the same discipline, instructed with the same kindness; and although the real sweetness of her temper, and her constant industry in improvement, might have rendered her valuable as a peace-maker to the quarrelsome, or an assistant to the indolent, neither, in general, sought her interference, because they held her to be governed by the same rules which bound themselves, and referred all matters of moment to their governess.

But wherever a proper favour was to be obtained, a childish error to be forgiven, an indulgence desired, Janetta was always applied to, less on account of her supposed powers of persuasion, than in order to confer on her the pleasure she evidently felt; so far from being a selfish child (the great error of only children) she might be said to live *in* and *for others*, to the utter exclusion of that usually most interesting person, *self*; and the circumstance of being surrounded by so large a family circle, of course offered abundant means for the exercise of that kindness and generosity which was inherent by nature, fostered by education, and become habitual from situation.

Such was Janetta, when she walked off with her prize of jujubes, recalling to mind all who had colds, or were likely to have them, yet coming to the very false conclusion, that so large a supply could not, by possibility, be wanted; but it furnished a proof of her mamma's great kindness to every body, and elicited a hope, that 'surely that dear mamma would not have occasion for them herself.'

It did however so happen, that when Mrs Alston was retiring for the night, she thought it prudent to have a few jujubes under her pillow, and entered her daughter's room which joined her own, for the purpose of taking them, but she did not find any; and not liking to disturb her, retired without them; and having an indifferent night, had the pain of hearing her daughter cough very frequently, without, as she thought, taking the means of relief she had so abundantly provided.

On Janetta entering her room in the morning, as was her custom, the first inquiry was—'Where did you put the jujubes, my dear?' and next, 'Why did you not take them yourself, in the night?'

'Dear mamma, I had not one left; therefore, I could not put any under my pillow, as you directed.'

'What could you possibly have done with them, Janetta? I insist upon knowing.'

'I think jujubes are very odd things, for they really went in the strangest way imaginable: but I will tell you exactly all I know.'

Of this, Mrs Alston could have no doubt, for Janetta's integrity was always able to bear examination, and she listened with a calm but somewhat serious air, to the explanation which followed.

'When I left you, I recalled to mind who amongst the young ladies were troubled with colds like myself, and I counted seven; so I got seven pieces of paper, mamma, and made up seven parcels—*good, handsome* parcels, and gave one to each of them. I thought I did very right, and was taking proper care of the young ladies.'

'So you were, Janetta; go on with your account.'

'Then I got two little papers, and put a few into each, for the two little ones, mamma, because I thought it would please them; and I made a package for Miss Jessop, because she was a stranger; and then I handed them about to the rest, and laid them open on the table, and though nobody seemed to like them, or care for them, when I returned from practising, I found there was not half a dozen left; but I wrapt those up for myself, remembering also you had said, it was possible you might want some, but, in the course of the evening, somebody asked for them, and so *all* were gone before bed-time.'

'You are the most imprudent girl, I have ever known, Janetta. Had the jujubes been husbanded as they ought, for those who required them, they would have lasted several days, for I bought all the confectioner had; and, living so far from the town, I shall be some time before I can get more. Go down immediately, and see if you can beg a few for me. I hope I shall find some person in the house who will have more thought for my wants than my own daughter has had.'

Poor Janetta burst into tears; her heart was so full of love to every creature around her, and so especially fond of her parents, that she had never, in her short life, received before a reproach on the score of deficient affection; nor could she acknowledge its justice, though she was agonized with the sense of its severity. With lingering footsteps she, however, sought to obey the command she had received, and had some consolation in soon returning with a plentiful supply of jujubes from those she had dealt them to so freely, and who were happy in offering them to the governess they loved.

Janetta found her papa in the dressing-room when she returned, and she laid them down on the table, with an eager anxious air.

'I am much obliged to my young friends, and glad to see that they have used my gift wisely,' said Mrs Alston.

'But, mamma, dear—*dear* mamma, do not think they love you better than I do, or that they think more about you than *me*, pray, *pray* do not say such words to me again; punish me any other way. I am naughty—I am foolish; but surely I always love *you*? Oh, papa, pray, speak for me!'

Mrs Alston had risen and turned away, too much affected to reply, yet desirous to make a deep impression on the mind and memory of her beloved daughter, whom it was really necessary to wound for her future benefit.

'My dear Janetta,' said the fond and anxious father, 'be assured your mamma cannot say one severe word to you, that does not wound herself much more. Judge, therefore, how much she feels at this very moment, and then you will see the necessity, for her sake and mine, of—I will not say conquering a fault, but attaining a virtue.'

'I did not think the jujubes were so very, *very* valuable,' said poor Janetta, sobbing; 'I did not remember they were to cure dear mamma; and, for myself, I did not mind my cough.'

'No, my child, in that consists your error, an *uncommon* one; but it is one, nevertheless. You cannot suppose, my love, that we think the loss of a pound of jujubes material; on the contrary, I shall sincerely rejoice if I can impress upon your mind a lesson I have long desired to teach you, Janetta. You have, my dear, contracted a love for *giving*, which, to a certain point, you must conquer; because, otherwise you will always keep yourself *poor*, and by that means be incapable of fulfilling your duties. Do you understand me?'

Janetta shook the curls from her brow, and gazed through her tears with something like returning confidence, in her father's face, as she answered—'I know very well, papa, that every body must be *just*, before they are generous; and mamma I am sure will say for me, that I never borrowed the least thing in my life, to a needleful of sewing silk, that I didn't pay it again as soon as possible; but I did think one might give away their own. I now see the jujubes were not my own; they were given, as it were, in trust for the sick, and I was a careless girl to do as I did; yet I meant to be careful and prudent, and every thing—indeed I did.'

'I believe you, my child, but with all these good intentions, you did a very unjust thing, Janetta—unjust to me.'

'You mean to dear mamma; I will never forgive myself for forgetting she might want them.'

'No, I mean to us both, by entirely omitting due and proper care to our *daughter*, who really required care, and whose cough the whole night through, has made our hearts ache in a manner those only who are parents themselves can sympathize with.'

Janetta appeared equally puzzled and distressed. Naturally acute as her mind was, she did not, at first, comprehend who was the person alluded to; but the moment she did, darting into her father's arms, she cried—'*your* daughter! dear *mamma's* daughter! I did not think, I did not consider—oh! I had no right to forget you loved me,' and again the poor child wept.

'This want of due consideration for yourself, my love is what I complain of,' said Mrs Alston, sitting down, and drawing her tenderly towards her; 'in your extreme kindness to others, you forget your own rights and wants so entirely, that if this disposition is not checked, or I ought rather to say *regulated*, in early life, my love, when the time comes for us to be taken from you, we shall have every reason to fear that you will give away all we have laboured to procure for you, and our old age will be oppressed with the dread of our only child being impoverished, aged, infirm, and friendless.'

It is not easy for the very young to conceive it possible they can become old and infirm. Janetta was excessively shocked at the idea of her dear parents being grieved on her account; but the latter part of the picture did not come home to her feelings, save in the last word, which absolutely astonished her; for as the whole wealth of her situation consisted in her daily exercise of her affections, and the grand business of her life was promoting the happiness of others, she had no idea of the possibility of losing kindness under circumstances when it would be most valuable and she eagerly exclaimed—'Friendless! surely, mamma, I can never be friendless! people would not forsake me because I had done my best to serve them.'

'Not *because* you had done your best to serve them; but, my love, the friends of your youth will, as you already know, be soon scattered abroad in the world, and, depend upon it, *other* people will be more likely to blame you for extravagance than commend you for generosity. You may say, perhaps truly, "I spend nothing on myself." They will answer—"No matter, you spent more than you could afford; you have forfeited the situation in life to which you were born, and which your education fitted you to enjoy. We will give you alms, but cannot admit you to our society." Do you not see the possibility of all this Janetta? nay, its extreme probability, unless you correct yourself?'

Janetta sat seriously a long time, and then said—'I meant to do right, but I dare say I have been wrong. I should not like to be poor myself, though I like poor people, and pity them very much; for I should be obliged to feel all along the same sort of misery I had just now, when I went from one to another, begging jujubes—so ashamed! so distressed!'

'Only much *more* ashamed—much *more* distressed.'

'The catechism says—"I must do my duty in that state of life unto which it shall please God to call me." From what you say, mamma, it means also, that I must *preserve* myself in that state or situation of life in which it has pleased God to place me?'

'I do, my love, and for that reason recommend you to be prudent, and to remember, that there are cares and duties belonging to yourself, as well as to your fellow creatures, and that if they are not performed, others must suffer from your self-neglect—indeed, with whom you are connected.'

'But you must not conclude, from any thing your mamma now says, that you are to run into an opposite extreme, Janetta,' said her papa; 'for that would be much the greater error of the two.'

'There is no fear of that dear papa; for I shall have a good deal to do to cure myself of giving away every thing I have given to me, because it is so pleasant and comes so natural as it were; but indeed I *will* reason upon it—I will think about it, and remember, for your sakes, not to strip *your* little girl of *every* thing, as I used to do.'

Away went Janetta, with the light step and the light heart of childhood, to water every one's garden, and cherish every one's flowers, without, as heretofore, neglecting her own. She was at that period of life when the lessons and impressions of religion are received with the warmest sensibility, and excite the purest gratitude, but do not therefore check (for any length of time) that happy buoyancy of spirit which seems granted to every young creature, as the especial boon of its early existence. Her father praised her labours, more especially as they regarded the improvements in her own garden, repeating, as he had often done before, 'that her kind attentions to others, her consideration for them, and her generosity to them, had his warmest approval, except in its *excess*, which was, as she well knew, a daily increasing evil, until her mamma took up the affair of the jujubes, as the foundation of a very needful remonstrance.'

'Needful, indeed, dear papa; for when I look back, I see clearly how foolish and imprudent I have been in my generosity, even destroying my power of charity; yet one is only a pleasure, and the other a positive duty; but I hope to be a great deal better before I am a woman; for I am determined strictly to imitate you and mamma, whom every body knows to be liberal and kind, and then cakes, fruit, and pocket-money, will be much more wisely distributed than the jujubes were.'

SAMUEL GRISWOLD GOODRICH (1793–1860), PETER PARLEY (pseudonym)
From *Make the Best of It; or, Cheerful Cherry and Other Tales* (1843)

A prolific publisher, Samuel Goodrich was the most successful Connecticut Yankee in the field of juvenile literature during the mid-eighteenth century. The son of a Congregational minister, he was born in the small farming community of Ridgefield; after a short education and a period of clerking in a country store, he bounded into the publishing trade at the ripe age of eighteen. His numerous books all purported to be factual not fantastic, realistic not romantic. His campaign against make-believe was very spirited—whether mounted by such creations as Gilbert Goahead and Robert Merry, or presented in the textbook chatter of his most famous persona, Peter Parley. This old white-haired fund of information—leaning on his wooden cane to support a bandaged, gouty foot—enjoyed a loyal following on both sides of the Atlantic; there were 116 Parley titles. The short tales in *Parley's Magazine* (1833–44) , collections of stories like *Make the Best of It*, and countless little

textbooks on subjects ranging from history and geography to arithmetic and spelling, were all eagerly awaited—and even imitated by several spurious 'Parleys'. The children's writer Goodrich most admired was Hannah More (see chapter 7); he visited her at her home, 'Barley Wood', outside Bristol, when she was in her eighties. (He may have dimly remembered More's tract, 'Parley the Porter', when he settled on the alliterative Peter Parley, which was both a pseudonym and an aptly named fictional character of great loquacity.) A good-natured go-getter himself, Goodrich observed in the Conclusion to *Make the Best of It*, that 'it has been my chief object . . . to set forth the excellence of good temper and cheerfulness, united with energy and perseverance; to show that sources of proper enjoyment will be found all around us if we but look for them in a right spirit'. Each of his stories has a clear-cut moral having to do with such topics as obedience to parents, caution, and material success, but they are not over-serious; like the author himself, they are sunny and energetic. In fact, as in the resuscitation of a presumed-drowned brother (without CPR!) in the story that follows, Goodrich's narratives can be close-to-miraculous.

The Pleasure Boat: or, The Broken Promise

A Gentleman, who lived in a fine house upon the banks of a beautiful lake, had five children, the two youngest of whom were twins—a boy and girl: these were four years old; while the others, a brother and two sisters, were much older.

The father of this family had a very pretty boat, and it was one of the greatest pleasures that the children could enjoy, to sail in it upon the lake. It was delightful to glide over the blue water; to see the fishes playing down deep in its bosom; to see the birds shooting over its surface, and often dipping their wings in the wave; and above all—it was delightful to visit a little island in the lake, upon which a pair of swans had hatched a brood of young ones, and which were now able to swim with their parents over the water.

One fine summer day these children begged their parents to let them go to the lake, and sail upon it in the boat; but the parents were afraid that they would get drowned, and refused their consent. The children then requested permission to go and walk along the border of the lake, saying that they would not go out in the boat. Upon this promise, the parents consented to the request, and accordingly the children started for their ramble.

They strolled along the edge of the water for some time, picking flowers upon the banks, or gathering shells and pebbles on the beach. By and by they saw the swans near the island, at a little distance, and they looked so quiet, beautiful and happy, that the children longed to get into the boat, and go out and see them. At last Thomas, the eldest of the group, proposed that they should do so, saying that the water was so smooth, no doubt their parents would be willing to let them go.

Now as Thomas was the eldest, he had influence over the others, and as he promised to be very careful, they consented. Having all got into the boat, Thomas took the paddle, placed it at the stern, and shoved the little vessel briskly through the water.

Directing its course at the same time that he urged it forward, he took the party from place to place, and at last they came to the island of the swans. Close by its margin they found the flock, consisting of the two parent birds, and their three young ones.

The swans were well acquainted with the children, and seemed to regard them as friends; so that when the boat approached, they arched their long necks, and came up close to it. The old ones even put their heads forward and ate some corn out of the hands of the twins, which they had brought for the purpose. The young ones ate the pieces of bread which were given to them in the water, and dived down to seize the grains of corn that were thrown out.

The twins, who were named Frank and Fanny, were greatly charmed with all this, but they seemed to enjoy it in different ways. Fanny was mild and gentle in her feelings, and her happiness seemed to partake of her general character. She regarded the swans with a pleased but tranquil look, and spoke to them in soft and tender tones.

But Frank was more ardent in his temper. He could not conduct himself with much order. He threw up his arms, and clapped his hands, and shouted till the borders of the lake echoed with his merry cries. Nor was all this enough. He was very anxious to take hold of one of the little swans. His sisters both warned him against this, and told him that in stooping over as he had done several times, he was in danger of falling into the water.

But most children are thoughtless, and seldom fear danger, till they have had some experience of evil. So it was with our joyous little boy of the boat. He heeded not the caution of his sisters, but continued his pranks, and at last, reaching forward to seize one of the young swans, fell headlong into the water!

There was a wild shriek from all the children as their little brother plunged into the lake and disappeared beneath the water. In a few seconds the poor boy came to the surface, and being very near the boat, the two sisters reached suddenly forward to take hold of him; this turned the boat on its side, and in an instant it was upset and all the party were thrown into the water.

Fortunately the water at this place was not deep, and Thomas soon succeeded in getting his sisters, including little Fanny, to the island, which was close at hand. But Frank, who was the cause of the accident, was still in the water, and had disappeared beneath its surface.

I cannot tell you with what agony Thomas searched about in the water for his dear little brother. I cannot tell you how his older sisters, standing on the shore, wrung their hands in anxiety and grief. I cannot tell you how little Fanny too cried out to Thomas to bring brother Frank out of the water.

Already Frank had been two or three minutes in the lake, and Thomas knew that if he was not very soon taken out he would never breathe again. It was, therefore, with a degree of distress which I cannot describe, that he plunged into the water, and searched along the bottom for his little brother. At last he felt something upon the sand, and, laying hold of it, he drew it forth, and lo! it was little Frank. Thomas brought him to the land, but how pale and deathlike was the face of the child!

One of the sisters took him in her arms, and held him to her bosom, seeking to bring back the colour and warmth to his cold cheek. She sat down with him in her lap, and they all knelt around, and while they wept they took his little cold hands in theirs, and with streaming eyes kissed him over and over again.

It was heart-rending to see little Fanny, looking into his face with terror at seeing it so white and so still. It seemed to her like sleep, but oh, how fearful seemed that strange, cold sleep, in one, but a few minutes before, the very image and impress of love and life and joy.

With timid and trembling fingers, Fanny at length took the hand of her brother, and lifting it to her lips, kissed it tenderly; and then she kissed his cheek; and then she spoke gently to him, saying, 'Dear Frank, do you not know little Fanny? will you not speak to Fanny? will you not open your eyes, and look at me?' There was no answer, and the child burst into a gush of tears. But at this moment there was a slight movement in the little boy's frame, and he opened his eyes.

These signs of life gave inexpressible joy to the children. They even sobbed aloud, and clapped their hands, and wept, and jumped up and down, all in the same moment. After some minutes, and symptoms of great distress, Frank recovered, and looking round, seemed to know his sisters, and to become conscious of his situation. Soon after this, Thomas swam to the boat, and having pushed it to the shore and baled out the water, the little party returned towards their home.

Now these children loved their parents very much, but they were afraid to meet them, and really did not wish to go home. The reason was that they were conscious of their error, and saw that their disobedience had put to risk the life of their little brother. It was proposed by one of the unhappy party to conceal the fact, and account for the condition of Frank by saying that he had slipped into the water while walking along the bank. Thus it is that one fault begets another. Disobedience brings about accident, and this leads to falsehood: nay, it makes children, who before loved father and mother, dread their presence, seek to avoid them, and at last to deceive them.

But I am glad to say, that in this instance the little party did not act thus: they went straight to their mother, told the truth, confessed their faults, and begged forgiveness. This was granted, and then the father knelt down, and they all knelt with him, and they thanked God that the life of the little boy had been saved, and prayed that the erring boys and girls might be kept from further disobedience.

7. SUNDAY SCHOOL MORALISTS

I must have religion in your hearts, as well as in your outward behaviour;
you must walk by faith as well as by sight; religion must govern your thoughts,
and your affections, and your tempers.

—*Mrs Sherwood,* The Sunday-School Teachers (1821)

For the writers who took up the cause of the education of the poor, the authorities were not Locke and Rousseau. Lay and clerical author-activists who embraced the mission of forming a God-fearing nation, who viewed education as redemptive and religion as counter-revolutionary, fastened on the touchstones of the Bible, Dr Watts, Bunyan, and *The Whole Duty of Man.* Distinct from (though often supported by) the Rational Moralists, who were primarily concerned to dispense information to their child readers on the understanding that reason, the discreet guidance of their elders, and natural piety would groom them to enjoy happiness, the authors to be examined in this chapter were convinced that happiness was wholly spiritual.

Involved in the establishment of Britain's first Sunday schools, leading participants in the Evangelical movement, and initiators of domestic and missionary charities, these writers produced a vast amount of literature designed, as Hannah More put it, 'to persuade children of the absolute claim of religion'. Much of it belongs to an enormous body of literary ephemera—religious tracts and minor tales. However, the amazing circulation of this work and the breadth of its support mean that it is also an important lens through which to view—and attempt to understand—ideas and attitudes, markets and institutions, and specific works and creators. In addition to an army of individual texts devoted to religious instruction, there was a whole sub-genre of periodical writing; in the first half of the nineteenth century, for instance, over forty youth magazines, some with monthly circulations of close to 50,000, emerged from various Sunday schools and charitable organizations. The range of abilities and tones in periodical writing is predictably very wide—from the sentimental gentility of 'Old Humphrey' (George Mogridge, 1787–1854) to the ferocious terror of the 'Children's Friend', the Reverend William Carus Wilson (1792–1859), who may have been the model for Charlotte Brontë's repressive Mr Brocklehurst.

Foremost among the influences on these writers, both the gentle and the terrifying, was Evangelicalism, which embraced all Dissenters, with some exceptions among Quakers and Unitarians. Beginning within the established churches—of high and low degree—this movement of the masses believed in the transforming experience of conversion, as a sudden or an agonizingly prolonged recognition of the work of the spirit. Among the most moving accounts of conversion is *The Authentic Narrative* (1764) of John Newton, a former captain of slave ships who was ordained a priest and who collaborated with the poet William Cowper on the Olney Hymns (1779); from this collection Newton's 'Amazing Grace' has exerted a lasting appeal. The movement closely associated with the spread of Evangelicalism is Methodism. Under the practical direction of John Wesley (1703–91) Methodism resorted strongly to religious sentiment, which found its most conspicuous expression in camp-meetings and revivals.

Evangelicals were fervent believers whose enthusiasm was expressed in active ways. In seeking to restore the authority of the Bible and encourage evangelization at home and abroad, they practised self-discipline and performed good works among the poor in the ever-growing industrial districts of England. They advocated such social reforms as abolitionism and child-labour legislation; they endeavored to help landless labourers dispossessed by the enclosure movement; and without state support but on the basis of their religious convictions, they established schools for the children of mill and mine workers, who had little chance of admission to a grammar or a private academy. What charity schools, under the auspices of the Society for Promoting Christian Knowledge (SPCK), had provided for the children of the poor at the beginning of the eighteenth century, the Sunday schools, run on a similar joint-stock scheme of endowments from the rich and subscriptions from the middling ranks, offered at the close of the eighteenth and throughout the nineteenth centuries.

Although Robert Raikes, the wealthy Evangelical layman and publisher from Gloucester, is usually hailed as the father of the Sunday school movement, there were in fact many forerunners—from Nicholas Ferrar's early seventeenth-century community of Little Gidding, which offered a penny and food to children who learned the Psalms, to the eighteenth-century Sunday schools established by Hannah Ball at High Wycombe, Henry Venn at Huddersfield, and Sophia Cooke in the rough Pye Corner district of Gloucester. The initiative of Raikes, who distributed primers and catechisms, coordinated these efforts with an effect comparable to the influence of John Newbery on the juvenile book trade. In the *Gloucester Journal* (3 November 1783) he announced his 'little experiment' to employ instructors to teach children to read the catechism and conduct them to church so that the children's 'minds [are] engaged, the day passes profitably, . . . and the behaviour of the children is greatly civilised.' In London, the Baptist William Fox spearheaded the formation of the inter-denominational Society for the Support and Encouragement of Sunday Schools in 1785. At York in 1786 a Church of England Sunday School Society was formed, with more than 500 children attending the opening Sunday programs in ten schools.

The High Church principles of Sarah Trimmer, therefore, were not in the least compromised when she endorsed the Sunday school movement in *The Economy of Charity* (1787). Dedicating her treatise to Queen Charlotte, who had requested her assistance in setting up Sunday schools in Windsor, and fixing her gaze on her own sex, Mrs Trimmer outlined the benefits of the Sunday school in general and of her own short-lived experiments with 'sabbath schools' in the town of Brentford. Though her concern for the poor was genuine, her literary manner was self-righteous and she was not above snobbery. 'God only knows', she warned, 'what the lower classes of people will become if Sunday-Schools are suffered to drop, and something farther is not done for their reformation.' Her Sunday school was open from 8 a.m. to 6 p.m., during which time the children read, spelled, recited, sang, and played outdoors. Mrs Trimmer's chief objectives were 'the reformation of manners, the implanting of religious knowledge, and the proper observance of the Sabbath-Day'. An ideological debate about allowing or discouraging writing, to accompany reading, lasted throughout the Sunday school movement.

The dialogues, sermons, hymns, verse, family stories, and plebeian narratives in the selections that follow represent the work of four influential female writers (Anna Letitia Barbauld, Sarah Trimmer, Hannah More, and Mary Sherwood), two pastoral activists who were the first leaders of the Religious Tract Society (George Burder and Rowland Hill), and three maternal catechists whose names are virtually forgotten today (Favell Lee Mortimer, Lucy Leman Rede, and Mrs Dalby). Their work has certainly not escaped attack for narrowness and artificiality. In a letter (23 October 1802) Charles Lamb lashed out at Barbauld and Trimmer's 'nonsense', which he cursed as 'Blights and Blasts of all that is human in man and child'. Lamb's remarks, as related by Coleridge, were misogynist as well as disapproving; he found intellectual, or 'bluestocking', women unfeminine, allowing that Anna Barbauld was 'only just tinted blue'. Historian J.H. Plumb has expressed his sympathies with the objectified children in the Sunday school moralists' stories who were 'to stay firmly in Eden with their hands off the apples and deaf to the serpents'. While it is necessary to look critically at the moralists' philanthropy, which, in its attempts to teach the labouring poor and inure them to their drudgery, sounds to us like paternalism, it is simplistic, as M.G. Jones has advised, to dismiss their writing as mere 'mental pabulum'.

There is a good deal of strengthening fibre in the moralists' work. George Burder extracts the spiritual meaning from gallery pictures and reproduces engravings of the originals too. Anna Barbauld provides comforting but acute word-pictures of the hierarchies of material and eternal worlds, not without an awareness of the need to reform. Sarah Trimmer extends the genre of the animal tale to serve as a parable of parental love. Rowland Hill enlarges on Watts's themes. Hannah More does not stint on the carefully observed details of village life to underscore the contrasts between a godless poacher and his maligned victims; the tract allows her to combine a catechism lesson with unforgettable examples from real life. With a similar fervour Mrs Sherwood does not suppress the gruesome particulars of the last hours of neglected, unchurched Augusta Noble. In poems and dialogues Favell Lee Mortimer, Lucy Leman Rede, and Mrs Dalby all convey the painstaking patience of maternal instruction.

As with the Rational moralists, women writers predominated among the Sunday school moralists. Whether biological or ideological mothers, their influence spread far beyond individual families and communities. Anna Barbauld's most recent editors, William McCarthy and Elizabeth Kraft, characterize this reformer adroitly as 'a civic mother', while in the nineteenth century Hannah More, who established and maintained sixteen Sunday schools in the poorest villages of the Mendips, was recognized—through an allusion to the biblical Deborah—as a 'mother in Israel' (Judges 5. 7).

Evangelical books and tracts, often given as gifts to the poor or prizes to the well behaved, throbbed with an active, felt religion. Espousing a vocational, methodical, utilitarian learning which was tailored to prejudged capacities, they nevertheless succeeded in educating tens of thousands of youngsters—before the era of National Education Acts. Protected in the 'armour of God' (Ephesians 6. 13), their creators, who lobbied for reforms of conduct and commerce, assumed the role of fearless soldiers.

GEORGE BURDER (1752–1832)

From *Early Piety; or, Memoirs of Children Eminently Serious, Interspersed with Familiar Dialogues, Emblematical Pictures and Hymns* (1777)

A London-born engraver who became a Congregational minister, Burder was a man of fervent conviction who used his considerable organizational ability in the service of the church. After a period as a travelling preacher in England and Wales, he started Sunday schools at Coventry in 1785; was a founding member of the Religious Tract Society in 1799, and of the British and Foreign Bible Society in 1804; edited the *Evangelical Magazine* for many years; and served as secretary of the London Missionary Society from 1803 to 1827. He versified Bunyan's *The Pilgrim's Progress*, edited *The Holy War*, supple-mented Watts's hymns, and published sermons on exegetical and missionary topics. *Early Piety* was his first publication, designed to 'profit and please' young readers, as his Preface announced, by teaching them to 'love prayer', 'hate sin', and 'be fit to die'. Billy and Betsey Goodchild, home from boarding school for the Christmas holidays, are supremely docile, willing sponges, absorbing Squire Benevolent's commentary on the 'spiritual meaning' of his pictures. Illustrated with eight handsome copper plates, *Early Piety* may also showcase Burder's own engraving expertise.

Chapter II. Of the Gallery of Pictures.

Master and Miss *Goodchild*, behaving themselves so well, deserved indulgence; and they had what they deserved:—for they had not been at home long, when a great man, *John Benevolent*, Esq., hearing of them, invited them to his country house, at a very pleasant village near London; and he sent his own coach for them too. They were most cordially received, and kindly entertained indeed. Among the many curious things they saw, nothing pleased them better than a gallery of fine pictures, each of which had a *spiritual meaning*; and the Esquire was so obliging as to point out to them the instructive lessons, they were designed to teach. In order, therefore, to convey to our young readers some idea of the beautiful originals, we have been permitted, at no small expense, to have three of them elegantly engraved.

The first picture, which struck their attention, was a beautiful historical piece, very highly finished by a capital hand—of which the annexed plate is a copy.

The little folks (as you will naturally suppose) were anxious to know the meaning of it—which gave rise to the following dialogue.

Master G. Pray, Sir, what does this picture represent?

Esq. My dears, you perceive a poor man almost drowned.

Miss G. Yes, sir. And how came he there?

Esq. He was going over that great piece of water, in a little pasteboard boat. Being deluded by a man in black (who *ought* to have known better) he foolishly thought that his boat would keep out the water, and convey him safely to the opposite shore. But, as soon as the wind blew, and the waves arose, his boat overset (you may just see the top of it), and the man fell into the water.

Miss G. Poor man! But pray, Sir, who is that gentleman on the bank?

Esq. My dear, that is a tender-hearted good Prince: though he looks so plain, he lives in yonder fine palace on the high hill: and seeing (for he can see a great way) this poor creature fall in, he ran immediately to his relief—flung in the rope as you can see, and bid the poor man lay fast hold, and he would draw him out.

Master G. Dear Sir, how kind! How very kind that was!

Esq. It was indeed.—The man can never be sufficiently thankful to him.

Miss G. And how excessively tight he seems to hold the rope!

Esq. My dear, he would not let it go for all the world; his life is at stake— and if it had not been for the gentleman, he must certainly have perished—And now children (added Mr Benevolent), I'll tell you what spiritual instruction it is intended to convey. The man in his paper boat, is to shew you how every man by nature (till taught of God) is ready to think that he may get to heaven, by what he can do himself. But it is absolutely impossible, for this reason. The HOLY LAW of God insists upon PERFECT OBEDIENCE, and nothing short of that will do.—But no man is *now* able to obey perfectly.

Therefore, unless the *perfect righteousness* of another is imputed to him, he must fall under the curse of the broken law—his *own best righteousness* will fail him, as this man's paper boat has done,—and if immediate assistance is not afforded, he must perish for ever and ever. But that dear Prince, is to represent JESUS CHRIST, the King of kings and Lord of lords, who came from glory on purpose to seek and save the lost. The rope shews you how we are saved by FAITH. (Faith is taking God at his word.) There is no merit in the man, nor in his holding the rope. His deliverance from death is entirely owing to the Gentleman; and thus the whole glory of salvation is due alone to Christ.

Master G. I dare say the poor man will not brag of saving himself.—I am sure he ought to be very thankful.

Esq. You say right, and so he was. The Gentleman took him afterwards, and gave him fresh cloaths, his own handsome livery, white turned up with red—and he dwells now in his palace, as happy as a prince.

Miss G. I believe, Sir, I know the meaning of that—Thus Jesus brings to heaven, all whom he converts and forgives; so that he can say—*Not one of them is lost.*

Master G. How dearly the man must love him, how desirous must he be to *please* him! I dare say the prince has no need to bid him *twice* do anything, or to threaten to turn him out of doors if he is not good.—I think if I was in his place, it would be *my meat and drink to do his will*, and I should want no other wages than his approbation.

Esq. Well said, indeed.—O my dear children, remember then, thus chearfully to love and obey a precious Saviour, who has redeemed us FROM THE CURSE of the Law, by becoming a CURSE FOR US.

In the next picture, you see two boys; he on the left-hand is named PASSION, the other's name is PATIENCE. You may perceive, *Passion* is much disquieted; but, *Patience* sits, with a bible in his hand, as quiet as a lamb; and he is so happy, because he is content to wait till next year, for several pretty things his guardian has promised him. But Passion is thus disturbed, because he is determined to have all now. He is indeed a very wicked child—he is descended from *Dives*, whom you read of in the bible; and *Patience* is descended from *Lazarus*, a very good, though a very poor man. They take after their ancestors very much; for, as Mr *Bunyan* informs us in his *Pilgrim's Progress*, a man came and brought to Passion a great bag of money, which he seized with prodigious eagerness; and, at the same time laughing at *Patience*, called him a *sorry beggar*: but however, it was not long before he spent all he had, *in riotous living*; lost his friends and his cash together, and has been seen himself not long ago begging about the streets. Whereas *Patience*, in time, by diligence and industry, got a very comfortable estate, upon which he lives, and does a great deal of good with it.

Master G. And pray, Sir, what is this to teach us?

Esq. My dear, it is this—Never to covet present things, things which regard only this world, but both quietly wait, and patiently hope for your portion of *better things in a better world.* All this world calls good or great must either leave us, or be left by us: And, it is better to have our portion in heaven than on earth, for this reason also, because, if it is on earth, we are going *from* it; but if it be in heaven, we are going *to* it.

Esq. What do you observe, Miss *Goodchild*, in this next picture?

Miss G. Sir, I observe a man with a rake in his hand, raking together all the muck and straw; and he seems to be very busy indeed.

Esq. But do not you observe something else?

Miss G. Yes, Sir, there is an angel over his head, that seems to want him to look up at a fine crown in his hand. How sweetly the angel smiles! But the man takes no notice. Will you please, Sir, tell us its meaning?

Esq. My dears—The man who seems so busy in raking together nothing but dirt, is an emblem of the men of *this* world, *who rise early and sit up late, eating the bread of carefulness,* and all to get money. The angel represents the faithful ministers of Jesus Christ, who are using all the means they can, to engage poor careless sinners to think of eternal things; and shewing them what a crown they are despising for mere trash.—But, after all, as you observed, the man takes no notice of the angel, nor of the glorious crown, tho' it is worth a thousand times more than he will ever scrape together as long as he lives. And thus, dear children, too, too many, labor and study only for the meat which perisheth, while

they neglect the unspeakably important concerns of SALVATION; and thus ministers *labor in vain, and spend their strength for nought.—Few believe their report,
and to few is the arm of the Lord revealed.*

The very kind Gentleman, after having shewn them several other pictures of
equal merit, dismissed them, with some pretty presents, especially a neat pocket
bible to each, which (to them) was the most precious gift they could possibly
receive.

When they returned home, they gave so distinct and pleasing an account of
all they had seen, as highly delighted their parents; especially as they took care to
remember the instructive *explanation* of each piece, and were not, like most children, pleased with them merely as pictures.

Master *Goodchild* particularly observed to his Papa, with what earnestness the
man in the water kept hold the rope; and said, He hoped the Lord would help
him, ever to hold Jesus fast by faith, for his Saviour, with the same degree of
stedfastness.

Mr *Goodchild* was so pleased with their remarks, that he promised they should
see every thing that might be likely to advance their best interests; and, accordingly the next day, they went to the *Museum*. An account of which you have in
the following chapter.

ANNA LETITIA BARBAULD (1743–1825)
From *Hymns in Prose for Children* (1781) and *Lessons for Children: Part Four* (1788)

Presbyterian poet, essayist, and teacher, Mrs
Barbauld was also a remarkable innovator
in the field of children's literature. The four
small volumes of her *Lessons for Children*
(1778–88), whose gentle maternal teaching
about the material world influenced Maria
Edgeworth and was fondly recalled by
Elizabeth Barrett Browning, were a popular
series of graduated readers for children
from two to six years of age. The first volume opens with a two-year-old sitting on
his mother's lap and sounding out mono-
syllables, while the fourth volume,
extracted here, features a confident young
reader who learns about both the network
of labour that provides his slice of bread and
butter and the patterns of animal and
human consumption. With *Hymns in Prose*
the horizon of lessons widens. Designed for
recitation by the boys at Palgrave School, in
Suffolk, which Barbauld ran with her
husband Rochemont, the twelve hymns
adapted the tone of the 'deservedly honoured' Dr Watts, but changed the medium,
since Barbauld did not consider it proper to
lower poetry 'to the capacities of children'.
Priscilla Wakefield's Harcourt family, in
Mental Improvement (see chapter 6), clearly
followed Barbauld's intention that her
hymns 'be committed to memory', for
Henry Harcourt recites the 'Negro woman's
lament' from Hymn VIII. Its picture of the
hierarchy of the world—from the cottage
labourer and weeping slave to the august
king—opens and closes with praise of God.
The sense of divine superintendence and
benevolence was likely influenced by the
uplifting philosophy of the Scottish Francis
Hutcheson (1694–1746). In her *Thoughts
on the Education of Daughters* Mary Wollstonecraft recommended *Hymns in Prose*,
which was reprinted for over a century.

Barbauld also contributed selections (fourteen out of ninety-nine) to *Evenings at Home* (1792–6), six volumes of dialogues, tales, and poetry by her brother, John Aikin. As well as being a surrogate mother to the 130 pupils at Palgrave School, Barbauld was an adoptive mother to her nephew.

From *Hymns in Prose for Children* (1781)

Hymn VIII

See where stands the cottage of the labourer, covered with warm thatch; the mother is spinning at the door; the young children sport before her on the grass; the elder ones learn to labour, and are obedient; the father worketh to provide them food: either he tilleth the ground, or he gathereth in the corn, or shaketh his ripe apples from the tree: his children run to meet him when he cometh home, and his wife prepareth the wholesome meal.

The father, the mother, and the children, make a family; the father is the master thereof. If the family is numerous, and the grounds large, there are servants to help to do the work: all these dwell in one house; they sleep beneath one roof; they eat of the same bread; they kneel down together and praise God every night and every morning with one voice; they are very closely united, and are dearer to each other than any strangers. If one is sick, they mourn together; and if one is happy, they rejoice together.

Many houses are built together; many families live near one another; they meet together on the green, and in pleasant walks, and to buy and sell, and in the house of justice; and the sound of the bell calleth them to the house of God, in company. If one is poor, his neighbour helpeth him; if he is sad, he comforteth him. This is a village; see where it stands enclosed in a green shade, and the tall spire peeps above the trees. If there be very many houses, it is a town—it is governed by a magistrate.

Many towns, and a large extent of country, make a kingdom: it is enclosed by mountains; it is divided by rivers; it is washed by seas; the inhabitants thereof are countrymen; they speak the same language; they make war and peace together— a king is the ruler thereof.

Many kingdoms, and countries full of people, and islands, and large continents, and different climates, make up this whole world—God governeth it. The people swarm upon the face of it like ants upon a hillock: some are black with the hot sun; some cover themselves with furs against the sharp cold; some drink of the fruit of the vine; some the pleasant milk of the cocoanut; and others quench their thirst with the running stream.

All are God's family; he knoweth every one of them, as a shepherd knoweth his flock; they pray to him in different languages, but he understandeth them all; he heareth them all; he taketh care of all; none are so great, that he cannot punish them; none are so mean, that he will not protect them.

Negro woman, who sittest pining in captivity, and weepest over thy sick child; though no one seeth thee, God seeth thee; though no one pitieth thee, God pitieth thee: raise thy voice, forlorn and abandoned one; call upon him from amidst thy bonds, for assuredly he will hear thee.

Monarch, that rulest over an hundred states; whose frown is terrible as death, and whose armies cover the land, boast not thyself as though there were none above thee:—God is above thee; his powerful arm is always over thee; and if thou doest ill, assuredly he will punish thee.

Nations of the earth, fear the Lord; families of men, call upon the name of your God.

Is there any one whom God hath not made? let him not worship him: is there any one whom he hath not blessed? let him not praise him.

From *Lessons for Children: Part Four* (1788)

Charles, what a clever thing it is to read! A little while ago, you know, you could only read little words; and you were forced to spell them—c-a-t, cat; d-o-g, dog. Now you can read pretty stories, and I am going to write you some.

Do you know why you are better than Puss? Puss can play as well as you; and Puss can drink milk, and lie upon the carpet; and she can run as fast as you, and faster too, a great deal; and she can climb trees better; and she can catch mice, which you cannot do. But can Puss talk? No. Can Puss read? No. Then that is the reason why you are better than Puss—because you can talk and read. Can Pierrot, your dog, read? No. Will you teach him? Take the pin, and point to the words. No—he will not learn. I never saw a little dog or cat learn to read. But little boys can learn. If you do not learn, Charles, you are not good for half as much as Puss. You had better learn your lesson.

———

Charles wants some bread and butter.—But the bread is not baked. Then bid Christopher Clump heat his oven and bake it.—But the loaf is not kneaded. Then bid little Margery take the dough and knead it.—But the flour is not ground. Then take it to the mill, and bid Roger the miller grind it.—But the corn is not threshed. Then bid John Dobbins take his flail and thrash it.—But the corn is not reaped. Then bid Dick Clodpole take his sickle and cut it.—But the wheat is not sown. Then bid farmer Diggory take the seed and sow it.—But the field is not ploughed. Then bid Ralph Wiseacre take the horses and plough it.—But the plough is not made. Then go to Humphrey Hiccory the carpenter, and bid him make one.—But there is never a plough-share. Then bid Firebrass the smith go to his anvil and beat one.—But we have no butter. Then go to market, Susan, and buy some.—But the butter is not churned. Then take your churn, Dolly, and churn some.—But the cow is not milked. The take your pail, Cicely, and milk it. Now, Betty, pray spread Charles a slice of bread and butter.

———

Little birds eat seeds and fruit.
Partridges eat corn.
Wolves devour sheep.
Blackbirds peck cherries.
The otter eats fish.
The calf sucks milk.
The weasel sucks eggs.
Squirrels crack nuts.
Foxes eat chickens.
Men eat every thing, corn, and fruit, and mutton, and fish, and eggs, and milk, and chickens.

SARAH TRIMMER (1741–1810)
From *Fabulous Histories, designed for the Instruction of Children, respecting their treatment of animals* (1786) and *The Charity School Spelling Book* (1798)

Mother of twelve children, Mrs Trimmer was also an energetic writer of religious and instructional literature. Her first juvenile book, *An Easy Introduction to the Knowledge of Nature, and Reading the Holy Scriptures* (1780), set the tone for her subsequent work, always informed by High Church principles. She wrote an account of infant baptism, a companion to the Book of Common Prayer, abridgements of the Old and New Testaments, and a scriptural catechism. In the early 1780s Trimmer established separate schools for poor girls and boys at Brentford, in Middlesex, where, as the graduated readers of her *Charity School Spelling Books, Parts I and II* (1798) make clear, girls spun yarn and sewed, while boys headed pins, carded wool, and mended their coats. According to the Sunday School Hymn in Part II, young scholars were prompted to praise 'this refuge from want, from ignorance, and vice . . . with grateful hearts'. Trimmer addressed like-minded Anglican middle-class women in *The Economy of Charity* (1787) in her 'wish to see established in every parish, Schools of Industry for poor girls'. As a periodical writer she edited *The Family Magazine* (1788–9), contributing most of its improving tales for the poor. She singlehandedly ran *The Guardian of Education* (1802–6), the first review of children's literature. Her views were strict and censorious: Gay's Fables, though 'a favourite book', were deemed 'too political for children'; geography, writing, and arithmetic were to be 'made subservient to religious instruction'; novels should not be allowed until young persons 'are in some measure acquainted with real life' (Section XIV). Although Trimmer was in the vanguard of the Sunday School movement, she also endorsed parental instruction as natural and paramount. In *Fabulous Histories*, published frequently in the next century under the title *The History of the Robins*, Trimmer presented a series of fables using a family of robins to teach about a human family. The conscientious and sympathetic Mrs Benson leads her two children, eleven-year-old Harriet and six-year-old Frederick, to an understanding of the compassionate care of these birds for their offspring as a paradigm of parents' benevolent concern for their children.

From *Fabulous Histories* (1786)

Chapter XXIV

For three successive days nothing remarkable happened, either at Mr Benson's or the Redbreasts' nest. The little family came daily to the breakfast-table, and Robin daily recovered from his accident, though not sufficiently to fly well; but Dicky, Flapsy, and Pecksy, continued so healthy, and improved so fast, that they required no further care; and the third morning after their tour to the grove, &c. they did not commit the least error. When they retired from the parlour into the court-yard, to which Robin accompanied them, the father expressed great delight, that they were at length able to shift for themselves. And now a wonderful change took place in his own heart. That ardent affection for his young, which had hitherto made him, for their sakes, patient of toil, and fearless of danger, was on a sudden quenched; but, from the goodness of his disposition, he still felt a kind solicitude for their future welfare; therefore called them around him, and thus addressed them.

'You must be sensible, my dear young ones, that from the time you left the egg-shell, till the present instant, both your mother and I have nourished you with the tenderest love. We have taught you all the arts of life which are necessary to procure you subsistence, and preserve you from danger. We have shewn you a variety of characters in the different classes of birds; and pointed out those which are to be imitated, and those which are to be shunned. You must now shift for yourselves; but before we part, let me repeat my admonition, to use industry, avoid contention, cultivate peace, and be contented with your condition. Let none of your own species excel you in any amiable quality, for want of your endeavours to equal the best; and do your duty in every relation of life, as we have done ours by you. Prefer a calm retirement to the gay scenes of levity and dissipation, for there is the greatest degree of happiness to be found. You, Robin, I would advise, on account of your infirmity, to attach yourself to Mr Benson's family, where you have been so kindly cherished.'

Whilst he thus spake, his mate stood by, who finding the same change beginning to take place in her own breast, she viewed her family with tender regret; and when he ceased, cried out: 'Adieu, ye dear objects of my late cares and solicitude! may ye never more stand in need of a mother's assistance! Though nature now dismisses me from the arduous task, which I have long daily performed, I rejoice not, but would gladly continue my toil, for the sake of its attendant pleasures. Oh! delightful sentiments of maternal love, how can I part with you? Let me, my nestlings, give you a last embrace.' Then spreading her wings, she folded them successively to her bosom, and instantly recovered her tranquillity. Each young one expressed its grateful thanks to both father and mother, and with these acknowledgments filial affection expired in their breasts; instead of which, a respectful friendship succeeded. Thus was that tender tie dissolved, which had hitherto bound this little family together; for the parents had performed their duty, and the young ones had no need of farther assistance.

The old Redbreasts having now only themselves to provide for, resolved to be no longer burthensome to their benefactors, and after pouring forth their gratitude in the most lively strains, they took their flight together, resolving never to separate. Every care now vanished, and their little hearts felt no sentiments but those of cheerfulness and joy. They ranged the fields and gardens, sipped at the coolest springs, and indulged themselves in the pleasures of society, joining their cheerful notes with those of other gay choristers, who animate and heighten the delightful scenes of rural life.

The first morning that the old Redbreasts were missing from Mrs Benson's breakfast-table, Frederick and his sister were greatly alarmed for their safety; but their mamma said, she was of opinion that they had left their nestlings; as it was the nature of animals in general to dismiss their young, as soon as they were able to provide for themselves. That is very strange, replied Miss Harriet; I wonder what would become of my brother and me, were you and papa to serve us so? And is a boy of six, or a girl of eleven years old, capable of shifting for themselves? said her mamma. No, my dear child, you have need of a much longer continuance of our care than birds and other animals; and therefore God has ordained that parental affection, when once awakened, should always remain in the human breast, unless extinguished by the undutiful behaviour of the child.

And shall we see the old Redbreasts no more? cried Frederick. I do not know that you will, replied Mrs Benson, though it is not unlikely that they may visit us again in the winter; but let not their absence grieve you, my love, for I dare say they are very safe and happy.

At that instant the young ones arrived, and met with a very joyful reception. The amusement they afforded to Master Benson, reconciled him to the loss of their parents; but Harriet declared, she could not help being sorry that they were gone. I shall, for the future, mamma, said she, take a great deal of notice of animals; for I have had much entertainment in observing the ways of these Robins. I highly approve your resolution, my dear, said Mrs Benson, and hope the occasional instruction I have at different times given you, has furnished you with general ideas respecting the proper treatment of animals. I will now inform you, upon what principles the rules of conduct I prescribe to myself on this subject are founded.

I consider, that the same almighty and good God, who created mankind, made all other living creatures likewise; and appointed them their different ranks in the creation, that they might form together a community, receiving and conferring reciprocal benefits.

There is no doubt that the Almighty designed all beings for happiness, proportionable to the faculties he endued them with; therefore, whoever wantonly destroys that happiness, acts contrary to the will of his Maker.

The world we live in seems to have been principally designed for the use and comfort of mankind, who, by the divine appointment, have dominion over the inferior creatures; in the exercise of which, it is certainly their duty to imitate the *supreme Lord of the Universe*, by being merciful to the utmost of their power. They are endued with Reason, which enables them to discover the different natures of brutes, the faculties they possess, and how they may be made serviceable in the world; and as beasts cannot apply these faculties to their own use in so extensive a way, and numbers of them (being unable to provide for their own sustenance) are indebted to men for many of the necessaries of life, men have an undoubted right to their labour in return.

Several other kinds of animals, which are sustained at the expense of mankind, cannot labour for them; from such they have a natural claim to whatever they can supply towards the food and raiment of their benefactors; and therefore, when we take the wool and milk of the flocks and herds, we take no more than our due, and what they can very well spare; as they seem to have an over-abundance given them, that they may be able to return their obligations to us.

Some creatures have nothing to give us but their own bodies; these have been expressly destined, by the *supreme Governor*, as food for mankind, and he has appointed an extraordinary increase of them for this very purpose; such an increase, as would be very injurious to us if all were suffered to live. These we have an undoubted right to kill; but we should make their short lives as comfortable as possible.

Other creatures seem to be of no particular use to mankind, but as they serve to furnish our minds with contemplations on the wisdom, power, and goodness of God, and to exhilarate our spirits by their cheerfulness. These should not be wantonly killed, nor treated with the least degree of cruelty, but should be at full liberty to enjoy the blessings assigned them; unless they abound to such a degree, as to become injurious, by devouring the food which is designed for man, or for animals more immediately beneficial to him, whom it is his duty to protect.

Some animals, such as wild beasts, serpents, &c. are in their nature ferocious, noxious, or venomous, and capable of injuring the health, or even of destroying the lives of men, and other creatures of a higher rank than themselves: these, if they leave the secret abodes which are allotted them, and become offensive, certainly may with justice be killed.

In a word, my dear, we should endeavour to regulate our regards according to the utility and necessities of every living creature with which we are any ways connected; and consequently should prefer the happiness of *mankind* to that of any *animal* whatever. Next to these (who being partakers of the same nature with ourselves, are more properly our *fellow-creatures*) we should consider our cattle and domestick animals, and take care to supply every creature that is dependent on us with proper food, and keep it in its proper place: after their wants are supplied, we should extend our benevolence and compassion as far as possible to the inferior ranks of beings; and if nothing farther is in our power, should at least refrain from exercising cruelties on them. For my own part, I never willingly put to death, or cause to be put to death, any creature but when there is a real necessity for it; and have my food dressed in a plain manner, that no more lives may be sacrificed for me, than nature requires for my subsistence in that way which God has allotted me. But I fear I have tired you with my long lecture, so will now dismiss you.

Whilst Mrs Benson was giving these instructions to her daughter, Frederick diverted himself with the young Robins, who having no kind parents now to admonish them, made a longer visit than usual; so that Mrs Benson would have been obliged to drive them away, had not Pecksy, on seeing her move from her seat, recollected that she and her brother and sister had been guilty of an impropriety; she therefore reminded them that they should no longer intrude, and led the way out at the window; the others followed her, and Mrs Benson gave permission to her children to take their morning's walk before they began their lessons.

From *The Charity School Spelling Book; Containing the Alphabet, Spelling Lessons, and Short Stories of Good and Bad Boys and Girls in Words of One Syllable only* (c. 1798)

Story 9: Ruth Ward

Ruth Ward was one of those cross girls no one loves to be with.

When she was at home she was cross to the babe. If the babe was out of the way, she would tease the poor cat; and hurt it so, it would have made you grieve to see the poor dumb beast.

If there was no cat to tease, she would catch flies and pull their legs, or tear their wings off, and laugh to see them in pain.

Her friends sent her to school, for they could pay for her; but she was so bad there, that no one could have any peace for her; she did all she could to tease the rest of the girls, and spoilt their work and their books; so she did not go long to school you may be sure, but was sent off as not fit to be with good girls.

When she had gone on in this way for a good while, she had the ill luck to break her leg, and it was so bad that it was cut off.

While Ruth Ward lay a-bed, Betsy Poole, who went to school with her, and who was one of those she had been cross to, said to the rest of the girls, Have you heard that poor Ruth Ward has broke her leg? Has she, said one; I don't care, she was cross to me, and I will not go near her; and so said the rest. If none of you will go, I will, said Betsy Poole; I grieve for her, though she was cross to me. We should not leave folks when they are sick and bad, if they have been cross to us; may be Ruth Ward may mend. Well, said Ann Read, I will go with you, Betsy, to see how she goes on, poor soul; I think it is right to do as you say. So they both went; and there lay poor Ruth in bed quite bad, in sad pain; but it gave her joy to see these two girls; for she thought as she had been cross, no one would go near her. How do you do, poor Ruth, said Betsy Poole. Quite bad! Quite bad! Said Ruth. I grieve for you, said Ann Read. You are too good, said Ruth Ward, both of you, to grieve for me who have been so cross to you; but if it please God I get well, I will do so no more. I will not hurt or tease so much as a fly, if I get well. No, no, my dear girls, I know what it is to lose a leg. I shall pull no more legs off as long as I live.

It did please God that Ruth should get as well as she could be with one leg; and she kept her word, and was so good and so kind, as to gain the love of all; and she went to the school again, and kept to her work, and made shift when she grew up to earn her bread though she was lame.

ROWLAND HILL (1744–1833)
From *Divine Hymns Attempted in Easy Language for the Use of Children* (1790) and *Instructions for Children* (1794)

Despite his Cambridge education, Hill's earnest Evangelical views and preaching delayed his ordination until 1773. Although his background was more privileged than George Burder's, they were similarly tireless philanthropists. Hill superintended the establishment of thirteen Sunday schools, supported by his Surrey Chapel, in London, which enrolled over 3,000 children. The first Chairman of the Religious Tract Society, he also promoted the work of the British and Foreign Bible Society, and advocated the as-yet-unpopular practice of vaccination. Hill designed *Divine Hymns* as 'an appendix' to Watts's *Songs*, which, as he recalls in the Preface, was the first present he received as a child: 'even in those early days, the sound of the words left a secret something upon my mind that was pleasant, profitable, and good.' He aims for the same effects in his forty-four hymns, recommended especially for Sunday school children, but 'not less acceptable for children of a superior description,' he notes. His simplified verse is written clearly from the point of view of the angels: even the child 'that has ungodly parents' (in Hymn XXIV, added 'by the gentleman that corrected the publication') pities and prays for their carelessness. The collection reached its sixth edition in 1804. Hill's 'fear that in many families and congregations [children] are too much neglected' prompted his *Instructions for Children*, consisting of interpreted Bible stories, obituaries of holy children, and prayers. While *The Evangelical Penny Magazine and Bible Illustrator* (24 November 1832) praised Hill as 'one of that evangelical class, . . . truly and characteristically the preacher of the poor,' his attitude toward poor Sabbath scapegraces in *Instructions for Children* likely impresses today's reader as paternalistic and authoritarian.

From *Divine Hymns Attempted in Easy Language for the Use of Children*

A Sabbath Day's Hymn

I

Jesus our holy Lord,
Thy name we join to sing,
Who didst on this glad day
Complete salvation bring.
We bless the Lord, who from the grave
Arose again lost man to save.

II

Thro' mercy we are call'd
Tho' young in years, to praise
The conquests of thy love,
The riches of thy grace.
O may our hearts in thee rejoice,
And take thee as our only choice!

III

In humble love we wait
To know thy righteous will
Instruct our feeble minds
To be obedient still.
O what a day of love and grace
To hear of Christ, and sing his praise!

IV

Dear Lord, forgive the child
That plays, and sins away
The mercies we enjoy
On this most blessed day
For here we love, and serve the Lord,
And sing his praise, and hear his word.

V

Thro' thy redeeming blood,
Dear Savior, set us free;
And by thy Spirit's grace
O let us live to thee.
Then take us, Lord, when we shall die,
To dwell with thee, above the sky.

A Child's Confession to be Said When Sorry for a Sin Newly Committed

I

O what a wretched heart have I,
　　How full of sin and shame!
How justly I deserve to lie
　　In one eternal flame!

II

Dear Jesus, can a child so vile
　　Be number'd with thy own?
No grace but thine can reconcile,
　　No blood but thine atone.

III

In that most precious fountain, cleanse
　　My crimson guilt away,
And make me grieve for that offence
　　Which I have done to-day.

IV

When thou, dear Jesus, wast a child,
　　Thou didst not sin like me:
No sinful words thy lips defil'd;
　　No faults appear'd in thee.

V

Thou wast more spotless than a dove,
　　More harmless than a lamb;
Obedient, humble full of love,
　　And never once to blame.

VI

But I am proud, and ever prone
　　From duty's path to start;
I am not meek, but oft have shewn
　　The vileness of my heart.

VII

Imprint thine image on my breast,
　　Thine Holy Spirit give;
A mind, with true repentance blest,
　　That I may turn and live.

A Child's Thanskgiving for Good Parents

I

Born a sinful helpless babe;
Born but to weep, and groan, and die;
Ne'er had I liv'd to bless thy name,
Had not thy pity, Lord, been nigh.

II

Beasts that can graze around the field,
Birds that can take the wing and fly;
Yea, every insect thou hast made,
Could better help themselves than I.

III

Ne'er had I known a Father's care,
Nor rested on a Mother's breast,
Had not thy providential love,
With tenderness their hearts possess'd.

IV

Their watchful care still leads me on:
From their kind hand I still receive
The raiment that I daily wear,
The food on which I daily live.

V

Their mild correction for each fault,
Their kind instruction for my good;
Are all design'd in love to bring.
My wandering spirit near to God.

VI

O holy Saviour, may that day
Of future love and grace appear,
In which my parents both shall reap
The harvest of their faithful care.

A Hymn for a Child That Has Ungodly Parents

I

How happy are those little ones,
    Whose parents fear the Lord,
And shew their daughters, and their sons
    The treasures of his word.

II

Instructed, not at school alone,
    But at their home beside:
With quicker pace they travel on,
    And never want a guide.

III

I know that scripture tells me true,
    There is a place of woe,
(My parents! I am pain'd for you)
    To which the careless go.

IV

O Lord, who causest babes to see
    And leav'st the antient blind,
Their case, who being gave to me,
    Sits heavy on my mind.

V

Must we, and shall we, when the date
    Of this short life is o'er,
Be fix'd in such a diff'rent state,
    And meet in love no more?

VI

Forbid it, Lord, and change a pray'r
    In trembling hope preferr'd,
To praise, and thank, for saving care
    And supplication heard.

From *Instructions for Children; or, A Token of Love for the Rising Generation* (1794)

Come, ye children, hearken unto me, and I will teach you the fear of the Lord

(Psalm 34. 11)

1. Now from this text, I shall first observe that the great God who made heaven and earth, and all mankind, sees us wherever we are, and knows all we say and do.

2. And then I observe, that this God is *holy, just,* and *good*; and that he has revealed his blessed law, which forbids us all to sin against him. This holy law, you must all be taught, as written in the ten commandments: the substance of which is, *thou shalt love the Lord thy God with all thy heart, with all thy mind, with all thy soul, and with all thy strength*; and the second is a very loving commandment also; *thou shalt love thy neighbour as thyself.*

3. Now this law we should all obey in our hearts and lives: and our first parents, Adam and Eve, lived very happy in the garden of Paradise till they sinned against this good law; and then they were turned out of Paradise, and lost the blessed favour of God.

4. For the Lord hath planted in that garden, such rich fruit as never grew in any garden besides, only forbidding our first parents to taste of one tree, that he might prove their love towards him; but through the temptations of the wicked one, who now dwells in hell, they despised the commandment of God, and ate the forbidden fruit; and by this their hearts were given over to be corrupted by sin.

5. They being corrupted parents, their children were corrupted also; insomuch that we read in the bible, that their first son Cain was a bloody murderer, and murdered his own good brother, Abel, only because he was a better man than himself.

6. Afterwards we are told how all sinners corrupted each other, and filled the whole world with wickedness; so that God himself, though all mercy and love, was *grieved at his very heart that he had made man*, and was determined to punish them by sending a most dreadful flood, which drowned the whole earth.

7. But Noah being a righteous man, was saved in his ark, which was a large ship that Almighty God ordered him to build for himself and his family, while all the world of ungodly sinners besides, were destroyed for their sins.

8. O how dreadful must sin be to deserve such punishment at the hand of God! And as you go on to read the bible, you will find how soon man's wicked heart taught him to be bad again: and how the Lord sent down fire and brimstone from heaven upon Sodom and Gomorrah; how he made earthquakes to swallow up wicked men alive; how he ordered the sea to drown all the rebellious Egyptians for persecuting and abusing those people that he loved, *even his Israel that he had chosen*; how he has made his angels to strike others dead by thousands, for despising his people, and blaspheming his name; and how even at this present day, he permits bad men to fight till they cover each other with blood; and how he lets whole armies go to war till they kill one another by hundreds and thousands without mercy.

9. Now from the bad lives of mankind, you may surely know that their hearts are bad also; for the wickedness of our actions always comes from the wickedness of our hearts: none but the wicked do that which is wicked.

10. And now dear children, let me see if I cannot shew you somewhat of the wickedness of your own hearts, that our merciful God may give you repentance for your sins, and bless you with his forgiving love, through Jesus Christ; for all children are born in sin, and therefore cannot be saved without his grace and mercy.

11. First you have been taught that you should love the Lord your God, with all your hearts, and souls, and minds, and strength; and how happy are all they that thus love the dear Lord, and are thus beloved by him!

12. But how is it that many children had rather go to play, than to the Lord's house to hear his word, and sing his praise: and when at the Lord's house, how little do they attend upon what is spoken, but often behave indecently, and thereby set an example to other children, to make them as bad as themselves. O did but such children remember that God hears all they say, and sees all they do, surely they would tremble at their sin, and fear, lest his righteous judgement should overtake them!

13. Why is it that poor children do not look upon it as a great mercy, that they are relieved from hard labour on a sabbath day, that they may learn to read their bibles, and be taught thereby the Lord's great compassion in saving vile sinners, through *Jesus Christ*.

HANNAH MORE (1745–1833)
From *Cheap Repository Tracts* (1795–7)

[handwritten annotation: published by S. Hazard her pseudonym was "Z"]

The second youngest of the five daughters of a schoolmaster, Hannah More—poet, playwright, essayist, tract writer, novelist, and polemicist—gained fame and notoriety throughout her long life because of the provocative power of her writing. As an adolescent she wrote a pastoral drama, *The Search After Happiness* (first published in 1773) for performance by the girls at the Bristol school run by her sisters. In the style of the Rational Moralists, the play features a virtuous widow who dispenses advice and warns the young searchers against frivolity and waste. More herself, a prolific writer who devoted several hours each day to writing, never wasted time. Her three tragedies were produced in the late 1770s; the second, *Percy* (1777), had a spectacular run at Covent Garden. Though not written for performance, *Sacred Dramas* (1782), based on biblical texts and aimed at young readers, was reprinted often. More renounced the stage early in her career, yet she retained a remarkable ability to cater for particular audiences—whether advocating moral reform of the privileged classes (*Thoughts on the Importance of the Manners of the Great*, 1788), criticizing the education of girls as decorative ornaments (*Strictures on the Modern System of Female Education*, 1799), or creating an Evangelical paragon, Lucilla Stanley, in her only novel (*Coelebs in Search of a Wife*, 1808). A firm believer in social ranks, More also wrote for the lower orders, using the language of the chapbooks and broadsides of popular culture to provide anti-revolutionary reading material for the young and the newly literate. *The Cheap Repository for Moral and Religious Tracts*, the three-year project she edited, superintended, and largely wrote, consisted of the regular monthly production of three numbers—stories, ballads, and Sunday readings—stressing restraint on the part of the poor and praising the paternalistic philanthropy of the gentry. When the Repository was formed at the urging of the Bishop of London, More was already well known as the initiator of Sunday schools in poor Mendip villages, institutions which she visited regularly. The tracts were intended for wide distribution: shopkeepers and hawkers bought them in bulk at reduced rates, while the gentry bought them in quantities to distribute to the poor. They were shipped by the thousands to America, circulated in the West Indies, Sierra Leone, and Asia, and even translated into Russian. Narratives were often serialized. The first part of Black Giles's story appeared in November 1796; the second, in December. The carefully observed details of village life in the tracts serve a strict and formulaic design: unlike the virtuous poor, such as the Shepherd of Salisbury Plain (Parts I and II, 1795), the godless are not only unregenerate, but wasteful and doomed. Giles the poacher lives in a mud cottage that is the essence of dinginess and neglect, 'with broken windows stuffed with dirty rags'; although the shepherd's hovel is no more commodious, it is the epitome of 'perfect neatness'. Giles's wife, the fortune teller Tawney Rachel, is as deceiving as her mate and a 'wretched manager' too; the shepherd's patched clothing and multicoloured darned socks illustrate his partner's 'good housewifery'. Giles dies 'in great misery' and Rachel is transported to Botany Bay; by contrast, the shepherd acquires a better cottage and job, and his wife is rewarded with the position of schoolmistress. In the second part of Giles the poacher's story, More complicates the tidy narrative formula by introducing a dawning conscience in Giles's son and by making clear that Giles's maligned victims, like Tom Price, are not interested in retribution. Virtue—when accompanied by industry—is its own reward.

Black Giles, the Poacher
Part II. History of Widow Brown's Apple Tree (1796)

I think my readers got so well acquainted last month with Black Giles, the poacher, that they will not expect this month to hear any great good either of Giles himself, his wife Rachel, or any of their family. I am sorry to expose their tricks, but it is their fault, not mine. If I pretend to speak about people at all, I must tell the truth. I am sure, if folks would but turn about and mend, it would be a thousand times pleasanter to me to write their histories; for it is no comfort to tell of any body's faults. If the world would but grow good, I should be glad enough to publish it; but till it really becomes so, I must go on describing it as it is; otherwise, I should only mislead my readers, instead of instructing them. It is the duty of a faithful historian to relate the evil with the good.

As to Giles and his boys, I am sure old widow Brown has good reason to remember their dexterity. Poor woman! She had a fine little bed of onions in her neat and well-kept garden: she was very fond of her onions; and many a rheumatism had she caught by kneeling down to weed them in a damp day, notwithstanding the little flannel cloak and a bit of an old mat which Madam Wilson gave her, because the old woman would needs weed in wet weather. Her onions she always carefully treasured up for her winter's store; for an onion makes a little broth very relishing, and is, indeed, the only savoury thing poor people are used to get. She had also a small orchard, containing about a dozen apple trees, with which in a good year she has been known to make a couple of barrels of cider, which she sold to the landlord towards paying her rent, besides having a little keg which she was able to keep back for her own drinking. Well! would you believe it? Giles and his boys marked both onions and apples for their own; indeed, a man who stole so many rabbits from the warren was likely enough to steal onions for sauce. One day, when the widow was abroad on a little business, Giles and his boys made a clear riddance of the onion bed; and when they had pulled up every single onion, they then turned a couple of pigs into the garden, who, allured by the smell, tore up the bed in such a manner, that the widow, when she came home, had not the least doubt but the pigs had been the thieves. To confirm this opinion, they took care to leave the little hatch half open at one end of the garden, and to break down a slight fence at the other end.

I wonder how anybody can find in his heart not to pity and respect poor old widows! There is something so forlorn and helpless in their condition, that, methinks, it is a call on every body, men, women, and children, to do them all the kind services that fall in their way. Surely their having no one to take their part is an additional reason for kind-hearted people not to hurt and oppress them. But it was this very reason which led Giles to do this woman an injury.

With what a touching simplicity is it recorded in Scripture of the youth whom our blessed Saviour raised from the dead, that he was the only son of his mother, *and she a widow!*

It happened unluckily for poor widow Brown that her cottage stood quite alone. On several mornings together (for roguery gets up much earlier than industry) Giles and his boys stole regularly into her orchard, followed by their jackasses. She was so deaf that she could not hear the asses if they brayed ever so loud, and to this Giles trusted; for he was very cautious in his rogueries; since he could not otherwise have contrived so long to keep out of prison; for though he was almost always suspected, he had seldom been taken up, and never convicted. The boys used to fill their bags, load their asses, and then march off; and if in their way into the town where the apples were to be sold they chanced to pass by one of their neighbours who might be likely to suspect them, they then all at once began to scream out, 'Buy my coal!—buy my sand!'

Besides the trees in her orchard, poor widow Brown had in her small garden one apple tree particularly fine; it was a redstreak, so tempting and so lovely, that Giles's family had watched it with longing eyes, till at last they resolved on a plan for carrying off all this fine fruit in their bags. But it was a nice point to manage. The tree stood directly under her chamber window, so that there was some danger she might spy them at the work. They therefore determined to wait till next Sunday morning, when they knew she would not fail to be at church. Sunday came, and during service Giles attended. It was a lone house, as I said before, and the rest of the parish were safe at church. In a trice the tree was cleared, the bags were filled, the asses were whipped, the thieves were off, the coast was clear, and all was safe and quiet by the time the sermon was over.

Unluckily, however, it happened that this tree was so beautiful, and the fruit so fine, that the people as they used to pass to and from the church were very apt to stop and admire widow Brown's redstreaks; and some of the farmers rather envied her, that in that scarce season, when they hardly expected to make a pie out of a large orchard, she was likely to make a cask of cider from a single tree. I am afraid, indeed, if I must speak out, she herself set her heart too much upon this fruit, and had felt as much pride in her tree as gratitude to a good Providence for it; but this failing of hers was no excuse for Giles. The covetousness of this thief had for once got the better of his caution; the tree was too completely stripped, though the youngest boy Dick did beg hard that his father would leave the poor old woman enough for a few dumplings; and when Giles ordered Dick in his turn to shake the tree, the boy did it so gently that hardly any apples fell, for which he got a good stroke of the stick with which the old man was beating down the apples.

The neighbours on their return from church stopped as usual, but it was—not, alas! To admire the apples, for apples there were none left, but to lament the robbery, and console the widow; meantime the redstreaks were safely lodged in Giles's hovel under a few bundles of new hay which he had contrived to pull from the farmer's mow the night before, for the use of his jackasses. Such a stir, however, began to be made about the widow's apple tree, that Giles, who knew how much his character laid him open to suspicion, as soon as he saw the people safe in church again in the afternoon, ordered his boys to carry each a hatful of the apples and thrust them in at a little casement window which happened to be open in the house of Samuel Price, a very honest carpenter in that parish, who was at church with his whole family. Giles's plan, by this contrivance, was to lay the theft on Price's sons, in case the thing should come to be further enquired into. Here Dick put in a word, and begged and prayed his father not to force them to carry the apples to Price's. But all that he got by his begging was such a knock as had nearly laid him on the earth. 'What, you cowardly rascal,' said Giles, 'you will go and '*peach*, I suppose, and get your father sent to gaol.'

Poor widow Brown, though her trouble had made her still weaker than she was, went to church again in the afternoon; indeed, she rightly thought that her being in trouble was a new reason why she ought to go. During the service she tried with all her might not to think of her redstreaks; and whenever they would come into her head, she took up her Prayer-book directly, and so she forgot them a little; and, indeed, she found herself much easier when she came out of the church than when she went in; an effect so commonly produced by prayer, that, methinks it is a pity people do not try it oftener. Now it happened oddly enough, that on that Sunday, of all the Sundays of the year, the widow should call in to rest a little at Samuel Price's, to tell over again the lamentable story of the apples, and to consult with him how the thief might be brought to justice. But, oh reader! guess if you can, for I am sure I cannot tell you, what was her surprise when, on going into Samuel Price's kitchen, she saw her own redstreaks lying in the window! The apples were of a sort too remarkable, for colour, shape, and size, to be mistaken. There was not such another tree in the parish. Widow Brown immediately screamed out, 'Alas-a-day! as sure as can be here are my redstreaks; I could swear to them in any court.' Samuel Price, who believed his sons to be as honest as himself, was shocked and troubled at the sight. He knew he had no redstreaks of his own; he knew there were no apples in the window when he went to church; he did verily believe these apples to be the widow's. But how they came there he could not possibly guess. He called for Tom, the only one of his sons who now lived at home. Tom was at the Sunday school, which he had never once missed since Mr Wilson the minister had set up one in the parish. Was such a boy likely to do such a deed?

A crowd was by this time got about Price's door, among which were Giles and his boys, who had already taken care to spread the news that Tom Price was the thief. Most people were unwilling to believe it. His character was very good, but appearances were strongly against him. Mr Wilson, who had staid to christen a child, now came in. He was much concerned that Tom Price, the best boy in his school, should stand accused of such a crime. He sent for the boy, examined and cross-examined him. No marks of guilt appeared. But still, though he pleaded not guilty, there lay the redstreaks in his father's window. All the idle fellows in the place, who were most likely to have committed such a theft themselves, were the very people who fell with vengeance on poor Tom. The wicked seldom give any quarter. 'This is one of your sanctified ones!' cried they. 'This was all the good that Sunday schools did! For their parts they never saw any good come by religion. Sunday was the only day for a little pastime; and if poor boys must be shut up with their godly books, when they ought to be out taking a little pleasure, it was no wonder they made themselves amends by such tricks.' Another said, he would like to see Parson Wilson's righteous one well whipped. A third hoped he would be clapped in the stocks for a young hypocrite as he was; while old Giles, who thought the only way to avoid suspicion was by being more violent than the rest, declared, 'that he hoped the young dog would be transported for life.'

Mr Wilson was too wise and too just to proceed against Tom without full proof. He declared the crime was a very heavy one, and he feared that heavy must be the punishment. Tom, who knew his own innocence, earnestly prayed to God that it might be made to appear as clear as the noonday; and very fervent were his secret devotions on that night.

Black Giles passed his night in a very different manner. He set off as soon as it was dark, with his sons and their jackasses laden with their stolen goods. As such a cry was raised about the apples he did not think it safe to keep them longer at home, but resolved to go and sell them at the next town; borrowing without leave a lame colt out of the moor to assist in carrying off his booty.

Giles and his eldest sons had rare sport all the way in thinking, that while they were enjoying the profit of their plunder, Tom Price would be whipped round the market place at least, if not sent beyond sea. But the younger boy, Dick, who had naturally a tender heart, though hardened by his long familiarity with sin, could not help crying when he thought that Tom Price might, perhaps, be transported for a crime which he himself had helped to commit. He had had no compunction about the robbery, for he had not been instructed in the great principles of truth and justice; nor would he, therefore, perhaps, have had much remorse about accusing an innocent boy. But, though utterly devoid of principle, he had some remains of natural feeling and of gratitude. Tom Price had often given him a bit of his own bread and cheese; and once, when Dick was like to be drowned, Tom had jumped into the pond with his clothes on, and saved his life when he was just sinking: the remembrance of all this made his heart heavy. He said nothing; but as he trotted barefoot after the asses, he heard his father and brothers laugh at having outwitted the godly ones; and he grieved to think how poor Tom would suffer for his wickedness, yet fear kept him silent: they called him sulky dog, and lashed the asses till they bled.

In the mean time, Tom Price kept up his spirits as well as he could. He worked hard all day, and prayed heartily night and morning. 'It is true,' said he to himself, 'as I am not guilty of this sin; but yet this accusation set me examining myself, and truly repenting of all my other sins; for I find enough to repent of, though I thank God I did not steal the widow's apples.'

At length Sunday came, and Tom went to school as usual. As soon as he walked in, there was a great deal of whispering and laughing among the worst boys; and he overheard them say, 'Who would have thought it? This is master's favourite! This is Parson's Wilson's sober Tommy! We sha'n't have Tommy thrown in our teeth again if we go to get a bird's nest, or gather a few nuts on a Sunday.'—'Your demure ones are always hypocrites,' says another.—'The still sow sucks all the milk,' says a third.

Giles's family had always kept clear of the school. Dick, indeed, had sometimes wished to go; not that he had much sense of sin, or desire after goodness, but he thought if he could once read, he might rise in the world, and not be forced to drive asses all his life. Through this whole Saturday night he could not sleep. He longed to know what would be done to Tom. He began to wish to go to school, but he had not courage; sin is very cowardly. So on the Sunday morning he went and sat himself down under the church wall. Mr Wilson passed by. It was not his way to reject the most wicked, till he had tried every means to bring them over; and even then he pitied and prayed for them. He had, indeed, long left off talking to Giles's sons; but, seeing Dick sitting by himself, he once more spoke to him, desired him to leave off his vagabond life, and go with him into the school. The boy hung down his head, but made no answer. He did not, however, either rise up and run away, or look sulky as he used to do. The minister desired him once more to go. 'Sir,' said the boy, 'I can't go; I am so big I am ashamed.'—'The bigger you are, the less time you have to lose.'—'But, sir, I can't read.'—'Then it is high time you should learn.'—'I should be ashamed to begin to learn my letters.'—'The shame is not in beginning to learn them, but in being contented never to know them.'—'But, sir, I am so ragged!'—'God looks at the heart, and not at the coat.'—'But, sir I have no shoes or stockings.'—'So much the worse. I remember who gave you both. (Here Dick coloured.) It is bad to want shoes and stockings; but still if you can drive your asses a dozen miles without them, you may certainly walk a hundred yards to school without them.'—'But, sir, the good boys will hate me, and won't speak to me.'—'Good boys hate nobody; and as to not speaking to you, to be sure they will not keep you company while you go on in your present evil courses; but as soon as they see you wish to reform, they will help you, and pity you, and teach you, and so come along.' Here Mr Wilson took this dirty boy by the hand, and gently pulled him forward, kindly talking to him all the way, in the most condescending manner.

How the whole school stared to see Dick Giles come in! No one, however, dared to say what he thought. The business went on, and Dick slunk into a corner, partly to hide his rags, and partly to hide his sin; for last Sunday's transaction sat heavy on his heart, not because he had stolen the apples, but because Tom Price had been accused. This, I say, made him slink behind. Poor boy! He little thought there was ONE saw him who sees all things, and from whose eye no hole nor corner can hide the sinner; 'for he is about our bed, and about our paths, and spieth out all our ways.'

It was the custom in that school, and an excellent custom it is, for the master, who was a good and wise man, to mark down in his pocket-book all the events of the week, that he might turn them to some account in his Sunday evening instructions; such as any useful story in the newspaper, any account of boys being drowned as they were out in a pleasure-boat on Sundays, any sudden death in the parish, or any other remarkable visitation of Providence; insomuch, that many young people in the place, who did not belong to the school, and many parents also, used to drop in for an hour on Sunday evening, when they were sure to hear something profitable. The minister greatly approved this practice, and often called in himself, which was a great support to the master, and encouragement to the people who attended.

The master had taken a deep concern in the story of widow Brown's apple tree. He could not believe Tom Price was guilty, nor dared he pronounce him innocent; but he resolved to turn the instructions of the present evening to this subject. He began thus:—'My dear boys, however light some of you might make of robbing an orchard, yet I have often told you there is no such thing as a *little* sin, if it be wilful or habitual. I wish now to explain to you, also, that there is hardly such a thing as a *single* solitary sin. You know I teach you not merely to repeat the commandments as an exercise for your memory, but as a rule for your conduct. If you were to come here only to learn to read and spell on a Sunday, I should think that was not employing God's day for God's work; but I teach you to read, that you may, by this means, come so to understand the Bible and the Catechism, as to make every text in the one, and every question and answer in the other, to be so fixed in your hearts, that they may bring forth in you the fruits of good living.'

Master. How many commandments are there?

Boy. Ten.

Master. How many commandments did that boy break who stole widow Brown's apples?

Boy. Only one, master; the eighth.

Master. What is the eighth?

Boy. Thou shalt not steal.

Master. And you are very sure that this was the only one he broke? Now suppose I could prove to you that he probably broke not less than six out of those ten commandments, which the great Lord of heaven himself stooped down from his eternal glory to deliver to men, would you not, then, think it is a terrible thing to steal, whether apples or guineas?

Boy. Yes, master.

Master. I will put the case. Some wicked boy has robbed widow Brown's orchard. (Here the eyes of every one were turned on poor Tom Price, except those of Dick Giles, who fixed his on the ground.) I accuse no one, continued the master, Tom Price is a good boy, and was not missing at the time of the robbery; these are two reasons why I presume he is innocent; but whoever it was, you allow that by stealing these apples he broke the *eighth* commandment?

Boy. Yes, master.

Master. On what day were these apples stolen?

Boy. On Sunday.

Master. What is the fourth commandment?

Boy. Thou shalt keep holy the Sabbath-day.

Master. Does that person keep holy the Sabbath-day who loiters in an orchard on Sunday, when he should be at church, and steals apples when he ought to be saying his prayers?

Boy. No, master.

Master. What command does he break?

Boy. The fourth.

Master. Suppose this boy had parents who had sent him to church, and that he had disobeyed them by not going, would that be keeping the fifth commandment?

Boy. No, master; for the fifth commandment says, *Thou shalt honour thy father and thy mother.*

This was the only part of the case in which poor Dick Giles's heart did not smite him: he knew he had disobeyed no father! for his father, alas! was, still wickeder than himself, and had brought him up to commit the sin. But what a wretched comfort was this! The master went on.

Master. Suppose this boy earnestly coveted this fruit, though it belonged to another person, would that be right?

Boy. No, master; for the tenth commandment says, *Thou shalt not covet.*

Master. Very well. Here are four of God's positive commands already broken. Now do you think thieves ever scruple to use wicked words?

Boy. I am afraid not, master.

Here Dick Giles was not so hardened but that he remembered how many curses had passed between him and his father while they were filling the bags, and he was afraid to look up. The Master went on.

'I will go one step further. If the thief, to all his other sins, has added that of accusing the innocent to save himself, if he should break the *ninth* commandment, by *bearing false witness against a harmless neighbour*, then six commandments are broken for an *apple*! But if it be otherwise, if Tom Price should be found guilty, it is not his good character shall save him. I shall shed tears over him, but punish him I must, and that severely.'—'No, that you sha'n't,' roared out Dick Giles, who sprung from his hiding-place, fell on his knees, and burst out a-crying, 'Tom Price is as good a boy as ever lived: it was father and I who stole the apples!'

It would have done your heart good to have seen the joy of the master, the modest blushes of Tom Price, and the satisfaction of every honest boy in the school. All shook hands with Tom, and even Dick got some portion of pity. I wish I had room to give my readers the moving exhortation which the master gave. But while Mr Wilson left the guilty boy to the management of the master, he thought it became himself, as a minister and a magistrate, to go to the extent of the law in punishing the father. Early on the Monday morning he sent to apprehend Giles. In the mean time Mr Wilson was sent for to a gardener's house two miles distant, to attend a man who was dying. This was a duty to which all others gave way in his mind. He set out directly; but what was his surprise, on his arrival, to see, on a little bed on the floor, poaching Giles lying in all the agonies of death! Jack Weston, the same poor young man against whom Giles had informed for killing a hare, was kneeling by him, offering him some broth, and talking to him in the kindest manner. Mr Wilson begged to know the meaning of all this; and Jack Weston spoke as follows:—

'At four this morning, as I was going out to mow, passing under the high wall of this garden, I heard a most dismal moaning. The nearer I came the more dismal it grew. At last, who should I see but poor Giles groaning, and struggling under a quantity of bricks and stones, but not able to stir. The day before he had marked a fine large net on this old wall, and resolved to steal it, for he thought it might do as well to catch partridges as to preserve cherries; so, sir, standing on the very top of this wall, and tugging with all his might to loosen the net from the hooks which fastened it, down came Giles, net, wall, and all; for the wall was gone to decay. It was very high indeed, and poor Giles not only broke his thigh, but has got a terrible blow on his head, and is bruised all over like a mummy. On seeing me, sir, poor Giles cried out, "Oh, Jack! I did try to ruin thee by lodging that information, and now thou wilt be revenged by letting me lie here and perish."— "God forbid, Giles!" cried I: "thou shalt see what sort of revenge a Christian takes." So, sir, I sent off the gardener's boy to fetch a surgeon, while I scampered home and brought back this bit of a hammock, which is, indeed, my own bed, and put Giles upon it; we then lifted him up, bed and all, as tenderly as if he had been a gentleman, and brought him in here. My wife has just brought him a drop of nice broth; and now, sir, as I have done what I could for his poor perishing body, it was I who took the liberty to send to you to come to try to help his poor soul, for the doctor says he can't live.'

Mr Wilson could not help saying to himself, 'Such an action as this is worth a whole volume of comments on that precept of our blessed Master, *Love your enemies; do good to them that hate you.*' Giles's dying groans confirmed the sad account Weston had just given. The poor wretch could neither pray himself nor attend to the minister. He could only cry out, 'Oh! sir, what will become of me? I don't know how to repent. Oh, my poor wicked children! Sir I have bred them all up in sin and ignorance. Have mercy on them, sir; let me not meet them in the place of torment to which I am going. Lord grant them that time for repentance which I have thrown away!' He languished a few days, and died in great misery:—a fresh and sad instance that people who abuse the grace of God and resist his Spirit find it difficult to repent when they will.

Except the minister and Jack Weston, no one came to see poor Giles, besides Tommy Price, who had been so sadly wronged by him. Tom often brought him his own rice-milk or apple-dumpling; and Giles, ignorant and depraved as he was, often cried out, 'That he thought now there must be some truth in religion, since it taught even a boy to *deny himself* and to *forgive an injury.*' Mr Wilson, the next Sunday, made a moving discourse on the danger of what are called *petty offenses.* This, together with the awful death of Giles, produced such an effect that no poacher has been able to show his head in that parish ever since.

MARY MARTHA SHERWOOD (1775–1851)
From *This History of the Fairchild Family; or, The Child's Manual* (1818)

Author of over 400 publications (tracts, family and catechetical stories, and novels), Mrs Sherwood was born in the same year as Jane Austen, and was a clergyman's daughter as well. She was educated in a prosperous but strict home. Wearing an iron collar to which a blackboard was attached, she stood uncomplainingly for daily lessons from her mother. She and her sister Lucy took charge of a Sunday school, where Mary read successive chapters of her early novel, *Susan Grey* (1802), to the older girls as warnings against the promises of military men, 'who were there today and gone tomorrow'. In 1803 she married her cousin, Captain Henry Sherwood, of the 53rd Foot Regiment, and accompanied him when he was ordered to India in 1805, reluctantly leaving her firstborn in England. In their ten-year stay in India, the growing Sherwood family of biological (four daughters and two sons) and adopted children moved often; in each posting she set up schools and wrote about family life. *Little Henry and His Bearer* (1815; 37th edition by 1850), the tale of an angelic, dying eight-year-old British orphan who catechizes and directs the conversion of his Hindu bearer Boosy, was an amazing success; in her lifetime it was translated into French, German, Spanish, Hindustani, Chinese, and Sinhalese. The complementary tract, *Little Lucy and her Dhaye* (1825), highlights a similar turn from Sinbad stories to sacred texts, along with the conversion of the Indian nurse. India remained a rich resource throughout her long career, as evidenced in tracts and novels such as *The Indian Pilgrim* (1818), *George Desmond* (1821), *Henry Milner* (1823) and its sequel *John Marten* (1844), and *The Indian Orphans* (1839). On a family voyage to Meerut, Sherwood drafted *The Fairchild Family* (second part, 1842; third part, 1847), whose first instalment was published on their return to England; consisting of related stories, each closing with a prayer and a hymn, and all 'calculated to show the importance and effects of a religious education', as the title page announced, the book was the quintessential reading experience, according to F.J. Harvey Darton, for every nineteenth-century middle-class child. In the chapter included here, the demise of the foolish but neglected Augusta Noble underscores the author's solemn purpose, and borrows Dr Watts's twenty-third Divine Song for emphasis. Whether writing for children or adults, Sherwood was unwilling to temper her conviction of inherent human corruption. Mr Fairchild conducts his quarrelling youngsters to view the rotting corpse of a fratricide on a gibbet to teach them 'that our hearts by nature are full of hatred'. At Wick, Worcestershire, Sherwood established a boarding school for young ladies and continued to publish prodigiously. With dogmatic fervour she edited Sarah Fielding's *The Governess* (1820)—sans fairy tales. The dynamics of family life, always reflecting the foundational importance of Christian principles, inform her work, from the piety of the English boarder in *The Flowers of the Forest* (1830), the Christian education of the boy-narrator in *The Babes in the Wood of the New World* (1830), and the fond memories of *The Happy Family* (1838), to the instructive contrasts between siblings in her long historical novels, *The Mirror of Maidens* (1851) and *The Two Knights* (1851). An abolitionist whose attitude toward the indigene was condescending but occasionally sympathetic, she succeeded in creating compelling portraits of Dazee in *The Recaptured Negro* (1821) and Thomas Wilson in *The Poor Man of Colour* (1830).

Fatal Effect of Disobedience to Parents

When Mr and Mrs Fairchild returned from the old gardener's, they found John ready with the cart; so, wishing Mrs Goodwill a good evening, and thanking her for all her kindness, they returned home.

The next morning Mr Fairchild got up early, and went down to the village. Breakfast was ready, and Mrs Fairchild and the children waiting at the table, when he came back. 'Get your breakfast, my dear,' said he to Mrs Fairchild; 'don't wait for me.' So saying, he went into his study, and shut the door. Mrs Fairchild supposing that he had some letters to write, got her breakfast quietly: after which, she sent Lucy to ask her Papa if he would not choose any breakfast. When

Mr Fairchild heard Lucy's voice at the study door, he came out, and followed her into the parlour.

When Mrs Fairchild looked at her husband's face, she saw that something had grieved him very much. She was frightened, and said, 'My dear, I am sure something is the matter: what is it? Tell me the worst at once: pray do?'

'Indeed, my dear,' said Mr Fairchild, 'I have heard something this morning which has shocked me dreadfully. I was not willing to tell you before you had breakfast. I know what you will feel when you hear it.'

'Do, do, tell it me,' said Mrs Fairchild, turning quite white.

'Poor Augusta Noble!' said Mr Fairchild.

'What! Papa?' said Lucy and Emily and Henry.

'She is dead!' said Mr Fairchild.

The children turned as pale as their mother; and poor Mrs Fairchild would have dropped off her chair, if Betty, guessing what was the matter (for she had heard the news too, though she had not chosen to tell it), had not run in, and held her in her arms.

'Oh, poor Lady Noble! poor Lady Noble!' said Mrs Fairchild, as soon as she could speak: 'Poor Lady Noble!'

As soon as their mamma spoke, the children all together began to cry and sob, which affected Mr Fairchild so much that he hastened into his study again, and shut the door.

Whilst the children were crying, and Betty holding Mrs Fairchild, for she continued very faint and sick, Mrs Barker came into the parlour. Mrs Barker was a kind woman; and as she lived by herself, was always at liberty to go amongst her neighbours in times of trouble. 'Ah, Mrs Fairchild!' she said, 'I know what troubles you: we are all in grief, through the whole village.'

When Mrs Fairchild saw Mrs Barker, she began to shed tears, which did her much good; after which she was able to ask Mrs Barker what was the cause of the poor child's death, 'as', said she, 'I never heard that she was ill.'

'Ah Mrs Fairchild, the manner of her death is the worst part of the story, and that which must grieve her parents' hearts. You know that poor Miss Augusta was always the darling of her mother, who brought her up in great pride, without fear of God or knowledge of religion: nay, Lady Noble would even mock at religion and religious people in her presence; and she chose a governess for her who had no more of God about her than herself.'

'I never thought much of that governess,' said Mrs Fairchild.

'As Miss Augusta was brought up without the fear of God,' continued Mrs Barker, 'she had, of course, no notion of obedience to her parents, farther than just striving to please them in their presence: she lived in the constant practice of disobeying them; and the governess continually concealed her disobedience from Lady Noble. And what is the consequence? The poor child has lost her life, and the governess is turned out of doors in disgrace.'

'But,' said Mrs Fairchild, 'how did she lose her life through disobedience to her parents? Pray tell me, Mrs Barker.'

'The story is so shocking I hardly dare tell it you,' answered Mrs Barker: 'but you must know it.—Miss Augusta had a custom of playing with fire, and carrying candles about, though Lady Noble had often warned her of the danger of this, and had strictly charged the governess to prevent it. But it seems that the governess, being afraid of offending, had suffered her very often to be guilty of this piece of disobedience, without telling Lady Noble. And the night before last, when Lady Noble was playing cards in the drawing-room, with some visitors, Miss Augusta took a candle off the hall table, and carried it up stairs to the governess's room. The governess was not in the room. Miss Augusta went to the closet, and it is supposed was looking in the glass, with the candle in her hand: but this is not known. Lady Noble's maid, who was in a room not far off, was frightened by dreadful screamings: she ran into the governess's room, and there found poor Augusta all in a blaze, from head to foot! The maid burnt herself very much in putting out the fire; and poor Miss Augusta was so dreadfully burnt, that she never spoke afterwards, but died in agonies last night—a warning to all children how they presume to disobey their parents! "The eye that mocketh at his father, and refuses to obey his mother, the ravens of the valley shall pick it out, and the young eagles shall eat it." (Prov. xxx. 17).'

When Mrs Fairchild and the children heard this dreadful story, they were very much grieved. Mrs Barker staid with them all day; and it was, indeed, a day of mourning through all the house. This was Wednesday; and on Saturday poor Miss Augusta was to be buried. Mr Fairchild was invited to attend the funeral; and the children also were desired to go, as they had been sometimes the play-fellows of poor Miss Augusta. Mrs Fairchild dressed them in white; and at four o'clock in the afternoon a coach covered with black cloth came to the door of Mr Fairchild's house, to take them to Sir Charles Noble's.

When Lucy and Emily and Henry got into the coach, with their papa, they felt very sorrowful; and not one of them spoke one word all the while the coach-man was driving to Sir Charles Noble's. When they came into the park, they saw a hearse, and a great many coaches and other carriages, standing at the door of the house, besides many persons on horseback in black clothes with white scarfs and hat-bands. The hearse was hung with black, and so were several of the coaches; and at the top of the hearse were plumes of white feathers.—Perhaps you may never have seen a hearse; in case you have not, I shall try to describe it to you. It is a long close coach, without windows, used for carrying the dead from their houses to their graves. Sometimes black and sometimes white plumes of feathers are fixed at the top of these hearses, according to the age of the person to be borne. Hearses are always painted or hung with black, and are in general drawn by black horses: so that they make a very dismal appearance.

When the children came near to Sir Charles's house, and saw all the people and carriages waiting to accompany their poor little playmate to her grave, they began to cry afresh, and Mr Fairchild himself looked very sad. 'The eye of him that hath seen me shall see me no more: thine eyes are upon me, and I am not' (Job vii. 8).

When the coach came to the house-door, a footman came out, dressed in black, and took them into the hall, where white gloves and scarfs were given to them, and they were led into the dining-room. There, upon a large table covered with black cloth, was the coffin of poor Augusta, covered with white velvet, and ornamented with silver. Almost all the gentlemen and ladies of the neighbour-hood were in the room; but Sir Charles and Lady Noble were not there. When

Emily and Lucy saw the coffin, they began to cry more and more; and little Henry too cried, though he rubbed his eyes, and tried to hide his tears.

When every thing was ready, the coffin was lifted up, and put into the hearse; the company got into the coaches; and they all moved slowly to the parish church, which was close to the village, about two miles distant. As the children passed back through the park in the mourning-coach, they saw many places where they had walked and played with poor Augusta; and this made them the more sorrowful. As for man, 'all flesh is grass, and all the goodliness thereof as the flower of the field' (Isa. xl. 6).—When they passed through the park gate, they could hear the church bell tolling very plainly. The carriages moved on very slowly, so that it was between five and six when the funeral reached the church. The churchyard was full of people. The coffin was taken out of the hearse and carried into the church, the clergyman going before and all the people following. The coffin was placed on a bier in the middle of the church whilst the clergyman read the first part of the Funeral Service. Lucy and Emily and Henry stood all the time close to the coffin, crying very bitterly.—Perhaps you have never read the Funeral Service with attention: if you have not, I would advise you to read it immediately, and consider it well; for there are many things in it which may make you wise unto salvation.—Poor Augusta's coffin was then lifted up, and carried, not into the church-yard, but to the door of a vault under the church, which was the burying-place of all the Nobles: and as the people were letting down the coffin into the vault, earth was cast upon it, and the clergyman repeated these words: 'Forasmuch as it hath pleased Almighty God of his great mercy to take unto himself the soul of our dear sister here departed, we therefore commit her body to the ground; earth to earth, ashes to ashes, dust to dust; in sure and certain hope of the resurrection to eternal life, through our Lord Jesus Christ; who shall change our vile body, that it may be like his glorious body, according to the mighty working whereby he is able to subdue all things to himself.' The coffin then was removed into a dark place in the vault, and Lucy and Emily and Henry saw it no more.

When the service was done, Mr Fairchild returned sorrowfully to the coach, with his children; but before the coachman drove away, the clergyman himself came to the door, and said, 'Mr Fairchild, if you are going home, I will take a seat with you in the coach, and drink a dish of tea with Mrs Fairchild this evening; for I feel in want of a little Christian society.' Mr Fairchild gladly made room for Mr Somers—for that was the clergyman's name—and the coach drove back to Mr Fairchild's house.

As they were going along, they talked of nothing but poor Miss Augusta and her parents; and Mr Fairchild asked Mr Somers if he knew in what state of mind the poor child died. 'Ah, sir!' said Mr Somers, 'you have touched upon the very worst part of the whole business. From the time of the accident till the time that the breath left her body, she was insensible: she had not one moment for thought or repentance; and it is well known that Lady Noble never taught her any thing concerning God and her Redeemer, and never would let any body else: nay, she was taught to mock at religion and pious people. She knew nothing of the evil of her own heart, and nothing of the Redeemer, nor of the sin of disobedience to her parents.'

'Oh, Mr Somers!' said Mr Fairchild, 'what a dreadful story is this! Had this poor child been brought up in the fear of God, she might now have been living, a blessing to her parents and the delight of their eyes. "Withhold not correction from the child; for if thou beatest him with the rod, he shall not die: thou shalt beat him with the rod, and shalt deliver his soul from hell." (Prov. xxiii. 13, 14).'

'Poor little Augusta!' said Mr Somers: 'Lady Noble would never hearken to me, when I spoke to her on the duty of bringing up her children in the fear of God. I believe she thought me very impertinent, to speak to her upon the subject.'

By this time the coach was arrived at Mr Fairchild's door. Mrs Fairchild and Mrs Barker were waiting tea for them: they had both been crying, as might be seen by their eyes. After tea, Mr Somers gave out a hymn, and prayed. I shall put down both the hymn and the prayer in this place; altering only a few words, to suit any little child who wishes to use the prayer by himself.

A Prayer Against the Sin of Disobedience to Parents

O Almighty Father! thou who didst command all children to honour their parents, and didst promise to bless those who obeyed this Commandment, give me a heart to keep this law. I know that I ought to do all that my father and mother and masters bid me do, if they do not order me to do any thing wicked; and yet my heart, O Lord God, is so bad, that I do not like to obey them. Sometimes, when they give me an order, I am obstinate and passionate, and refuse to do it even in their sight, and would rather be punished than obey them; and sometimes I try to disobey them slily, when I think that they do not see me; forgetting that thine eye, O Lord God, is always upon me; and though thou, O Lord God, mayest not punish me immediately, yet thou markest all my sins in a book: and I know that the dreadful day will come, when the dead shall be raised, and the books shall be opened; and all I have done, unless I repent and turn unto the Lord, will be read aloud before men and angels, and I shall be cast into hell fire for my sins.

O holy Father! I am sorry for my disobedience. O make me more and more sorry for it; and send thy Holy Spirit to give me a clean heart, that I may obey this thy Commandment. I know that disobedient children, unless they repent, always come to an ill end: there is no blessing on such as do not honour their parents. O then, dear Saviour, hear my prayer! Thou, that diedst for poor sinners, save a wicked child! Give me a new heart; teach me to be obedient to my parents, and to honour and respect them; that I may be blessed in this present life, and may, through the merits of my dying Redeemer, be received into everlasting glory in the world to come.

Now to God the Father, God the Son, and God the Holy Ghost, be all glory and honour, for ever and ever. *Amen* 'Our Father,' &c.

Hymn XXIII

Let children that would fear the Lord
   Hear what their teachers say,
With reverence meet their parents' word,
   And with delight obey.

Have you not heard what dreadful plagues
   Are threat'ned by the Lord
To him that breaks his father's law,
   Or mocks his mother's word?

What heavy guilt upon him lies?
   How cursed is his name?
The ravens shall pick out his eyes,
   And eagles eat the same!

But those who worship God, and give
   Their parents honour due,
Here on this earth they long shall live,
   And live hereafter too.

FAVELL LEE MORTIMER (1802–1878)

From *The Peep of Day; or, A Series of the Earliest Religious Instruction the Infant Mind is Capable of Receiving* (1833)

Daughter of the banker David Bevan, of the firm of Barclay, Bevan, & Co, London, Mrs Mortimer, though religiously educated, experienced an intense conversion at the age of twenty-five, after which she devoted herself to charitable work. Thomas Mortimer, whom she married in 1841, was a chapel minister in London. She wrote many Bible tracts and educational works about travel to Europe (*Near Home*, 1849), Asia and Australia (*Far Off*, 1852–4), learning to read (*Reading Without Tears*, 1857), and learning Latin (*Latin Without Tears*, 1877). But her most famous works are a series of instructive religious dialogues. The first of these, The Peep of Day, which was translated into French, German, Russian, Samoan, and Chinese, was followed by *Line upon Line* (1837–8), *Lines left out*, and *Precept upon Precept*. Favell Lee Bevan directed *The Peep of Day* to children in school-rooms and cottages, 'who have no nurseries'. Convinced that children as young as three were eager to talk about 'the Invisible, the Eternal, the Infinite', she offered them her 'humble work . . . of systematic instruction'.

Lesson IV. Of the Soul

Has God been kind to dogs?

Has he given them bodies?—Yes.

Have they bones, and flesh, and blood, and skin?—Yes.

The dog has a body as well as you. Is the dog's body like yours?—No.

How many legs have you?—Two.

How many legs has the dog?—Four.

Have you got arms?—Yes, two.

Has the dog got arms?—No; it has got no arms, nor hands. But the dog has legs instead. Your skin is smooth, but the dog is covered with hair.

Is the cat's body like yours?—No; it is covered with fur.

Is a chicken's body like yours? How many legs has the chicken?—Two.

And so have you. But are its legs like yours?—No; the chicken has very thin, dark legs, and it has claws instead of feet.

Have you feathers on your skin? Have you wings? Is your mouth like a chicken's beak? Has the chicken any teeth?—No; the chicken's body is not at all like yours. Yet the chicken has a body—for it has flesh, and bones, and blood, and skin.

Has a fly got a body?—Yes, it has a black body, and six black legs, and two wings like glass. Its body is not at all like yours.

Who gave bodies to dogs, horses, chickens, and flies? Who keeps them alive? God thinks of all these creatures every moment.[1] Can a dog thank God?

No; dogs and horses, sheep and cows, cannot thank God.

Why cannot they thank God?

Is it because they cannot talk?

That is not the reason.

---

1 'Are not five sparrows sold for two farthings, and not one of them is forgotten before God?' Luke xii. 6

The reason is, they cannot think of God. They never heard of God. They cannot understand about God.[2]

Why not?—Because they have no souls, or spirits, like yours.

Have you got a soul?—Yes, in your body there is a soul which will never die. Your soul can think of God.

When God made your body, he put your soul inside. Are you glad of that? When God made the dogs, he put no soul like yours inside their bodies, and they cannot think of God.

Can I see your soul?—No; I cannot see it. No one can see it but God.[3] He knows what you are thinking of now.

Which is the best, your soul or your body?—Your soul is a great deal the best.

Why is your soul the best?—Your body can die, but your soul cannot die.[4]

Shall I tell you what your body is made of?—Of dust. God made the dust into flesh and blood.

What is your soul made of?

Your soul, or spirit, is made of the breath of God.[5]

That little dog will die some day. Its body will be thrown away.[6] The dog will be quite gone when its body is dead. But when your body dies, your soul will be alive, and you will not be quite gone.[7]

Where would you be put if you were dead?—Your body would be put into a hole in the ground, but your soul would not be in the hole.[8]

Even a baby has a soul, or a spirit.

One day as I was walking in the streets, I saw a man carrying a box. Some people were walking behind, crying. There was a dead baby in the box—Was the soul of the baby in the box?

No, its soul was gone up to God.[9]

Will you not thank God for giving you a spirit? Will you not ask him to take your spirit to live with him when your body dies?[10]

Say to God, 'Pray, take my spirit to live with thee when my body dies and turns to dust.'

2 'Be ye not as the horse or the mule, which have no understanding.' Ps. xxxii. 9

3 'Thou, even thou only, knowest the hearts of all the children of men.' 1 Kgs. viii. 39

4 'What shall a man give in exchange for his soul?' Matt. xvi. 26

5 'And the Lord God formed man of the dust of the ground, and breathed into his nostrils the breath of life; and man became a living soul.' Gen. ii. 7

6 'The beasts that perish.' Ps. xlix. 20

7 'Who knoweth the spirit of man that goeth upward, and the spirit of the beast that goeth downward to the earth?' Eccles. iii. 21

8 'Then shall the dust return to the earth as it was: and the spirit shall return unto God who gave it.' Eccles. xii. 7

9 'I shall go to him, but he shall not return to me.' 2 Sam. xii. 23

10 'We are all willing rather to be absent from the body, and to be present with the Lord.' 2 Cor. v. 8

CHILD

Tell me, mamma, if I must die
    One day, as little baby died;
And look so very pale, and lie
    Down in the pit-hole by his side?

Shall I leave dear papa and you,
    And never see you any more?
Tell me, mamma, if this is true;
    I did not know it was before.

MAMMA

'Tis true, my love, that you must die;
    The God who made you says you must,
And every one of us shall lie,
    Like the dear baby, in the dust.

These hands and feet, and busy head,
    Shall waste and crumble quite away;
But though your body shall be dead,
    There is a part which can't decay.

Jane Taylor's Hymns for Infant Minds.

What is that part which can't decay?
It is your soul.
Your body will decay; it will turn into dust; but your soul will live for ever: it will never decay.

LUCY LEMAN REDE
From *Flowers That Never Fade* (1838)

Accompanied by hand-coloured illustrations, these placid verses, the work of a little-known English writer, convey the Sunday school teaching that obedience, service, and perseverance are their own rewards; their scenes are comfortably removed from real pain and want.

Going to Bed

'And so you will not go to bed,
You naughty girl?' her mother said
   To Fanny, who was crying:
'You see how quickly Charles and John,
And baby, too, to bed have gone,
   Without this sobbing, sighing.

Come, kiss mamma, and go up stairs,
And dry your eyes, and say your prayers,
   And don't make all this riot.'
Then little Fanny kissed mamma,
And bade good night to her papa,
   And went to bed quite quiet.

The Fisherman

Serene was the morn when the fisherman went
    In his trim little boat out to sea:
His bosom was happy with hope and content,
    As the breast of the good man must be.

He cast out his net, and the fish he soon won,
    And came cheerily home before night:
He hung up his nets to be dried in the sun,
    When it rose in the morn with fresh light.

Then he went to his cot where his supper was spread,
    Rejoiced from his labours to rest;
Thanked God for his blessings; retired to bed,
    With pleasure and peace in his breast.

The Match-Woman

Oh! see that poor woman with matches to sell,
    And think how severe is her fate!
She must roam through the streets, although often unwell,
And in heart-rending accents her sad story tell,
    As she lingers in tears at each gate.

Her poor little boy, and the babe at her breast,
    Hunger's craving, I fear, often stings:
Think, then, and be grateful that Heaven has blest
You with parents so good, and by whom you're carest,
    And pray for these poor little things.

The Idle Boy

Rise, Edward, rise, the morning sun
Its early race has long begun;
Hark! on ev'ry vernal spray
The little birds sing blithe and gay;
And ev'ry herb that decks the sod,
Breathes forth a morning prayer to God.
And shall you, then, to whom kind Heaven,
Health, strength, and partial friends has given,
Lie, like a sluggard, and forget
To whom you owe so great a debt?
Have you no duties to fulfil?
No tasks on which to try your skill?
Yes, yes, you have, then rise in haste,
And not another moment waste.

MRS THOMAS DALBY

From *Dutch Tiles: Being Narratives of Holy Scripture; with numerous appropriate engravings for the use of children and young persons* (1842)

This posthumous publication spotlights the role of the maternal instructor who teaches her son Bible history lessons from the scenes depicted on fireplace tiles. In a letter (17 February 1842) inserted in the Osborne Collection copy, Thomas Dalby, the author's widowed husband, explains the book's purpose to his nephew: 'The reason this book is called Dutch Tiles is because a little boy, like yourself, was taught by his Mamma, many things out of the bible, relating to God and Jesus Christ by means of Dutch tiles round her fireplace.' The model for this instruction was the mother of Philip Doddridge (1702–51), the nonconformist divine; Doddridge, who ran an Evangelical academy and established a charity school at Northampton, wrote approximately 400 hymns in the style of Watts. Doddridge's mother, the daughter of a Lutheran émigré, began his education, as the frontispiece to *Dutch Tiles* indicates, at the fireplace in the well-to-do family's parlour. This mother's scriptural commentary does not soften the terror of sin or the fury of the primal scene of fratricide. In its blackness and enormity sin is a constant threat, while Old and New Testaments together provide interlocking warnings and directives.

Cain and Abel

The next tile represent two brothers, whose names were Cain and Abel. They were sons of Adam and Eve. Cain was the oldest, and was the very first person born into the world. He was born after the fall, and exhibited a mournful proof of the change that had thereby passed upon human nature. When Cain grew up, his employment was like his father's, to dig and cultivate the ground; his brother Abel's was, to tend sheep. They each presented an offering to God. Cain brought of his fruits; and Abel of his flock. But there was a marked difference in the quality or kind of their offering. It is recorded of Abel, that he 'brought of the firstlings of his flock, and of the fat thereof,' namely, the first and best; but of Cain, merely that he 'brought of fruit of the ground.' Lambs were offered as types or emblems of the promised Saviour; and Abel's offering was presented as a token of his faith in that Saviour: he brought his lamb as a type or emblem and therefore brought the very best he had in his flock. Cain brought no lamb, nor was his offering presented in faith; and it was not accepted.

Of these offerings it was recorded (thousands of years afterwards, as you may read in the Epistle to the Hebrews, chap. xi. 4), 'By faith' (faith in the promised Saviour) 'Abel offered unto God a more excellent sacrifice than Cain.'

Abel 'obtained the witness that he was righteous,' for God was pleased to testify his acceptance of Abel's offerings. It was impossible that God could mistake the offerers' hearts: and 'to Abel and his offering God had respect,' but to Cain and his offering he had not. On perceiving this, Cain became very angry, and his countenance changed, or fell. Had he felt this unworthiness, grieved that his offering was not accepted, humbly inquired into the cause, and sought to know how he might present it acceptably another time, what might he not have hoped, wrong as he had done, from a God so plenteous in mercy? But Cain was not humbled, not sorry, not desirous of doing better: on the contrary, he became full of rage and resentment.

The eye of God beheld what was in Cain's heart before it broke forth into expression; and God condescended to remonstrate with him, and to tell him that if he did well he should be accepted; but at the same time warned him that, if not, sin (his worst adversary) lay at the door—lay like a fierce lion ready to spring upon him, if he yielded to wicked passions that were working in his heart. Notwithstanding this solemn warning on the one hand, and encouragement on the other, from God himself, Cain yielded to the wicked passions that were working in his heart, and they became (as wicked passions yielded to always do) stronger and stronger. He 'talked with Abel'; (and doubtless talked as he felt); and when they were alone in a field one day, apart from their father and mother, his rage burst forth, so that while talking with Abel, he furiously rose up and slew him! Slew his brother, his own brother! Whose only offence appears to have been that he and his offering were accepted of God, while himself and his offering were not.

We are not informed in the bible what Adam and Eve said when this dreadful outrage came to their knowledge: but it is not difficult to imagine what their feelings were; nor how greatly their sorrow was embittered by the sad reflection that this enormous sin was a consequence of their own transgression in the Garden of Eden.

Do you ask what became of wicked Cain? You need not to be told that the eye of God was upon him, and saw what he had done. God also spoke to him, and said, 'Where is Abel thy brother?' We might have supposed that at the mention of his poor brother's name, Cain's heart would be ready to break with anguish; but this was not the case: he was not sorry, nor did he even say he was. Though he was speaking to the all-seeing God, he pretended not to know, and insolently asked, 'Am I my brother's keeper?' O what words these to be uttered by guilty Cain to his Creator and Judge! Enormous as his sin had been, Cain showed nothing like repentance, nor did he even confess that he had sinned. He was speaking to God, yet his words were words of sullenness and falsehood. Thus did Cain add sin to sin, even in the face of God. Such was the patience exercised towards this hardened sinner, that he was not made to feel the immediate vengeance of the Almighty; but the false covering of his sin was instantly removed, and he was shown what he had done, and what his punishment should be. The voice of his brother's blood had cried unto God, and Cain was cursed from the earth which had received it from his murderous hand. Though he tilled it, it should henceforth refuse to yield to his culture; and a fugitive and vagabond should he be upon it.

When Cain heard this, he again opened his lips, but not to lament his atrocious sin and entreat forgiveness: he only complained of the greatness of his punishment, and expressed his fear that everyone he met would attempt to take away his life. This was his dread, and it pleased God to remove it; for a mandate was issued, to forbid the taking away of his life, and a mark was set upon him to prevent it. When Cain had succeeded in having his life preserved, which was the only thing he appeared to be anxious about, 'he went from the presence of the Lord.'

This is one of the darkest pictures of fallen human nature; a most dreadful example of the effects of unresisted sin. Cain's history is short: very little more is recorded of him. But this short story is written in black characters from beginning to end.

It has already been remarked, that sin hardens the heart; and that one sin prepares the way for another and another. It was so in this case. How hard was the heart of Cain! And doubtless it became harder and harder, as his sins increased upon him. Of Cain it is elsewhere written, that 'his works were evil'; of Abel, that 'his works were righteous.' Yet Cain was angry because God, who knew their hearts, accepted Abel's offering, and rejected his. His unjust anger grew into hatred, and hatred led to murder. Nor did his sin end even here; for it remained rooted in his heart, nor did he ask to be forgiven. Standing before his offended Creator, he sought the preservation of his life; and when that was granted, he went out from his presence, with all his guilt upon him, unhumbled, and unfeeling as a stone.

That sin hardens the heart, you have the strongest proof you can have in wicked Cain, who, after the preservation of his life was granted at his desire, went out from the presence of the Lord without once entreating mercy for his guilty soul.

While reflecting upon Cain, pray to be preserved from hardness of heart; and remember to watch against the first beginnings of what you know to be sinful. Angry words, angry thoughts, and angry looks you know to be so: watch against them, pray against them. Prayer, humble, earnest, believing prayer, is never offered in vain.

Commit to memory these three short texts of Scripture: 'Resist the devil, and he will flee from you.' (James iv. 7) 'Draw nigh to God, and he will draw nigh to you.' (James iv. 8) 'Watch and pray, that ye enter not into temptation.' (Matt. xxvi. 41)

8. HARBINGERS OF THE GOLDEN AGE

And I made a rural pen,
And I stain'd the water clear,
And I wrote my happy songs,
Every child may joy to hear.

—*William Blake*, Songs of Innocence (1789)

By the mid-nineteenth century there had appeared several talented writers, working in the same milieu as the Rational Moralists and the Sunday school writers, who began to signal important and long-lasting changes in literature for children. Unlike their doctrinaire contemporaries they were willing to endorse entertainment as a creditable goal in their works for the young, and were capable of fashioning delightful vehicles to ensure success. In special and diverse ways, these poets and storytellers ushered in the Golden Age of children's literature.

Happily the numerous poets in this group did not share Mrs Barbauld's fear that adapting poetry to a child's understanding would lessen its strength and beauty. They roamed widely in their poignantly expressive art to create poems—or, more modestly, colourful ditties—for and about children. Some of this verse is still enjoyed today. Such charming, tuneful, simple poems as Jane Taylor's 'The Star', Clement Moore's 'A Visit from Saint Nicholas', Sarah Hale's 'Mary's Lamb', Mary Howitt's 'The Spider and the Fly', and Eliza Follen's 'Three Little Kittens' have comforted and amused generations of readers. Christopher Smart transported the act of expressing Christian sentiments in rhyme to truly sublime heights in his luminous *Hymns for the Amusement of Children*. William Blake, whose vision of childhood was profound, etched on copper plates his texts and illustrations of 'the two contrary states of the human soul'. This poet-prophet could never be accused of idealizing childhood as a time of pastoral innocence: he dared, on occasion, to let the child's voice utter scathing social criticism.

Exploring both joy and sorrow with exquisite delicacy, most of the poets in this group are acute observers of their society and themselves. But their lightness of touch, and in some cases their artistry, remove them almost completely from the solemn world of instruction and preaching, and the stance of complacent moral rectitude, that are associated with their forerunners. The tongue-twisters in *Peter Piper's Practical Principles* and the sometimes uproarious cautionary examples in *The English Struwwelpeter* stand learning on its head. Sheer delight in the recognizable social mores of insect and bird worlds characterizes Roscoe's magical account of *The Butterfly's Ball* and Dorset's companion piece, *The Peacock 'At Home'*. The juvenilia of Roscoe's son's protégée, fifteen-year-old Felicia Browne, inquiring into the topics of fame, sorrow, and artistic expression, holds the promise of many future volumes. Edward Lear's nonsense limericks show the courage and singularity of an artist pursuing entertainment—however wry or eccentric—for its own sake. Charmingly illustrated manuscript gift books by Eleanor Mure and Jane Cotton Boucher de Montizambert underscore the adult's intuitive delight in amusing children—whether in a ludicrous early version of *The Three Bears* or in a witty fable of domestic sentiment and over-zealous cookery, *Mrs Mole and Mrs Mouse*.

Several publishers and editors were keenly aware of a mushrooming interest in entertaining the young—though, of course, never to the exclusion of instructing them. John Marshall's *Infant's Library*, the work of a shrewd promoter who clearly knew how to attract middle-class buyers and young readers, has the visual appeal of a beautiful but useful toy. Another London publisher, John Harris, issued over fifty colour-illustrated books in a series entitled, significantly, *The Cabinet of Amusement and Instruction* (*c*. 1810–30), which he advertised as 'consisting of the most approved Novelties for the Nursery'. Such titles as *Peter Piper's Practical Principles, Sir Harry Harold's View of the Dignitaries of England, The Infant's Grammar; or, A Picnic Party of the Parts of Speech, The Picturesque Primer*, and *The Monkey's Frolic* reflect Harris's wish to make every sort of lesson textually and visually amusing. Another influential proponent of attractive and imaginative literature for the young was Henry Cole (1802–82). For his *Home Treasury* (1841–9)—a later series of nursery rhymes, traditional ballads, tales, fables, and fairy stories—he adopted two happy/benign names for his pseudonym, 'Felix Summerly'. His 'Original Announcement' in 1843 stated the purpose of his Treasury as 'anti-Peter Parleyism', which expressed Cole's opposition to the Parley school of facts without fancy. Speaking of the restricted state of children's literature in his day, he regretted that 'the many tales sung or said—from time immemorial, which appealed to the other and certainly not less important elements of a little child's mind, its fancy, imagination, sympathies, affections, are almost all gone out of memory, and are scarcely to be obtained.' Cole intended his *Home Treasury* to be the antidote to a 'narrow' cultivation of the understanding. Inspired by William Blake's book productions, he had his series carefully designed for maximum visual stimulation.

In addition to these publishing endeavours, another indication of the considerable energies that were being channelled into the twin objectives of amusing and instructing children is visible in the works of certain literary artists whose reputations extend far beyond the field of children's literature. The personal symbolism and mythology of William Blake's prophetic books and the rhapsodic genius of Christopher Smart's lengthy poems are primarily adult fare. But the achievement of Charles Lamb, a prominent man of letters who wrote a great deal for the young, stands without comparison in the development of reading material for them. Filling what he saw as an unfortunate gap in the experience of children, he paraphrased Chapman's *Odyssey* and, with his sister, summarized Shakespeare's plays. In his letter to Coleridge (23 October 1802) he deplored the dismal reality that 'Science has succeeded to Poetry no less in the little walks of children than with men,' and asked: 'Is there no possibility of averting this sore evil?' His abridgements and original works for children were a resoundingly affirmative reply.

A further strategy directed against Mrs Barbauld and Mrs Trimmer was the beginning of a modern tradition of the fairy tale. John Newbery had deflated the importance of fairies; the Rational Moralists had worried about their misleading children; the Sunday school writers had simply expunged them from juvenile writing. But, in *Holiday House* Catherine Sinclair presents a charming 'instructress', Fairy Teach-all. Not a sententious hired tutor or stern governess, Teach-all conveys essential yet entertaining precepts to youngsters who are hardly paragons of sense and virtue. In fact Sinclair was among the first storytellers to write about real and therefore imperfect children. As she explained in her preface:

In these pages the author has endeavoured to paint that species of noisy, frolicsome, mischievous children which is now almost extinct, wishing to preserve a sort of fabulous remembrance of days long past, when young people were like wild horses on the prairies, rather than like well broken hacks on the road; and when

amidst many faults and eccentricities, there was still some individuality of character and feeling allowed to remain.

Writing for the entertainment of her own niece, nephew, and young brother, Miss Sinclair created a genuinely amusing picture of Victorian children—in this case undisciplined ones. The novelty of such a subject made the book very popular. The lessons are imparted by Uncle David and Lady Harriet—as well, in Uncle David's story reproduced in this chapter, by Fairy Teach-all—but the fun-loving, even somewhat destructive Graham children learn more through their own experience than through dispensed instruction. The boy heroes of another modern fairy tale, Francis Paget's *The Hope of the Katzekopfs: A Fairy Tale* (1844), rely on the magical, prescient guidance of the good fairy Lady Abracadabra to direct their adventures.

These fairy instructresses, Teach-all and Abracadabra, were probably known to Charles Kingsley when he introduced Mrs Doasyouwouldbedoneby and Mrs Bedonebyasyoudid to his underwater seminary in *The Water Babies* (1863). William Thackeray may have had both Abracadabra and the silly goings-on of the Katzekopf court in mind when, in *The Rose and the Ring* (1854), he created the Fairy Blackstick, the deceptive Angelica, bumbling Bulbo, indolent Giglio, and the surprise heroine Betsinda-Rosalba. Beginning with *At the Back of the North Wind* (1871) and on into the *Curdie* books (1872, 1882), George MacDonald mined the rich vein of the fairy convention. Even Oscar Wilde and Rudyard Kipling introduced a range of non-corporeal beings, as in 'The Happy Prince' and 'The Selfish Giant' (1886), and *Puck of Pook's Hill* (1906) and *Rewards and Fairies* (1909).

The writers featured in this chapter were by no means typical of the authors who wrote for children in the pre-1850 period: the moralists and those who pandered to a recently literate market with crude chapbooks and saw their task as disciplining socially subordinate populations were in the majority. But, in assuming the role of guardians of children's hopes with true and insightful understanding, the work of Smart, Blake, the Taylors, Roscoe, Lamb, Moore, Hale, Sinclair, Lear, Hoffmann, and others exerted an enormous influence. Exploring such Romantic values as creativity, spontaneity, and intuitive sympathy, these artists created poems and stories that tasted more of honey than medicine. Significantly, their experiments, which intensified at the dawn of the Victorian era, expanded the range of projects to educate and cultivate the young by accustoming them to wit, playfulness, ironic humour, and zany frivolity. Furthermore, by this time a new genre that excluded overt instruction had been introduced: the action-filled adventure story. (Space limitations prevent the inclusion of extracts from three of the best of these: Harriet Martineau's *The Playfellow* [1841] and Captain Frederick Marryat's *Mr Midshipman Easy* [1826] and *Masterman Ready* [1841].) By the opening of the Golden Age a felt need had developed, and was beginning to be satisfied, not just for children's books, but for children's literature: works of the imagination clothed in delight.

CHRISTOPHER SMART (1722–71)
From *Hymns for the Amusement of Children* (1772)

Christopher Smart is a figure of contradictions: a Cambridge scholar who published in plebeian periodicals; a debt-ridden, alcoholic husband and father who wrote hymns of praise; and a labelled madman who challenged eighteenth-century practices of diagnosis and confinement. With penury constantly facing him, Smart composed libretti for oratorios, wrote satires under the name of Ebenezer Pentweazle, contributed to a three-penny journal as 'Mary Midnight' (a pseudonym borrowed from Delarivier Manley), and found employment in various other forms of hack work for his father-in-law, John Newbery. For a period of seven years (1757–63) he was incarcerated in St Luke's Hospital and then in Mr Potter's asylum in Bethnal Green. The conflicted musings of his friend Dr Johnson, who was not convinced that Smart was mad, point to an understanding of madness as a cultural construct. Johnson remarked: 'I did not think he ought to be shut up. His infirmities were not noxious to society. He insisted on people praying with him; and I'd as lief pray with Kit Smart as any one else.' On the subject of Smart's supposed madness, Boswell quotes Johnson's ironic observations: 'Madness frequently discovers itself merely by unnecessary deviation from the usual modes of the world. My poor friend Smart shewed the disturbance of his mind, by falling on his knees, and saying his prayers in the street, or in any other unusual place.

Now although, rationally speaking, it is greater madness not to pray at all, than to pray as Smart did, I am afraid there are so many who do not pray, that their understanding is not called in question.' One of Smart's most recent biographers, Chris Mounsey, calls him 'clown of God'.

In spite of his 'unhappy vacillation of mind' (Boswell's words), Smart was capable of writing illuminating Christian verse, whose amazingly simple language disrupts such Enlightenment values as rational thought and practical business. *Hymns for the Amusement of Children*—containing thirty-nine hymns that were written wholly or largely while he was in debtor's prison (where he died), and were published posthumously—stands as the intermediary text between Watts's *Divine and Moral Songs* and Blake's *Songs of Innocence and of Experience*. Smart enlarges the Christian spirit of Watts by concentrating on an escape from the ordinary and access to self-transcendence, aspects of his hymns that anticipate the personal symbolism and lyrical rendering of childhood in Blake's songs. Smart's observations of his cat, 'My Cat Jeoffry' from *Jubilate Agno* (Rejoice in the Lamb), written during his madhouse confinement (and not published until 1939), adroitly blend simple empiricism and spiritual deduction: both the human being and his cat are touched by—and expressions of—the divine.

Hymn X
Truth

'Tis thus the holy Scriptures ends,
   'Whoever loves or makes a lie,
'On heavens felicity depends
   'In vain, for he shall surely die.'

5 The stars, the firmament, the sun,
   God's glorious work, God's great design,
All, all was finish'd as begun,
   By rule, by compass, and by line.

Hence David unto heaven appeals,
10   'Ye heav'ns his righteousness declare';
His signet their duration seals,
   And bids them be as firm, as fair.

Then give me grace, celestial Sire,
   The truth to love, the truth to tell;
15 Let everlasting sweets aspire,
   And filth and falshood sink to hell.

Hymn XI
Beauty. *For a Damsel.*

Christ, keep me from the self-survey
    Of beauties all thine own;
If there is beauty, let me pray
    And praise the Lord alone.

5 Pray—that I may the fiend withstand,
    Where'er his serpents be;
Praise—that the Lord's almighty hand
    Is manifest in me.

It is not so—my features are
10   Much meaner than the rest;
A glow-worm cannot be a star,
    And I am plain at best.

Then come, my love thy grace impart,
    Great Saviour of mankind;
15 O come, and purify my heart,
    And beautify my mind.

Then will I thy carnations nurse,
    And cherish every role;
And empty to the poor my purse,
20   Till grace to glory grows.

Hymn XVI
Learning

Come, come with emulative strife,
To learn the way, the truth, and life,
    Which Jesus is in one;
In all sound doctrine he proceeds,
5 From Alpha to Omega leads,
    E'en Spirit, Sire, and Son.

Sure of th' exceeding great reward,
Midst all your learning learn the Lord—
    This was thy doctrine, Paul;
10 And this thy lecture shou'd persuade,
Tho' thou hadst more of human aid,
    Than blest brethren all.

Humanity's a charming thing,
And every science of the ring,
15   Good is the classic lore;
For these are helps along the road,
That leads to Zion's blest abode,
    And heav'nly muse's store.

But greater still in each respect,
20 He that communicates direct
    The tutor of the soul;
Who without pain, degrees or parts,
While he illuminates our hearts,
    Can teach at once the whole.

Hymn XXV
Mirth

If you are merry sing away,
   And touch the organs sweet;
This is the Lord's triumphant day,
Ye children in the gall'ries gay,
5   Shout from each goodly seat.

It shall be May to-morrow's morn,
   A field then let us run,
And deck us in the blooming thorn,
Soon as the cock begins to warn,
10   And long before the sun.

—I give the praise to Christ Alone,
   My pinks already show;
And my streak'd roses fully blown,
The sweetness of the Lord make known,
15   And to his glory grow.

Ye little prattlers that repair
   For cowslips in the mead,
Of those exulting colts beware,
But blythe security is there,
20   Where skipping lambkins feed.

With white and crimson laughs the sky,
   With birds the hedge-rows ring;
To give the praise to God most High,
And all the sulky fiends defy,
25   Is a most joyful thing.

Hymn XXXV
At Dressing in the Morning

Now I arise, impow'r'd by Thee,
    The glorious sun to face;
O cloath me with humility,
    Adorn me with thy grace.

5 All evil of the day forefend,
    Prevent the Tempter's snare;
Thine Angel on my steps attend,
    And give me fruit to pray'r,

O make me useful as I go
10   My pilgrimage along;
And sweetly sooth this vale of woe
    By charity and song.

Let me from Christ obedience learn
    To Christ obedience pay;
15 Each parent duteous love return,
    And consecrate the day.

Hymn XXXVI
At Undressing in the Evening

These cloaths, of which I now devest
    Myself, ALL-SEEING EYE,
Must be one day (that day be blest)
    Relinquish'd and laid by.

5 Thou cordial sleep, to death akin,
    I court thee on my knee;
O let my exit, free from sin,
    Be little more than Thee.

But if much agonizing pain
10   My dying hour await,
The Lord be with me to sustain,
    To help and to abate.

O let me meet Thee undeterr'd
    By no foul stains defil'd!
15 According to thy Holy Word,
    Receive me as a Child.

My Cat Jeoffry

For I will consider my Cat Jeoffry.

For he is the servant of the Living God, duly and daily serving him.

For at the first glance of the glory of God in the East he worships in his way.

For is this done by wreathing his body seven times round with elegant quickness.

5 For then he leaps up to catch the musk, which is the blessing of God upon his prayer.

For he rolls upon prank to work it in.

For having done duty and received blessing he begins to consider himself.

For this he performs in ten degrees.

For first he looks upon his fore-paws to see if they are clean.

10 For secondly he kicks up behind to clear away there.

For thirdly he works it upon stretch with the fore-paws extended.

For fourthly he sharpens his paws by wood.

For fifthly he washes himself.

For sixthly he rolls upon wash.

15 For seventhly he fleas himself, that he may not be interrupted upon the beat.

For eighthly he rubs himself against a post.

For ninthly he looks up for his instructions.

For tenthly he goes in quest of food.

For having consider'd God and himself he will consider his neighbour.

20 For if he meets another cat he will kiss her in kindness.

For when he takes his prey he plays with it to give it a chance.

For one mouse in seven escapes by his dallying.

For when his day's work is done his business more properly begins.

For he keeps the Lord's watch in the night against the adversary.

25 For he counteracts the powers of darkness by his electrical skin & glaring eyes.

For he counteracts the Devil, who is death, by brisking about the life.

For in his morning orisons he loves the sun and the sun loves him.

For he is of the tribe of Tiger.

For the Cherub Cat is a term of the Angel Tiger.

30 For he has the subtlety and hissing of a serpent, which in goodness he suppresses.

For he will not do destruction, if he is well-fed, neither will he spit without provocation.

For he purrs in thankfulness, when God tells him he's a good Cat.

For he is an instrument for the children to learn benevolence upon.

For every house is incomplete without him & a blessing is lacking in the spirit.

35 For the Lord commanded Moses concerning the cats at the departure of the Children of Israel from Egypt.

For every family had one cat at least in the bag.

For the English Cats are the best in Europe.

For he is the cleanest in the use of his fore-paws of any quadrupede.

For the dexterity of his defence is an instance of the love of God to him exceedingly.

40 For he is the quickest to his mark of any creature.

For he is tenacious of his point.

For he is a mixture of gravity and waggery.

For he knows that God is his Saviour.
For there is nothing sweeter than his peace when at rest.
45 For there is nothing brisker than his life when in motion.
For he is of the Lord's poor and so indeed is he called by benevolence perpetually—
    Poor Jeoffry! poor Jeoffry! the rat has bit thy throat.
For I bless the name of the Lord Jesus that Jeoffry is better.
For the divine spirit comes about his body to sustain it in complete cat.
For his tongue is exceeding pure so that it has in purity what it wants in music.
50 For he is docile and can learn certain things.
For he can set up with gravity which is patience upon approbation.
For he can fetch and carry, which is patience in employment.
For he can jump over a stick which is patience upon proof positive.
For he can spraggle upon waggle at the word of command.
55 For he can jump from an eminence into his master's bosom.
For he can catch the cork and toss it again.
For he is hated by the hypocrite and miser.
For the former is afraid of detection.
For the latter refuses the charge.
60 For he camels his back to bear the first notion of business.
For he is good to think on, if a man would express himself neatly.
For he made a great figure in Egypt for his signal services.
For he killed the Icneumon-rat very pernicious by land.
For his ears are so acute that they sting again.
65 For from this proceeds the passing quickness of his attention.
For by stroking of him I have found out electricity.
For I perceived God's light about him both wax and fire.
For the Electrical fire is the spiritual substance, which God sends from heaven to
    sustain the bodies both of man and beast.
For God has blessed him in the variety of his movements.
70 For, though he cannot fly, he is an excellent clamberer.
For his motions upon the face of the earth are more than any other quadrupede.
For he can tread to all the measures upon the music.
For he can swim for life.
For he can creep.

WILLIAM BLAKE (1757–1857)
From *Songs of Innocence and of Experience Shewing the Two Contrary States of the Human Soul* (1794)

Poet, engraver, painter, and mystic, Blake spent his life as an obscure, eccentric artist in London; though greatly gifted, he was neglected and even ridiculed in his lifetime. Like Wordsworth and Coleridge he supported the radical cause of the French Revolution. Never complacently at ease with other artists, however, he was determined to found an art of his own: 'I must Create a System or be enslav'd by another Man's. I will not Reason & Compare; my business is to Create' (Jerusalem: 10, 20–1).

At approximately the same time as *Songs*, he composed *The French Revolution, America: A Prophecy, Europe: A Prophecy*, and the satire *A Marriage of Heaven and Hell*. His prophetic writing reformulates biblical narrative, which Blake called 'the Great Code of Art'. His marriage was childless; his wife assisted him in engraving and painting. For the *Songs* he etched his texts and illustrations together on a copper plate and handcoloured each print, thus producing a harmonious, aesthetic whole that illustrated his view of poetry as 'allegory addressed to the intellectual powers'. In 1794 he added *Songs of Experience* to his *Songs of Innocence* of 1789. The poems' compression of metaphor and symbol, their combination of words and design, and the importance of the child-figure in representing joy as well as misery—often through paired contrasts—continue to entrance readers of all ages. The songs' child-like imagery and lyrical simplicity ensure that many of them have entered the domain of children's literature.

Songs of Innocence (1789)

The Lamb

    Little Lamb who made thee?
    Dost thou know who made thee?
Gave thee life & bid thee feed,
By the stream & o'er the mead;
5 Gave thee clothing of delight,
Softest clothing wooly bright;
Gave thee such a tender voice,
Making all the vales rejoice:
    Little Lamb who made thee?
10   Dost thou know who made thee?

    Little Lamb I'll tell thee,
    Little Lamb I'll tell thee:
He is called by thy name,
For he calls himself a Lamb.
15 He is meek, and he is mild;
He became a little child.
I a child, and thou a lamb,
We are callèd by his name.
    Little Lamb, God bless thee!
20   Little Lamb, God bless thee!

Infant Joy

'I have no name:
I am but two days old.'
What shall I call thee?
'I happy am
5 Joy is my name.'
Sweet joy befall thee!

Pretty joy!
Sweet Joy, but two days old,
Sweet Joy I call thee!
10 Thou dost smile,
I sing the while,
Sweet joy befall thee!

Spring

Sound the Flute!
Now it's mute.
Birds delight
Day and Night.
5 Nightingale
In the dale
Lark in Sky
Merrily
Merrily, merrily to welcome in the Year.

10 Little Boy
Full of joy.
Little Girl
Sweet and small.
Cock does crow
15 So do you.
Merry voice
Infant noise
Merrily, merrily to welcome in the Year.

Little Lamb,
20 Here I am.
Come and lick
My white neck.
Let me pull
Your soft Wool.
25 Let me kiss
Your soft face.
Merrily, merrily we welcome in the Year.

Holy Thursday

'Twas on a Holy Thursday, their innocent faces clean,
The children walking two and two, in red and blue and green,
Grey-headed beadles walked before, with wands as white as snow,
Till into the high dome of Paul's they like Thames' waters flow.

5 O what a multitude they seemed, these flowers of London town!
Seated in companies they sit with radiance all their own.
The hum of multitudes was there, but multitudes of lambs,
Thousands of little boys and girls raising their innocent hands.

Now like a mighty wind they raise to Heaven the voice of song,
10 Or like harmonious thunderings the seats of Heaven among.
Beneath them sit the aged men, wise guardians of the poor;
Then cherish pity; lest you drive an angel from your door.

The Chimney Sweeper

When my mother died, I was very young,
And my father sold me while yet my tongue
Could scarcely cry ''weep! 'weep! 'weep! 'weep!'
So your chimneys I sweep, and in soot I sleep.

5 There's little Tom Dacre, who cried when his head,
That curled like a lamb's back, was shav'd: so I said,
'Hush, Tom! never mind it, for when your head's bare,
You know that the soot cannot spoil your white hair.'

And so he was quiet, and that very night,
10 As Tom was a-sleeping, he had such a sight!
That thousands of sweepers, Dick, Joe, Ned, and Jack,
Were all of them locked up in coffins of black.

And by came an Angel who had a bright key,
And he opened the coffins and set them all free;
15 Then down a green plain leaping, laughing, they run,
And wash in a river, and shine in the Sun.

Then naked and white, all their bags left behind,
They rise upon clouds, and sport in the wind;
And the Angel told Tom, if he'd be a good boy,
20 He'd have God for his father, and never want joy.

And so Tom awoke; and we rose in the dark,
And got with our bags and our brushes to work.
Though the morning was cold, Tom was happy and warm;
So if all do their duty they need not fear harm.

Songs of Experience (1794)

The Tyger

Tyger! Tyger! burning bright,
In the forests of the night;
What immortal hand or eye,
Could frame thy fearful symmetry?

5 In what distant deeps or skies,
Burnt the fire of thine eyes?
On what wings dare he aspire?
What the hand dare seize the fire?

And what shoulder, and what art,
10 Could twist the sinews of thy heart?
And when thy heart began to beat,
What dread hand? And what dread feet?

What the hammer? what the chain,
In what furnace was thy brain?
15 What the anvil? what dread grasp,
Dare its deadly terrors clasp?

When the stars threw down their spears
And watered heaven with their tears:
Did he smile his work to see?
20 Did he who made the Lamb make thee?

Tyger! Tyger! burning bright,
In the forests of the night:
What immortal hand or eye,
Dare frame thy fearful symmetry?

Infant Sorrow

My mother groaned! my father wept.
Into the dangerous world I leapt:
Helpless, naked, piping loud:
Like a fiend hid in a cloud.

5 Struggling in my father's hands:
Striving against my swaddling-bands:
Bound and weary I thought best
To sulk upon my mother's breast.

The Chimney Sweeper

A little black thing among the snow,
Crying "'weep! 'weep!' in notes of woe!
'Where are thy father and mother? say?'
'They are both gone up to the church to pray.'

5 'Because I was happy upon the heath,
And smiled among the winter's snow,
They clothed me in the clothes of death,
And taught me to sing the notes of woe.

'And because I am happy, and dance and sing,
10 They think they have done me no injury,
And are gone to praise God and his Priest and King,
Who make up a heaven of our misery.'

Holy Thursday

Is this a holy thing to see,
In a rich and fruitful land,
Babes reduced to misery,
Fed with cold and usurous hand?

5 Is that trembling cry a song?
Can it be a song of joy?
And so many children poor?
It is a land of poverty!

And their sun does never shine,
10 And their fields are bleak and bare,
And their ways are filled with thorns:
It is eternal winter there.

For where'er the sun does shine,
And where'er the rain does fall,
15 Babe can never hunger there,
Nor poverty the mind appall.

JOHN MARSHALL (*fl.* 1783–1823)
From *The Infant's Library* (*c.* 1800)

This 'library' of sixteen miniature books is itself a delightful object—a decorated wooden box divided into four compartments with a sliding front panel. Printer and bookseller John Marshall was an astute promoter of what children wanted to see and what their parents were willing to buy. He dedicated 'these little volumes principally intended for amusement' to youngsters, never missing an opportunity to remind his clientele where 'a great variety of books and schemes for the Instruction and Amusement of young people' could be purchased. The little books—sixty-four pages each, with pastel boards, centre stitching, and an illustration per opening—deal with the alphabet, common nouns, animals, rural and urban scenes, flowers, birds, games for girls and boys, and a brief catalogue of kings and queens from William the Conqueror to George III. Though the textual accompaniments—by Marshall or a hack in his employ—were not polished, they successfully engaged a young audience by speaking to them directly. As Emma Laws notes in her curated exhibit of Miniature Libraries, Marshall hoped to galvanize the children's book market by producing three small gems simultaneously: *The Infant's Library, The Juvenile; or Child's Library,* and *The Doll's Library* <www.nal.vam.ac.uk/exhibits/miniaturelibraries/introduction.html>. Marshall also published *The Infant's Library* in Latin, German, and French. One of his last publications, a book of limericks entitled *Anecdotes and Adventures of Fifteen Gentlemen* (*c.* 1822)—possibly by Richard Scraften Sharpe (*c.* 1775–1852)—contains the verse 'There was a rich man of Tobago', which is held to have inspired Edward Lear's *Book of Nonsense* over two decades later.

The illustrations that follow are from a copy donated to the Osborne Collection of Early Children's Books, Toronto Public Library, by Dr Elizabeth Budd Bentley.

From *The Infant's Library*

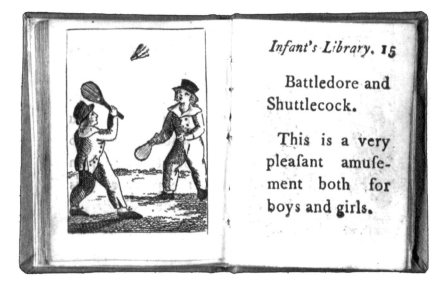

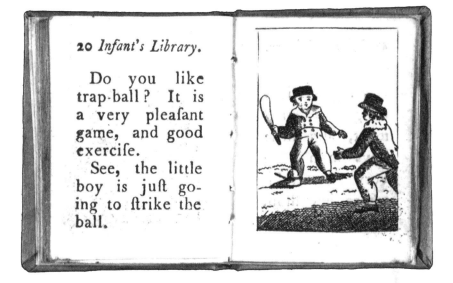

20 *Infant's Library.*

Do you like trap-ball? It is a very pleasant game, and good exercise.

See, the little boy is just going to strike the ball.

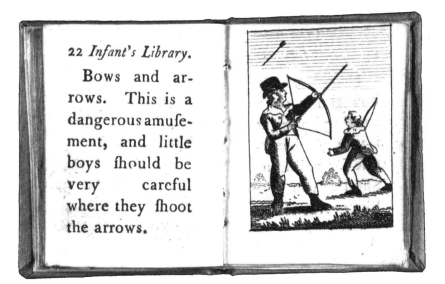

22 *Infant's Library.*

Bows and arrows. This is a dangerous amusement, and little boys should be very careful where they shoot the arrows.

24 *Infant's Library.*

I will practife a minuet, and when Harriet and Matilda come in the evening, they will dance to it.

24 *Infant's Library.*

Here is a little boy riding on a rocking-horfe; it is very good exercife for children. Should you not like to ride too?

26 *Infant's Library.*

I will be the governeſs.

Learn your book well, Kitty, or you will be correɛted.

Maria, you are a good girl, and ſhall be rewarded.

28 *Infant's Library.*

Three little boys playing at marbles. See, they have placed them in a ring; I believe this play is called taw.

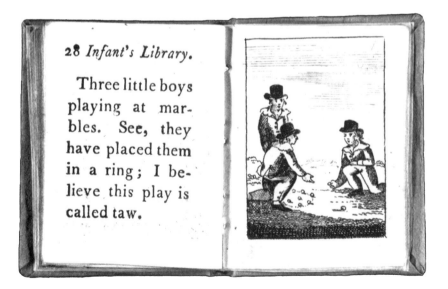

ANN TAYLOR GILBERT (1782–1866) and
JANE TAYLOR (1783–1824)
From *Original Poems for Infant Minds* (1804–5) and
Rhymes for the Nursery (1806)

The daughters of Isaac Taylor were vivacious girls who as children composed stories, plays, and verse for their own amusement. The whole family had an inclination to write; indeed, their father and brother made contributions to *Original Poems*. The publisher Darton and Harvey added further poems by Adelaide O'Keefe (1776–1855) to make up this well-loved collection of ditties that blend caution, justice, humour, and sentiment, and do so in a graceful conversational style. In their preface to *Rhymes for the Nursery* they asked respectfully to be allowed to show 'whether ideas adapted to the comprehension of infancy, admit the restrictions of rhyme and metre.' As the illustration from an 1868 edition testifies, their work remained popular for many decades.

From *Original Poems for Infant Minds*

Meddlesome Matty

One ugly trick has often spoil'd
    The sweetest and the best;
Matilda, though a pleasant child,
    One ugly trick possessed,
5 Which, like a cloud before the skies,
Hid all her better qualities.

Sometimes she'd lift the tea-pot lid,
    To peep at what was in it;
Or tilt the kettle, if you did
10   But turn your back a minute.
In vain you told her not to touch,
Her trick of meddling grew so much.

Her grandmamma went out one day,
    And by mistake she laid
15 Her spectacles and snuff-box gay
    Too near the little maid;
'Ah! well,' thought she, 'I'll try them on,
As soon as grandmamma is gone.'

Forthwith she placed upon her nose
20   The glasses large and wide;
And looking round, as I suppose,
    The snuff-box too she spied:
'Oh! what a pretty box is that;
I'll open it,' said little Matt.

25 'I know that grandmamma would say,
    "Don't meddle with it, dear;"
But then, she's far enough away,
    And no one else is near:
Besides, what can there be amiss
30 In opening such a box as this?'

So thumb and finger went to work
    To move the stubborn lid,
And presently a mighty jerk
    The mighty mischief did;
35 For all at once, ah! woeful case,
The snuff came puffing in her face.

Poor eyes, and nose, and mouth, beside
    A dismal sight presented;
In vain, as bitterly she cried,
40   Her folly she repented.
In vain she ran about for ease,
She could do nothing now but sneeze.

She dash'd the spectacles away,
　　To wipe her tingling eyes,
45 And as in twenty bits they lay,
　　Her grandmamma she spies.
'Heyday! and what's the matter now?'
Says grandmamma, with lifted brow.

　　Matilda, smarting with the pain,
50 　　And tingling still, and sore,
Made many a promise to refrain
　　From meddling evermore.
And 'tis a fact, as I have heard,
She ever since has kept her word.

The Wooden Doll and the Wax Doll

There were two friends, a very charming pair!
Brunette the brown, and Blanchidine the fair;
And she to love Brunette did constantly incline,
Nor less did Brunette love sweet Blanchidine.
5 Brunette in dress was neat, yet always plain;
But Blanchidine of finery was vain.

Now Blanchidine a new acquaintance made—
A little girl most sumptuously arrayed,
In plumes and ribbons, gaudy to behold,
10 And India frock, with spots of shining gold.
Said Blanchidine, 'A girl so richly dress'd
Should surely be by every one caress'd.
To play with me if she will condescend,
Henceforth 'tis she alone shall be my friend.'

15 And so for this new friend in silks adorn'd,
Her poor Brunette was slighted, left, and scorn'd.
Of Blanchidine's vast stock of pretty toys,
A wooden doll her every thought employs;
Its neck so white, so smooth, its cheeks so red—
20 She kiss'd, she fondled, and she took to bed.

Mamma now brought her home a doll of wax,
Its hair in ringlets white, and soft as flax;
Its eyes could open and its eyes could shut;
And on it, too, with taste its clothes were put,
25 'My dear wax doll!' sweet Blanchidine would cry—
Her doll of wood was thrown neglected by.

One summer's day,—'twas in the month of June,—
The sun blazed out in all the heat of noon:
'My waxen doll,' she cried, 'my dear, my charmer!
30 What, are you cold? but you shall soon be warmer.'
She laid it in the sun—misfortune dire!
The wax ran down as if before the fire!
Each beauteous feature quickly disappear'd,
And melting, left a blank all soil'd and smear'd.

35 Her doll disfigured she beheld amazed,
And thus express'd her sorrow as she gazed:
'Is it for you my heart I have estranged
From that I fondly loved, which has not changed?
Just so may change my new acquaintance fine,
40 For whom I left Brunette, that friend of mine.
No more by outside show will I be lured;
Of such capricious whims I think I'm cured:
To plain old friends my heart shall still be true,
Nor change for every face because 'tis new.'
45 Her slighted wooden doll resumed its charms,
And wrong'd Brunette she clasp' d within her arms.

ADELAIDE O'KEEFE

My Mother

Who fed me from her gentle breasts,
And hushed me in her arms to rest,
And on my cheek sweet kisses prest?
        My Mother.

5 When sleep forsook my open eye,
Who was it sung sweet hushaby,
And rocked me that I should not cry?
        My Mother.

Who sat and watched my infant head,
10 When sleeping on my cradle bed,
And tears of sweet affection shed?
        My Mother.

When pain and sickness made me cry,
Who gazed upon my heavy eye,
15 And wept, for fear that I should die?
        My Mother.

Who dressed my doll in clothes so gay,
And fondly taught me how to play,
And minded all I had to say?
20   My Mother.

Who ran to help me when I fell,
And would some pretty story tell,
Or kiss the place to make it well?
                My Mother.

25 Who taught my infant lips to pray,
And love God's holy book and day,
And walk in wisdom's pleasant way?
                My Mother.

And can I ever cease to be
30 Affectionate and kind to thee,
Who was so very kind to me?
                My Mother.

Ah no! the thought I cannot bear,
And if God please my life to spare,
35 I hope I shall reward thy care,
                My Mother.

When thou art feeble, old, and grey,
My healthy arm shall be thy stay,
And I will soothe thy pains away,
40   My Mother.

And when I see thee hang thy head,
'Twill be my turn to watch thy bed,
And tears of sweet affection shed,
                My Mother.

45 For could our Father in the skies
Look down with pleased or loving eyes,
If ever I could dare despise
                My Mother?

From *Rhymes for the Nursery*

The Field Daisy

I'm a pretty little thing,
Always coming with the spring,
In the meadows green, I'm found,
Peeping just above the ground,
5　And my stalk is cover'd flat,
With a white and yellow hat.

Little lady, when you pass
Lightly o'er the tender grass,
Skip about, but do not tread
10　On my meek and healthy head,
For I always seem to say,
'Surly winter's gone away.'

ANN

The Baby's Dance

Dance little baby, dance up high,
Never mind baby, mother is by;
Crow and caper, caper and crow,
There little baby, there you go;
15　Up to the ceiling, down to the ground,
Backwards and forwards, round and round;
Dance little baby, and mother shall sing,
With the merry coral, ding, ding, ding.

ANN

The Star

Twinkle, twinkle, little star,
How I wonder what you are!
Up above the world so high,
Like a diamond in the sky.

5　When the blazing sun is gone,
When he nothing shines upon,
Then you show your little light,
Twinkle, twinkle, all the night.

Then the traveller in the dark,
10　Thanks you for your tiny spark,
He could not see which way to go,
If you did not twinkle so.

In the dark blue sky you keep,
And often through my curtains peep,
15 For you never shut your eye,
Till the sun is in the sky.

'Tis your bright and tiny spark,
Lights the traveller in the dark;
Though I know not what you are,
20 Twinkle, twinkle, little star.

JANE

The Michaelmas Daisy

I am very pale and dim,
With my faint and bluish rim;
Standing on my narrow stalk,
By the litter'd gravel walk,
5 And the withered leaves, aloft,
Fall upon me, very oft.

But I show my lonely head,
When the other flowers are dead,
And you're even glad to spy
10 Such a homely thing as I;
For I seem to smile, and say,
'Summer is not quite away.'

ANN

The Little Girl to her Dolly

There, go to sleep dolly, in own mother's lap;
I've put on your night-gown and neat little cap;
So sleep, pretty baby, and shut up your eye,
Bye bye, little dolly, lie still, and bye bye.

I'll lay my clean handkerchief over your head,
And then make believe that my lap is your bed;
So hush, little dear, and be sure you don't cry,
Bye bye, little dolly, lie still, and bye bye.

There,—now it is morning, and time to get up,
And I'll crumb you a mess, in my doll's china cup;
So wake little baby, and open your eye,
For I think it high time to have done with bye bye.

ANN

ELIZABETH TURNER (d. 1846)

From *The Daisy; or, Cautionary Stories in Verse Adapted to the Ideas of Children from Four to Eight Years Old* (1807)

Elizabeth Turner's collection of enjoyably facile doggerel has a strong moralistic flavour: the results of misbehaviour are swift and predictable. As the first 'cautionary stories in verse', it acquired a degree of fame; it was adapted by Heinrich Hoffmann in *Struwwelpeter* (1848) and parodied by Hilaire Belloc in his *Cautionary Tales* (1907).

The Giddy Girl

Miss Helen was always too giddy to heed
    What her mother had told her to shun;
For frequently, over the street in full speed,
    She would cross where the carriages run.

And out she would go to a very deep well,
    To look at the water below;
How naughty! to run to a dangerous well,
    Where her mother forbade her to go!

One morning, intending to take but one peep,
    Her foot slipp'd away from the ground;
Unhappy misfortune! the water was deep,
    And giddy Miss Helen was drown'd.

Dressed or Undressed

When children are naughty, and will not be dressed,
  Pray, what do you think is the way?
Why, often I really believe it is best
  To keep them in night-clothes all day!

But then they can have no good breakfast to eat,
  Nor walk with their mother or aunt;
At dinner they'll have neither pudding nor meat,
  Nor any thing else that they want.

Then who would be naughty, and sit all the day
  In night-clothes unfit to be seen?
And pray, who would lose all their pudding and play,
  For not being dressed neat and clean?

Careless Maria

Maria was a careless child,
   And grieved her friends by this:
      Where'er she went,
      Her clothes were rent,
Her hat and bonnet spoil'd,
   A careless little Miss!

Her gloves and mits were often lost,
   Her tippet sadly soil'd;
      You might have seen,
      Where she had been,
For toys all round were toss'd,
   Oh, what a careless child!

One day her uncle bought a toy,
   That round and round would twirl
      But when he found
      The litter'd ground,
He said, 'I don't tee-totums buy
   For such a careless girl!'

The New Penny

Miss Ann saw a man,
Quite poor, at a door,
And Ann had a pretty new Penny;
Now this the kind Miss
Threw pat in his hat,
Although she was left without any.

She meant, as she went,
To stop at a shop,
Where cakes she had seen a great many;
And buy a fruit-pie,
Or take home a cake,
By spending her pretty new penny.

But well I can tell,
When Ann gave the man
Her money, she wish'd not for any;
He said, 'I've no bread,'
She heard, and preferr'd
To give him her pretty new penny.

Dangerous Sport

Poor Peter was burnt by the poker one day,
  When he made it look pretty and red;
For the beautiful sparks made him think it fine play,
  To lift it as high as his head.

But somehow it happen'd, his finger and thumb
  Were terribly scorch'd by the heat;
And he scream'd out aloud for his Mother to come,
  And stamp'd on the floor with his feet.

Now if Peter had minded his Mother's command,
  His fingers would not have been sore;
And he promised again, as she bound up his hand,
  To play with hot pokers no more.

The Chimney Sweeper

Sweep! sweep! sweep! sweep! cries little Jack,
With brush and bag upon his back,
  And black from head to foot;
While daily as he goes along,
Sweep! sweep! sweep! sweep! is all his song,
  Beneath his load of soot.

But then he was not always black,
Oh, no! he once was pretty Jack,
   And had a kind Papa;
But, silly child! he ran to play
Too far from home, a long, long way,
   And did not ask Mamma.

So he was lost, and now must creep
Up chimneys, crying, Sweep! sweep! sweep!

Miss Sophia

Miss Sophy, one fine sunny day,
Left her work and ran away;
When soon she reached the garden-gate,
Which finding lock'd, she would not wait,
But tried to climb and scramble o'er
A gate as high as any door.

But little girls should never climb,
And Sophy won't another time;
For when, upon the highest rail,
Her frock was caught upon a nail,
She lost her hold, and, sad to tell,
Was hurt and bruised—for down she fell.

WILLIAM ROSCOE (1753–1831)
The Butterfly's Ball and the Grasshopper's Feast (1807)

Historian, attorney, banker, rare-book collector, and reform campaigner, William Roscoe of Liverpool was a leader of the cosmopolitan Enlightenment in that city. He had a keen interest in Italian culture and wrote the lives of Lorenzo de Medici (1796) and Leo X (1805). An amateur botanist as well, he was elected a fellow of the Linnaean Society (1805); he was also elected as the city's Whig member of Parliament (1806–7). Roscoe wrote *The Butterfly's Ball* as an amusement for his youngest son, Robert, and contributed it to *The Gentleman's Magazine* in 1806. The next year the publisher John Harris issued the rhyme, along with commissioned illustrations by William Mulready, in chapbook form. Whimsical, non-moral, and popular, *The Butterfly's Ball* appeared in many publications in the nineteenth century and was frequently paired in one volume with Catherine Dorset's *The Peacock 'At Home'* (which follows in this anthology). Just as Roscoe's later botanical research led to the naming of an order of one-stamen plants, 'Roscoea', his inventiveness in composing *The Butterfly's Ball* was honoured with a whole series of imitations.

The Butterfly's Ball *and the* Grasshopper's Feast

COME, take up your hats, and away let us haste
To the *Butterfly's* Ball and the *Grasshopper's* Feast:
The Trumpeter, *Gadfly*, has summoned the Crew,
And the Revels are now only waiting for you.
5   So said little Robert, and pacing along,
His merry Companions came forth in a throng,
And on the smooth Grass, by the side of a Wood,
Beneath a broad Oak that for ages had stood,

Saw the Children of Earth, and the Tenants of Air,
10 For an Evening's Amusement together repair.
And there came the *Beetle*, so blind and so black,
Who carried the *Emmet*, his Friend, on his back.
And there was the *Gnat*, and the *Dragon-fly* too,
With all their Relations, Green, Orange, and Blue.
15 And there came the *Moth*, with his plumage of down,
And the *Hornet*, in Jacket of Yellow and Brown,

Who with him the *Wasp*, his Companion, did bring,
But they promised that Evening to lay by their Sting.
And the sly little *Dormouse* crept out of his hole,
20 And brought to the Feast his blind Brother, the *Mole*.
And the *Snail*, with his Horns peeping out of his Shell,
Came from a great distance, the Length of an Ell.
A Mushroom their Table, and on it was laid
A Water-dock Leaf, which a Table-cloth made.

25 The Viands were various, to each of their taste,
And the *Bee* brought her Honey to crown the Repast.
Then close on his haunches, so solemn and wise,
The *Frog* from a corner look'd up to the Skies;
And the *Squirrel*, well pleased such diversions to see,
30 Mounted high over-head, and look'd down from a Tree.
Then out came the *Spider*, with finger so fine,
To shew his dexterity on the tight line.

From one branch to another, his Cobwebs he slung,
Then quick as an arrow he darted along;
35 But just in the middle,—Oh! shocking to tell,
From his Rope, in an instant, poor Harlequin fell.
Yet he touch'd not the ground, but with talons outspread,
Hung suspended in air, at the end of a thread.
Then the *Grasshopper* came with a jerk and a spring;
40 Very long was his Leg, though but short was his Wing;

He took but three leaps, and was soon out of sight,
Then chirp' d his own praises the rest of the night.
With step so majestic the *Snail* did advance,
And promised the Gazers a Minuet to dance.
45 But they all laugh'd so loud that he pull'd in his head,
And went in his own little chamber to bed.
Then, as Evening gave way to the Shadows of Night,
Their Watchman, the *Glow-worm*, came out with a light.

Then Home let us hasten, while yet we can see,
50 For no Watchman is waiting for you and for me.
So said little Robert, and pacing along,
His merry Companions returned in a throng.

CATHERINE ANN DORSET (1750–1817)
The Peacock 'At Home' (1807)

The second number of John Harris's *Cabinet of Amusement and Instruction series*, Dorset's *The Peacock 'At Home'* presents the rousing response of the birds to Roscoe's insect fête. It is an ornithological comedy of manners, full of gossipy asides, details of costumes, comments on dance partners, and tantalizing menus.

The Peacock 'At Home'

The Butterfly's Ball, and the Grasshopper's Feasts,
Excited the spleen of the Birds and the Beasts:

For their mirth and good cheer—of the Bee was the theme,
And the Gnat blew his horn, as he danc'd in the beam.

5 'Twas humm'd by the Beetle, 'twas buzz'd by the Fly,
And sung by the myriads that sport 'neath the sky.

The Quadrupeds listen'd with sullen displeasure,
But the Tenants of Air were enrag'd beyond measure.

The Peacock display'd his bright plumes to the Sun,
10 And, addressing his Mates, thus indignant begun:

'Shall we, like domestic, inelegant Fowls,
'As unpolish'd as Geese, and as stupid as Owls,

'Sit tamely at home, hum drum, with our Spouses,
'While Crickets, and Butterflies, open their houses?

15 'Shall such mean little Insects pretend to the fashion?
'Cousin Turkey-cock, well may you be in a passion!

'If I suffer such insolent airs to prevail,
'May Juno pluck out all the eyes in my tail;

'So a Fête I will give, and my taste I'll display,
20 'And send out my cards for Saint Valentine's Day.'

—This determin'd, six fleet Carrier Pigeons went out,
To invite all the Birds to Sir Argus's Rout.

The nest-loving TURTLE-DOVE sent an excuse;
DAME PARTLET lay in, as did good Mrs GOOSE.

25 The TURKEY, poor soul! was confin'd to the rip:
    For all her young Brood had just fail'd with the pip.

    And the PARTRIDGE was ask'd; but a Neighbour hard by,
    Had engag'd a snug party to meet in a Pye;

    The WHEAT'EAR declin'd, recollecting her Cousins,
30 Last year, to a Feast were invited by dozens;

    But alas! they return'd not; and she had no taste
    To appear in a costume of vine-leaves or paste.

    The WOODCOCK preferr'd his lone haunt on the moor;
    And the Traveller, SWALLOW, was still on his tour.

35 The CUCKOO, who should have been one of the guests,
    Was rambling on visits to other Birds' Nests.

    But the rest, all accepted the kind invitation,
    And much bustle it caus'd in the plumed creation:

    Such ruffling of feathers, such pruning of coats!
40 Such chirping, such whistling, such clearing of throats!

    Such polishing bills, and such oiling of pinions!
    Had never been known in the biped dominions.

    The TAYLOR BIRD offer'd to make up new clothes;
    For all the young Birdlings, who wish'd to be Beaux:

45 He made for the ROBIN a doublet of red
    And a new velvet cap for the GOLDFINCH's head;

    He added a plume to the WREN's golden crest,
    And spangled with silver the GUINEA-FOWL's breast;

    While the HALCYON bent over the streamlet to view,
50 How pretty she look'd in her bodice of blue!

    Thus adorn'd, they set off for the Peacock's abode,
    With the Guide INDICATOR, who shew'd them the road:

From all points of the compass, came Birds of all feather;
And the PARROT can tell who and who were together.

55 There came LORD CASSOWARY, and General FLAMINGO,
And DON PEREQUETO, escap'd from Domingo;

From his high rock-built eyrie the EAGLE came forth,
And the Duchess of PTARMIGAN flew from the north.

The GREBE and the EIDER DUCK came up by water,
60 With the SWAN, who brought out the young CYGNET, her daughter.

From his woodland abode came the PHEASANT, to meet
Two kindred, arrived by the last India fleet:

The one, like a Nabob, in habit most splendid,
Where gold with each hue of the Rainbow was blended:

65 In silver and black, like a fair pensive Maid,
Who mourns for her love! was the other array'd.

The CHOUGH came from Cornwall, and brought up his Wife;
The GROUSE travell'd south, from his Lairdship in Fife;

The BUNTING forsook her soft nest in the reeds;
70 And the WIDOW-BIRD came, though she still wore her weeds;

Sir John HERON, of the Lakes, strutted in a *grand pas*,
But no card had been sent to the pilfering DAW,

As the Peacock kept up his progenitors' quarrel,
Which Esop relates, about cast-off apparel;

75 For Birds are like Men in their contests together,
And, in questions of right, can dispute for a feather.

The PEACOCK, Imperial, the pride of his race.
Receiv'd all his guests with an infinite grace,

Wav'd high his blue neck, and his train he display'd,
80 Embroider'd with gold, and with em'ralds inlaid.

Then with all the gay troup to the shrubb'ry repair'd,
Where the musical Birds had a concert prepar'd;

A holly-bush form'd the Orchestra, and in it
Sat the Black-bird, the Thrush, the Lark, and the Linnet;

85 A BULL-FINCH, a captive! almost from the nest,
Now escap'd from his cage, and, with liberty blest,

In a sweet mellow tone, join'd the lessons of art
With the accents of nature, which flow'd from his heart.

The CANARY, a much-admir'd foreign musician,
90 Condescended to sing to the Fowls of condition,

While the NIGHTINGALE warbled, and quaver'd so fine,
That they all clapp'd their wings, and pronounc'd it divine!

The SKY LARK, in extacy, sang from a cloud,
And CHANTICLEER crow'd, and the YAFFIL laugh'd loud.

95 The dancing began, when the singing was over;
A DOTTEREL first open'd the ball with the PLOVER,

Baron STORK, in a waltz, was allow'd to excel,
With his beautiful Partner, the fair DEMOISELLE;

And a newly-fledg'd GOSLING, so spruce and genteel,
100 A minuet swam with young Mr TEAL.

A London-bred SPARROW—a pert forward Cit!
Danc'd a reel with Miss WAGTAIL, and little TOM TIT.

And the Sieur GUILLEMOT next perform'd a *pas seul,*
While the elderly Bipeds were playing a Pool.

105 The Dowager Lady TOUCAN first cut in,
With old Doctor BUZZARD, and Adm'ral PENGUIN.

From Ivy-bush Tow'r came Dame OWLET the Wise,
And Counsellor CROSSBILL sat by to advise.

Some Birds past their prime, o'er whose *heads* it was fated,
110 Should pass many St Valentines—yet be unmated,

Look'd on, and remark'd, that the prudent and sage,
Were quite overlook'd in this frivolous age,

When Birds, scarce pen-feather'd, were brought to a rout,
Forward Chits! from the egg-shell but newly come out;

115 That in their youthful days, they ne'er witness'd such frisking,
And how wrong! in the GREENFINCH to flirt with the SISKIN.

So thought Lady MACKAW, and her Friend COCKATOO,
And the RAVEN foretold that 'no good could ensue!'

They censur'd the BANTAM for strutting and crowing,
120 In those vile pantaloons, which he fancied look'd knowing;

And a want of decorum caus'd many demurs,
Against the GAME CHICKEN, for coming in spurs.

Old Alderman CORM'RANT, for supper impatient,
At the Eating-room door, for an hour, had been station'd,

125 Till a MAGPIE, at length, the banquet announcing,
Gave the signal, long wish'd for, a clamouring and pouncing

At the well-furnish'd board all were eager to perch;
But the little Miss CREEPERS were left in the lurch.

Description must fail; and the pen is unable
130 To describe all the lux'ries which cover'd the table.

Each delicate viand that taste could denote,
Wasps *a la sauce piquante*, and Flies *en compôte*;

Worms and Frogs *en friture*, for the web-footed Fowl,
And a barbecued Mouse was prepared for the Owls.

135 Nuts, grain, fruit, and fish, to regale ev'ry palate,
And groundsel and chick-weed serv'd up in a salad.

The RAZOR-BILL carv'd for the famishing group,
And the SPOONBILL obligingly ladled the soup;

So they fill'd all their crops with the dainties before 'em,
140 And the tables were cleared with the utmost decorum.

When they gaily had caroll'd till peep of the dawn,
The Lark gently hinted, 'twas time to be gone;

And his clarion, so shrill, gave the company warning,
That Chanticleer scented the gales of the morning.

145 So they chirp'd, in full chorus, a friendly adieu;
And, with hearts quite as light as the plumage that grew
On their merry-thought bosoms, away they all flew. . . .

Then long live the PEACOCK, in splendor unmatch'd,
Whose Ball shall be talk'd of, by Birds yet unhatch'd;

150 His praise let the Trumpeter loudly proclaim,
And the Goose lend her quill to transmit it to Fame.

FELICIA DOROTHEA BROWNE, later HEMANS (1793–1835)
From *Poems* (1808)

Born in Liverpool and raised in north Wales, near Abergele, Denbighshire, Felicia Browne was a precocious child. Thanks to the support of William Roscoe the younger, her first quarto volume—consisting of poems about family life, emotional states, and natural descriptions—was published when she was only fifteen. Although *Poems* was severely reviewed, it remains a remarkable anthology of sentimental themes, as Hemans' most recent editor, Gary Kelly, puts it, 'couched in forms familiar from approved eighteenth-century authors'. With their intense love of nature, ingenuous displays of family affection, and pursuit of artistic expressivity, the poems started the career of this tremendously prolific and popular artist, who published over twenty volumes of poetry in her lifetime—many of which were reprinted throughout the nineteenth century.

Invocation to the Fairies

For My Sister's Grotto

> Fays and Fairies haste away!
> This is Harriet's holiday:
> Bring the lyre, and bring the lute,
> Bring the sweetly-breathing flute;
> 5 Wreaths of cowslips hither bring,
> All the honours of the spring;
> Adorn the grot with all that's gay,
> Fays and Fairies haste away.
> Bring the vine to Bacchus dear,
> 10 Bring the purple lilac here,

Festoons of roses, sweetest flower,
The yellow primrose of the bower,
Blue-ey'd violets wet with dew,
Bring the clustering woodbine too.
15 Bring in baskets made of rush,
The cherry with its ripen'd blush,
The downy peach, so soft, so fair,
The luscious grape, the mellow pear:
These to Harriet hither bring,
20 And sweetly in return she'll sing.
Be the brilliant grotto scene
The palace of the Fairy Queen.
Form the sprightly circling dance,
Fairies here your steps advance;
25 To the harp's soft dulcet sound,
Let your footsteps lightly bound.
Unveil your forms to mortal eye;
Let Harriet view your revelry.

Wisdom

All Wisdom's ways are smooth and fair,
No treasures can with hers compare;
More precious than the ruby bright,
She leads to honour and delight.
5 Seek her, and she is quickly found,
With never-fading olives crown'd.
Riches may fly within an hour,
Pale sickness wither beauty's flower,
Death may our dearest friendships sever,
10 And rend the social tie for ever;
Ah! what but Wisdom then remains,
To cheer the heart beneath its pains!
To bid each murmuring thought arise,
And soar with rapture to the skies.
15 She calms the passions of the breast,
With soothing hopes of future rest;
And like a minister of heaven,
She tells us 'mortals are forgiven.'
Then Ophir's gold to her is nought,
20 Nor polished silver finely wrought;
Nor all the jewels of the mine,
Compar'd with Wisdom's gem divine.

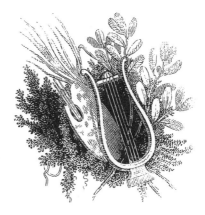

Lines to Major Cox

On Receiving from Him an Elegant Box of Colours

Tho' youthful ardour fires my glowing heart,
To copy Nature with enchanting Art;
Ah! still I fondly strive with effort vain,
The pencil's flowing graces to attain.
5   But when Instruction guides my roving feet,
To reach the Muse of Painting's lofty seat;
Where Genius learns in magic colours warm,
To join Expression's fire and Beauty's form;
If then 'tis mine with energy to trace
10 The varied charms of Nature's blooming face;
To dress the mimic flowers in rainbow dyes,
Bright as the blushes of the orient skies;
In glowing hues to bid the landscape live,
Or to the figure animation give;
15 Oh! then, my pencil's tribute justly due,
Sweet Gratitude shall consecrate to you.

CHARLES and MARY LAMB (1775–1834; 1764–1847)
From *Poetry for Children* (1809)

Charles Lamb, whose pen-name was Elia, was an essayist, poet, and critic. Devoted companion and custodian, through his whole adult life, of his sometimes mentally unbalanced sister Mary, Lamb enjoyed close friendships with Coleridge, Wordsworth, Hazlitt, and Crabb Robinson. The Lambs had produced some notable works for children prior to the appearance of *Poetry for Children*. Charles had adapted and expanded the familiar nursery rhyme about the exploit of a pack of cards in *The King of Hearts with the Rogueries of the Knave who stole away the Queen's Pies* (1805). Brother and sister together had composed summaries of Shakespeare's plays, with Mary doing the comedies and Charles the tragedies, in *Tales from Shakespeare* (1807). Charles had synopsized Chapman's *Odyssey* as *The Adventures of Ulysses* (1808) and had contributed three stories to his sister's collection of stories about young ladies, *Mrs Leicester's School* (1809). *Poetry for Children* contains brother–sister dialogues, one of them alluding to William Roscoe, and a slightly uneasy treatment of fancy. For the most part these poems on childlike subjects are contrived and wooden—they lack the light touch and literary grace of the Lambs' prose for children—but the book was well received in its day.

Chusing a Name

I have got a new-born sister;
I was nigh the first that kiss'd her.
When the nursing woman brought her
To Papa, his infant daughter,
5 How Papa's dear eyes did glisten!—
She will shortly be to christen:
And Papa has made the offer,
I shall have the naming of her.

Now I wonder what would please her,
10 Charlotte, Julia, or Louisa.
Ann and Mary, they're too common;
Joan's too formal for a woman;
Jane's a prettier name beside;
But we had a Jane that died.
15 They would say, if 'twas Rebecca,
That she was a little Quaker.
Edith's pretty, but that looks
Better in old English books;
Ellen's left off long ago;
20 Blanch is out of fashion now.
None that I have nam'd as yet
Are so good as Margaret.

Emily is neat and fine.
What do you think of Caroline?
25 How I'm puzzled and perplext
What to chuse or think of next!
I am in a little fever.
Lest the name that I shall give her
Should disgrace her or defame her,
30 I will leave Papa to name her.

What is Fancy?

SISTER

I am to write three lines, and you
Three others that will rhyme.
There—now I've done my task.

BROTHER

Three stupid lines as e'er I knew.
When you've the pen next time,
Some Question of me ask.

SISTER

Then tell me, brother, and pray mind,
Brother, you tell me true:
What sort of thing is *fancy*?

BROTHER

By all that I can ever find,
'Tis something that is very new,
And what no dunces *can see*.

SISTER

That is not half the way to tell
What *fancy* is about;
So pray now tell me more.

BROTHER

Sister, I think 'twere quite as well
That you should find it out;
So think the matter o'er.

SISTER

It's what comes in our heads when we
Play at 'Let's make believe',
And when we play at 'Guessing'.

BROTHER

And I have heard it said to be
A talent often makes us grieve,
And sometimes proves a blessing.

The Butterfly

SISTER

Do, my dearest brother John,
Let that Butterfly alone.

BROTHER

What harm now do I do?
You're always making such a noise—

SISTER

O fie, John; none but naughty boys
Say such rude words as you.

BROTHER

Because you're always speaking sharp:
On the same thing you always harp.
A bird one may not catch,
Nor find a nest, nor angle neither,
Nor from the peacock pluck a feather,
But you are on the watch
To moralize and lecture still.

SISTER

And ever lecture, John, I will,
When such sad things I hear.
But talk not now of what is past;
The moments fly away too fast,
Though endlessly they seem to last
To that poor soul in fear.

BROTHER

Well, soon (I say) I'll let it loose;
But, sister, you talk like a goose,
There's no soul in a fly.

SISTER

It has a form and fibres fine,
Were temper'd by the hand divine
Who dwells beyond the sky.

Look, brother, you have hurt its wing—
And plainly by its fluttering
    You see it's in distress.
Gay painted Coxcomb, spangled Beau,
A Butterfly is call'd you know,
    That's always in full dress;
The finest gentleman of all
Insects he is—he gave a Ball,
    You know the Poet wrote.
Let's fancy this the very same,
And then you'll own you've been to blame
    To spoil his silken coat.

BROTHER

Your dancing, spangled, powder'd Beau,
Look, through the air I've let him go:
    And now we're friends again.
As sure as he is in the air,
From this time, Ann, I will take care,
    And try to be humane.

From *Peter Piper's Practical Principles of Plain and Perfect Pronunciation* (1813)

This ingeniously alliterative abecedary was the eighth number in the *Cabinet of Amusement and Instruction* series published by John Harris. Later additions—*Marmaduke Multiply's Merry Method of Making Mathematicians* (1816) and *Punctuation Personified* (1824)—are simply lessons in rhyme; they lack the rollicking inventiveness and sense of abandoned fun of *Peter Piper's Principles*. The book opens with 'Peter Piper's Polite Preface: PETER PIPER Puts Pen to Paper, to produce his Peerless Production, Proudly Presuming it will Please Princes, Peers, and Parliaments, and Procure him the Praise and Plaudits of their Progeny and Posterity, as he can prove it Positively to be a Paragon, or Playful, Palatable, Proverbial, Panegyrical, Philosophical, Philanthropical Phaenomenon of Productions.' The excerpts included here are reproduced from the Osborne Collection's edition of 1820, in which the first line of the second rhyme, 'Bobby Blubber blew a Bullock's Bladder', was changed to the more genteel (and easier to pronounce) 'Billy Button bought a butter'd Biscuit'.

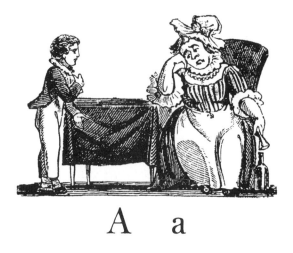

A a

Andrew Airpump ask'd his Aunt her Ailment:
Did Andrew Airpump ask his Aunt her Ailment?
If Andrew Airpump ask'd his Aunt her Ailment,
Where was the Ailment of Andrew Airpump's Aunt?

B b

Billy Button bought a butter'd Biscuit:
Did Billy Button buy a butter'd Biscuit?
If Billy Button bought a butter'd Biscuit,
Where's the butter'd Biscuit Billy Button bought?

C c

Captain Crackskull crack'd a Catchpoll's[1] Cockscomb[2]:
Did Captain Crackskull crack a Catchpoll's Cockscomb?
If Captain Crackskull crack'd a Catchpoll's Cockscomb,
Where's the Catchpoll's Cockscomb Captain Crackskull crack'd?

1 Catchpoll: sheriff's bailiff
2 Cockscomb: fool's cap or ludicrous term for head

M m

Matthew Mendlegs miss'd a mangled Monkey:
Did Matthew Mendlegs miss a mangled Monkey?
If Matthew Mendlegs miss'd a mangled Monkey,
Where's the mangled Monkey Matthew Mendlegs miss'd?

N n

Neddy Noodle nipp'd his Neighbour's Nutmegs;
Did Neddy Noodle nip his Neighbour's Nutmegs?
If Neddy Noodle nipp'd his Neighbour's Nutmegs,
Where are the Neighbour's Nutmegs Neddy Noodle nipp'd?

O o

Oliver Oglethorpe ogled an Owl and Oyster:
Did Oliver Oglethorpe ogle an Owl and Oyster?
If Oliver Oglethorpe ogled an Owl and Oyster,
Where are the Owl and Oyster Oliver Oglethorpe ogled?

P p

Peter Piper pick'd a Peck of Pepper:
Did Peter Piper pick a Peck of Pepper?
If Peter Piper pick'd a Peck of Pepper,
Where's the Peck of Pepper Peter Piper pick'd?

CLEMENT CLARKE MOORE (1779–1863)
'A Visit from Saint Nicholas' (1823)

A professor of Greek and Hebrew at the General Theological Seminary of the Episcopalian church in New York, Moore wrote this poem for his own children. 'A Visit from Saint Nicholas' appeared anonymously in *The Troy Sentinel* on 23 December 1823, and later in Moore's collection, *Poems* (1844). Whether submitted to faltering recitation at children's Christmas concerts or to the sonorous declamation of a great actor, it continues to charm with its dramatic narrative, rollicking anapestic metre, and vivid diction: Moore's images nest securely in our minds.

A Visit from Saint Nicholas

'Twas the night before Christmas, when all through the house
Not a creature was stirring, not even a mouse;
The stockings were hung by the chimney with care,
In hopes that St Nicholas soon would be there;
5 The children were nestled all snug in their beds,
While visions of sugar plums danced in their heads;
And mamma in her 'kerchief, and I in my cap,
Had just settled our brains for a long winter's nap,

When out on the lawn there arose such a clatter,
10 I sprang from the bed to see what was the matter.
Away to the window I flew like a flash,
Tore open the shutters and threw up the sash.

The moon on the breast of the new-fallen snow
Gave the lustre of midday to objects below,
15 When, what to my wondering eyes should appear,
But a miniature sleigh, and eight tiny reindeer,
With a little old driver, so lively and quick,
I knew in a moment it must be St Nick.
More rapid than eagles his coursers they came,
20 And he whistled, and shouted, and called them by name:
'Now, Dasher! now, Dancer! now, Prancer and Vixen!
On, Comet! on, Cupid! on, Donder and Blitzen!
To the top of the porch! to the top of the wall!
Now dash away! dash away! dash away all!'
25 As dry leaves that before the wild hurricane fly,
When they meet with an obstacle, mount to the sky,
So up to the house-top the coursers they flew,
With the sleigh full of toys, and St Nicholas too.

And then, in a twinkling, I heard on the roof
30 The prancing and pawing of each little hoof.
As I drew in my head, and was turning around,
Down the chimney St Nicholas came with a bound.
He was dressed all in fur, from his head to his foot,
And his clothes were all tarnished with ashes and soot;
35 A bundle of toys he had flung on his back,
And he looked like a peddler just opening his pack.
His eyes—how they twinkled, his dimples how merry!
His cheeks were like roses, his nose like a cherry!
His droll little mouth was drawn up like a bow,
40 And the beard of his chin was as white as the snow;
The stump of a pipe he held tight in his teeth,
And the smoke it encircled his head like a wreath;
He had a broad face and a little round belly,
That shook, when he laughed, like a bowlful of jelly.
45 He was chubby and plump, a right jolly old elf,
And I laughed when I saw him, in spite of myself:

A wink of his eyes and a twist of his head,
Soon gave me to know I had nothing to dread;
He spoke not a word, but went straight to his work,
50 And filled all the stockings, then turned with a jerk,
And laying his finger aside of his nose,
And giving a nod, up the chimney he rose;

He sprang to his sleigh, to his team gave a whistle,
And away they all flew like the down of a thistle.
55 But I heard him exclaim, ere he drove out of sight,
'Happy Christmas to all, and to all a good night.'

SARAH JOSEPHA HALE (1788–1879)
From *Poems for Our Children* (1830)

When she was widowed in 1822 with five young children to support and educate, Sarah Hale turned to writing, producing work for a variety of periodicals, a book of poetry, *The Genius of Oblivion* (1823), and a highly successful novel, *Northwood* (1827), which was critical of the system of slavery. In 1828 she became editor of the Boston-based *Ladies' Magazine*, devoted exclusively to original material. Hale incorporated the *Ladies' Magazine* into the Philadelphia-based *Godey's Lady's Book*, a periodical which she edited for a remarkable period (1837–77). She supported many causes to advance the education of women: among them, housing co-operatives, normal schools, and female seminaries, and the hiring of women faculty at Vassar College.

'Mary's Lamb' first appeared in a periodical she edited, *Juvenile Miscellany*, in 1830, later that year becoming part of her collection, *Poems for our Children Designed for Families, Sabbath Schools and Infant Schools*. Within two years it had been set to music; it was reprinted often in the *McGuffey Readers*, thus implanting itself in the consciousness of generations of youngsters.

Mary's Lamb

Mary had a little lamb,
    Its fleece was white as snow,
And everywhere that Mary went
    The lamb was sure to go;
He followed her to school one day—
    That was against the rule,
It made the children laugh and play
    To see a lamb at school.

And so the teacher turned him out,
    But still he lingered near,
And waited patiently about,
    Till Mary did appear.
And then he ran to her and laid
    His head upon her arm,
As if he said, 'I'm not afraid—
    You'll shield me from all harm.'

'What makes the lamb love Mary so?'
   The little children cry;
'Oh, Mary loves the lamb, you know,'
   The teacher did reply,
'And you each gentle animal
   In confidence may bind,
And make it follow at your call,
   If you are always kind.'

ELEANOR MURE (1779–1885)
The Story of the Three Bears (1831)

As the dedication page of her illustrated manuscript declares, this was Miss Mure's 'Birthday Present to Horace Broke, Sept. 26: 1831'. Four-year-old Horace, or 'Horbook', as he called himself, was the nephew of the author-illustrator, 'Aunt Nello'. Her *Three Bears* antedates Robert Southey's prose version in *The Doctor* (vol. iv, chapter CXXIX) by six years. Both Mure and Southey have a meddlesome old woman as the central character. The young fair-haired heroine familiar to today's children did not appear until Joseph Cundall's version of the story in *A Treasury of Pleasure Books* (1850), and she did not receive the name 'Goldilocks' until the early twentieth century. Southey sent the old woman 'to the House of Correction for a vagrant as she was', but Mure devised a farcical ending.

The Story of the Three Bears

Many ages ago, it was common, I find,
For dumb creatures to talk just as well as mankind:
Birds and Beasts met together t'arrange their affairs;
Nay! the Frogs of the day, must needs give themselves airs,
5 And apeing their betters, not pleas'd with their station,
Talk'd of having a King to rule over their nation.

In these curious days, it did raise no surprise,
(Though now 'twould make ev'ry one open their eyes)
That three Bears, very sick of their woods and their den,
10 Should fancy a home 'mongst the dwellings of men;
So not caring a fig for what any one said,
They bought a large house already furnished.

An old woman liv'd near them, who to their house went,
As to make their acquaintance she was fully bent.
15 They refused to receive her; and at this rebuff,
The angry old woman went home in a huff;

'Adzooks!' she exclaim'd, 'what impertinent Bears!
'I would fain know their title to give themselves airs.'

20 She, without more reflection, resolved not to let
The matter rest here; and work'd into a pet.
She made up her mind to watch them safe out,
Then not at all thinking what she was about,
She determin'd, without the Bears' leave, to explore
Each part of the house; so popp'd in at the door.

25 She went to the parlour; and there she did see
Some bowls of good milk, by one, two, and three:
She tasted the first, and then spit it about;
She drank some of the second, and threw it all out,
But when of the third, she had taken one sup,
30 Oh! greedy old woman! she drank it all up.

She went to the drawing-room, and she found there,
For each of the Bears, a most ponderous chair;
She sat down in the first, but she found it too rough;
She sat down in the second but that she felt tough;
She sat down in the third, without much ado;
35 When, good lack-a-day! the bottom burst through.

She went to the bedrooms, and there she did find
Three nice-looking beds, the best of their kind;
She lay down in the first; but she found little ease:
She lay down in the second, which still less did please;
40 She lay down in the third, without much ado,
When, good lack-a-day! the bottom burst through!

She look'd out of the window, and there she descried
The bears coming homewards, with dignified stride.
45 'Oh!' quoth she, I am lost, if the bears find me here.'
So forthwith in a closet, all trembling with fear,
She hid herself; hoping she might get away,
Before the three Bruins could find where she lay.

Meanwhile the poor bears who had been out to roam,
50 Were coming as fast as they could to their home:
Tired, hungry, and longing for food and rest,
Unsuspicious of harm, to the parlour they prest;
As they opened the door, a sight greeted their eyes,
Which fill'd their rough breasts both with wrath & surprise.

55 The first bear, roaring loud, exclaim'd, 'What do I see?'
'Who's been tasting my good milk, without leave of me?'
The second more gently said; 'I can't conceive

'Who's been drinking my milk without asking my leave?'
The little bear scream'd, looking into his cup,
60 'Who's been drinking my milk, and drunk it all up?'

They went to the drawing-room; where the first bear
Roar'd, 'Who, without leave, has sat down in my chair?'
The second, astonish'd, more mildly did say,
'Who's been sitting in my chair when I was away?'
65 The little bear madly cried; 'What shall I do?
'Who has sat in my chair, and the bottom burst thro'?'

To the bedroom they went; and the first bear then said
'Who since I've been out, has lain down in my bed?'
The second bear, quite aghast, fiercely did say,
70 'Who has had the presumption in my bed to lay?'
The little bear scream'd out, 'Oh! What shall I do?'
'Who in my bed has lain, and the bottom burst thro'?"

Indignant they run the delinquent to find;
Each corner they search, and each door look behind:
75 The closet they open, exclaiming; 'She's here!'
And drag forth the dame, half expiring with fear;
Quite determin'd to punish her, long they debate
What, in justice, should be their old enemy's fate.

On the fire they throw her, but burn her they couldn't;
80 In the water they put her, but drown there she wouldn't;
They seize her before all the wondering people,
And chuck her aloft on St Paul's churchyard steeple;
And if she's still there when you earnestly look,
You will see her quite plainly—my little Horbrook!

MARY BOTHAM HOWITT (1799–1888)
From *Sketches of Natural History* (1834)

As Quakers and professional writers, both Mary Howitt and her husband William, author of *The Boy's Country Book* (1839), made distinctive contributions to children's literature. In addition to serving as an early translator of Hans Andersen's *Fairy Tales*, Mary edited a collection of cautionary poems (*The Pink*) by the redoubtable moralist Elizabeth Turner, and herself wrote much popular verse and the well-liked *Strive and Thrive* (1840) and *Little Coin, Much Care* (1842), two children's novels that, as the titles suggest, have a strongly moral tone. The moral envoi of 'The Spider and the Fly'—whose subtitle, 'An Apologue', means moral fable—is thus entirely fitting for her time and outlook. The verse first appeared in *The New Year's Gift* of 1829 and was later incorporated in *Sketches of Natural History*, a collection of poems about animals and insects that was illustrated with the finely detailed engravings of Ebenezer Landells. Howitt sought to introduce the leavening agents of charm and humour to strict cautionary preachments; as a result the dialogue between the wily, flattering spider and the cautious but gullible fly has been a timeless nursery favourite. The Howitts pressed for reforms within the Society of Friends and, growing less and less content with its restrictions, eventually withdrew.

The Spider and the Fly: An Apologue

A New Version of an Old Story

'Will you walk into my parlour?' said the Spider to the Fly,
''Tis the prettiest little parlour that ever you did spy;
The way into my parlour is up a winding stair,
And I've a many curious thing to shew when you are there.'
5 'Oh no, no,' said the little Fly, 'to ask me is in vain,
For who goes up your winding stair can ne'er come down again.'

'I'm sure you must be weary, dear, with soaring up so high;
Will you rest upon my little bed?' said the Spider to the Fly.
'There are pretty curtains drawn around; the sheets are fine and thin,
10 And if you like to rest awhile, I'll snugly tuck you in!'
'Oh no, no,' said the little Fly, 'for I've often heard it said,
They never, never wake again, who sleep upon your bed!'

Said the cunning Spider to the Fly, 'Dear friend what can I do,
To prove the warm affection I've always felt for you?
15 I have within my pantry, good store of all that's nice;
I'm sure you're very welcome—will you please to take a slice?'
'Oh no, no,' said the little Fly, 'kind sir, that cannot be,
I've heard what's in your pantry, and I do not wish to see!'

'Sweet creature!' said the Spider, 'you're witty and you're wise,
20 How handsome are your gauzy wings, how brilliant are your eyes!
I've a little looking-glass upon my parlour shelf,
If you'll step in one moment, dear, you shall behold yourself.'
'I thank you, gentle sir,' she said, 'for what you're pleased to say,
And bidding you good morning now, I'll call another day.'

25 The Spider turned him round about, and went into his den,
For well he knew the silly Fly would soon come back again:
So he wove a subtle web, in a little corner sly,
And set his table ready, to dine upon the Fly.
Then he came out to his door again, and merrily did sing,
30 'Come hither, hither, pretty Fly, with the pearl and silver wing;
Your robes are green and purple—there's a crest upon your head;
Your eyes are like the diamond bright, but mine are dull as lead!'

Alas, alas! how very soon this silly little Fly,
Hearing his wily, flattering words, came slowly flitting by;
35 With buzzing wings she hung aloft, then near and nearer drew,
Thinking only of her brilliant eyes, and green and purple hue—
Thinking only of her crested head—poor foolish thing! At last,
Up Jumped the cunning Spider, and fiercely held her fast.
He dragged her up his winding stair, into his dismal den,
40 Within his little parlour—but she ne'er came out again!

And now dear little children, who may this story read,
To idle, silly flattering words, I pray you ne'er give heed:
Unto an evil counsellor, close heart and ear and eye,
And take a lesson from this tale, of the Spider and the Fly.

CATHERINE SINCLAIR (1800–1864)
From *Holiday House: A Series of Tales* (1839)

These are the stories about the extremely lively Graham children, Laura and Harry, who live with their grandmother, Lady Harriet, a fond Uncle David, and a demanding nurse called Crabtree, whose sternness is usually modified by avuncular indulgence and the calm wisdom of Lady Harriet. As the children grow older and the book nears its end, the madcap tenor of domestic adventures lessens. In fact *Holiday House* closes with the most sobering of all experiences. Laura and Harry, along with Crabtree and their invalid father, gather round the deathbed of their older brother, Frank, a fatally wounded midshipman.

At the time of Uncle David's fairy story, reproduced below, high seriousness and pathos of this order have not yet overtaken the narrative. Master No-book, Giant Snap-'em-up, and Fairy Teach-all draw on the well-established Newbery tradition of personified abstractions like Graspall, Gripe, and Meanwell—though Sinclair's characters are exaggerated. She also borrows from recognizable conventions, with Fairy Do-nothing's picture of pleasure derived from the medieval imaginary country of the Land of Cockaigne and the giant's cannibalistic diet recalling Thomas Boreman's *Gigantick Histories*. *Holiday House*'s 'nonsensical story about giants and fairies' transmits Uncle David's lesson on the importance of reading with absolute clarity. It is convincing and somehow reassuring that the younger Grahams do not convert immediately to his cause.

Chapter IX
Uncle David's Nonsensical Story about Giants and Fairies

'Pie-crust and pastry-crust, that was the wall;
The windows were made of black-puddings and white,
And slated with pancakes—you ne'er saw the like!'

In the days of yore, children were not all such clever, good sensible people as they are now! Lessons were then considered rather a plague—sugar-plums were still in demand—holidays continued yet in fashion—and toys were not then made to teach mathematics, nor story-books to give instruction in chemistry and navigation. These were very strange times, and there existed at that period, a very idle, greedy, naughty boy, such as we never hear of in the present day. His papa and mama were—no matter who,—and he lived, no matter where. His name was Master No-book, and he seemed to think his eyes were made for nothing but to stare out of the windows, and his mouth for no other purpose but to eat. This young gentleman hated lessons like mustard, both of which brought tears into his eyes, and during school-hours, he sat gazing at his books, pretending to be busy, while his mind wandered away to wish impatiently for dinner, and to consider where he could get the nicest pies, pastry, ices, and jellies, while he smacked his lips at the very thoughts of them. I think he must have been first cousin to Peter Grey, but that is not perfectly certain.

Whenever Master No-book spoke, it was always to ask for something, and you might continually hear him say, in a whining tone of voice, 'Papa! may I take this piece of cake? Aunt Sarah! will you give me an apple? Mama! do send me the whole of that plum-pudding!' Indeed, very frequently when he did not get permission to gormandize, this naughty glutton helped himself without leave. Even his dreams were like his waking hours, for he had often a horrible nightmare about lessons, thinking he was smothered with Greek Lexicons, or pelted out of the school with a shower of English Grammars, while one night he fancied himself sitting down to devour an enormous plum-cake, and that all on a sudden it became transformed into a Latin Dictionary!

One afternoon, Master No-book, having played truant all day from school, was lolling on his mama's best sofa in the drawing-room, with his leather boots tucked up on the satin cushions, and nothing to do, but to suck a few oranges, and nothing to think of but how much sugar to put upon them, when suddenly an event took place which filled him with astonishment.

A sound of soft music stole into the room, becoming louder and louder the longer he listened, till at length, in a few moments afterwards, a large hole burst open in the wall of his room, and there stepped into his presence two magnificent fairies, just arrived from their castles in the air, to pay him a visit. They had travelled all the way on purpose to have some conversation with Master No-book, and immediately introduced themselves in a very ceremonious manner.

The fairy Do-nothing was gorgeously dressed with a wreath of flaming gas round her head, a robe of gold tissue, a necklace of rubies, and a bouquet in her hand, of glittering diamonds. Her cheeks were rouged to the very eyes,—her teeth were set in gold, and her hair was of a most brilliant purple; in short, so fine and fashionable-looking a fairy never was seen in a drawing-room before.

The fairy Teach-all, who followed next, was simply dressed in white muslin, with bunches of natural flowers in her light brown hair, and she carried in her hand a few neat small books, which Master No-book looked at with a shudder of aversion.

The two fairies now informed him, that they very often invited large parties of children to spend some time at their palaces, but as they lived in quite an opposite direction, it was necessary for their young guests to choose which it would be best to visit first; therefore now they had come to inquire of Master No-book, whom he thought it would be most agreeable to accompany on the present occasion.

'In my house', said the fairy Teach-all, speaking with a very sweet smile, and a soft, pleasing voice, 'you shall be taught to find pleasure in every sort of exertion, for I delight in activity and diligence. My young friends rise at seven every morning, and amuse themselves with working in a beautiful garden of flowers,—rearing whatever fruit they wish to eat,—visiting among the poor,—associating pleasantly together,—studying the arts and sciences,—and learning to know the world in which they live, and to fulfil the purposes for which they have been brought into it. In short, all our amusements tend to some useful object, either for our own improvement or the good of others, and you will grow wiser, better, and happier every day you remain in the Palace of Knowledge.'

'But in Castle Needless, where I live,' interrupted the fairy Do-nothing, rudely pushing her companion aside, with an angry contemptuous look, 'we never think of exerting ourselves for anything. You may put your head in your pocket, and your hands in your sides as long as you choose to stay. No one is ever even asked a question, that he may be spared the trouble of answering. We lead the most fashionable life imaginable, for nobody speaks to anybody! Each of my visitors is quite an exclusive, and sits with his back to as many of the company as possible, in the most comfortable arm-chair that can be contrived. There, if you are only so good as to take the trouble of wishing for anything, it is yours, without even turning an eye round to look where it comes from. Dresses are provided of the most magnificent kind, which go on of themselves, without your having the smallest annoyance with either buttons or strings,—games which you can play without an effort of thought,—and dishes dressed by a French cook, smoking hot under your nose, from morning till night,—while any rain we have, is either made of cherry brandy, lemonade, or lavender water,—and in winter it generally snows iced-punch for an hour during the forenoon.'

Nobody need be told which fairy Master No-book preferred; and quite charmed at his own good fortune in receiving so agreeable an invitation, he eagerly gave his hand to the splendid new acquaintance who promised him so much pleasure and ease, and gladly proceeded, in a carriage lined with velvet, stuffed with downy pillows, and drawn by milk-white swans, to that magnificent residence Castle Needless, which was lighted by a thousand windows during the day, and by a million of lamps every night.

Here Master No-book enjoyed a constant holiday and a constant feast, while a beautiful lady covered with jewels, was ready to tell him stories from morning till night, and servants waited to pick up his playthings if they fell, or to draw out his purse or his pocket-handkerchief when he wished to use them.

Thus Master No-book lay dozing for hours and days on rich embroidered cushions, never stirring from his place, but admiring the view of trees covered with the richest burned almonds, grottoes of sugar-candy, a jet d'eau of champagne, a wide sea which tasted of sugar instead of salt, and a bright clear pond, filled with gold-fish, that let themselves be caught whenever he pleased. Nothing could be more complete, and yet, very strange to say, Master No-book did not seem particularly happy! This appears exceedingly unreasonable, when so much trouble was taken to please him; but the truth is, that every day he became more fretful and peevish. No sweet-meats were worth the trouble of eating, nothing was pleasant to play at, and in the end he wished it were possible to sleep all day, as well as all night.

Not a hundred miles from the fairy Do-nothing's palace, there lived a most cruel monster called the giant Snap-'em-up, who looked, when he stood up, like the tall steeple of a great church, raising his head so high, that he could peep over the loftiest mountains, and was obliged to climb up a ladder to comb his own hair.

Every morning regularly, this prodigiously great giant walked round the world before breakfast for an appetite, after which, he made tea in a large lake, used the sea as a slop-basin, and boiled his kettle on Mount Vesuvius. He lived in great style, and his dinners were most magnificent, consisting very often of an elephant roasted whole, ostrich patties, a tiger smothered in onions, stewed lions, and whale soup; but for a side-dish his greatest favourite consisted of little boys, as fat as possible, fried in crumbs of bread, with plenty of pepper and salt.

No children were so well fed, or in such good condition for eating as those in the fairy Do-nothing's garden, who was a very particular friend of the giant Snap-'em-up's, and who sometimes laughingly said she would give him a license, and call her own garden his 'preserve', because she allowed him to help himself, whenever he pleased, to as many of her visitors as he chose, without taking the trouble even to count them, and in return for such extreme civility, the giant very frequently invited her to dinner.

Snap-'em-up's favourite sport was, to see how many brace of little boys he could bag in a morning; so in passing along the streets, he peeped into all the drawing-rooms without having occasion to get upon tiptoe, and picked up every young gentleman who was idly looking out of the windows, and even a few occasionally who were playing truant from school, but busy children seemed always somehow quite out of his reach.

One day, when Master No-book felt even more lazy, more idle, and more miserable than ever, he lay beside a perfect mountain of toys and cakes, wondering what to wish for next, and hating the very sight of everything and everybody. At last he gave so loud a yawn of weariness and disgust, that his jaw very nearly fell out of joint, and then he sighed so deeply, that the giant Snap-'em-up heard the sound as he passed along the road after breakfast, and instantly stepped into the garden, with his glass at his eye, to see what was the matter. Immediately on observing a large, fat, over-grown boy, as round as a dumpling, lying on a bed of roses, he gave a cry of delight, followed by a gigantic peal of laughter, which was heard three miles off, and picking up Master No-book between his finger and his thumb, with a pinch that very nearly broke his ribs, he carried him rapidly towards his own castle, while the fairy Do-nothing laughingly shook her head as he passed, saying, 'That little man does me great credit!—he has only been fed for a week, and is as fat already as a prize ox! What a dainty morsel he will be! When do you dine to-day, in case I should have time to look in upon you?'

On reaching home, the giant immediately hung up Master No-book by the hair of his head, on a prodigious hook in the larder, having first taken some large lumps of nasty suet, forcing them down his throat to make him become still fatter, and then stirring the fire, that he might be almost melted with heat, to make his liver grow larger. On a shelf quite near, Master No-book perceived the dead bodies of six other boys, whom he remembered to have seen fattening in the fair Do-nothing's garden, while he recollected how some of them had rejoiced at thoughts of leading a long, useless, idle life, with no one to please but themselves.

The enormous cook now seized hold of Master No-book, brandishing her knife, with an aspect of horrible determination, intending to kill him, while he took the trouble of screaming and kicking in the most desperate manner, when the giant turned gravely round and said, that as pigs were considered a much greater dainty when whipped to death than killed in any other way, he meant to see whether children might not be improved by it also; therefore she might leave that great hog of a boy till he had time to try the experiment, especially as his own appetite would be improved by the exercise. This was a dreadful prospect for the unhappy prisoner; but meantime it prolonged his life a few hours, as he was immediately hung up again in the larder, and left to himself. There, in torture of mind and body,—like a fish upon a hook, the wretched boy began at last to reflect seriously upon his former ways, and to consider what a happy home he might have had, if he could only have been satisfied with business and pleasure succeeding each other, like day and night, while lessons might have come in, as a pleasant sauce to his play-hours, and his play-hours as a sauce to his lessons.

In the midst of many reflections, which were all very sensible, though rather too late, Master No-book's attention became attracted by the sound of many voices laughing, talking, and singing, which caused him to turn his eyes in a new direction, when, for the first time, he observed that the fairy Teach-all's garden lay upon a beautiful sloping bank not far off. There a crowd of merry, noisy, rosy-cheeked boys, were busily employed, and seemed happier than the day was long; while poor Master No-book watched them during his own miserable hours, envying the enjoyment with which they raked the flower borders, gathered the fruit, carried baskets of vegetables to the poor, worked with carpenter's tools, drew pictures, shot with bows and arrows, played at cricket, and then sat in the sunny arbours learning their tasks, or talking agreeably together, till at length, a dinner-bell having been rung, the whole party sat merrily down with hearty appetites, and cheerful good-humour, to an entertainment of plain roast meat and pudding, where the fairy Teach-all presided herself, and helped her guests moderately, to as much as was good for each.

Large tears rolled down the cheeks of Master No-book while watching this scene; and remembering that if he had known what was best for him, he might have been as happy as the happiest of these excellent boys, instead of suffering ennui and weariness, as he had done at the fairy Do-nothing's, ending in a miserable death; but his attention was soon after most alarmingly roused by hearing the giant Snap-'em-up again in conversation with his cook, who said, that if he wished for a good large dish of scolloped children at dinner, it would be necessary to catch a few more, as those he had already provided would scarcely be a mouthful.

As the giant kept very fashionable hours, and always waited dinner for himself till nine o'clock, there was still plenty of time; so, with a loud grumble about the trouble, he seized a large basket in his hand, and set off at a rapid pace towards the fairy Teach-all's garden. It was very seldom that Snap-'em-up ventured to think of foraging in this direction, as he had never once succeeded in carrying off a single captive from the enclosure, it was so well fortified and so bravely defended; but on this occasion, being desperately hungry, he felt as bold as a lion, and walked, with outstretched hands, straight towards the fairy Teach-all's dinner-table, taking such prodigious strides, that he seemed almost as if he would trample on himself.

A cry of consternation arose the instant this tremendous giant appeared; and as usual on such occasions, when he had made the same attempt before, a dreadful battle took place. Fifty active little boys bravely flew upon the enemy, armed with their dinner knives, and looked like a nest of hornets, stinging him in every direction, till he roared with pain, and would have run away, but the fairy Teach-all, seeing his intention, rushed forward with the carving knife, and brandishing it high over her head, she most courageously stabbed him to the heart!

If a great mountain had fallen to the earth, it would have seemed like nothing in comparison of the giant Snap-'em-up, who crushed two or three houses to powder beneath him, and upset several fine monuments that were to have made people remembered for ever; but all this would have seemed scarcely worth mentioning, had it not been for a still greater event which occurred on the occasion, no less than the death of the fairy Do-nothing, who had been indolently looking on at this great battle, without taking the trouble to interfere, or even to care who was victorious, but being also lazy about running away, when the giant fell, his sword came with so violent a stroke on her head, that she instantly expired.

Thus, luckily for the whole world, the fairy Teach-all got possession of immense property, which she proceeded without delay to make the best use of in her power. In the first place, however, she lost no time in liberating Master No-book from his hook in the larder, and gave him a lecture on activity, moderation, and good conduct, which he never afterwards forgot; and it was astonishing to see the change that took place immediately in his whole thoughts and actions. From this very hour, Master No-book became the most diligent, active, happy boy in the fairy Teach-all's garden; and on returning home a month afterwards, he astonished all the masters at school by his extraordinary reformation. The most difficult lessons were a pleasure to him,—he scarcely ever stirred without a book in his hand,—never lay on a sofa again,—would scarcely even sit on a chair with a back to it, but preferred a three-legged stool,—detested holidays,—never thought any exertion a trouble,—preferred climbing over the top of a hill to creeping round the bottom,—always ate the plainest food in very small quantities,—joined a Temperance Society!—and never tasted a morsel till he had worked very hard and got an appetite.

Not long after this, an old uncle, who had formerly been ashamed of Master No-book's indolence and gluttony, became so pleased at the wonderful change, that, on his death, he left him a magnificent estate, desiring that he should take his name; therefore, instead of being any longer one of the No-book family, he is now called Sir Timothy Bluestocking,—a pattern to the whole country round, for the good he does to every one, and especially for his extraordinary activity, appearing as if he could do twenty things at once. Though generally very good natured and agreeable, Sir Timothy is occasionally observed in a violent passion, laying about him with his walking-stick in the most terrific manner, and beating little boys within an inch of their lives; but on inquiry, it invariably appears that he has found them out to be lazy, idle, or greedy, for all the industrious boys in the parish are sent to get employment from him, while he assures them that they are far happier breaking stones on the road, than if they were sitting idly in a drawing room with nothing to do. Sir Timothy cares very little for poetry in general; but the following are his favourite verses, which he has placed over the chimney-piece at a school that he built for the poor, and every scholar is obliged, the very day he begins his education, to learn them:—

Some people complain they have nothing to do,
And time passes slowly away;
They saunter about with no object in view,
And long for the end of the day.

In vain are the trifles and toys they desire,
For nothing they truly enjoy;
Of trifles, and toys, and amusements they tire,
For want of some useful employ.

Although for transgression the ground was accursed,
Yet gratefully man must allow,
'Twas really a blessing which doom'd him at first,
To live by the sweat of his brow.

ELIZA LEE FOLLEN (1787–1860)
From *New Nursery Songs for All Good Children* (1843)

Eliza Follen, a New Englander dedicated to the cause of preserving traditional nursery rhymes, used them as models for her own ditties for children. In her preface to *Little Songs* (1856), she observed: 'It has been my object . . . to endeavour to catch something of the good-humoured pleasantry, the musical nonsense which makes Mother Goose attractive to all ages.' It is to Mrs Follen's credit that in her collection of relatively mediocre verse one poem has entered oral literature: 'Three Little Kittens'. As in the exploits of Trimmer's young Redbreasts, Follen's cat family experiences both rewards and punishments. In contrast to the sentimentally charged narrative of Trimmer, however, the tidy marching rhythm with which the kittens' deeds are related evokes the reader's smiles rather than emotional involvement.

Three Little Kittens

Three little kittens they lost their mittens,
And they began to cry,
Oh, mother dear, we sadly fear
Our mittens we have lost.
5 What! lost your mittens, you naughty kittens!
Then you shall have no pie.
Mee-ow, mee-ow, mee-ow.
No, you shall have no pie.
The three little kittens they found their mittens,
10 And they began to cry,
Oh, mother dear, see here, see here,
Our mittens we have found!
Put on your mittens, you silly kittens,
And you shall have some pie.
15 Purr-r, purr-r, purr-r.
Oh, let us have some pie.
The three little kittens put on their mittens,
And soon ate up the pie;
Oh, mother dear, we greatly fear
20 Our mittens we have soiled.
What! soiled your mittens, you naughty kittens!
Then they began to sigh.
Mee-ow, mee-ow, mee-ow.
Then they began to sigh.
25 The three little kittens they washed their mittens,
And hung them out to dry;
Oh! mother dear, do you not hear,
Our mittens we have washed!

What! washed your mittens, then you're good kittens,
But I smell a rat close by.
30 Mee-ow, mee-ow, mee-ow.
We smell a rat close by.

EDWARD LEAR (1812–1888)
From *The Book of Nonsense* (1846)

The English painter Edward Lear wrote and illustrated these first nonsense limericks for the grandchildren of his early patron, the Earl of Derby. He had already gained some respect for his precisely detailed and coloured ornithological drawings; and since 1837, and the start of his European and Asian travels, he had sketched landscapes and compiled travel journals. He was esteemed by such contemporaries as Queen Victoria, to whom in 1845 he gave drawing lessons, and Tennyson, with whom he kept up a lengthy correspondence. Lear is remembered most often today for his nonsense literature—works he wrote for recreation and amusement. His limericks, songs, alphabets, 'botanies', and stories—all marked by his inimitable whimsy and absurd humour—continue to divert young and old readers alike.

There was an Old Man of Coblenz,
The length of whose legs was immense;
He went with one prance, from Turkey to France,
That surprising Old Man of Coblenz.

There was an Old Man of the West,
Who never could get any rest;
So they set him to spin, on his nose and his chin,
Which cured that Old Man of the West.

There was an Old Man of Marseilles,
Whose daughters wore bottle-green veils;
They caught several Fish, which they put in a dish,
And sent to their Pa' at Marseilles.

There was on Old Person of Sparta,
Who had twenty-five sons and one daughter;
He fed them on snails, and weighed them in scales,
That wonderful person of Sparta.

There was a young Lady of Tyre,
Who swept the loud chords of a lyre;
At the sound of each sweep, she enraptured the deep,
And enchanted the city of Tyre.

There was a Young Lady of Welling,
Whose praise all the world was a telling;
She played on the harp, and caught several carp,
That accomplished Young Lady of Welling.

HEINRICH HOFFMANN (1809–1894)
From *The English Struwwelpeter; or, Pretty Stories and Funny Pictures for Little Children* (1848)

A Frankfurt pediatrician, psychiatrist, and watercolourist, Hoffmann composed and illustrated *Lustige Geschichten und drolige Bilder* (Pretty Stories and Funny Pictures) for his three-year-old son in 1844. He wrote five works for children in all and expressed his preference for *Koenig Nussknacker und der Arme Rheinhold* (King Nutcracker or the Dream of Poor Reinhold). But his reputation among English readers rests firmly on his first book. After friends had convinced him to publish it, the ten stories—in particular the last about Slovenly Peter—became so popular that by its fifth edition in 1847 the title was changed to *Der Struwwelpeter*. English translations in Britain (1848) and America (1850) followed shortly; the book has since been translated into a total of thirty-one languages and has inspired a number of political satires, the most memorable being *Struwwelhitler*. Parents frequently find these exaggerated cautionary tales frightening and disturbing; children, on the other hand, usually warm to their humorous, albeit grisly, caricature of wrong-doing.

SLOVENLY PETER

See Slovenly Peter! Here he stands,
With his dirty hair and hands.
See! his nails are never cut;
They are grim'd as black as soot;
No water for many weeks,
Has been near his cheeks;
And the sloven, I declare,
Not once this year has combed his hair!
Anything to me is sweeter
Than to see shock-headed Peter.

THE STORY OF AUGUSTUS WHO WOULD NOT HAVE ANY SOUP

Augustus was a chubby lad;
Fat ruddy cheeks Augustus had;
And everybody saw with joy
The plump and hearty healthy boy.
He ate and drank as he was told,
And never let his soup get cold.
But one day, one cold winter's day,
He threw away the spoon and screamed:
"O take the nasty soup away!
I won't have any soup to-day:
I will not, will not eat my soup!
I will not eat it, no!"

Next day, now look, the picture shows
How lank and lean Augustus grows!
Yet, though he feels so weak and ill,
The naughty fellow cries out still—
"Not any soup for me, I say!
O take the nasty soup away!
I will not, will not eat my soup!
I will not eat it, no!"

The third day comes. O what a sin!
To make himself so pale and thin.
Yet, when the soup is put on table,
He screams, as loud as he is able—
"Not any soup for me, I say!
O take the nasty soup away!
I won't have any soup to-day!"

Look at him, now the fourth
    day's come!
He scarce outweighs a sugar-plum;
He's like a little bit of thread;
And on the fifth day he was—dead!

THE DREADFUL STORY OF PAULINE AND THE MATCHES

Mamma and Nurse went out one day,
And left Pauline alone at play;
Around the room she gayly sprung,
Clapp'd her hands, and danced, and sung.
Now, on the table close at hand,
A box of matches chanc'd to stand,
And kind Mamma and Nurse had told her,
That if she touch'd them they would scold
  her;
But Pauline said, "Oh, what a pity!
For, when they burn, it is so pretty;
They crackle so, and spit, and flame;
And Mamma often burns the same.
I'll just light a match or two
As I have often seen my mother do."

When Minz and Maunz, the pussy-cats,
  heard this
They held up their paws and began to hiss.
"Me-ow!" they said, "me-ow, me-o!
You'll burn to death, if you do so,
Your parents have forbidden you, you
  know."

But Pauline would not take advice,
She lit a match, it was so nice!
It crackled so, it burn'd so clear,—
Exactly like the picture here.
She jump'd for joy and ran about,
And was too pleas'd to put it out.

When Minz and Maunz, the little cats,
  saw this,
They said, "Oh, naughty, naughty Miss!"
And stretch'd their claws,
And rais'd their paws;
" 'Tis very, very wrong, you know;
Me-ow, me-o, me-ow, me-o!
You will be burnt if you do so,
Your mother has forbidden you, you
  know."

Now see! oh! see, what a dreadful thing
The fire has caught her apron-string;
Her apron burns, her arms, her hair;
She burns all over, everywhere.

Then how the pussy-cats did mew,
What else, poor pussies, could they do?
They scream'd for help, 'twas all in vain,
So then, they said, "We'll scream again.
Make haste, make haste! me-ow! me-o!
She'll burn to death,—we told her so."

So she was burnt with all her clothes,
And arms and hands, and eyes and nose;
Till she had nothing more to lose
Except her little scarlet shoes;
And nothing else but these was found
Among her ashes on the ground.

And when the good cats sat beside
The smoking ashes, how they cried!
"Me-ow, me-o! Me-ow, me-oo!
What will Mamma and Nursy do?"
Their tears ran down their cheeks so fast,
They made a little pond at last.

JANE VAUGHAN COTTON BOUCHER de MONTIZAMBERT
The Sad Tale of Mrs Mole and Mrs Mouse (*c.* 1849)

Jane Cotton wrote and illustrated this charming tale for her child, Caroline Elizabeth. Cotton was the daughter of the Archdeacon of Cashel, Ireland, Dr Henry Cotton, an Oxford-educated scholar who published many biblical studies. In 1846, in Lismore, Ireland, where her father was then dean, Jane Cotton married G.S. Niverville Boucher de Montizambert, a Quebecker from a prominent Lower Canada family; her husband's ancestors, who were involved in the fur trade and various campaigns in the Ohio Valley and Acadia, had sworn allegiance to the British crown in the eighteenth century. Their only child was born in India in 1847. Major de Montizambert was killed in a conflict in the Punjab.

Although Jane Cotton was probably raised on Mrs Trimmer's improving blends of fable and domestic tale, this young mother clearly also knew the zesty amusements of John Harris's *Cabinet*. The entertainment in verse couplets that she concocted for her nursery-age daughter aims at fun without thumping a moral lesson. Humorously exaggerated details of the Martha-like domesticity of Mrs Mouse, who wears brooms to stumps, climax in the kitchen accident. Many of the witty observations—about the preacher's perplexing sermon and the silent furniture that offers no explanation of her sister's whereabouts to the churchgoing Mrs Mole—indicate that adult as well as child readers would chortle at this seriocomic tale.

The manuscript poem was a gift to the Osborne Collection of Early Children's Books, Toronto Public Library, by Joan Winters.

Mrs Mole and Mrs Mouse
Lived together in a house.
One Sunday morning Mrs Mole,
A quiet calm devout old soul,
5 Her breakfast over, walked up stairs,
Put on her cloak and trudged to prayers.

Not so her sister Mrs Mouse,
She stayed at home to mind the house,
More of a Martha than a Mary.
10 Her pigs, her poultry, and her Dairy
Engrossed her thoughts, nor time had she
To spend upon Eternity.

Soon as her sister's back was turn'd
She fussed, and bustled; first she churned
15 Then swept and tidied all the rooms,
And wore to stumps two carpet brooms.

And next came on her weightiest care
The Sunday's dinner to prepare.
She killed, and plucked, and cleaned a Hen,
20 Picked, trussed, and spitted it, and then
She made full many a forced meat Ball
Of divers cates divided small.

And then the kind but worldly soul,
Thinking of absent sister Mole,
25 (Loved with an only sister's love,
E'en as herself, or perhaps above)
Resolved to give her meal a zest,
With fare her sister loved the best.

Yes! Dumplings twain their board should crown,
30 Of apples from the tree blown down;
With zeal she to the garden hies,
Bent her dear sister to surprise.
Laden returns with choicest freight,
Whose worth is spoken by its weight.

35 The fruit to peel, the core extract
Yet keep the apples round, compact,
Skilled she proceeds, and last inclose
In paste wherein no juncture shows
To mortals reasoning on their fare
40 How Apples found an entrance there.

Moulded by cunning hand, the paste
Plastic yet firm, is sweet to taste.
A pot stood boiling on the fire,
The water sputtering in its ire.
45 Undaunted by the steam or din,
She plunged her dainty dumplings in.
But oh! She lost her equipoise,
And headlong sank with gurgling noise.

The sermon over, Mrs Mole
50 Trudged homeward, seeking to unroll,
The hidden things the Priest expounded,
Whose exposition but confounded—
Labouring to harmonize, perplexed,
Dark comments on a simple text.

55 Within the house sad silence dwells,
She knows not why her bosom swells,
But something whispers woe is near,
Sorrow is heralded by fear.

She sees no sign of thrifty care,
60 No table neatly spread is there,
No sister's voice and smile to greet,
And bid her seat herself and eat.
Viands undressed, untempting stand,
Left by the now swoln torpid hand,
65 Fit for the spit, and glowing fire,
Now waning, ready to expire:

At such an hour unwonted sight
Of ill prophetic, in affright
She calls her sister—no reply!
70 She sees not, tears have dimmed her eye.
She sinks into her sister's chair,
And cries—where is my sister—where?
The sullen chair declined to vouch,
'Twas not a conversation couch.

75 Where is my sister? Mistress Table,
Tell me for pity, if you're able:
More true than any Sibyl leaves,
The Table both its own upheaves.
Then lets them fall with crashing sound
80 And falls dismembered to the ground.

Warn'd—yet but half instructed, quick
She cries, 'Good Clock, forbear to tick
With that distracting nonchalance.
Tell me, for you can tell perchance,
85 Where is my ——, but hear me, Clock
And spare my nerves a further shock.'

The clock gave one loud tick, no more.
Struck One: Struck Two: Struck Three: Struck Four:
Struck Five: Struck Six, more slowly Seven:
90 Struck Eight: Nine: Ten: then Struck Eleven;
Then Twelve, its round of hours complete,
And then, unheard, appalling feat
It struck Thirteen!! Struck never more
Thenceforth as mute as neighbour Door.

95 Meanwhile from out the fire there came
A dying faint funereal flame:
Soon as the flame was seen t'emerge
The pot set up a wailing dirge
Irregular, and feeble, slow
100 In minor key like infant woe

Diminuendo slow in time
It mourned th' involuntary crime
And on the waning fire to stand,
It seemed in dread of Deodand.[1]

105 Poor Mrs Mole with frantic gaze
Its hollow fatal depths surveys;
The pitying eddying haze conceals
What ruthless light at length reveals.
Poor Mrs Mouse, oh sight of woe!
110 Boiled tender in a shroud of dough.

Conclusion

Since that sad day poor Mrs Mole
Lives in some dark secluded hole,
Blinded by sorrow; and a prey
To care, she shuns the light of day;
115 The life of a recluse she leads, and frugal feeds
On dew worms, grapes, leaves or weeds;
Thinks on her sister's careful ways
With fond regret, and on the days
When happily within a house
120 She dwelt with her dear Sister Mouse.

---

1 An expiatory offering to God of a thing which has caused the death of a person

BIBLIOGRAPHY

CRITICAL AND HISTORICAL STUDIES

Ariès, Philippe. *Centuries of Childhood: A Social History of Family Life.* Trans. R. Baldick. London: Jonathan Cape, 1962.

Avery, Gillian and Julia Briggs, eds. *Children and Their Books.* Oxford: Clarendon, 1989.

Boas, George. *The Cult of Childhood.* London: Warburg Institute, 1966.

Boswell, John. *The Kindness of Strangers: The Abandonment of Children in Western Europe from Late Antiquity to the Renaissance.* New York: Random House, 1988.

Butts, Dennis. *Stories and Society: Children's Literature in Its Social Context.* London: Macmillan, 1992.

Carpenter, Humphrey and Mari Prichard. *The Oxford Companion to Children's Literature.* Oxford: Oxford University Press, 1984.

Coveney, Peter. *Poor Monkey: The Child in Literature.* London: Rockcliff, 1957.

Cunningham, Hugh. *Children and Childhood in Western Society Since 1500.* London: Longman, 1995.

Darton, F.J. Harvey. *Children's Books in England: Five Centuries of Social Life.* 3rd edition rev. B. Alderson. Cambridge: Cambridge University Press, 1982.

de Mause, Lloyd, ed. *The History of Childhood.* New York: Psychohistory Press, 1974.

Egoff, Sheila. *The Republic of Childhood: A Critical Guide to Canadian Children's Literature in English.* 2nd ed. Toronto: Oxford University Press, 1975.

Elias, Norbert. *The History of Manners: The Civilizing Process.* Vol 1. (1939) Trans. E. Jephcott. New York: Urizen Books, 1978.

Ellis, Alec. *A History of Children's Reading and Literature.* Oxford: Pergammon Press, 1968.

Field, Mrs. E.M. *The Child and His Book: Some Account of the History and Progress of Children's Literature in England.* London: Wells Gardner, Darton & Co., 1892.

Fraser, James H., ed. *Society and Children's Literature.* Boston: David Godine, 1978.

Gottlieb, Beatrice. *The Family in the Western World from the Black Death to the Industrial Age.* New York: Oxford University Press, 1993.

Green, Roger Lancelyn. *Tellers of Tales: Children's Books and Their Authors from 1800 to 1968.* London: Kaye & Ward, 1969.

Hazard, Paul. *Books, Children and Men.* Trans. M. Mitchell. Boston: Horn Book, 1947.

Hürlimann, Bettina. *Three Centuries of Children's Books in Europe.* Trans. and ed. B. Alderson. New York: World Publishing, 1959.

Hunt, Peter, ed. *An Illustrated History of Children's Literature.* Oxford: Oxford University Press, 1995.

Jackson, Mary V. *Engines of Instruction, Mischief, and Magic: Children's Literature in England from Its Beginnings to 1839.* Lincoln: University of Nebraska Press, 1989.

Kiefer, Monica. *American Children Through Their Books, 1700–1835.* Philadephia: University of Pennsylvania Press, 1948.

MacLeod, Anne Scott. *A Moral Tale: Children's Fiction and American Culture, 1820–1860*. Hamden: Shoe String Press, 1975.

Meigs, Cornelia, et al. *A Critical History of Children's Literature in English*. New York: Macmillan, 1953.

Muir, Percy. *English Children's Books 1600 to 1900*. New York: F.A. Praeger, 1954.

O'Day, Rosemary. *Education and Society 1500–1800*. London: Longman, 1982.

Opie, Iona and Peter. *The Lore and Language of Schoolchildren*. Oxford: Clarendon, 1959.

———. *The Oxford Dictionary of Nursery Rhymes*. Oxford: Oxford University Press, 1951, 1980.

Pinchbeck, Ivy and M. Hewitt. *Children in English Society from Tudor Times to the Eighteenth Century*. 2 vols. London: Routledge and Kegan Paul, 1969–73.

Pollock, Linda. *Forgotten Children: Parent-Child Relations from 1500 to 1900*. Cambridge: Cambridge University Press, 1983.

Saxby, H.M. *A History of Australian Children's Literature, 1841–1941*. Sydney: Wentworth Books, 1969.

Shavit, Zohar. *Poetics of Children's Literature*. Athens, GA: University of Georgia Press, 1986.

Sloane, William. *Children's Books in England and America in the Seventeenth Century: A History and a Checklist*. New York: King's Crown, 1955.

Snook, Edith. ' "His open side our book": Meditation and Education in Elizabeth Grymeston's Miscelanea Meditations Memoratives," in *Maternal Measures; Figuring Caregiving in the Early Modern Period*, ed. Naomi Miller and Naomi Yavneh. Aldershot: Ashgate, 2000; 16375.

Thwaite, Mary F. *From Primer to Pleasure in Reading: An Introduction to the History of Children's Books in England*. Boston: Horn Book, 1972.

Topsell, Edward. *The Elizabethan Zoo: A Book of Beasts Both Fabulous and Authentic*. London: F. Etchells and H. Macdonald, 1926.

Townsend, John Rowe. *Written for Children: An Outline of English Children's Literature*. London: Garnet Miller, 1965.

Whalley, Joyce. *Cobwebs to Catch Flies: Illustrated books for the Nursery and Schoolroom 1700–1900*. London: Elek Books, 1974.

Wrightson, Keith. *English Society 1580–1680*. New Brunswick, N.J.: Rutgers University Press, 1982.

ANTHOLOGIES AND WEBSITES OF EARLY CHILDREN'S LITERATURE

Arnold, Arnold. *Pictures and Stories from Forgotten Children's Books*. New York: Dover, 1969.

Barry, Florence. *A Century of Children's Books*. London: Methuen, 1929.

Brand, Christiana, ed. *Naughty Children*. London: Victor Gollancz, 1962.

Cott, Jonathan, general editor. *Masterworks of Children's Literature*. 8 vols in 9. New York: Stonehill Publishing in association with Chelsea House, 1983.

de Vries, Leonard, ed. *Flowers of Delight*. London: Dennis Dobson, 1965.

———. *Little Wide-Awake*. London: Arthur Barker Ltd., 1967.

Early children's Books and Their Ilustration. Boston: David Godine, 1975.

Freeman, Ruth. *Yesterday's School Books*. Watkins Glen, N.Y.: Century House, 1960.

Haviland, Virginia. *Yankee Doodle's Literary Sampler of Prose, Poetry and Pictures*. Washington: Library of Congress, 1974.

Opie, Iona and Peter. *A Nursery Companion*. London: Oxford University Ptress, 1980.

Tuer, Andrew W. *Forgotten Children's Books.* New York: Benjamin Blom, 1898.

———. *Stories from Old-fashioned Children's Books.* London: Leadenhall Press, 1900.

<www.oup.com/ca/he/companion/demers>

1. EARLY LESSONS AT HOME AND SCHOOL

Ascham, Roger. *The Scholemaster.* Ed. D.C. Whimster. London: Methuen, 1934.

Black, L. "Some Renaissance Children's Verse," *Review of English Studies* 24 (1973): 1–16.

Butterworth, Charles C. *The English Primers (1529–1545).* Philadelphia: University of Pennsylvania Press, 1953.

Charlton, Kenneth. *Education in Renaissance England.* London: Routledge and Kegan Paul 1965.

Chudleigh, Mary, Lady. *Poems and Prose.* Ed. M.J.M. Ezell. New York: Oxford University Press, 1993.

Clarke, Elizabeth. ' "A heart terrifying Sorrow": the Deaths of Children in Seventeenth-Century Women's Manuscript Journals' in *Representations of Childhood Death,* ed. Gillian Avery and Kimberley Reynolds. New York: Macmillan-St. Martin's, 2000.

Comenius, John Amos. *Orbis Pictus.* Intro. John E. Sadler. London: Oxford University Press, 1968.

Davies, W.J. Frank. *Teaching Reading in Early England.* London: Pitman Publishing, 1973.

Erasmus, Desiderius. *De Pueris Instituendis, Early Liberal Education for Children,* ed. J.K. Sowards. *Collected Works of Erasmus,* vol 26. Toronto: University of Toronto Press, 1985.

Folmsbee, Beulah. *A Little History of the Horn-book.* Boston: Horn Book, 1942.

Furnivall, F.J., ed. *The Babees Book.* Early English Text Society no. 32. London: Trübner & Co, 1868.

———. *Caxton's Book of Curteyse 1477–8.* E.E.T.S. no. 3. London: Trübner & Co., 1868.

Garmonsway, G.N., ed. *Aelfric's Colloquy.* London: Methuen, 1939.

Goodich, Michael. 'Bartholomaeus Anglicus on Child-rearing' *History of Childhood Quarterly* 3 (1975): 75–84.

Green, Ian. ' "For Children in Yeeres and Children in Understanding": The Emergence of the English Catechism under Elizabeth and the Early Stuarts,' *Journal of Ecclesiastical History* 37 (1986): 397–425.

Grymeston, Elizabeth. *Miscelanea. Meditations. Memoratives.* London: M Bradford, 1604.

Hardman, Phillipa. 'A Mediaeval "Library in Parvo"', *Medium Aevum* 47 (1978): 262–73.

Harrison, Molly and O.M. Royston. *How They Lived, Vol II: An Anthology of original accounts written between 1485 and 1700.* Oxford: Basil Blackwell, 1963.

Hassall, W.O. *How They Lived: An Anthology of original accounts written before 1485.* Oxford: Basil Blackwell, 1962.

Joscelin, Elizabeth. *The Mothers Legacy to her unborne Childe.* Ed. J. LeDrew Metcalfe. Toronto: University of Toronto Press, 2000.

Kroll, Jerome. 'The Concept of Childhood in the Middle Ages', *Journal of the History of the Behavioural Sciences* 13 (1977): 384–93.

Lee, Brian S. 'Seen and Sometimes Heard: Piteous and Pert Children in Medieval English Literature', *Children's Literature Association Quarterly* 23 (1998): 40–8.

Leigh, Dorothy. *The Mothers Blessing.* London: John Budge, 1616.

Lenaghan, R.T., ed. *Caxton's Aesop.* Cambridge: Harvard University Press, 1967.

More, Thomas. *Latin Poems*, ed. C.H. Miller et al. *Collected Works of St Thomas More*, vol 3, Part 11. New Haven: Yale University Press, 1963.

Mulcaster, Richard. *Positions Concerning the Training Up of Children*. Ed. W. Barker. Toronto: University of Toronto Press, 1994.

Richardson, Elizabeth. *A Ladies Legacie to Her Daughters*. London: Thomas Harper, 1645.

Seymour, M.C., general editor. *On the Properties of Things: John Trevisa's translation of Bartholomaeus Anglicus De Proprietatibus Rerum*. 3 vols Oxford: Clarendon, 1975.

Shahar, Shulamith. *Childhood in the Middle Ages*. London: Routledge, 1990.

Shaner, Mary E. 'Instruction and Delight: Medieval Romances as Children's Literature', *Poetics Today* 13 (1992): 5–15.

Spufford, Margaret. 'First steps in literacy: the reading and writing experiences of the humblest seventeenth-century spiritual autobiographers', *Social History* 4 (1979): 407–35.

Swanson, Jenny. 'Childhood and child-rearing in *ad status* sermons by later thirteenth century friars', *Journal of Medieval History* 16 (1990): 309–31.

Topsell, Edward. *The History of Four-footed Beasts and Serpents*. London: G. Sawbridge, 1658. (Bruce Peel Special Collections Library, University of Alberta)

Tudor, Philippa. 'Religious Instruction for Children and Adolescents in the Early English Reformation', *Journal of Ecclesiastical History* 35 (1984): 391–413.

Tuer, Andrew W. *History of the Horn-Book*. 2 vols London: Leadenhall Press, 1896.

Winthrop Papers. 5 vols. Vol III: 1631–37. Boston: The Massachusetts Historical Society, 1943.

2. PURITAN 'HELL-FIRE': WARNINGS AND WARMTH

Bunyan, John. *A Book for Boys and Girls; or, Country Rhymes for Children*. Facsimile of unique first edition, 1686. Introduction by John Brown. London: E. Stock, 1889.

———. *Sighs from Hell; or, The Groans of a Damned Soul*. New edition. Leeds: J. Binns, 1795.

Collinson, Patrick. *The Elizabethan Puritan Movement*. Oxford: Clarendon, 1967, 1990.

Cotton, John. *Milk for Babes, Drawn out of the Breasts of Both Testaments*. London: Henry Overton, 1646.

Danielson, Dennis. 'Catechism, *The Pilgrim's Progress*, and the Pilgrim's Progress,' *Journal of English and Germanic Philology* 94 (1995): 42–58.

Delbanco, Andrew. *The Real American Dream*. Cambridge: Harvard University Press, 1999.

Ford, Paul Leicester, ed. *The New England Primer; A History of its Origin and Development with a reprint of the unique copy of the earliest known edition and many facsimile illustrations*. New York: Dodd & Mead, 1897.

Heartman, Charles F. *The New-England Primer Issued Prior to 1830: A Bibliographical Check-List*. New York: R.R. Bowker, 1934.

Heimert, Alan and Andrew Delbanco, editors. *The Puritans in America*. Cambridge: Harvard University Press, 1985.

Hensley, Jeannine, ed. *The Works of Anne Bradstreet*. Cambridge: Harvard University Press, 1967.

Hill, Christopher. *The English Bible and the Seventeenth Century Revolution*. London: Penguin, 1993.

Janeway, James. *A Token for Children, being an exact account of the conversion, holy and exemplary lives and joyful deaths of several young children.* London: Dorman Newman, 1672.

Kaufman, U. Milo. *The Pilgrim's Progress and Traditions in Puritan Meditation.* New Haven: Yale University Press, 1966.

Keach, Benjamin. *War With the Devil; or, the Young Man's Conflict with the Powers of Darkness.* London: Benjamin Harris, 1684.

Lutes, Jean Marie. 'Negotiating Theology and Gynecology: Anne Bradstreet's Representations of the Female Body,' *Signs* 22 (1997): 309–40.

Marcus, Leah S. *Childhood and Cultural Despair.* Pittsburgh: University of Pittsburgh Press, 1978.

Morison, Samuel E. *The Puritan Pronaos: Studies in the Intellectual Life of New England in the Seventeenth Century.* New York: New York University Press, 1936.

Rosenmeier, Rosamund. *Anne Bradstreet Revisited.* Boston: Twayne, 1991.

Trim, Mary. 'A Rediscovery of John Bunyan's *Book for Boys and Girls,*' *International Review of Children's Literature and Librarianship* 8 (1993): 149–67.

3. LYRICAL INSTRUCTION: ISAAC WATTS AND HIS CONTEMPORARIES

Adey, Lionel. *Hymns and the Christian 'Myth'.* Vancouver: University of British Columbia Press, 1986.

Barber, Mary. *A Tale.* Dublin: George Ewing, 1728.

———. *Poems on Several Occasions.* London: C. Rivington, 1735.

Bishop, Selma L. *Isaac Watts Hymns and Spiritual Songs 1707–1748: A Study in Early Eighteenth-Century Language Changes.* London: The Faith Press, 1962.

Escott, Harry. *Isaac Watts, Hymnographer: A Study of the Beginnings, Development, and Philosophy of the English Hymn.* London: Independent Press, 1962.

Gay, John. *Fables.* London: J. Tonson and J. Watts, 1727.

Nokes, David. *John Gay: A Profession of Friendship.* Oxford: Oxford University Press, 1995.

Watts, Isaac. *Divine Songs Attempted in Easy Language for the Use of Children.* Introduction J.H.P. Pafford. London: Oxford University Press, 1971.

4. CHAPBOOKS AND PENNY HISTORIES

Ashton, John. *Chap-Books of the Eighteenth Century.* London: Chatto & Windus, 1882.

Brewer, John. *The Pleasures of the Imagination. English Culture in the Eighteenth Century.* New York: Farrar Straus Giroux, 1997

Federer, Charles., ed. *Yorkshire Chapbooks.* London: Elliot Stock, 1889.

McKendrick, Neil, J. Brewer, and J.H. Plumb. *The Birth of a Consumer Society: The Commercialization of Eighteenth-Century England.* London: Europa Publications, 1982.

Neuberg, Victor E. *Chapbooks: A Bibliography of References to English and American Chapbook Literature of the Eighteenth and Nineteenth Centuries.* London: Vine Press, 1964.

———. *Popular Literature: A History and Guide from the Beginning of Printing to the year 1897.* London: Woburn Press, 1977.

Nursery Rhymes and Chapbooks 1805–1814. Preface Justin G. Schiller. New York: Garland, 1978.

The Penny Histories: A Study of Chapbooks for young readers over two centuries. Introduction Victor E. Neuberg.

London: Oxford University Press, 1968.

Spufford, Margaret. *Small Books and Pleasant Histories; Popular fiction and its readership in seventeenth-century England.* Athens: University of Georgia Press, 1981.

Thompson, Roger, ed. *Samuel Pepys' Penny Merriments.* New York: Columbia University Press, 1977.

The Trial of an Ox, for Killing a Man. Banbury: J.G. Rusher, n.d. (Bruce Peel Special Collections Library, University of Alberta)

Zall, P.M., ed. *A Nest of Ninnies and Other English Jestbooks of the Seventeenth Century.* Lincoln: University of Nebraska Press, 1970.

5. BOREMAN, COOPER, AND NEWBERY: 'INSTRUCTION WITH DELIGHT'

Boreman, Thomas. *A Description of Three Hundred Animals.* Preface C.D. Stewart. New York: S.R. Publishers Limited, Johnson Reprint Corporation, 1968.

———. *The Gigantick History of the Two Famous Giants and Other Curiosities in Guildhall, London.* London: T. Boreman, 1740

———. *Curiosities in the Tower of London.* Second edition. London: T. Boreman, 1741.

The Child's New Play-Thing: Being a Spelling-Book Intended to Make the Learning to Read, A Diversion instead of a Task. London: M. Cooper, 1745.

Dawson, Janis. 'Trade and Plumb-Cake in Lilliput: The Origins of Juvenile Consumerism and Early English Children's Periodicals,' *Children's Literature in Education* 29 (1998): 175–98.

The History of Little Goody Two-Shoes. A Facsimile Reproduction of the 1776 Edition. Introduction Charles Welsh. London: Griffith & Farran, 1881.

Lisney, Arthur A. *A Bibliography of British Lepidoptera 1608–1799.* London: Chiswick Press, 1960.

Newbery, John. *A Little Pretty Pocket-Book.* Introduction M.F. Thwaite. London: Oxford University Press, 1966.

O'Malley, Andrew. 'The Coach and Six: Chapbook Residue in Late Eighteenth-Century Children's Literature,' *The Lion and the Unicorn* 24 (2000): 18–44.

Roscoe, S. *John Newbery and His Successors 1740–1814, A Bibliography.* Wormley: Five Owls Press, 1973.

———. *Newbery, Carnan, Power.* London: Dawsons of Pall Mall, 1966.

Stone, Wilbur Macey. *The Gigantick Histories of Thomas Boreman.* Portland, Maine: Southworth Press, 1933.

Townsend, John Rowe. 'John Newbery and Tom Telescope,' *Signal* 78 (1995): 207–14.

6. RATIONAL MORALISTS

Abbott, Reverend Jacob. *Rollo at School.* London: James S. Hodson, 1839.

Armes, Ethel, ed. *Nancy Shippen Her Journal Book.* Philadelphia: Lippincott, 1935.

Butler, Marilyn. *Maria Edgeworth. A Literary Biography.* Oxford: Clarendon, 1972.

Cave, Jane. *Poems on Various Subjects, Entertaining, Elegiac and Religious.* Winchester: L. Sadler, 1783.

Day, Thomas. *The History of Sandford and Merton.* 3 vols. London: John Stockdale, 1791–1801.

Edgeworth, Maria. *Early Lessons.* 4 vols. 16th Edition. London: Longman & Co., 1845.

Ezell, Margaret J.M. 'John Locke's Images of Childhood: Early Eighteenth Century Response to *Some Thoughts Concerning Education,*' *Eighteenth-Century Studies* 17 (1983): 139–55.

Fenn, Lady Eleanor. *Cobwebs to Catch Flies; or, Dialogues in Short Sentences Adapted for Children from the Age of Three to Eight Years.* 2 vols. London: John Marshall, *c.* 1800.

Fielding, Sarah. *The Governess; or, Little Female Academy. Facsimile reproduction of the first edition of 1749.* Introduction Jill E. Grey. London: Oxford University Press, 1968.

Fyfe, Aileen. 'Young Readers and the Sciences,' *Books and the Sciences in History,* ed. M. Frasca-Spada and N. Jardine. Cambridge: Cambridge University Press, 2000; 276–90.

Goodrich, Samuel G. ('Peter Parley'). *Make the Best of It; or, Cheerful Cherry and Other Tales.* New York: Sheldon & Co., 1863.

Hill, Bridget. 'Priscilla Wakefield as a Writer of Children's Educational Books,' *Women's Writing* 4 (1997): 3–14.

Hofland, Barbara. *Farewell Tales Founded on Facts.* New York: W.E. Dean, n.d.

Horsley, Henry S. *The Affectionate Parent's Gift, and the Good Child's Reward; Consisting of a series of poems and essays on natural, moral and religious subjects.* London: T. Kelly, 1828.

Jordan, Alice M. *From Rollo to Tom Sawyer.* Boston: The Horn Book, 1948.

Kilner, Dorothy. *The Village School; or, a Collection of Entertaining Histories, for the Instruction and Amusement of all Good children.* London: John Marshall, [1795?].

Kilner, Mary Ann. *The Adventures of a Pin-cushion chiefly for the Use of Young Ladies.* London: John Marshall, [1780?].

———. *Jemima Placid; or, The Advantage of Good-Nature.* London: John Marshall, 1783.

Kramnick, Isaac. 'Children's Literature and Bourgeois Ideology: Observations on Culture and Industrial Capitalism in the Later Eighteenth Century.' In *Culture and Politics from Puritanism to the Enlightenment.* Ed. Perez Zagorin. Berkeley: University of Calfornia Press, 1980; 203–40.

Locke, John. *Some Thoughts Concerning Education.* Edited with Introduction John W. and Jean S. Yolton. Oxford: Clarendon, 1989.

Marcet, Jane. *Mary's Grammar; interspersed with stories and intended for the use of children.* 2nd Edition. London: Longman, Rees, Orme, Brown, Green & Longman, 1836.

Messem, Catherine. 'Irreconcilable Tensions: Gender, Class and the Welsh Question in the Poetry of Jane Cave,' *Welsh Writing in English* 2 (1996): 1–21.

Myers, Mitzi. 'Impeccable Governesses, Rational Dames, and Moral Mothers: Mary Wollstonecraft and the Female Tradition in Georgian Children's Books,' *Children's Literature* 14 (1986): 31–59.

———. 'Socializing Rosamond: Educational Ideology and Fictional Form.' *Children's Literature Association Quarterly* 14 (1989): 52–8.

———. 'Romancing the Moral Tale: Maria Edgeworth and the Problematics of Pedagogy.' In *Romanticism and Children's Literature in Nineteenth-Century England.* Ed. James Holt McGavran, Jr. Athens: University of Georgia Press, 1991; 96–128.

Patterson, Sylvia W. *Rousseau's Émile and Early Children's Literature.* Metuchen, N.J.: Scarecrow Press, 1971.

Pickering, Samuel F., Jr. *John Locke and Children's Books in Eighteenth-Century England.* Knoxville: University of Tennessee Press, 1981.

Rede, Lucy Leman. *Flowers That Never Fade.* London: Dean and Munday, [1838].

Roselle, Daniel. *Samuel Griswold Goodrich, Creator of Peter Parley; A Study of His Life and Work*. Albany: State University of New York Press, 1968.

Rousseau, Jean-Jacques. *Émile*. Trans. B. Foxley. London: Dent, 1911.

Shteir, Ann B., ed. 'Introduction,' *Priscilla Wakefield, Mental Improvement*. East Lansing: Colleagues Press, 1995.

Summerfield, Geoffrey. *Fantasy and Reason: Children's Literature in the Eighteenth Century*. Athens, GA: University of Georgia Press, 1985.

Suzuki, Mika. 'The Little Female Academy and The Governess,' *Women's Writing* 1 (1994): 325–39.

Todd, Janet. *Mary Wollstonecraft: A Revolutionary Life*. London: Weidenfeld and Nicolson, 2000.

Traill, Catharine Parr. *The Young Emigrants; or, Pictures of Canada. Calculated to Amuse and Instruct the Minds of Youth*. London: Harvey and Darton, 1826.

Wakefield, Priscilla. *Mental Improvement: or, the Beauties and Wonders of Nature and Art, Conveyed in a series of Instructive Conversations*. Volume 1. London: Darton and Harvey, 1794.

———. *Reflections on the Present Condition of the Female Sex; with Suggestions for Its Improvement*. London: Darton and Harvey, 1798.

Wollstonecraft, Mary. *Original Stories from Real Life; with Conversations, Calculated to Regulate the Affections and From the Mind to Truth and Goodness*. London: J. Johnson, 1791.

———. *Collected Letters*. Ed. Ralph W. Wardle. Ithaca: Cornell University Press, 1979.

7. SUNDAY SCHOOL MORALISTS

Barbauld, Anna Letitia. *Hymns in Prose for Children*. 27th Edition. London: Harvey and Darton, 1832.

———. *Lessons for Children*. In Four Parts. New Edition. London: Baldwin & Craddock, 1834.

———. *The Poems*. Ed. W. McCarthy and E. Kraft. Athens, GA: University of Georgia Press, 1994.

———. *Selected Poetry and Prose*. Ed. W. McCarthy and E. Kraft. Peterborough, ON: Broadview Press, 2002.

Burder, Reverend George. *Early Piety; or Memoirs of Children Eminently Serious, interspersed with Familiar Dialogues, Emblematical Pictures and Hymns*. London: H. Trapp and Vallance and Simmons, 1777.

Cliff, Philip B. *The Rise and Development of the Sunday School Movement in England 1780–1980*. Nutfield, Redhill, Surrey: Robert Denholm House, National Christian Education Council, 1986.

Coleridge, Samuel Taylor. *Letters, Conversations and Recollections*. Ed. T. Allsop. Vol 1. London: Moxon, 1836.

Cutt, Margaret Nancy. *Mrs Sherwood and Her Books for Children*. London: Oxford University Press, 1974.

Dalby, Mrs. *Dutch Tiles, Being Narratives of Holy Scripture, with numerous appropriate engravings for the use of children and young persons*. London: John Mason, 1842.

Demers, Patricia. *Heaven upon Earth: The Form of Moral and Religious Children's Literature to 1850*. Knoxville: University of Tennessee Press, 1993.

———. *The World of Hannah More*. Lexington: University Press of Kentucky, 1996.

Hill, Rowland. *Divine Hymns, Attempted in Easy Language for the Use of Children*. London: T. Wilkins, 1790.

———. *Instructions for Children; or, A Token of Love for the Rising Generation*. London: G. Thompson, 1794.

Jones, M.G. *The Charity School Movement: A Study of Eighteenth Century*

Puritanism in Action. Cambridge: Cambridge University Press, 1938; rpt. 1964.

Kennedy, Thomas C. 'From Anna Barbauld's *Hymns in Prose* to William Blake's *Songs of Innocence and Experience,*' *Philological Quarterly* 77(1998): 359–76.

Lamb, Charles. *The Letters of Charles Lamb.* Ed. E.V. Lucas. London: Dent, 1935.

Laqueur, Thomas Walter. *Religion and Respectability: Sunday Schools and Working Class Culture 1780–1850.* New Haven: Yale University Press, 1976.

McCarthy, William. 'Mother of All Discourses: Anna Barbauld's Lessons for Children,' *Princeton University Library Chronicle* 60 (1999): 196–219.

More, Hannah. *The Works of Hannah More.* 11 vols. Vol. IV, *Stories and Tales.* London: T. Cadell, 1830.

Mortimer, Favell Lee. *The Peep of Day; or, a Series of the Earliest Religious Instruction the Infant Mind is Capable of Receiving.* London: Hatchards, 1886.

Newell, A.G. 'Early Evangelical Fiction,' *Evangelical Quarterly* 38 (1966): 3–21; 81–98.

Plumb, J.H. 'The New World of Children in Eighteenth-Century England.' *Past and Present* 67 (1975): 64–95.

Rosman, Doreen. *Evangelicals and Culture.* London: Croom Helm, 1984.

Sherwood, Mary Martha. *The History of the Fairchild Family; or, The Child's Manual; being a collection of stories calculated to show the importance and effects of a religious education.* 3 vols. London: J. Hatchard, 1847–48.

Trimmer, Sarah. *Fabulous Histories. Designed for the Instruction of Children, Respecting their Treatment of Animals.* London: T. Longman, 1786.

———. *The Economy of Charity; or, An Address to Ladies Concerning Sunday Schools; the Establishment of Schools of Industry under Female Inspection; and the Distribution of Voluntary Benefaction.* London: T. Bensley, 1787.

———. *The Charity School Spelling Book.* Parts I and II. 4th Edition. London: F. & C. Rivington, 1798.

———. *The Guardian of Education, A Periodical Work; Consisting of a Practical Essay on Christian Education, Founded immediately on the Scriptures and the Sacred Offices of the Church of England.* 5 vols. London: J. Hatchard, 1802–06.

Vallone, Lynne. ' "A Humble Spirit under Correction": Tracts, Hymns, and the Ideology of Evangelical Fiction for Children, 1780–1820,' *The Lion and the Unicorn* 15 (1991): 72–95.

Zunshine, Lisa. 'Rhetoric, Cognition, and Ideology in A.L. Barbauld's *Hymns in Prose for Children* (1781)," *Poetics Today* 23 (2002): 123–39.

8. HARBINGERS OF THE GOLDEN AGE

Bindman, David. *William Blake; His Arts and Times.* London: Thames and Hudson Ltd., 1982.

Blake, William. *The Poems of William Blake, Comprising Songs of Innocence and of Experience.* London: B.M. Picketing, 1874.

———. *Songs of Innocence and of Experience,* A Facsimile Edition. London: Trianon Press, 1955.

Boucher de Montizambert, Jane Vaughan Cotton. *The Sad Tale of Mrs Mole and Mrs Mouse.* MS *c.* 1849. The Osborne Collection of Early Children's Books, Toronto Public Library.

Brimmell, R.A. 'A Note on John Marshall & Richard Marshall,' *Antiquarian Book Monthly Review* (February 1991): 68–9.

Browne, Felicia Dorothea. *Poems*. Liverpool: G.F. Harris and London: T. Cadell and W. Davies, 1808. (Bruce Peel Special Collections Library, University of Alberta)

Davidson, Angus. *Edward Lear Landscape Painter and Nonsense Poet (1812–1888)*. London: John Murray, 1938.

Dorset, Catherine A. *The Peacock 'At Home'*. London: J. Harris, 1808. (Osborne Collection)

Hawes, Clement, ed. *Christopher Smart and the English Enlightenment*. New York: St. Martin's, 1999.

Hemans. Felicia. *Selected Poems, Prose, and Letters*. Ed. Gary Kelly. Broadview: Peterborough, ON, 2002.

Hoffmann, Heinrich. *Slovenly Peter, or Cheerful Stories and Funny Pictures for Good Little Folks*. Philadelphia: J.C. Winston, n.d.

Howitt, Mary. *Sketches of Natural History*. Boston: Weeks, Jordan & Co., 1839.

Hurst, Clive. ' "From a Great Distance": The Early Text of *The Butterfly's Ball*,' *Bodleian Library Record* 13 (1990): 415–22.

Lamb, Charles and Mary. *Poetry for Children*. London: Leadenhall Press, 1892.

Lear, Edward. *A Book of Nonsense*. Fourteenth Edition. London: Dalziel Brothers, 1863.

Moon, Marjorie. *John Harris's Books for Youth 1801–1843*. Cambridge: Five Owls Press, 1976.

———. *Benjamin Tabart's Juvenile Library*. Winchester, Hampshire: St. Paul's Bibliographies, 1990.

Mounsey, Chris. *Christopher Smart Clown of God*. Lewisburg: Bucknell University Press, 2001.

Mure, Eleanor. *The Story of the Three Bears*. Toronto: Oxford University Press, 1967. For the Friends of the Osborne and Lillian H. Smith Collections.

Ober, Warren U. *The Story of the Three Bears: The Evolution of an International Classic*. Delmar, NY: Scholars' Facsimiles and Reprints, 1981.

Peter Piper's Practical Principles of Plain and Perfect Pronunciation. To which is added, A Collection of moral and entertaining conundrums London: J. Harris, 1820. (Osborne Collection)

Philips, Adam. *The Beast in the Nursery; On Curiosity and Other Appetites*. New York: Vintage Books, 1998.

Richardson, Alan. *Literature, Education, and Romanticism: Reading as Social Practice, 1780–1832*. Cambridge: Cambridge University Press, 1994

Roscoe, S. 'Some Uncollected Authors: John Marshall and "The Infant's Library," ' *The Book Collector* 4 (1955): 148–57.

Roscoe, William. *The Butterfly's Ball and the Grasshopper's Feast*. London: J. Harris, 1807. (Osborne Collection)

Sinclair, Catherine. *Holiday House: A Series of Tales*. Edinburgh: William Whyte and Co., 1851.

Smart, Christopher. *The Complete Poetical Works*. Ed. Karina Williamson and Marcus Walsh. 6 vols. Oxford: Clarendon, 1980–96.

Taylor, Ann and Jane. *Hymns for Infant Minds*. New Edition. London: Jackson and Walford, 1846.

———. *Original Poems*. Illustrated. London and New York: George Routledge & Sons, 1868.

Turner, Elizabeth. *The Daisy; or, Cautionary Stories in Verse*. Adapted to the Ideas of Children from Four to Eight Years Old. London: J. Harris, 1807.

INDEX